Return to Eden

Return to Eden

A Journey
through the Aboriginal Promised Landscape
of Amagalyuagba

THIRD EDITION

David H. Turner

Rock's Mills Press
Rock's Mills, Ontario • Oakville, Ontario
2025

The following Library of Congress Cataloging-in-Publication Data
appeared in the second edition of this book:

Turner, David H.
Return to Eden: a journey through the aboriginal
promised landscape of Amagalyuagba/ David H. Turner—Rev. ed.
p. cm. — (Toronto studies in religion; vol. 21)
Includes bibliographical references and index.
1. Australian aborigines—Religion. I. Title. II. Series.
BL2610.T87 306'.089'9915094295—dc20 96-6088

Published by
Rock's Mills Press

Copyright © 2025 by David H. Turner.
Previous editions copyright © 1996, 1989 by Peter Lang Publishing, Inc., New York.
All rights reserved. No part of this publication may be reproduced, distributed, or transmitted in any form or by any means, including photocopying, recording, or other electronic or mechanical methods, without the prior written permission of the publisher, except in the case of brief quotations embodied in critical reviews and certain other noncommercial uses permitted by copyright law. For permission requests, contact the publisher at: customer.service@rocksmillspress.com

This book was originally published by Peter Lang Publishing, Inc., as volume 21 in the series *Toronto Studies in Religion*, Donald Wiebe, general editor. The text of this edition follows that of the second edition, with the correction of minor typographical errors.

in memory
of Iain and Bryan

"And what of the secret of the Tree of Life? It remains half-hidden within the world of the first Australians."
(*Life Before Genesis*)

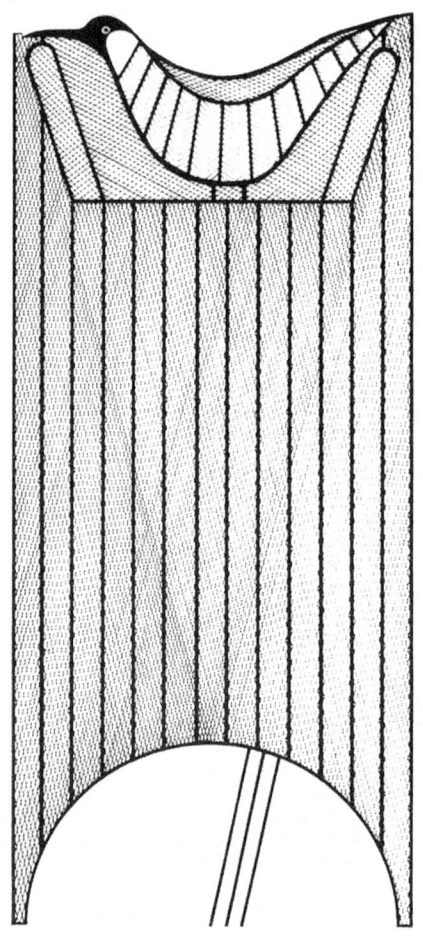

Editor's Preface

In the first edition of *Return to Eden* David Turner used the theoretical insights of his first book in this series, *Life Before Genesis*, as a lens through which to review the way of life of the Aboriginal people of Amagalyuagba on his return to Bickerton Island in northern Australia in 1986. On this visit, Turner claims to have found more than a simple confirmation of his original theoretical speculations. The Aborigines, he insists, not only possess the same theoretical insights but do so in a more profound fashion. Turner recounted his experience of this return to Amagalyuagba (having first become acquainted with these people between 1969 and 1974), in narrative style in the form of a journey back to their "promised lands".

Although in some respects this book represents a departure from the others in this series, including Turner's first volume, it is a wholly appropriate contribution. This study fits well within the broad parameters of the series which aims to publish empirical, analytical and theoretical studies of religion and religions, for Turner's study offers a phenomenological account of the world's oldest continuing religious tradition, that of the Australian Aborigines.

In this second edition Turner has written a new Preface, updating the situation of the Warnungamagalyuagba to 1995, has added a glossary of Aboriginal terms, an index, and a new chapter on his 1971 attempt to undertake post-doctoral work among these people; he has also clarified and extended parts of his description and his analyses of the Aboriginal way of life in response to readers' suggestions on reading the first edition of this work. Turner sees himself engaged in a continuing process of translating Aboriginal culture into English both in terms that English readers will be able to understand and that will do justice to the Aboriginal reality. The reviews of the first edition of this book seem to indicate that he bas had considerable success in this task and this revised edition will, I have no doubt, further increase our understanding and appreciation of this remarkable religious tradition.

Donald Wiebe
Trinity College
University of Toronto
September 1995

Contents

List of Maps	xiii
List of Tables	xiv
List of Plates	xv
Acknowledgments	xvii
Preface to the Third Edition	xxi
Preface to the Second Edition	xxxiii
Glossary of Important Aboriginal Terms	xli
Introduction	1

Part I: EXODUS

I	1971: Return and Expulsion	7

PRELIMINARY REMARKS • 7   SUBSEQUENT EVENTS • 8

II	1974: Return and Withdrawal	19
III	1985/86: Return and Regrouping	

Part II: EDENS

IV	The More Things Change, the More Things Remain the Same	55

THE TERMS OF RELATIONSHIP • 68

V	The Promised Lands	93

PILGRIMAGE TO ARUMANDJA • 93   SURVEYING, ABORIGINAL STYLE • 110

VI	The Economics of the Dreaming	139
VII	Songstreams	165

AGWILYUNGGGWA • 165   LIFE'S LOGIC PRESENT • 184
OF SHIPS AND DOVES AND SPIDERS AND THINGS • 193

VIII	Cosmo-logic	213

ARUMANDJA REVISITED • 213   THE LANGUAGE OF THE GODS • 233

Part III: THE FALL

IX	Malara Muwurrariya (Manganese Nightmare)	247
X	Broken Promises	257

LAND (?) RIGHTS • 258

XI	Life's Logic Lost	275

EDENS? • 279

THEORETICAL POSTLUDE	281
References	291
Thematic Index	297

List of Maps

1. Amagalyuagba, Bickerton Island, in relation to Groote Eylandt and mainland Australia — 1
2. The Promised Landscape of Amagalyuagba: Songstreams — 118
3. The Promised Landscape of Amagalyuagba: Placenames — 119
4. The Promised Landscape of Amagalyuagba: Resources — 120
5. Songstreams of the Western Gulf — 121

List of Figures

1. The Warnungamagalyuagba Relationship System — 67
2. Galiyawa's and "Crosby's" Drawings of Amagalyuagba — 137
3. Gula's Drawings of Sharks — 185
4. Wind Songs and their People/Lands — 208
5. Particle Interpenetration — 215
6. Yin and Yang — 218
7. Murabuda's Drawing of Amagalyuagba — 264

List of Tables

1.	Warnungamagalyuagba Relationship Terms	68
2.	Songstream Companies of the Western Gulf	71
3.	Key to the Promised Landscape of Amagaalyuagba	122
4.	Important Food Resources of Amagalyuagba	149

List of Plates

1.	Stylized representation of Djabargwa's bark painting of Bara, West Wind, inset with Yingwa, Crow	viii
	Photorecord: Groote Eylandt and Bickerton Island, 1986	xlv
2.	Murabuda Wurramarrba and Bobby Nungumadjbar at the Angurugu Community Government Council office	xlv
3.	Murabuda Wurramarrba and others on his Songstream	xlv
4.	Processing the Spirit to the gravesite at Balalya's funeral	xlvi
5.	Dancing the Spirit to the gravesite on Curlew	xlvi
6.	Gula Lalara singing Balalya's Spirit to her Agwilyunggwa	xlvii
7.	Gudigba Lalara	xlvii
8.	The Place where Nambirrirrma descended on Bickerton	xlviii
9.	Graeme at A:nemurramadja, "Laughing Waves", Place	xlviii
10.	Ruth and Iain chopping wood at Milya:gburra campsite	xlix
11.	Iain and Michelle and Milya:gburra Outstation	xlix
12.	Hokusai's "Great Wave off Kangawa"	169
13.	Lawren Harris's "Pic Island Lake Superior"	169
14.	Gegenda Durila's bark painting of "Turtle Food"	205
15.	Iain Baxter's "Reflected Landscape"	205

Acknowledgments

Many individuals and organizations have made this work possible. Funding for the 1996, 1987 and 1988 visits to Groote Eylandt and Bickerton Island was provided by the Social Sciences and Humanities Research Council of Canada and the Research Board of the University of Toronto. My consultancy for the Minister of Community Development in the Northern Territory of Australia, first Barry Coulter and then Don Dale, permitted me to broaden my general experience of Aborigines in Australia and placed additional funds at my disposal which facilitated my work on Bickerton and Groote. By the same token, officers of the Northern Land Council, in particular Frank McKeowan and Michael Duffy, have been supportive of my work, first on the issue of Aboriginal land tenure and then on the question of manganese toxicity on Groote. For the opportunity to contribute to research into this latter issue I am indebted to Professor John Cawte and Dr. Charles Kilburn of the University of New South Wales whose pioneering work in this field may well save lives on Groote, Bickerton and elsewhere.

I would also like to thank Dr. Julie Waddy, an anthropologist affiliated with the Church Missionary Society (C.M.S.) on Groote for making her then-unpublished thesis on *Classification of Plants and Animals from a Groote Eylandt Aboriginal Point of View* available to me. All taxonomic referents are taken from this work. To Judith Stokes, the C.M.S. linguist at Angurugu on Groote, I again express my gratitude for the help she first gave me on the language back in 1969, though I am sure she will have been disappointed to see me backslide so much in my ability compared to my earlier days on Groote. For a technical description of the language I refer the reader to Miss Stokes' publications on Anindilyaugwa (1981, 1982).

The orthography used here is basically that employed in my 1974 book *Tradition and Transformation,* with some simplifications. Here, though, "rr" will designate a rolled r, "a:" a long *a* as in weigh. Anindilyaugwa is a prefixing, multiple noun classifying language with a complex system of noun and pro-noun incorporation. Verbs, adjectives and pronouns are prefixed to agree with the class of the noun of which there are eight.

The section of Chapter 10 entitled "The Language of the Gods" on Aboriginal music was written in collaboration with Hendrik Stephen Kossen, a linguistics student at the University of Toronto who just happened into my class on Aboriginal Australia the year I wrote this book and who also just happened to be a talented musician with an ear for quarter-tones. He developed the notational system and structurally analyzed the music. Without his collaboration my journey would have remained incomplete and to him I express a special thanks. The material in Chapter 9 on Nambirrirrma and Christ formed the basis of a paper I wrote for the book *Aboriginal Australians and Christian Missions* edited by Tony Swain and Deborah Rose.

I would also again like to thank the Netherlands Institute for Advanced Studies in Wassenaar and my colleague Professor P. E. de Josselin de Jong of Leiden University for providing me with a year at their wonderful facility to think through the implications of my anthropological work to that point in time (1980/81) and produce *Life Before Genesis*, a theoretical understanding of Australian Aboriginal culture. The present work represents a testing out in the field of many of the ideas contained within that book. I would also like to acknowledge my debt to Dr. Alan Barnard of Edinburgh University with whom I have corresponded on various aspects of this work for many years now. As well, I am indebted to Professor Donald Wiebe of Trinity College, University of Toronto, the editor of the series in which this and *Life Before Genesis,* appear. His "skeptical enthusiasm" for my approach to the study of religion continues to inform my work, as my skeptical enthusiasm for his, he tells me, continues to inform his own.

I am grateful to Christopher Myers, the Managing Director of Peter Lang Publishing in New York, for encouraging me to produce a revised, second edition of this book, and to Mr. Peter Lang himself, now in retirement in England, for his correspondence on the first edition of this volume as well as on *Life Before Genesis,* and for his personal interest in my project.

Thanks too to Ron Hughes who completed the final computer simulation of the Aboriginal system of kinship, marriage and Songstream affiliation, to Jane Davie who produced the maps and line drawings, to Siobhan Tarasick who typed the final manuscript of the first edition, to Elizabeth Rainsberry and Gilbert Verghese who proofed and formatted the second respectively, and to Lisa Dillon of Peter Lang Publishing for her work on the second edition.

Iain Baxter's photographic essay, "Reflected Landscape", is reproduced with the kind permission of the artist.

I thank Trinity College, the Centre for Religious Studies and the Research Board of the University of Toronto for their financial assistance in aid of publishing the first volume.

It goes without saying that nothing would have been possible without the forbearance of my Aboriginal colleagues on Groote Eylandt and Bickerton Island, in particular Gula, Murabuda, Nandjiwarra, Bobby Nungumadjbarr and the Angurugu Community Council – nor without that of Ruth (Charles), sons Graeme and Iain and daughter Michelle, who accompanied me to the field. The book is dedicated in part to Iain who subsequently died of cancer and represents a time when we were all together.

David Turner
Trinity College
University of Toronto
September 1995

Preface to the Third Edition
OUT OF TIME
with Jabeni Lalara

It has taken me quite some time to decide how to write a preface to a book first published in 1989 about an Aboriginal Way of Life that has now all but vanished but within which I was immersed during intermittent visits to the people (which actually made each one that more intense) between 1969 and 2003. It is now 2025, so, given my physical absence of 22 years, how did I manage a third edition? And absence from where exactly? (text, maps, pages 118–130).

Out of nowhere in September of 2019 the anthropologist Scott Cane of Iritijtira in South Australia contacted me to ask if I would help him put together a report for the Northern and Anindilyakwa Land Councils to help prevent seabed mining in the Groote Eylandt archipelago.

> I am currently researching and writing a native title sea claim around Groote Eylandt and the adjacent mainland. It's a complicated exercise! The reason I am emailing you is simply because I thought you might be interested in the investigation and to say that your work has been a massive help and is, basically, superb. It is (in my opinion) **the** research that has stood the test of time and I am completely impressed by its detail, accuracy and complexity. It is quite inspiring.

Scott is the author of *First Footprints: The Epic Story of the First Australians* (Allen & Unwin, Crow's Nest, New South Wales, 2013) and hosted the ABC TV series of the same name. He is blessed (if that is the right word) with a unique understanding of Aboriginal expressive culture acquired while investigating land claims on their behalf (*Pila Nguru, the Spinifex People*, Freemantle Arts Centre Press, Freemantle, 2002).

Scott's invitation was when it came back to mind all bundled up and focussed in a quite compact and summary form. Hence the three smaller books by Rock's Mills Press: *Life to the Power of N o t h i n g* (2019/21), *Pathway to the Stars, Playing for Alexa*, 2023 (a brief ceremony I performed for my former partner Alexa Ponomareff on her passing), and *"S e e i n g" the*

E t e r n a l (2026). The larger book in question, *Return to Eden: A Journey Through the Promised Landscape of Amagalyuagba*, was first published by Peter Lang Publishing in 1989 in New York with a second edition in 1996. The ethnographic material in both these editions, though, is basically from my 1986/7 visit.

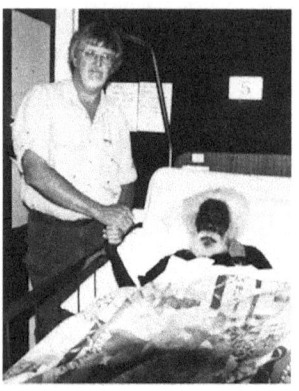

It was my visit to the archipelago in 2003 when I made a pact with Gula Lalara, my mentor, that whichever one of us passed first the other would "retire," that is, if me, Gula would "give up my tapping sticks" (i.e., Singing in ceremonies) and, if Gula, I would "give up my research." (i.e, he would not be here to teach me). Gula gave up his tapping sticks shortly thereafter complaining of losing the power in his voice and he passed first in 2005 (obviously, or I wouldn't be writing this). This photograph (by Alexa Ponomareff) was taken the last time I saw him—in 2003—in Darwin Hospital as his health was declining. He passed two years later.

An amazing person, I miss him.

As promised, I concluded my "research," at least in the archipelago which had become more of a participation than an observation in any case, and travelled instead to Pangnirtung on Baffin Island with Alexa and our son Liam as guests of Christopher Trott (now the teacher and I the student) and students in the University of Manitoba Summer School Program where I met Piona who came to me and asked if I would tell his story (*Eye of the Shaman: The Visions of Piona Keyuakjuk*, Rock's Mills Press, Oakville, 2019).

I did, however, keep in touch with Jabeni, my *na:niguma* or "younger brother" in our terms but much more in theirs (text, page 108), also Gula's "younger brother," thanks to Jennifer Baird Wurramara who was married to Warren, Jabeni's "younger brother." Jennifer now lives in Darwin.

These three editions of *Return to Eden* would not have appeared without the contributions of my wife Ruth Charles in 1969 and 1986 in particular, who was known at the time to the Aboriginal people as "the only *balanda*

(European) who spoke the language properly." She learned quickly: the women refused to speak to her in English in order to speed up the process. The Anindilyaugwa language (I prefer the softer "au" to the harsher "ak" as we learned it) was then pronounced one of the most complex on the planet. The first two editions of *Eden* are dedicated to the memory of our late children Iain and Bryan. Iain was beloved by the Aboriginal people you will encounter here and by everyone else who met him. He was with us when I was writing the second edition of *Eden*, though not for long, and is still a part of us all.

I would like to acknowledge again the friendship of Barry Coulter, the former Deputy Chief Minister of the Northern Territory, who has always managed to transcend any disagreements political or otherwise we might have had over the years. As recounted in *Eden* (text, pages 35–36) Barry was instrumental in our efforts on behalf of the Northern Territory and federal governments to retrieve "Australia's Crown Jewels," the Strehlow Collection of Central Australian Aboriginal ceremonial objects and lore, in the mid-1980s. The Collection is now housed in Alice Springs. Thereafter, Barry was instrumental in soliciting me to write a report on local government for Aboriginal people in the territory for the territory and federal governments which resulted in the establishment of Community Government Councils throughout the territory with provision for Aboriginal principles of representation (*Transformation and Tradition: A Report on Aboriginal Development in/on the Northern Territory of Australia*, Government Printer, Darwin, 1986). Alas, the Community Governments have since been absorbed into massive Shire Councils.

I would like to thank three former students for their friendships who have made waves elsewhere in their own right: Christopher Trott (on behalf of Inuit people), Guy Lanoue (on behalf of Athabaskan people), and Philippe Rouja (on behalf of Bardi people). Closer to home, long-term supporter and advisor, Dan Bajorek, friends Jesse Paglaroli, Rick Cowan, Glen Bishop, and Gord Mercier, and neighbours Ruth Hogan and Bonnie and Bill Blair. And my old hockey and baseball buddy Dennis Cordick who has just retired from goaltending (and always had my number).

At home, my son Liam who has had to deal directly with my "return" to "Eden," and down the 401 his equally accommodating grandparents, Barbara and Constantin Ponomareff. Up Highway 7 in Ottawa, my brother John and wife Shelley, Adam and Lindsay, and out west on the Trans-Canada in Vancouver my son Graeme, retired, and daughter Michelle, a midwife and PhD student at the University of British Columbia, both of whom are featured in this account. Ruth lives in her parents' former home in the Okanagan Valley. Outback in Australia, Jennifer Baird, of course, in Darwin, and Valerie Munt of Flinders University in Adelaide whose friendship developed during the course of the "return" part of this journey. Valerie is co-author with Peter Monteath of the book *Red Professor* on "the cold war life of Fred Rose," mentioned below.

To publisher David Stover of Rock's Mills Press who saw something about some t h i n g in *Life to the Power of N o t h i n g* and *Pathways to the Stars*, and persevered with *Eden* despite my hesitation to "return" to a world that basically no longer exists, I owe my sincere gratitude. It was David's suggestion to "p l u r a l i z e" the *N o t h i n g* of the title in *Life* as well as selected words in the Preface as as a "visual teaching" (see the Prologue to *"S e e i n g" the E t er n a l"* for the "reasoning").

The first two editions of *Eden*, published in 1989 and 1996 with Peter Lang Publishing, appeared in the series Toronto Studies in Religion edited by Professor Donald Wiebe of Trinity College Toronto whose foresight resulted in a sub-series in its own right.[1] Gratitude to Philip Dunshea of Peter Lang Press in Toronto for arranging the transfer of copyright of *Return to Eden* to Rock's Mills.

To Scott Cane who set all this this in motion, without your call to arms, so to speak, I likely would not have resumed this journey. I hope my "going back" then "forward" both at the same t i m e justifies your confidence in my work. And to Professor James Haire, the former national president-elect of the Uniting Church in Australia, head of the School of Theology at Griffith University, and principal of Trinity College, Brisbane: I regret I did not take up your insight and challenge at the time.

As he observed in a publisher's review of a book I wrote some years ago:[2]

In this volume Turner takes up the Aboriginal concept of R e n u n- c i a t i o n (with a capital R), specifically from the Aboriginal commun-

---

1. *Life Before Genesis: A Conclusion (An Understanding of the Significance of Australian Aboriginal Culture)*, 1985, second edition, 1987; *Afterlife Before Genesis: An Introduction (Accessing the Eternal through Australian Aboriginal Music)*, 1997; *Genesis Regained: Aboriginal Forms of Renunciation in Judaeo-Christian Scriptures and Other Major Traditions*, 1999; and *The Spirit Lives: A Personal Journey from Loss to Understanding Through Religious Experience*, 2002.
2. *Genesis Regained*, frontispiece.

ities of Groote Eylandt and Bickerton Island in northern Australia. Our conventional idea of renunciation may be seen as one end of a continuum—the other end of which is selfishness and accumulation. The Aboriginal concept of R e n u n c i a t i o n goes far beyond that, and indeed has a quite different basis. It is beyond any such continuum, in that it is posited on that basis that, in the transcendent dimension of reality, 'someNothing' continues to exist even after all has been given away.

The Aboriginal part of this journey began in 1969 with Ruth as a PhD student at the University of Western Australia in Perth (text, map opposite page 1). Perth-to-Perth if you will, the former a town in Ontario where I was raised when my father became managing editor of *The Perth Courier* in 1949 after emigrating with our family from England. It is a town to which I am still connected. The detour to Perth, W.A., occurred after an honours BA at Carleton University in Ottawa, followed by a year in graduate school at the University of Alberta where I met Ruth, then via the National Film Board to the London School of Film Technique in Covent Garden, England. There one evening, a chance encounter with Steve Burns and his wife on the tube as we were on our way to see a film, Steve enrolled in the PhD program in Philosophy at the University of London. This led to a social gathering with students at the university where the conversation revolved around the recent translation of a book by the French anthropologist Claude Lévi-Strauss titled *The Savage Mind* (English edition, University of Chicago Press, 1966), in which he wrote (among other things):

Australian societies have probably developed in isolation more than appears to have been the case elsewhere. Moreover, this development was not undergone passively. It was desired and conceptualization, for few civilizations seem to equal the Australians in their taste for erudition and speculation and what sometimes looks like intellectual dandyism, odd as this expression may appear when it is applied to people of so rudimentary a level of material life… (p. 89).

That did it!
Perhaps the incongruity of this from our materialist perspective. Or just that it seemed to him that these were the most difficult people on the planet

for us to understand. I had to know more. So with Ruth enthusiastically on board we set out to plot a course to Australia.

First, off to the Social Anthropology Department at the University of London and Professor Phyllis Kaberry, author of the book *Aboriginal Woman, Sacred and Profane* (Routledge, Oxfordshire, UK, 1939) to inquire about enrolling there. That would be possible, she said, but they could not finance research in Australia given the state of the British economy, currently in recession. But she would write to Professors Ronald and Catherine Berndt at the University of Western Australia to see about enrolling there.

The reply came back: if you can make your own way out here you can enrol in the Master's Preliminary Program and we'll go from there. But how to get there? Just happened that the P&O liner *Oriana* was in dry dock for repairs in Southhampton and many of the migrants destined for the next voyage to Australia had been sent by plane. There were now some vacancies. So, for 10 pounds Ruth and I enjoyed a three-week cruise to Perth, W.A., via South Africa where, as it chanced, my father "Norm" had been part of a group from newspapers in England that had travelled before the War to set up a moderately anti-segregation newspaper (so he told me) in Johannesburg. Failed. And as he and the crew were returning home on a German freighter, war broke out: Anti-Hitler captain lets the English passengers off in Gibraltar, Dad crosses into Spain, arrested, escapes, makes it home on a fishing boat, tries to enlist, rejected because of something he picked up in S.A., assigned to farm with his brother, later branches out on his own.

We arrived in Perth and I enrolled in the anthropology program already in progress, did well enough to skip the MA altogether and proceed directly to the PhD and, it being in the British tradition, there were no courses at that level, only preparation, so straight to fieldwork. The place chosen by Professor Ronald Berndt, my supervisor? Groote Eylandt in the Northern Territory. The reason? The previous research there was undertaken by two Marxist anthropologists, Peter Worsley and Frederick G. G. Rose, both British by origin, with Fred having defected to the German Democratic Republic during the Cold War. Their work might show a certain bias, thought Professor Berndt (it did not apart from that of any other approach at the time regarding the historical position of the First Australians).

So, in March of 1969 it was on a mail plane hopping up the coast on a run to Darwin, pick up our permit from the Welfare Branch of the Northern Territory government (not the Aborigines in those days), deposit all our main stuff like a motorbike on a barge, and fly over to Angurugu on Groote Eylandt on a mining flight.

The rest of that year, as they say, is history and recorded in *Tradition and Transformation: A Study of Aborigines in the Groote Eylandt Area, Northern Australia* (Australian Institute of Aboriginal Studies, Canberra, 1974, with audio tape). This book is now available at AIATSIS (personal communication, September 4, 2024). The tape contains Old Galiyawa Wurramarrba telling the story of Nambirrirrma who appears from "Nowhere" and sets down (reiterates what they already appear to know) a blueprint for the marriage and relationship system (text, pages 96–110).

Subsequent times in the area in 1971 and '74 between 1969 and 1986 are recounted in the preface to the second edition of *Return to Eden* and in Chapters I, II, and III, and I won't repeat them here except to say that by then I had returned to Canada[3] after a brief period at the Australian National University and a year at the University of Manitoba, finally settling in (more or less) at the Anthropology Department of the University of Toronto and Trinity College—later honoured with a Fellowship at the Netherlands Institute for Advanced Study (N.I.A.S.) in Wassenaar in 1980–81 as the Australian work circulated.

In 1986 I returned to the Groote Eylandt archipelago with Ruth and our children, Graeme, Michelle and Iain, where the events in *Return to Eden* unfolded. It was during this period that I was inducted into the Agwilyunggwa initiation ceremony by the Aboriginal people, a not-insignificant development (text, pages 172–184), considering I had already been symbolically put through the Marndiwala circumcision ceremony in 1969 so that I could talk to the elders. A second edition of *Eden* appeared with Peter Lang in 1996 that touches on the then political situation and briefly introduces some further insights post-1986/7 as visits had continued into the '90s, and on to 2001 and 2003 leading to the current understanding.

Historical Update

In early September of 2020 I received news from Jennifer in Darwin that

---

3. A note: when my family and I were about to return to Canada from Australia in 1974 I received letters from Lévi-Strauss in Paris and Rodney Needham at Oxford imploring me to remain in Australia and continue my work with Aboriginal people. They had been involved in a rather acrimonious debate about the nature of elementary systems of kinship and marriage that involved Aboriginal evidence and I was providing evidence. But that die was cast, at least for the moment.

Jabeni was not well, and then soon afterwards that he had suffered a heart attack. His loss would be devastating for the community. He was the *djunggwaiya:*, or "boss," of the *Mardaia:n* sacred ceremony (text, pages 262–265) and is one of the last "Aboriginal men and women of high degree" of the archipelago.

I couldn't be there with Jabeni in body, not in the midst of the coronavirus pandemic, nor with my son Liam enrolled in the first year of his Media Arts program at Loyalist College in Belleville—and with his mother, Alexa, having recently passed away. It was only a short time after his heart attack that Jabeni's condition was pronounced untreatable and he was flown back from Darwin to Angurugu on Groote Eylandt and placed in palliative care. On September 25 preparations were being made for his passing. Two days later he was gone, at least from his material existence. I played the *yiraga* (didjeridu) in a small ceremony for him as I had played for Alexa (*Pathway to the Stars*). It was he who had taught me in the bush during my visits (below, note the large rock as resonator), the reason for secrecy being that at the time it was forbidden to play—even practice—in public outside ceremony (Jabeni also graces the frontispiece of *Life to the Power of N o t h i n g*).

One of the things that contributed to Jabeni's decline in health, his heart attack and death, was indeed the loss of the traditional Way of Life within his own community due to a complex of factors, not the least of which was pressure by various governments and the Groote Eylandt Mining Company to expand operations on land in the archipelago, and now the seabed. On land they had all but succeeded with the consent of some traditional land owners,

but the Anindilyakwa Land Council (ALC) had apparently drawn the line at seabed mining, triggering Scott's inquiry into documenting what remained of the traditional Way of Life in order to justifying preventing it. The official reason given by the Land Council for opposing seabed mining thus far was that it would interfere with the "Songlines" that criss-crossed the archipelago (text, pages 118–130, 137). But, thing is, they also criss-cross the l/Land[4] as well as the water, so why not assert more jurisdiction there? One answer is that the less you assert on the l/Land,

---

4. I write l/Land this way to indicate its dual Nature as *material and transcendent, both at the same time.*

the more that is open to mining as "not sacred."

Surprisingly, with Scott's report confirming the validity of the material in *Tradition and Transformation*, later elaborated in *Return to Eden*, the ALC failed to file an objection to the seabed mining. That would seem to be against its interests unless, of course, none of these aspects were still present in which case there would be little grounds at all (except environmental degradation) to stop the mining. However, an attempt to rewrite the indigenous history of the archipelago was also afoot. The rewrite asserted that the foundations of the Way of Life rested on a dual (moiety) division between two intermarrying sets of "clans."[5] Yes, there *were* these dual divisions, they were positioned *over and above* (so to speak) an indigenous base-four marriage system whereby someone in one "clan" would marry someone in another "clan" every second generation—the ideal being the *same* "clan"—as recorded in the story of Nambirrirrma, a Law also followed by the Nunggubuyu people of the adjacent mainland.

According to Gula and others in my time, these dual divisions were, in fact, introduced from the mainland with Gula's people along with the sacred Mardaiya:n ceremony when they immigrated from the mainland to Groote Eylandt (via Bickerton Island) in the 1920s (text, pages 189–193, 262–265). Songs on each side of the dual division celebrated the respective travels of two Culture Heroes, one named Blaur, the other, Gilyiringilyiying (pl.). More to the point, by 1969 only the Blaur's Songline had reached Groote Eylandt proper which meant that only Blaur had "sat down" (made a physical impression somewhere) in certain l/Lands between Groote Eylandt and the mainland. This act designated the L a n d s in question as "sacred." And as "sacred" these p/Places would be closed to mining. But He did not "sit down" in all the "clan" l/Lands on the path, leaving their status ambiguous in relation to His journey. Should the moieties eventually become the only points of reference for people's relationships to one another, and alone contain Songs, then all the lands **not** on their paths would become open to mining.

My information from 1969 with the elders on the origins of the moieties and the primacy of the "clans" and their Songs was put down to "anthropologist's error." That was a mistake. Given Scott's report it left the Anind-

---

5. I have used many terms for the basic unit of social organization—local group, "clan," People/Land—finding all inadequate to express the Aboriginal reality. I finally settled on the indigenous term "Angalya" that Jabeni impressed upon me as of prime importance. See *Life to the Power of N o t h i n g*, Part 1.

ilyakwa Land Council little choice but to rethink its advice. But do nothing? They abstained.

In any event, the Northern Territory government granted petitions from other applicants around the coastal areas of the territory and called a moratorium on the mining. At least it is something and would preserve the marine environment in the archipelago as well as the Aborigines' fishing rights, and perhaps more importantly, protect those P e r s o n s with identities located in p/Places there still considered "sacred."

My point is that the trends I noted in the Preface to the second edition of *Return to Eden* simply continued more or less unabated with Jabeni and others like him, such as Gula and Nandjiwarra Amagula before him, unable to stem the tide.

Manganese mining leases on Groote Eylandt have been consistently expanded since the inception of mining in the mid-1960s extending down the western side of the island reaching the centre and southeast of Groote Eylandt and now, perhaps, Winchelsea Island to the north. One need only access the bird's eye view tour of Groote Eylandt available on the Anindilyakwa Council's own website to see the carnage wrought. With this levelling of the land, gone are many of the signs of Cosmic Intent that Aboriginal people had seen in the world around them—the differentiating features, or E s s e n t i a l   N a t u r e s, of things that they, by my account, transFormed into Songs from which, in turn, they had fashioned their Way of Life (see the Preface in "*S e e i n g the E t e r n a l*). Eliminate these and you are eliminating people's identities and connection to the E t e r n a l. In Aboriginal terms, this is genocide.

June 2, 2025, AI report: "The mine is an open-cut, strip-mining operation that produces high-grade manganese ore. While the mine has experienced disruptions due to infrastructure damage from Tropical Cyclone Megan, operations have since resumed with exports expected to restart."

Meanwhile, incidences of violence continue, some now directed against the mining company and its employees—with some more "modern" issues also arising.[6]

6. https://www.abc.net.au/news/2023-09-08/nt-police-groote-eylandt-peppimenarti/102831026; https://apple.news/ADoHXiNXgTYirHHXUrtIG8Q

The research project in which I was involved in 1987 with Professor John Cawte and his team into the causes of a neurological degenerative disease among Aboriginal people in the archipelago and its possible link to manganese pollution from the mining was inexplicably shelved by the Northern Territory government once Professor Cawte's initial findings were published (text, Chapter IX). Substituted was an alternative hypothesis, namely that the cause was the genetically transmitted Machado Joseph Disease (MJD) hypothetically introduced by Macassan traders from southeast Asia prior to European contact.

Valid or not, this turned attention away from any serious investigation into the health effects of the mining that we were undertaking, not only of the extraction and crushing processes, but also of the practice of spreading tailings on Angurugu's roads, confirmed during my times there but something the company of course denies (I have photos which are not for general publication as they show my young son enveloped in them). In any event, it was predicted at the time when the focus shifted from environment to genetics that if the described symptoms were transmitted *only* genetically, then in a very short space of time the illness would flood the whole archipelago. This has failed to materialize.

It seems that Aboriginal people long before contact knew there was "something bad" about manganese (*Malara Muwurawiya*) as they connected it to instigating acts of violence (text, page 127, #103).

With mining royalties came the trappings of modern Australian society—a money economy, consumer goods, computers, speedboats, four-wheel drives and the like. And who are we to argue with the attraction of that? But what also came was petrol-sniffing, alcoholism and violence and the constant pressure from government, the churches, and industry to assimilate—as well as opportunities for "white advisers" to manipulate. Plus an ongoing racism which judged their traditional Way of Life "Stone Age" and their culture "beyond understanding." That part was right—beyond our *ability* to understand i t.

A simple example of misunderstanding on my part: in an Aboriginal context the marriage system described in *Eden* (text, page 67) may appear to be one based on exchange where one "clan" gives a husband to the same "clan" in exchange for a wife every second generation. But this could easily (or even primarily) be "s e e n" as a construct in "collapsed time" designed to repeat its Form every second generation. Consistent with this view was a promise system of arranging marriages even before the prospective parties were born (text, pages 81–82).

The importance of the collection that Ruth and I donated to the Museum and Art Gallery (MAGNT) of the Northern Territory in 1999—there rather than back to the community on the advice of the elders because of the social problems at the time—now assumes added importance. Comprised not only of bark paintings and artifacts from the early days of our visits, but also of ("clan") histories recorded in 1969 and updated in 1986/7 which extended back into the 19th century from men and women some of whom were born in that era. And, perhaps most significantly, there are tape recordings of some 163 Songs recorded during mortuary ceremonies in 1969 and 1986 belonging to a wide range of "clans" in the archipelago, including the Wurramara who lost their Songs. These Gula rather remarkably later identified for me (*Life to the Power of Nothing,*," pages 34–35).

It was our time in the Groote Eylandt archipelago in 1986/7 that, I believe, revealed the dynamic underpinning of the day-to-day Way of Life of Aboriginal people in the pre-contact period and opened up the possibility of deeper levels of understanding and experience.

Originally i t was just hints in my notebooks" (text, page 1).

David Turner
Perth, Ontario
July 17, 2025

Preface to the Second Edition

Since writing this book I have revisited Amagalyuagba, Bickerton Island, and Groote Eylandt a number of times, first to help Dr. John Cawte with his research into a neurological degenerative disease there (1987 and 1988) and then in 1992, 1993 and 1995 to undertake a project on Aboriginal music that had to be abandoned in 1971 due to the politics of Aboriginal studies in the Northern Territory in that era (see Chapter 1).

The situation of the Groote and Bickerton people in 1995 is much the same as in 1986–88 with two notable exception: my close friend and original sponsor to Groote, Nandjiwarra Amagula (who can be seen, by the way, in the film *The Last Wave*), has died in the aftermath of his wife's death recounted in this volume, and as of 1991 Groote Eylandt and Bickerton Island now have their own Land Council separate from the Northern Land Council. Nandjiwarra's loss is a blow to the political aspirations of these people as he was a man of great foresight and a mediator with white society. Inauguration of the Land Council, while at first glance seeming to afford local people somewhat more control over their own affairs, in reality has potentially made them more susceptible to local interests originating on the outside such as Church Missionary Society (C.M.S.) affiliated personnel, the Groote Eylandt Mining Company (GEMCO) and the European manager of the Land Council itself.

The manager of the Land Council, for one, is bent on bringing Aboriginal notions of land tenure into line with the federal Land Rights Act (see Chapter X) and even on treating land as mere real estate – a business proposition. The mining company is pressing to expand its leases on Groote Eylandt and extend them to Bickerton Island and the adjacent mainland. Ex-C.M.S. and Church-affiliated personnel are waiting for Aboriginal culture to collapse so that they can pick up the pieces and turn these Aboriginal people into "good Christians". Situation of the Land Council here has also raised the question of the respective spheres of jurisdictions of the Land Council, the Angurugu Community Government Council and the Umbakumba Association Council on the island. The local councils are constituted by Northern Territory legislation, the Land Council by federal government legislation (see Chapter X).

On the other hand, Milya:gburra outstation on Bickerton Island is expanding as an alternative to the turmoil and pollution of Angurugu. The Warnungamadada People/Land are proceeding with plans to establish their own outstation at Armadadi on the adjacent mainland and in their country on Bickerton and perhaps shift off Groote Eylandt altogether.

While mortuary ceremonies are still being performed in the area, the process of abbreviation in their duration continues, with some deaths now being handled in just a few days. This has the disadvantage of collapsing the context affording young people the opportunity to learn their Songs and has placed the few old Songmen who are left, like Gula Lalara, in a very awkward position. They now know more about the Songs of certain other People/Lands than those people themselves and there is sometimes a reluctance to have them present at other People's ceremonies for this reason. With diminishment of knowledge and the Land Council manager's efforts, land ownership disputes are more frequent with some People/Lands pushing for more exclusive jurisdiction over some areas of value to Europeans such as mining sites. One such dispute between the Warnungwudjaragba and the Warnungwadarrbalangwa was settled with the intervention of a tape recording I made in 1969 of old Djabargwa recounting the Wamungwadarrbalangwa's migration from Bickerton Island to Groote Eylandt in the pre-European past where land was handed over to them in a ceremony by the Warnungwudjaragba (see pp. 32–34). Because of this intervention and others, my own situation has become precarious at least from the point of view of the Land Council manager and some People/Lands.

The neurological degenerative disease that has plagued the Groote and Bickerton Island people for a generation now, discussed in Chapter IX, has been counter-diagnosed as Machado-Joseph disease, a genetic disorder. I say "counter-diagnosed" because the issue of a possible connection to manganese pollution (manganese has been mined in the area since the mid-1960s) established by Professor John Cawte has now been downplayed and that of the general harmful effects of manganese pollution ignored. Unfortunately, the number of people with this disease is increasing and equally unfortunately there is as yet no way of predicting who will contract it and no cure for it once it is manifested. Dr. Tim Burt, who assumed control of the medical research from Professor Cawte, says that even if the cause is genetic, as he seems to believe, what with the extent of intermarriage in the region, eventually the whole Aboriginal population could end up with the disorder and die. The problem of translating the medical diagnosis of the disorder to Aboriginal people remains.

On this issue, after leaving Groote Eylandt in 1986 a letter came into my possession dated September 26, 1984, from Dr. John Cawte to Mr. Charles Perkins, then Secretary of the Department of Aboriginal Affairs in Canberra. In part it read,

> The most recent research indicates that manganese dust has toxic effects previously not recognized nor suspected. In brief, it is found to affect the nervous system, the development of the embryo, and the immune system, notably the defense against viral infections ... it is now my view that Angurugu should be regarded as an unsafe environment until proven otherwise. I believe that every man, woman and child, and especially unborn children, may be considered at risk.

This view still has not been made known "to the community, nor anybody else" by public officials as it was not in 1984. I have, however, communicated the danger myself to Aboriginal people on Groote and it is one of the reasons why a number of them have moved to Bickerton Island and to outstations away from the mining leases. GEMCO apparently has carried out a $1 million study of its own on manganese toxicity but will not release the results to the public. In an attempt to place the issue in the public domain I have written an article entitled "Genocide on Groote Eylandt?" for the journal *Indigenous Affairs* (Vol. No. 4, 1994), the voice of the International Work Group on Indigenous People, based in Denmark (IWGA, Rolstraede 10, DK-1171, Copenhagen). As well I have raised the matter with politicians and media people in Australia known to be sympathetic to the Aborigines' plight and who have said they would help. Time will tell.

On a more academic plane, a number of points have been raised by reviewers of the first edition and I would like to address some of them here. One is my use of the concept Promised Landscape with its allusions to the Book of Genesis in the Bible. This, of course, relates back to the first volume in my projected trilogy, *Life Before Genesis*, in which I argued that Australian Aboriginal culture, in outline form and removed from its historical context, represents the baseline from which the Book of Genesis proceeds. As I see it, "The Fall" in Judeo-Christian terms was *from* something akin to Australian Aboriginal culture, that is, a plurality of People/Lands in a relation of mutual interdependence, and *into* something akin to Euro-nationalism, a separation of independent peoples/lands each bent on autonomy and self-determination. The title of my second volume, then, should properly have been *Return to Eden̲s*.

The concept of "Promised Land" is the closest English equivalent we have to the Aboriginal conception of land. More than any other notion it expresses simultaneously land as material resource and Land as abstract, eternal, jurisdiction manifesting a "religious" quality, as in "God-given jurisdiction" (though the concept of God in our tradition has no meaning at all in the Aborigines'). Capitalized words in the text, like Land and Song, are meant to communicate this "religious" dimension. The fit between our concept and theirs, however, is far from perfect as in a Hebrew context the resources contained within that jurisdiction were meant for one's own exclusive use and enjoyment, whereas in an Aboriginal context those resources are for the benefit of someone outside one's own jurisdiction.

Another point raised about my book was my continuing use of the term "clan" for People/Land (really Land/People as Tony Swain has pointed out) when I rejected the use of that concept in an Aboriginal context because of its association with genealogy or blood ties by kinship. The reason I continued to use it, though with quotes around it, is that the term has crept into Aboriginal English (as have the equally inapplicable "tribe" and "totem"), though the Aborigines do not mean by these English terms what we mean by the terms when they employ them (the whole issue of the meaning of Aboriginal English could be a field of study in itself).

Another issue raised by reviewers was my apparent reluctance to situate my study within the history of Aboriginal studies as such. In terms of ethnographic precursors my debt to Rose, Worsley, Strehlow, Stanner, the Berndts and Maddock is obvious and acknowledged. However, when it comes to theoretical interpretation the situation is somewhat different. The theoretical "formula" (see Postlude) that in a sense "explains" Australian Aboriginal "culture" (really life-Forms) lies outside the gaze of Aboriginal studies as currently written. Indeed it is, I believe, outside the gaze of our history of ideas insofar as the theory transcends materialism and therefore most of our theories of society, history and culture. That is why, when it came to describing what that theory *was* rather than was *not* (e.g., Marxism, Hegelianism, evolutionism), I found antecedents in religious, rather than academic, traditions where the notion of "Nothingness", for instance, is treated experientially instead of philosophically or ideologically. I apologize, however, for my summary treatment of "Eastern mysticism" which, as Tony Swain pointed out, does not constitute a meaningful category and subsumes some traditions which do exhibit correspondences with the Aboriginal. I have since tried to remedy this in my paper "Prayer in Anthropological Perspective" (in Lawrence Brown, ed., *Toward a Psychology of Prayer*, Birmingham, Alabama: Religious Education Press, 1994), though I still conclude that the so-called "major traditions" are not quite "up to" the out- and in-sights of Aboriginal religion – if indeed it is a "religion" and not simply a more acute perception of reality.

Tony Swain has recently published a volume entiled *A Place for Strangers* (London: Cambridge University Press, 1993), suggesting that the general outlines of Aboriginal culture as presented in *Return to Eden* and *Life Before Genesis* may once have been the norm for at least the "top end" of Australia. He also puts forward the intriguing idea that Christian contact actually introduced the notions of evil and sorcery into Aboriginal society, thereby undermining the traditional idea that although people may become "bad" they can be rehabilitated through reindoctrination in ceremonies. That is, if "evil" as distinct from "badness" is something in our nature and our nature is basically spiritual, as Aborigines believe, then it follows that evil can only be fully eradicated by removing "it" from the person's body, precisely the purpose of sorcery. This, though, has the consequence of ending the person's life, something Aborigines were extremely reluctant to do in the pre-contact past. In the Groote and Bickerton area I have documented the recent introduction of sorcery during the Mission period and, indeed, I witnessed the first act performed there (see *Tradition and Transformation*, pp. 107–108).

In her *Dingo Makes Us Human* (London: Cambridge University Press, 1992), Deborah Bird Rose presents a picture of Yarralin Aboriginal life which, at least in outline, very much matches the one I have located in the Groote and Bickerton Island area. She phrases inter-group relations as between "promised lands" in an interdependent relation based on notions of giving if not "renunciation". As on Groote and Bickerton the contact situation has modified the Yarralin people's traditional design.

If the findings of this book do locate the essential outline of Aboriginal culture in a large part of Australia in pre-contact times, we will have to reject once and for all the presupposition that there was a uniform stage of development in human history at a hunter-gatherer level of subsistence. This is for the very good reason that the general outlines of Aboriginal culture presented here locate essential differences from "band society" characteristic of most other peoples at a hunter-gatherer level of subsistence of which we have evidence. In the Australian case I am thinking of determination of socio-economic institutions and behaviour by transcendent Forms rather than material conditions, land as bounded jurisdiction abstractly owned rather than occupied and held, federative rather than incorporative social processes, renunciative otherness rather than competition or sharing, interdependence rather than autonomy and self sufficiency.

What the findings and perspective of *Return to Eden* do, I hope, is not only steer new research into Aboriginal culture in a somewhat different direction, but also situate existing research findings in Australia and elsewhere in a somewhat broader and deeper theoretical context to clarify and extend their meaning. With the perspective of *Return to Eden*, the often off-handed comments of ethnographers and observers – material they might relegate to footnotes – take on new meaning. Take, for example, Hiatt's remark in *Kinship and Conflict* (Canberra: The Australian National University Press, 1965) that "If every land-owning unit had to depend solely upon the resources of its own estate, some would certainly have perished... On occasion the members visited neighbouring communities, and at other times acted as their hosts" (p. 27). Within the framework of *Return to Eden*, the situation of people within Lands of limited resources may actually represent a conscious effort on their part to actually *prohibit* the consumption of even these limited resources to themselves, the "owners", by identifying with them "totemically". I argue that "totemism" and the prohibition on consuming one's species as well as abundances within one's own territory aimed to prevent self-sufficiency and force relations of a host guest nature between oneself and one's neighbours.

The perspective of *Eden* would lead us to reconsider reports like Hiatt's, not only in terms of the people/land relation but also the People/Land relation, that is, in terms of the process by which the Form of the Land (or of the Person) as an aesthetic or transcendent quality is constituted so as to "expel" resources and people from one Place to another. (It is this consideration of Forms that has led me to retitle Chapter 7 [now Chapter 8] "Cosmo-logic" rather than "Theo-logic" as the latter wrongly implies some notion of "God" in the Aboriginal scheme of things.)

As Don Wiebe mentions in his Preface, for this the second edition I have added a new chapter on my unsuccessful attempt in 1971 to return to the islands to conduct a comprehensive inquiry into Aboriginal music, a project to which I returned only recently. I have also included a glossary of important Aboriginal terms and an index organized along thematic lines so that the reader can readily locate and group material dealing with "religion", "economy", "polity" and the like.

Glossary of Important Aboriginal Terms

For a list of relationship terms and their meanings see Table 1.

For names of the People/Lands referred to in this book see Table 2.

Agwilyunggwa: phase of mortuary ceremonies where those closest to the deceased are painted up.

aiya:ba: reef.

alara: very impmiant place on each People/Land.

alarndarragawarriya: any physiologically disabling injury.

alawudawarra: activating aspect of spirit.

alumera: silt

ama:ba: song.

Amagalyuagba: Bickerton Island.

Amawurrena: Spirit or the Formal dimension of spirit.

Amawurrena-alawudawarra: Spirituality.

amugwa: a person's spirit when released; animating aspect of.

Amunduwurrarria: "remembrance" or final stage of mortuary ceremonies; now replaced by *Mardaiya:n*.

angalya: "country"; Land of People

angwura: fire/smoke.

Arumandja: important place on Bickerton Island where Nambirrirrma descended.

auguburda: spiritual contamination.

augwalya: animals, sea animals, fish, bony fish.

augwayagayama: tune.

awarrawalya: spirit = shadow, shade.

bara: west wind.

burra burra: any lethal disease; sometimes "sorcery".

Companies: Aboriginal English for People/Lands on the same Songstream.

derrarragugwa: peaceful dove/spider.

djunggwaiya: boss of ceremonial activities of a People/Land not your own, e.g., your mother's.

gemalyangarrengama: create = make something from nothing then slice off and twist in something from somewhere else.

Madalyuma: Sea Channel of a Dreamtime Being (e.g., Rainbow Serpent).

malara: manganese.

mamalagunda: fresh water spring in the sea.

mamariga: east wind.

mamera: tune with voice.

Mamungba: phase of mortuary ceremonies where a lock of the dead person's hair is sung into a dillybag and returned to country.

Mardaiya:n: sacred/secret ceremony introduced from the mainland.

mulgwa: womb, sometimes "bay".

midjiyanga: ship.

murndigrriya:rra: long yam.

Nambirrirrma: culture hero who descended from the sky on Bickerton Island to reiterate the Law.

nar'a:bina: nothing.

warnemaleda: a small bark container housing the remains of a dead child awaiting rebirth; doll.

warnigarangbidja: other-moiety relationship too close for marriage where man's father and woman's mother are from the same People/Land.

wurramugwa: ghosts, spirits of dead people on the "other side".

wurra:nigaberra: "their side" of Companies who "your side" marry.

Yabongwa: Rainbow Serpent.

Yandarranga: Central Hill.

yilyaugwa: wild honey.

yiraga: hollow log musical instrwnent played by circular breathing.

yirra:nigaberra: "our side" of Companies who may not intermarry

Photorecord:
Groote Eylandt and Bickerton Island, 1986

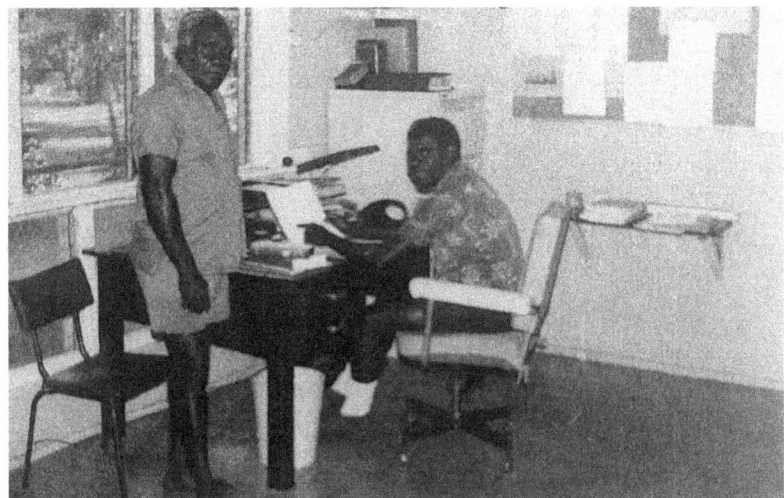

Plate 2. Murabuda Wurramarrba and Bobby Nungumadjbarr at the Angurugu Community Government Council office.

Plate 3. Murabuda Wurramarrba and others on his Songstream.

Plate 4. Processing the Spirit to the gravesite at Balaya's funeral.

Plate 5. Dancing the Spirit to the gravesite on Curlew.

Plate 6. Gula Lalara singing Balalya's Spirit to her Agwilyunggwa.

Plate 7. Gudigba Lalara.

Plate 8. The Place where Nambirrirrma descended on Bickerton.

Plate 9. Graeme at A:nemurramadja, "Laughing Waves", Place

Plate 10. Ruth and Iain chopping wood at Miya:gburra campsite.

Plate 11. Iain and Michelle at Milya:gburra Outstation.

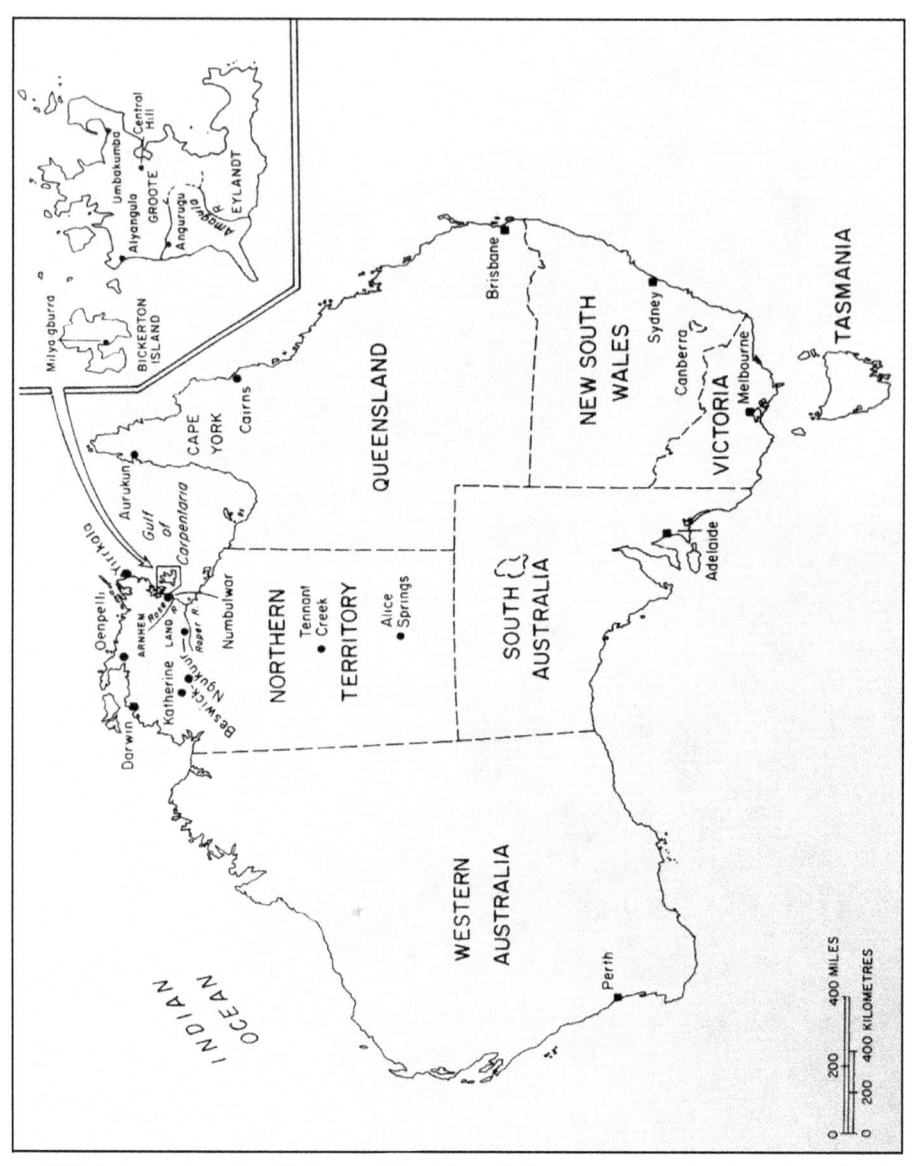

MAP 2. Amagalyuagba, Bickerton Island, in Relation to Groote Eylandt and Mainland Australia

INTRODUCTION

They were just hints in my notebooks. I had been told by the old men that the land belonging to one of the people of Amagalyuagba had the fresh water, another the yams and a third the wild apples. There were but four lands on the island – five if you counted the section of Wurra:nggilyangba (they-belonging-to A:nggilyangba) country on the north coast that had been carved out for the Warnungamadada some three generations ago. They belonging-to Armadadi, a place on the adjacent mainland, had come to Amagalyuagba or Bickerton Island about the same time the Warnungwadarrbalangwa (they-belonging-to-the place called Adarrba langwa). Both people, however, still retained jurisdiction over the lands they had left, despite their emigration.

The Warnungamadada were on the same Songstream as the Wurra:nggilyangba, connecting up by it to Wurruwa:ba, Parrots, and Yinemanenga, Wild Apples, through the travels of Yandarranga, Central Hill, and the Stingrays: Yimaduwaiya, Yilyanga and Yugurredangwa. This Songstream connected these people in turn to the Warnungang wurugwerigba on the eastern side of Groote Eylandt and to the Wurramaminyamandja on its central eastern side. When people in these groups died the men sang into this Songstream to find their Spirits and transported them through to the "other side" or what I will call a "fifth dimension".

The Warnungamadada, also called Lalara, were the people with whom I was affiliated when I was first on Groote Eylandt in Northern Australia in 1969 (Map I). My wife was affiliated with the Wurramara, the group the Warnungamadada marry, ideally in alternate generations. The association, far from incorporating us into their society, was merely to establish a point of reference from which we both could proceed to deal with each other as human beings. It was merely the polite way to treat guests.

Were the lands of the Bickerton Island people resource specific? Did the Aborigines draw boundaries around resources so that no one group of them could be self-sufficient? Yinemanenga, Wild Apples, was also a Wurra:nggilyangba Song. One normally wasn't allowed to consume what one sung. Were the old men referring to the symbolic relationship between people and resources and not to their location in bounded jurisdictions when they told me that one group had the fresh water, another the wild apples, a third the yams? But if fresh water was sung how could its consumption possibly be prohibited? The so-called "totemic" prohibition denied the resource in question to you even though it was within your bounds. Was the consequence, the purpose, of this thereby to make it available to someone else? If we, as Warnungamadada, can't eat *yilyanga,* the Wurramara can. Would drawing boundaries in such a way as to render countries resource specific be the obverse of this? That is, did this mean that someone else's resources would have to be made available to you if you were to have the full complement necessary to survival?

A lot of little things which had heretofore seemed relatively insignificant suddenly began to add up to a pattern. I would have to go back to confirm (or see denied) my impression. Supposing that people's lands did turn out to be resource specific, that people did draw their boundaries in such a way that no one had jurisdiction over all the critical resources. Why would this be so significant? For one thing, it would disprove Economists' (and the political Right's) claims that maximization of material self-interest is normal and natural and that our institutions should flow with, rather than against, this fact. If the Right was right, Bickerton would be an island of independent people competing for its diverse resources or it would be an island with but one group in control of all its resources. This would be the group that had out-competed all rivals over time.

Such a finding would also disprove Marxists' (and the political Left's) claim that co-operation and sharing were normal and natural and that our institutions should flow with, rather than against, this fact. If the Left were right, again Bickerton would be a one-people island, the outcome of groupings coming together peacefully to share its diverse resources. (It is also easy to see how both Left and Right could use the same evidence of a one-people island to justify their claims in the absence of historical data to demonstrate how the situation became that way.) If the resource-specific lands idea is true, it *would* also undermine the claim that the drive to autonomy and self-sufficiency/self-determination – common to both Left and Right thinking – is also natural to the human condition. By squeezing five peoples into such a small space as Bickerton Island and giving each control over a critical resource it would be as if these Aborigines were trying to prevent the very possibility of self-sufficiency/self-determination from arising.

Here then might be a hunting and gathering society that contradicted both the Left's vision of a primitive communist past and the Right's of an anarchistic individualist one. Instead would be what? A world of mutual respect and interdependence, the essence of what we call "civilization"? How could a Stone Age culture – the most materially impoverished on record – have achieved what we only aspire to? Yes, the hints I had in my notebooks, the directions in which they pointed, certainly did bear a second look. But I was being pulled back to the Wamungamagalyuagba, the people of Bickerton Island, reluctantly. The memory of my last visit in 1974, not to mention 1971, was still indelibly imprinted on my mind.

In the mid-1960s the Groote Eylandt Mining Company (GEMCO) had begun mining on the island. Between 1969 and 1974 the mining had accelerated, bringing in large numbers of Euro-Australians and more of the trappings of mainstream Australian society. Prior to the mid-1960s virtually the only Europeans on the island were the staff of the Church Missionary Society (C.M.S.). It was on their say-so that the Welfare Branch of the Northern Territory administration decided on my permit status on Groote Eylandt and they did so every two months during my stay in 1969. Having tolerated my presence for a year then, they were not about to let me test their patience again.

PART I

EXODUS

I

1971: Return and Expulsion

With completion of my first fieldwork period amongst the Aborigines of the Groote Eylandt and Bickerton Island area in 1969, I was appointed post doctoral research fellow at the Australian Institute of Aboriginal Studies (A.I.AS.) in Canberra and awarded a grant to carry out further fieldwork in the area, this time on Aboriginal ceremonies, songs and legends. In 1969 I had recorded some 40 tapes' worth of Aboriginal mortuary singing – over 600 songs – and this needed checking and analyzing. I had heard about but not seen a complete performance of the sacred Mardaiya:n ceremony and this needed further investigation. What seemed like a fairly apolitical and straightforward undertaking – and was that from the point of view of working with the Aborigines – soon turned out, however, to be anything but.

The following is the text of my report to the Institute of Aboriginal Studies of what transpired in my unsuccessful efforts to undertake this research project. The report is dated June 27, 1971, and edited only for style. It reflects a chapter of Australian history that is now, hopefully, forever closed.

Preliminary Remarks
With this (the goal of returning to Groote Eylandt) in view, I wrote to the superintendent of the Angurugu Mission on Groote Eylandt, via Judith Stokes, the Mission's linguist, informing him of my plans to return there to continue my research, and asking if accommodation were available for my wife, Ruth, and myself. I pointed out that, as we also intended going to Umbakumba (on Groote) and Rose River (on the adjacent mainland), our stay there would be much shorter than the previous 10 months' period we had spent in 1969 and suggested that if there were no Mission accommodation available, could they put us up for a few days while we worked out other arrangements privately. Shortly afterwards, on May 19, Professor Ronald Berndt (who had been my Ph.D. supervisor at the University of Western Australia in Perth) wrote to Mr. E. P. Milliken, Assistant Director of the Research Division of the Welfare Branch in the Northern Territory Administration, Darwin, explaining my plans to him.

When neither Mr. Milliken nor the Mission had replied by June 1, Professor Berndt and I decided to telegraph Mr. Milliken to find out whether they had any objections to my being issued a permit, hence any objections to my proceeding to Darwin. (At the time, a permit from the Northern Territory Administration was a necessary prerequisite to entering what was then the Arnhem Land/Groote Eylandt Aboriginal Reserve). I had expected the same reactions from both the Mission and Welfare as I had encountered during my first fieldtrip to Groote; namely that the Mission would say that no suitable accommodation could be made available to us by the Mission but that we might be able to arrange something privately with a Euro-Australian working on the island (given that we were "not to live like the Aborigines"), and that Welfare would issue me a week's permit to go to Groote and try to make these arrangements as well as to obtain the Aborigines' permission to work among them.

Mr. Milliken had told me when I left the field in 1969 that I would be able to return to Groote in the future and he had reaffirmed this assurance at a later meeting in Canberra in May 1970. Professor Berndt and I allowed a full week to elapse after sending the telegram and then, as no objection had been raised, and expecting none, Ruth and I left for Darwin on June 12.

Subsequent Events in Darwin:
June 12: I had originally planned to spend the weekend in Darwin looking for some of the Groote Aborigines who might be visiting there in order to sound them out regarding my return, before contacting Welfare the following week about my permit. However, a friend telephoned Mr. Milliken when we got in and told him that we had arrived in Darwin. Mr. Milliken left instructions that I was to phone him back at 4:00 p.m. that afternoon, and when I did so he denied having received Professor Berndt's telegram, but said he had received Professor Berndt's letter of May 19 only that day and said he was not even aware that I had received a grant from the A.I.A.S. to do further research on Groote. This was despite the fact that his superior Mr. Harry Giese, the Assistant Administrator of the Northern Territory, had been one of the persons who originally ratified my project with the Institute. The information had also appeared in the A.I.A.S's newsletter, and Professor Berndt had mentioned the awarding of my grant in his May 19th letter.

Mr. Milliken said that he would have to contact Mr. Leske of the Church Missionary Society (C.M.S.) in Darwin who administered the Angurugu Mission, regarding accommodation and permission to conduct my research. He said he would phone me back before noon the next day after contacting Mr. Leske. I told Mr. Milliken that I had written to the Mission regarding accommodation and that Mr. Leske would probably have been informed.

June 13: When Mr. Milliken had not phoned the next morning, I called *him* and he said he had not yet contacted Mr. Leske but would do so that afternoon and would call me back at 10:00 p.m. that evening. That afternoon Ruth and I went to "Open House" at the Baghot Aboriginal Reserve (in Darwin) and there we met seven Aboriginal men and eight women from Groote. They seemed very pleased to see us again and asked repeatedly when we were going over to the island.

When Mr. Milliken had not phoned by 10:00 p.m., I phoned *him* and he said he had not yet contacted Mr. Leske but would do so immediately and then telephone me back. When he did, he reported that Mr. Leske said he had not heard anything at all about my writing for accommodation and that he had no idea I was going back to Groote. Mr. Milliken then began to berate me for coming to Darwin and trying to get a permit without having first arranged accommodation. He then said that he and Mr. Leske agreed that I first must put my request for accommodation and research in writing and it would be sent to the Mission authorities and the Angurugu Aboriginal Station Council on Tuesday. As soon as this conversation ended, I phoned Mr. Leske to seek clarification, but a woman answered and, after asking my name, left the phone, returned and said that Mr. Leske was not available that night. At this point I decided I would try to contact Mr. Leske the following day and work on a draft to the Mission authorities and the Station Council regarding my work there.

June 14: Before I was able to contact Mr. Leske in the morning, I received a letter from Miss Stokes at the Mission addressed to me in Perth (Western Australia) but passed on to my Darwin address before mailing by C.M.S. authorities. This letter gave the impression that the Mission authorities were in favour of my return but that the local Aborigines were not and it said that, in any case, there was no accommodation available. It also said that Mr. Leske had read my original letter to Miss Stokes even before the Mission superintendent and thus knew that I had applied for accommodation and was planning to do research on Groote.

At this point I thought it best to apply for a two-day permit to allow me to travel to Groote and petition the Aborigines myself, if not those at the

Mission, then at Umbakumba settlement or Numbulwar on the adjacent mainland, both places included within the framework of my research proposal.

I phoned Mr. Leske of C.M.S. and asked if he would be willing to support an application for a two-day permit to the Mission so that I could seek private accommodation and put my case to the local Aboriginal people. He said that if I wanted to go to Groote even for two days, I would first have to apply in writing to the Aboriginal Station Council and also have accommodation arranged for the period. He went on to say that he had not heard anything about my wanting to return to Groote for further work until told by Mr. Milliken the previous night and began to berate me for not letting anyone know. I then mentioned the letter I had just received from Miss Stokes in which she said he had, in fact, seen the original letter and he admitted she had told him of my application. I then mentioned Miss Stokes' information regarding the Aboriginal meeting and the apparent refusal and explained why I thought I should present my application myself under these circumstances. I again asked if I could go out for two days to arrange accommodation and make formal application to the people in person. He said I could not, because the last time I went out (1969) I was supposed to re-apply for a permit if I found accommodation within the allotted time (one week) and I had failed to do so. (When I went to Groote in 1969 I was given a week's permit by Welfare to find suitable accommodation with the understanding that, if I did so, the pemlit would be extended. When I found accommodation – or rather the Aborigines found accommodation for me – I informed the superintendent who said he would inform Welfare and nothing more was said of the matter.) I asked Mr. Leske why other persons I knew who were connected with the church could go out for a few days without the Aborigines' permission, and be replied it was because they were doing worthwhile work.

Following this conversation I called Mr. Milliken and asked him if Welfare would be willing to issue me a two-day permit to go to the Mission to seek accommodation and the people's permission. The conversation went like this:

"I talked to Percy Leske and suggested getting a two-day permit to go to the Mission and petition the Station Council."

"All right, when would you like to go?" "Tomorrow."

"I won't be in the office early enough to issue you a permit."

"Okay. I'll go on Wednesday, then."

"Was this Percy's idea?"

"No, it was mine. He thought I should send it [the application] to the Aboriginal Council in writing."

"I'd better talk to Percy tomorrow. I'll call you before 8:30 a.m. If I don't, you call me. I'll be in the office early and I'm inundated with work and I might forget."

That evening outside the Darwin Hospital I met five Groote Aborigines and asked them about the meeting at the Mission when it was decided that we were not to return. They said that they knew of no such decision, but most of them would not have been on the island when the decision was apparently taken.

June 15: About half-past eight in the morning Mr. Milliken phoned saying that he had talked to Percy Leske and decided I could not go out on a two-day permit. Rather, I must make out my application in writing and send it to the Station Council. I then suggested going to Umbakumba first instead of Angurugu, and asked for a two-day permit to go there to find accommodation and ask permission of the local people. He said I had to proceed with the original plan to work at Angurugu and that Umbakumba was not within the terms of reference of my project. When I pointed out that it was, as was Nwnbulwar, he refused to talk about it further and if I wished to call back in the afternoon he would discuss writing an application to Umbakumba.

In this conversation with Mr. Milliken he revised his earlier statement about when he had received Professor Bemdt's letter, saying it had arrived June 2 but had only been mailed May 28 (in fact it had been mailed May 19.)

At this point I thought it wise to phone Professor Berndt and inform him of what was happening and seek his advice on what to do next. He felt that under the circumstances I should try to go to Umbakumba first, and when there, sort out things with the Mission Aborigines. He also agreed that to forward a written application would be unwise and could see no reason why I could not get a temporary permit to go out and see if arrangements could be made for both accommodation and the permission of the Aborigines. I again phoned Mr. Milliken and told him of Professor Bemdt's recommendations as well as the reasons for them. Mr. Milliken said he would be willing to give me a two-day permit to Umbakumba but would have to contact the superintendent first to see if there was accommodation, not only for a few days but also for a longer period. I asked if I could work this out for myself when I got there but he refused. (I had been told by a friend who had been to Umbakumba a week before that there were a number of houses vacant due to a shortage of staff and that I should be able to stay in one of these for a few days while I looked for something more permanent.) Under no circumstances, said Mr. Milliken, was I permitted to live in an Aboriginal style house or tent (as we had done in 1969). Mr. Milliken said that since he was going to be away for a few days he would instruct Anita Campbell, his assistant, to contact Umbakumba that afternoon regarding accommodation for myself and Ruth and that I was to call her back early the next morning for a reply.

June 16: I phoned Anita Campbell at 8:30 a.m. and asked her what the reply had been from Umbakumba regarding my accommodation there. She said that Mr. Milliken had never mentioned contacting Umbakumba to her or that I was even in Darwin or applying to go there. I explained to her that I was trying to get accommodation there for two or three days so that I could go out to see if more permanent arrangements could be made. I mentioned to her that I had been told by someone who had been there just a week ago that some of the houses were vacant because of a shortage of teachers. She said that she would try to contact Umbakumba for me on the morning radio schedule and would phone me back by 10:30 a.m. When she had not contacted me that morning I phoned her again and asked if she had received a reply. She said that the superintendent there had said that as they were presently very busy with the census and were having "internal troubles" they would prefer that my visit be deferred. During this conversation, however, Ms Campbell's tone completely changed compared to the previous occasion. Then she had been co-operative and friendly; now she seemed hostile. She berated me for not having told them I was coming to Darwin and for having arrived on the weekend. I said that a telegram had been sent on June 1 saying that I would be coming the following week and that we had allowed one full week to elapse in case any objections were raised before finally departing. I explained that I had not intended contacting Welfare until the beginning of the week but, since Mr. Milliken had been informed of my arrival by a friend and suggested I call him, I did so. At no time during the weekend did I suggest that anyone *do* anything for me. I was only seeking information as to what could be done. She said that I was only a minor consideration to them as there were more important things that had to be dealt with. I said that I knew of other people who had gone to Umbakumba for short periods recently and there had been no objections raised about their visits. She said that since Mr. Milliken was away, I should contact Mr. Giese who might be able to get permission from Umbakumba for me to go there. Consequently I made an appointment to see Mr. Giese at 4:00 p.m. the following day.

By now I was feeling very bewildered by what seemed extreme inconsistency on the part of the people with whom I had been dealing. In the first place, they rarely did what they said they were going to do; in the second, when I asked to go to the Mission for a few days to make the necessary arrangements I was told I first had to write the Aboriginal Station Council for permission, but when I made the same request to Umbakumba I was told I first had to contact the (government-appointed Euro-Australian) super-intendent; in the third place, on one occasion I was told I could have a two-day permit from Welfare to go to the Mission, but later was refused after consultation between Welfare and C.M.S. officials; and fourthly I had been told different things by the same individual on different occasions regarding whether or not or when they had received information about my project and arrival in Darwin.

June 17: That afternoon I went to see Mr. Giese and explained why I wanted to go to Umbakumba at this time rather than to the Mission. He agreed that I was right to have proceeded to Darwin after having sent the telegram and that it was within my frame of reference to begin work at Umbakumba. He said he would allow me to go to Umbakumba to try and find accommodation and petition the local people, but only if someone would agree to put Ruth and I up for the period. He asked how long I wanted to spend at Umbakumba and I replied that about two months would probably be sufficient (I had intended trying to spend this length of time at both Angurugu and Numbulwar.) He said he would also have to find someone to put us up at Umbakumba for this longer period and that under no circumstances was I to camp with the Aboriginal people in a tent or humpie (bark hut). I mentioned that I had heard that there were empty houses at the settlement but he said that I would not be able to use any of these as they would be given to additional staff who were to be going there in the very near future. He said he would see that my request for temporary accommodation for either my wife and I, or for myself alone, would be sent to Umbakumba the next morning and that I should phone his secretary at 4:00 p.m. the next day for the reply. He said that in the event I had to proceed initially myself and

I was successful in securing extended accommodation and the Aborigines' permission, my wife could fly out to join me. If I failed to come to any arrangement I was to return to Darwin.

June 18: I contacted Mr. Giese's secretary at 4:00 p.m. and she said that they had been unable to get in touch with Umbakumba and I would have to wait until Monday before the message could be sent. I was told to call back at 11 a.m. Monday morning. Later in the day I contacted Mr. Leske about the possibility of going to Numbulwar Mission in the event I was not able to go to Umbakumba. He said that there was no spare accommodation there and thought there was little point applying. Again, he would not agree to my going there for a few days to arrange something privately without first applying in writing. I again phoned Professor Berndt to keep him up-to date- on the proceedings.

June 19 and 20: No further contacts made.

June 21: When I phoned Mr. Giese's secretary at 11:00 a.m. she said that I was to contact Mr. Larkham who was now handling my case in Mr. Milliken's absence. Mr. Larkham told me that the District Welfare Officer (D.W.O.) on Groote, Mr. Casey, had been asked to telephone him that morning with an answer from Umbakumba but had not yet done so. I was to call back about two that afternoon. When I did, he told me that permission had been given for us to proceed but that I would be allowed to stay only if I agreed to the following conditions:

1. that a copy of the results of my research go to the assistant administrator of the Territory.
2. that I provide my own transport while on Groote. Transport was available for hire there.
3. that we get someone to put us up at Umbakumba.
4. that we were not to camp in the village with the Aborigines.
5. that we were to get permission from the village Council to do our research.

I agreed to meet these requirements and Mr. Larkham said that he would inform the Umbakumba superintendent and the D.W.O. that we were coming that afternoon and that I would not need a written permit for the time being. If I received permission and accommodation I was to have the Umbakumba superintendent inform Darwin.

We arrived on Groote that afternoon and drove back to the settlement in the Umbakumba supply truck which had met us at the plane. There I met the superintendent, Keith Smith, who said there was plenty of accommodation available. We were assigned a small house in the settlement which Mr. Smith said they usually retained for guests and he told us that we could move to another one on a permanent basis the next day. Mr. Smith had approached members of the village Council that day regarding permission to conduct my research and received their approval (which he put in writing). He said that he would contact Welfare in Darwin the following morning to say that I had met their requirements. He said that since there was no prospect of a full quota of staff arriving during my fieldwork period we would be able to stay in a particular house for the duration.

June 22: We moved into another house in the morning where we expected to be able to stay during our research period.

June 23: In the morning, one of the settlement staff contacted me and said that a message had come through from the D.W.O., Mr. Casey, that we were only to stay for three days then return to Darwin. He also said that a delegation from the Angurugu Station Council was coming to Umbakumba later in the day to see us. I immediately sought out Mr. Smith who said he had no further details and that he would take us to Alyangula (the mining township) that afternoon to see the D.W.O. When we arrived at the D.W.O.'s office he was not there but his secretary confirmed that such a message had been received. As she was in contact with Darwin on the radio I asked if I could send a message. I informed Darwin that I had fulfilled their conditions and asked for a two months' extension of my permit. Darwin replied asking for confirmation from the Umbakumba superintendent and this was given. There followed a delay while the information was being given to someone else present. Finally the reply came back that my permit was not to be extended until I fulfilled another condition (heretofore unmentioned), namely that I submit my research *proposal* to Welfare for approval. I replied that my project had already been passed by Mr. Giese as a member of the Institute of Aboriginal Studies review board and asked if I could simply write out a summary of my original proposal and lodge it with them. I was told that this would not suffice and that I was to return to Darwin. When the D.W.O. returned I asked if he could clarify the situation and suggest a possible course of action for me. He said that his instructions were clear and my wife and I were to be on the next morning's plane to Darwin (adding that if we were not, we would be placed under arrest and a plane flown out from Darwin for us). He also said that he had received an earlier message from Welfare in Darwin (which had not been passed on to the Umbakumba superintendent) which stated that we should not be allowed to stay in any government house at Umbakumba. Mr. Smith argued with the D.W.O. that houses were vacant there and would be for some time, but the D.W.O said that these were his instructions and I should not have been allowed to stay in the house I was in.

On the way back to Umbakumba from Alyangula we met Nandjiwarra Amagula who had been sent by the Angurugu Station Council to see me. He said that they had no objection to our coming to the Mission to conduct our work and put it in writing for me. This contradicted the earlier report from the Mission (officials) that the Aborigines there did not want us to come.

June 24: Ruth and I left Umbakumba in the morning to meet the Darwin plane and, knowing that the D.W.O. was also on his way to Darwin on the same flight, contacted him at the airport and asked if there had been any change in his instructions regarding my departure. He said there had not been and we were to leave the island. Immediately on reaching Darwin I telephoned Professor Berndt and told him what had happened and how I and my wife felt about the whole thing.

Both of us were emotionally and mentally drained by our experiences and decided that there was little to be gained by continuing discussions with Welfare officials, particularly with Mr. Milliken. We felt that we had fulfilled all the conditions imposed upon us by Welfare, and that the new stipulation that we had to submit a complete research proposal to them for approval seemed completely unreasonable and unethical. Considering what had transpired over the past six weeks since Professor Berndt had written to Mr. Milliken, we felt justified in lodging a formal complaint with the Institute regarding our treatment. Basically the same thing had happened (in 1969) when we tried to obtain our permit for our first field trip and only a fortunate set of circumstances had been responsible for our being able to stay on Groote (i.e., the absence of the Mission superintendent and pressure by the local Aborigines, led by Nandjiwarra, on the acting superintendent to give us one of their houses – a simple "staging house" across the river from the main settlement). Pressure from Welfare and Mission officials had continued throughout our fieldwork period and at times impeded our work (e.g., unfounded accusations that I was stirring up the Aborigines on a number of issues, particularly over Helen Wurm's visit and her attempt to obtain a sacred ceremonial object from the Numbulwar Aborigines which eventually resulted in the death of the leading *mardaiy;an* songman, Mack Mumiyowan, and over the location of a survey flag by the Navy on top of Central Hill without the Aborigines' permission; see my "On the Outside Looking In", in Smith and Turner, eds., *Challenging Anthropology).*

An attempt had also been made in 1969 to gain access to my research notes. During my stay on Groote, the Commonwealth Department of Aboriginal Affairs bought into my study by assuming part of its cost from the Institute of Aboriginal Studies without informing either Professor Berndt or myself and then approached me in the field through Jeremy Long for information on the Groote people on the grounds that I was now partially responsible to the Department. I refused and informed Professor Berndt who saw to it that their involvement was terminated.

Professor Berndt now agreed that it was not wise to try and continue my work under these circumstances, especially as it seemed likely that further obstacles were likely to be placed in my way. All things considered, this seemed to us a justifiable cut-off point and grounds for formal complaint. Consequently my wife and I returned to Perth to prepare this report.

As for my "formal complaint" about our treatment, Professor Berndt took it to the Institute of Aboriginal Studies who took it to the Commonwealth (Liberal-Country Party) Government and the Northern Territory Administration who refused to budge on the issue. Within a few weeks the whole matter was dropped. I headed off back to Canada with Ruth to regroup. The following year I returned at the invitation of the Australian National University to establish Aboriginal Studies in the teaching program there. In 1972 the government changed. The Labour Party under Whitlam was elected to power. They changed the rules on permits to Aboriginal communities. Henceforth you were allowed to appear in person before the Aboriginal people concerned to make your own case for conducting research among them.

[In 1986 I happened to encounter Mr. Milliken, now retired, in Darwin. We talked about these events. He was quite candid. The Church Mission Society, he said, were adamant that we were not to return to Groote Eylandt because we were interfering with their missionizing efforts there. Welfare did want access to my research findings as Groote was a sensitive area and the Aborigines' response to the mining which had just begun there was being closely monitored. Nothing personal. It was all purely political. That's just the way it was. Welcome to the Northern Territory of Australia!]

II

1974: Return and Withdrawal

In the winter of 1974 I planned a short research trip north to Roper River settlement and a brief revisit to Groote Eylandt before returning permanently to Canada for family reasons. The Roper river itself flows into the Gulf of Carpentaria on the coast to the south-west of Groote Eylandt and near its mouth the Church Missionary Society established a Mission in 1908. From here they branched north into the gulf country to spread not only the Christian message but also the material "benefits" of Western civilization. As John Bayton recounts the period in his *Cross Over Carpentaria* (p. 140):

> On Roper River the settlement was firmly established by 1920 and those people to whom the first missionaries went in 1908 – "frightened, dirty, (who) took no interest in themselves ignorant, (who) worshipped the 'debil debil' " and were given to a nomadic life had become a 'confident, developing' people whose ignorance had been dispelled by 'knowledge of the English language, writing, spelling and reading, arithmetic and some geography'. The mission was beginning to look outward and already prayer was being offered for the Aborigines of Groote Eylandt and plans in preparation for a survey to be made so soon as a suitable vessel was available....
>
> In 1922 the prayers for the extension of the work in Arnhem Land and the Gulf were answered and a small auxiliary vessel of 14 tons was presented to the mission, and in this the whole of the coast of Groote Eylandt was explored to find a suitable site for a mission. On the south-west corner and about two miles up a clear and beautiful river "a site was fixed and named Emerald".

The party then returned home to the Roper Mission to make plans for founding a Mission on Groote. This apparently uneventful voyage was anything but that for the local Aborigines. Murabuda Wurramarrba, a Bickerton Island man, recounts what happened:

> We were camped at Angurugu [on the river of the same name] getting

munenga (burrawang, *cycas angulata*, a staple food unavailable on Bickerton].

We were swimming in the river and having a good time when suddenly a boat appeared with something that looked human standing on it. It called out "Garamadalya ["you mob"], I am a messenger from God." We didn't know what it meant. And we didn't stop to listen. We just ran off into the bush. It called again, "Hallelujah children, don't run away, I've come with good news for you."

In the bush we talked about it. We thought it was a ghost. The old people said that when you smoke a place you can look deep into the smoke and see the faces of the old people. They are all shiny and white.

The old people had a story about a boat that had been anchored in the Bay at Alyangula [now the mining township] before this. They thought the human looking things on it had round feet. They'd seen their footprints on the sand and didn't know about shoes. They saw only from a distance and thought that they had round heads on top. They didn't know about hats. They knew they were humans, though, because they had hands and faces like ours.

Murabuda couldn't have remembered the details, he was only a small child at the time. It must have been a story told to him by his father and others much later as a joke, a retrospective laugh at their naiveté. Naiveté, however, has characterized the Aborigines' relationship to Europeans throughout the contact period, and it is no joke. They have suffered for it. On the other hand, their naiveté is born of an accommodating attitude which permitted Macassan traders from Indonesia before, and Europeans later, to set up shop in their midst even though the Europeans, at least, never asked permission to do so. It was an accommodation which, however, did demand some degree of distance. The Aborigines kept their women segregated from the Macassans, and when the Euro-Australian missionaries arrived, the Aborigines used the Mission as a trading post only, declining to settle down until the site was shifted from the Emerald River near the coast to Angurugu, inland, during the Second World War.

Both to save face and preserve their presence on the island, the Church Missionary Society reluctantly established the Emerald River site as a Mission for part-Aborigines from the mainland. Meanwhile they plied the local Aborigines with tobacco, sugar, tea and *dambala* (cloth) in an effort both to maintain their presence on the island and demonstrate the power behind their message. Soon they had the Aborigines funding most of the enterprise. This is a letter from M. L. Perriman to Lois Reed recalling his earlier experiences on Groote (in the Angurugu Mission Records, 19 August 1969).

> The policy of the mission was to pay for all work done or for articles purchased from the natives. To charge for all articles we supplied to the natives such as tobacco, knives, tomahawks, wire, cloth, etc. All medicines and treatment was to be free. We would purchase turtle shell and native-made articles at a fair price, then sell them. The difference between what we paid and received would be placed into an account or fund, from which we would purchase the tobacco and other items sold to the natives.

By this process the C.M.S. missionary subscribers' money would not be used for buying these items The Aborigines were paying for their own colonization.

Roper River Mission, now renamed Ngukurr, was far from being populated by "a developing confident people" when I arrived there in the summer of 1974. I had come to look at the so-called "semi-moiety" system of the Mara and Wanderang people there before going across to Groote. The "semi-moieties" were four in number, named Mumbali and Murungun on "the one side" (Urku "moiety"), and Kuial and Purdal (Ua "moiety") on "the other side". The Groote Eylandt, Bickerton Island, and adjacent mainland Nunggubuyu people didn't have them, though they were organized into four groupings of "mythologically-linked", so-called "clans". I wanted to see if the Mara and Wanderang "semi-moieties" were treated as "units", irrespective of the "clans" they contained and, if so, were they critical in determining people's relationships to one another in so-called "kinship and marriage" terms? Or were they merely ceremonial, song-stream, groupings as was the case among the Groote and Nunggubuyu people to the north, the individual "clan" as such being the critical unit in the definition of "kin"?

For instance, were only women with father's mothers in one's own "clan" called "wife", as on Groote, or did the term apply to all women with father's mothers in one's own "semi-moiety"? This may seem like an unimportant question until it is pointed out that differentiation and not "unity" is the rule in Aboriginal society and, as we shall see, the secret of their success in living relatively peacefully together not only on Groote Eylandt but also on the continent as a whole. If "clans" are present, then, we would not expect them to merge into "semi-moieties" or "moieties" and these latter categories should not be the reference points for people's personal identities.

Basically, the "integrity of the 'clan'" thesis was confirmed. What predicted relationships between people was the intersection of the "clan" affiliations of their respective cognates (father, mother, father's mother, mother's mother), rather than their cognates' respective "semi-moiety" affiliations. For instance, what defined another person as your "wife" was the fact that her father's mother was in your own "clan", not your "semi moiety".

What I also found was that, from the Aboriginal point of view, "semi moieties" were not subdivisions of "moieties" as these, our terms, imply. They were merely a grouping of "clans" into four divisions, whereas "moieties" were groupings of "clans" into two. "Four" did not derive from combining together a pre-existent, separate, "two". "Two" did not derive from combining a pre-existent separate, "four". "Semi-moieties" and "moieties" were simply different groupings of "clans" at different levels. "Four from two" or "two from four" is our linear way of thinking and should not be imposed on the Aboriginal reality. But more on this later, as well as on why the term "clan" and others like it ("family", "kinship") are also inappropriate impositions on Aboriginal reality.

I also found that the Aboriginal people of Ngukurr were singularly uninterested in the kind of "development" that was being imposed on them by Missionaries and Government officials. In the wake of this imposition they certainly weren't the "confident" people the Mission records had painted them out to be as a result of their work there. The settlement was run down and depressed in material terms; the Aboriginal people were insecure and unsure of their cultures compared to the people of Groote. At Ngukurr, besides Mara and Wanderang-speaking people, there were also Djinba, Ridarngu, Waliburrung, Ngandi, Ngalakan, Nunggubuyu, a scattering of part-Aborigines with no identifiable Aboriginal culture, and even a Groote Eylandt "family" – that of Gunbuli Wurramara, the resident Anglican minister!

These were all peoples attracted to the Roper River Mission by the prospect of tobacco and tea during its early years. Problems of intercommunication had led to the adoption of pidgin English as a common medium to the detriment of their own respective languages and now, cultures. Differences of social organization had given way to a uniformity anthropologists call the "section system" and which Aborigines refer to as "skins" (not human skins but the "skin" of the earth). These are generation divisions which cut across "clan" lines to link people far and wide into common categories. They combine people of alternate generations in the same "clan" into the same category (ego, grandfather and grandson would be in one category; father and son would be in another), a category that is common to all people in all mythically-linked "clans" irrespective of language differences. As a common medium of organization the section system was particularly suited to the circumstances in which the Aborigines who migrated to Roper found themselves. The problem is that the categories in question can be employed without reference to the "clans" themselves and, if used exclusively for organizing people over time, can cause them to lose touch with their respective lands or countries. This was the case at Ngukurr as I found out when I came to map the traditional territories of the Mara and Wanderang peoples.

The more southerly I proceeded from the lands of the Nunggubuyu people on the mainland adjacent to Groote, the more generalized and removed the affiliation with the land became, association being on the basis of language grouping and a general range of territory rather than on the basis of affiliation with the "clans" whose members spoke the language and with their specific territories. The lands just south of the Rose River, for instance, were associated with Nunggubuyu "clans", first the Nungumadjbarr, then the Murungun. But south of these was designated "Yukul" land and "Yukul" is a language group; Edward Island, off the coast, was designated "Wanderang" (language group); south of here, on the mainland, was designated "Warrakunta" (language group) and Nemamurdudi (a Nunggubuyu "clan"), and below this area, "Mara" (again, a language group). What complicated the situation even further was that Aborigines had heard that "land rights" were coming in and some of them, led by Dennis Daniels and Ray Jeffries, were pushing to have all the land between the Rose and Roper rivers declared "Yukul": "because if we split it we thought we wouldn't get it". Specific ties of "clans" to land within the general Yukul designation might have been known, but this was not something Europeans need worry themselves about. But this was not just politics. The Aborigines I talked to seemed unsure of the facts of their land rights and of their land boundaries on a "clan" to "clan" basis. After 70 years of European contact and in- and out- migration, this was understandable. Most of the Mara people whose traditional lands were in this area, for instance, lived at Borroloola settlement further to the south.

While I was in Ngukurr, however, I was able to gather information on one Nunggubuyu "clan" which I had missed out on in 1969. This was the Nemamurdudi. Unfortunately this complicated what I had thought was a fairly straightforward eastern Arnhem Land ethnographic situation. The Nemamurdudi hold principle jurisdiction over a stretch of territory to the north of Rose River. Most of them live, though, at Ngukurr. The following are their so-called "totems" (another foreign concept imposed on Aboriginal culture, this time by European observers who had taken the term from the Ojibwa Indians of Canada who had in turn been imposed on by Christopher Columbus who thought that he had discovered the Far East and named its inhabitants accordingly):

Ngarladja	– devil devil
Djamindji	– lightning
Ngaralu	– crab
Madjbarrawarra	– water snake
Nangwurru	– catfish
Ngaliyi	– turtle
Murlu	– a type of shark
Wurruwa:ba	– parrot
Yandarranga	– Central Hill

But the latter two "totems" also belong to the Lalara and Wurra:nggilyanba "clans" of Bickerton and the Wamungangwurugwerigba of Groote Eylandt as well as to another Nunggubuyu "clan", the Ngalmi. I knew that the "clans" in question were supposed to be linked to the Nemamurdudi as "brothers" and this appeared to confirm it. However, "lightning" was also on the Nemamurdudi list and it is associated with the Wurramara "clan" of Bickerton Island and the now extinct Warnungmurugulya of Groote. They are not only not in the same "clan" grouping as the Nemamurdudi and their "brother clans", but they are also in the opposite "moiety". That is, they are the "clans" the Nemamurdudi and their "brothers" should marry. The Nemamurdudi et. al. and the Wurramara et. al. should *not* share the same "totems".

A clue as to what really might be going on here was recorded in my notes, though I didn't realize the implications at the time. The murlu in the list was, in fact, two kinds of sharks, a white one and a black one. The black one belonged to the Nemamurdudi, the white one to the Murungun, a "clan" in the same "moiety" but different "semi-moiety". Perhaps there were two kinds of "lightning" too? But as I only realized this possibility much later after I had returned to Canada, I did not test this theory out at the time. The exercise did make me acutely aware, however, that henceforth I should be careful to record the specifics of species identification when eliciting "totems" from Aboriginal informants, something I took pains to do when I returned again to Groote Eylandt in 1986. And it heightened me to the fact that there might not always be a one-to-one correspondence between the name of a "totem" and its "totemic" referent.

Amongst these Ngukurr Aborigines there was a mercenary element I had not experienced while working on Groote. One day I was heading over to Joe Murdudi's to go fishing when I was intercepted by young Thompson (Ngandi) who was obviously drunk. He asked to see my permit and said if I made a wrong move they would kick me out. What he really wanted was for me to buy some petrol and run him up river in the settlement boat. I refused and continued on my way. Nothing happened as a consequence.

I learned from Joe that the Aborigines were not too pleased with the behaviour of some of the white staff and that there was a certain hostility to whites in general. The staff were always giving orders and were after Aboriginal women, he said. Indeed, one staff member – a teacher if I recall – bragged to me one day that sleeping with an Aboriginal woman was like sleeping with a can of worms. I don't know why he was telling me this unless he wanted to see it printed in a book in which case his ambition was realized. But I do know he was forced out by the Aborigines shortly after I left Ngukurr for Groote.

Through Gumbuli, the Aboriginal minister at Ngukurr, I let the Aborigines on Groote know I wanted to come, and when word came back to proceed, I flew north up along the Carpentaria coast to Numbulwar Mission then eastward out over the Gulf to Groote. It's incredibly beautiful from the air. Bickerton, the smaller island to the west of Groote, and the main island itself sit like two floating jewels in an emerald sea. The dark patches of shadow that appear here and there off-shore mark coral reefs deposited long, long ago, so legend has it, by such Creators as Stingray, Shovel-nosed Shark, Shark Ray and the Blind Woman Dimimba. If you know what to look for you can just make out a ripple in the water running like an umbilical cord between Bickerton Island and the southern coast of Groote at the mouth of the Amagula River. This is Madalyuma, Sea Channel, and home of the two great Snakes, Yabongwa:

nemelabelaba: na nemelabelaba: na.
the Snake is trying to get out of the Sea Channel, the snake is trying to get out of the Sea Channel.

nemagelarugwa magarda, nemelabelaba:na nemelabelaba:na.
the Snake reflecting in the Sea, the Snake is trying to get out of the Sea Channel, the Snake is trying to get out of the Sea Channel.

augwa muruwendinawa, nemelabelaba:na, nemelabelaba:na.
the Sea Channel is bending...

augwa munggwuredamandja, nemelabe/aba:na, nemelabelaba:na.
and we've come to a place belonging to our people...

augwa mamilyarrengga mandja, nemelabelaba:na, nemelabelaba:na.
and the Sea Channel is really muddy...

augwa nungwurrgwana ngawa, nemelabelaba:na, nemelabelaba:na.
and the Snake has already gone through...

augwa yimarrirramandja, nemelabelaba:na, nemelabelaba:na.
and the Snake is always traveling...

nemigauridja mamedagba, nemelabelaba:na, nemelabelaba:na.
the sea stretches out in front...

augwa nemagun1mbidja, nemelabelaba:na, nemelabelaba:na.
and the snake covers the whole Sea Channel with his body...

augwa nemigelerrada, nemelabelaba:na, nemelabelaba:na.
and the sea is glean1ing from his reflection...

augwa nanungwurrenggina, nemelabelaba:na, nemelabelaba:na.
and the spirits of the dead are looking at the Snake...

Where the two Snakes meet in the Channel is the boundary line between the land of the Wurramara people of Bickerton and that of the Amagula people of Groote Eylandt. Actually, where they meet shifts up and down the Channel. The two snakes are sometimes one. We passed over the zone of their/its transformation following our own, no less preordained, path to Groote.

It was not more than a few seconds after the 'plane touched down that word was out and around that I was back. Nandjiwarra suddenly appeared to take me where I wanted to go – Umbakumba settlement on the other side of the island. No pleasantries, no hellos (there are no words for hello or goodbye in the language), no emotion, just information: <<as soon as land rights come in the Amagula people are going back to the Amagula River area in the south; the Wurrawilya are already at Thompson Bay to the north of Umbakumba and some of the Wurramara have gone back to Bickerton. The old people are very upset about the young ones losing the law>>.

Many of the old men I had known before – Badjura, Balrumba, Borneo, Malgari, Nawenbaga, Mini Mini, Bugwanda, Mubana – had died since I was last here. Two, however, remained: Djabargwa and, perhaps the person I bad the greatest fondness for, "Old Charlie", Galiyawa. The Wurramarrba, his people, were trying to stop the Mining Company and the Government from establishing roads and base camps on Bickerton Island. They had already stopped the Mining Company from building a hotel on the island. They were not having much success, however, with their own young people. Six young girls were in Fanny Bay jail in Darwin for theft and selling liquor. One of them was Sally who still steadfastly refused to marry her promised husband, Grumadali, on Groote. Three other young women wanted to marry whites and meetings were currently being held by the elders on the issue. The problem of part-Aboriginal children of Aboriginal women and white men liaisons – six or seven since the first one born and allowed to live in 1969 – had been dealt with by now. Part of the problem was that Aboriginal conception beliefs hold that only the husband, the man in prolonged sexual contact with the woman, could be the father (in our sense of the term). How then could a fleeting association with a transient employee of the Mining Company produce a child that was observably part Aboriginal? More to the point, without an Aboriginal father the child in question could have no "totemic" identity, no rights in land, no permanent relationship to other Aboriginal people.

The eventual decision was that the children could stay on the island and be counted on the mother's side through the husband she should have married or who should have fathered the children, but that they would have to leave later on. The problem posed for conception beliefs was handled this way: it wasn't really one white man that was the father, but rather a whole collection of them. The babies had been made by many white men in succession. And it was true that none of the mothers had gone to the bush with just one white man before pregnancy. It didn't matter who the real father was – in Aboriginal terms the man in prolonged sexual contact with the women – because the Aborigines didn't want the women marrying white men. Hence the decision to raise the children themselves.

The Aborigines had now come to realize that the white man wasn't going to go away once they'd got what they'd come for as they had earlier been led to believe. Instead, "they'll stay and push us out." I had a lot of catching up to do.

By the time I arrived at Umbakumba with Nandjiwarra it was dark. He let me off near the Superintendent's office and headed back for home. He had been required to ask permission of the Umbakumba Council just to make this trip, something I found unusual considering the settlement was in a "clan" country closely related to his own. I didn't bother to check in with the white Superintendent out of habit (as I had never bothered to do so on my 1969 visits). Instead I made my way toward the Aboriginal camp. I reached the perimeter and found myself standing under one of the settlement's "street lights" illuminated by the gas generator over by the office. Suddenly there was noise in the dark before me. A figure burst out brandishing a knife and swinging a billy-can.

"White man, white man", slurred the voice, seemingly drunk: "I kill you." I recognized the face as it came within the range of the light. It was Samson, Nawaradidja's (Jock's) brother. Nawaradidja was my Nawarrga, in simple English, my elder brother – in Aboriginal terms, someone whose country was "totemically" linked to my own and who was eligible to marry women in the same "clan" as I was. He and Samson were of the Wurra:nggilyangba "clan". I knew that the word "kill" didn't mean that at all. It meant "hurt". I also knew that he was using it for effect, probably thinking that I would take the word literally and turn tail and run. Moreover I was pretty sure he didn't recognize me. And I was right. As soon as he was close enough to realize my features he stopped. The knife and billy-can slumped to his sides and he said: "Oh, Davida, Jockolie is over in the camp." Then he turned around in the other direction and ran off ranting and raving as before. What I didn't know was that he wasn't drunk. If he had been it might have been a different story. What was most disconcerting about the episode, though, was that here I was arriving completely unannounced after an absence of three years and being treated as if I had never left.

"Jockolie", Nawaradidja, and his brother were the last remaining males of their kind. Their father, now dead, had married into the Mirniyawan people of the mainland, custodians of the most important ceremony of the region – the Mardaiya:n. This made them *djunggwaiya:* or "bosses" of the ceremony. They had been taught its inner secrets, its law. The young man who had just confronted me had used his powers to "sing" the Umbakumba store so that no one was able to frequent it until it was released. That is, he had used his ritual powers to transport the Spirit of one of the ancestors of his "clan" to the store and station it on the doorstep so that no one would dare enter. He had done this by singing him there. Eventually elder ritual leaders were summoned to sing the Spirit back to where he had come from. Now Simon was threatening to bring him back again unless someone would drive him to the Angurugu Mission. Playing the drunk was all part of the act. If he sang the store while under the influence, his behaviour would be excused and no one would retaliate. He got his ride.

I never did reach the camp. Suddenly Jock was there to intercept me. He walked me in the other direction. Tempers were flaring and there might be trouble. Some of the men were drunk. Being white was a definite liability under the circumstances whether I was "Davida" or not. It would be best if I slept in one of the teacher's quarters. They were away on holidays. I spent most of the night lying awake beneath the window listening to the sounds of gunfire and bullets whistling around and occasionally through the buildings as the "drunken Aborigines" made their rounds.

What had happened? These were "the traditional people", the "real" Groote Eylandters, too strict even for the Aborigines at Angurugu. They were proud, tenacious, even fierce when it came to defending their way of life, especially against whites. Umbakumba was where the Northern Territory Administration sent its misfits in the hopes they would be persuaded to leave the service. It didn't matter what policies they dreamed up there because it would have no effect on the Aborigines anyway. The next day I found out and later confirmed from the records what had happened to change all this.

In December of 1972 two patrol officers traveled to Umbakumba to make inquiries into a breaking and entering episode at the mining company Recreation Club in Alyangula on the north-west corner of the island. The patrol officers suspected some Umbakumba Aborigines and had come to search them out. While questioning some people at Umbakumba, one of the patrol officers remembered he had left his gun in his vehicle and turned around to see it surrounded by a large group of Aborigines. He went over to retrieve his weapon but was "assaulted", the report later said, by the group. The second patrol officer came to his aid and the two of them fled to a nearby house in which they barricaded themselves until they were able to escape. Six patrol officers were afterwards sent to Umbakumba from Darwin and some 30 Aborigines were arrested. The majority were charged by the Magistrate with various offenses – though it was never proved they stole the liquor – and found guilty. They were sentenced to jail in Darwin for periods of between six and 18 months. This took the heart out of the Aboriginal community.

The young men, Jock said, now realized that Aboriginal law counted for nothing. Nor did their old men. Indeed, they were now in disrepute for not having told them about the real situation. White man's law was supreme. And white man's law was set by white men. Get drunk, fight, find a woman, this was the new way of life. You could see it in the faces of the old men: eyes averted, mumbled speech, disinterest. I paid old Na:engmenara of the Mamariga people to do a bark painting for me of his Dreaming the East Wind. His work had been admired far and wide by whites and Aborigines alike. What he turned out was plain crap. The lines weren't true, blotches of paint marred the design. He hadn't even dried the bark properly and it had begun to curl. It was how I imagined an Aboriginal child would draw a bark if Aboriginal children drew barks. Now I knew why Nandjiwarra was so upset. It was also why some of them were planning on moving out of the settlements and back to their countries "once land rights came in". Land rights was the work of the new Labour Government on the advice of Justice Woodward's Report. With some qualifications whites would hereafter be forced to respect the Aborigines' jurisdiction over their traditional lands, at least in the Northern Territory. The word had got around and many Aborigines were moving in anticipation. Meanwhile they had anarchy on their hands.

One symptom of the upheaval was the decision of a young woman, Emily of the Wurramara "clan", to refuse her promised husband Roy Wurrabadelamba and marry a white man, Fritz, who worked for GEMCO, the mining company. The Wurramara were split on the issue and all the other "clans" were against the marriage. The Wurrabadelamba had refused Fritz permission to enter their territory which meant he could no longer work at

Alyyangula where GEMCO's offices were located, and the Lalara and Wurramaminyamandja had barred him from theirs which meant he could not live at Angurugu. The couple were stranded and forced to move to Darwin. However, Joe, Emily's father, was making plans to set up an outstation on Bickerton Island "when land rights come in". The couple would be free to live there. In the meantime everyone agreed to allow Fritz a three-week permit so that he and Emily could come across together and visit once a year. Emily herself, of course, could come any time she wanted.

Of the 40-odd marriages that had taken place since my last prolonged stay in 1969, eight were *warnigarangbidja*, that is, the man's father and the woman's mother were from the same "clan". A number of these marriages had been allowed before I arrived on Groote in 1969, largely because of Mission influence. The missionaries didn't see why a man shouldn't marry a woman whose mother was from his own country so long as the man's father and the woman's mother weren't actual brother and sister. Shortly after these marriages were allowed they had been stopped. Now, apparently, they were on again, but not without some protest: a man from the same country as one of the women cut the prospective husband with a knife in an act of ritual protest before agreeing to allow one of the marriages.

Polygamy had now all but been abandoned at Angurugu, a notable exception being Gula Lalara who had three wives, though some of the older men were trying to claim wives who had been promised to them many years before. Five Umbakumba men, however, had more than one wife but there was pressure for the people here also to abandon the custom because it was causing problems for younger men who had increasingly had a smaller and smaller pool of "straight" single women to whom they were eligible for marriage. To stop their "promises" from running off with young Aboriginal men or with white men, the older men had been singing the women to sacred places (the obverse of singing an ancestor from a sacred place to the real world) where they would become "taboo", that is, unapproachable. Indeed, the practice had become so widespread that the Angurugu Community Council had decided to impose a fine of $100 on anyone resorting to the ploy.

I had returned to Groote Eylandt with copies of my book *Tradition and Transformation*, published by the Australian Institute of Aboriginal Studies in Canberra that same year, the result of my earlier researches on the island. In it were maps showing the boundaries of each "clan's" territory in the area. One map placed the south-eastern tip of Bickerton Island in the hands (or rather the minds) of the Warnungwadarrbalangwa people who also owned lands on the western side of the island as well as on Groote Eylandt. The book also contained the story of how that had come to be. A severe drought had driven the Wamungwadarrbalangwa from Bickerton to seek a haven on Groote. A "mythologically"-linked people there, the Wamungwudjaragba, agreed to subdivide a portion of their territory – the portion connected to Hollow Log Coffin which had traveled between their respective territories on the two islands – and reallocate it to the Warnungwadarrbalangwa. This done, the people moved over from Bickerton. I put the move at about 100 years ago.

Now what normally happens is that the old connections are conveniently "forgotten" and their former lands are, in turn, reallocated to other people through the same process. The lands on the western part of Bickerton Island were still well remembered, but not those on the eastern tip. In fact, only one old man knew for sure and it was on his evidence that I had reconstructed the story. I sat down with a group of people at Angurugu Mission and went through the book. When I came to page 7 showing the map of the general area and where each of the various "clan" lands was located, Wanaiya of the Warnungwadarrbalangwa stopped me and stretched out his finger toward the page. Was this a drawing of Groote Eylandt? Was that Bickerton? Then he pointed to the number 4 on the south-eastern tip of the smaller island.

"Miyamba:na magina?", What's that?, he asked.

"It's your territory on Bickerton Island," I replied.

Wanaiya looked up and around at his fellow Aborigines and smiled – a smug sort of smile that sent a small chill of realization down my spine. The perturbed looks on the faces of the people seated round about told me that what I had just done was "resolve" a debate that had been going on for a very very long time. The country wasn't really the Wurrawilya's who now claimed it but the Wamungwadarrbalangwa's – and would be forever now that I had recorded the fact in my book!

In 1969 Wanaiya had refused to talk to me until I could do so on his terms – in the local language, Anindilyaugwa. Then, when I had finally reached the requisite fluency and he did agree to talk, he immediately switched into near perfect English. He had been spotted by the missionaries as a particularly bright young man and, to put it bluntly, forced into school. Adulthood, however, had seen him "regress" to his "tribal ways". Now, though, he was well versed in our ways as well as his own. The pursuit of self-interest is not something one would associate with Aboriginal culture. Their institutions would prevent it. Not so ours, however, and Wanaiya knew it. If my book gave his people more land then my book was a good thing ("he asked the old people and then wrote it down," he had said to those seated around); if my book hadn't, it would have been a bad thing ("what could a white man know about our ways?").

The Mission bad worked with the Government to negotiate a royalties agreement with the Mining Company. The mining Township had been located in the country of the Wamungwadarrbalangwa – with their consent. Now that it was well established and not going anyplace, Wanaiya made his move. The mining Township would have to pay for the privilege of being there and, moreover, the money would go just to the Warnungwadarrbalangwa, not to any other Aborigines on the island despite their traditional interdependence. "Royalties" was white man's business and in business with white men, traditional Aboriginal rules just did not apply.

The Aboriginal blueprint in Wanaiya's mind was being stripped away and in its place was the possibility of "my land", "our land". That's why he chose to see the number 4 on the map in the book.

It wasn't long before I left Groote Eylandt for Canberra and from there departed for Canada. I professed a deep regret about leaving, about separating myself from Groote Eylandt. But that wasn't what I felt. What I felt was relief.

III

1985/86: Return and Regrouping

I thought I had put the Aborigines and my Australian experiences behind me and moved in another direction. On arriving at the University of Manitoba in Winnipeg in 1974 I had undertaken a study of the Cree in the northern part of the Province with Paul Wertman (1977). Then, in 1979, I had spent my sabbatical year in Yorkshire, England, researching the origins of the Industrial Revolution and the logic of English literature. This was to be part of a larger study involving a comparison of British and Canadian histories and cultural expressions – a comparison of the two places I knew first in the world, Lanark County, Ontario, Canada, and Halifax in the West Riding of Yorkshire. I had spent my first few years near Halifax and then was raised in Perth, Ontario, and thought these would be as good a reference point as any for making the transition from anthropology into the study of my own society.

However, that intended direction was deflected by Barry Coulter, the Minister for Community Development in the Northern Territory Government. I had met him in 1985 in Toronto during his efforts to secure the return of the T. G. H. Strehlow collection of Central Australian Aboriginal artifacts and cultural records to Australia. Strehlow, the son of a Lutheran missionary, born and raised among the Aranda of Central Australia, had become a Professor at the University of Adelaide and devoted his life to recording – indeed salvaging – their traditional culture. In the 1950s Aranda elders petitioned him to hold their sacred ceremonial object for safekeeping and out of the hands of their youth who were selling objects for money and alcohol and had turned their backs on the Law. Strehlow accepted the responsibility and housed the collection in his Adelaide home. However, unable to gain financial support for his proposed research facility there, he published secret-sacred photographs of Aranda ceremonies in the German magazine *Der Stern*, which in turn sold them to *People Magazine* in Australia which published them there for all Australians to see. Strehlow was denounced by Aborigines, politicians and anthropologists. He died a broken man. His second wife Cathy inherited the collection under the terms of Australian law and tried to carry on. She too was beset by difficulties, not the least of which was whose law applied in this case. Many Aranda insisted that the collection had been given in trust to Strehlow and could not be alienated.

I became involved, first through correspondence with Professor Strehlow before his death and then through Cathy who kept up the correspondence thereafter. I inventoried the collection at the Strehlow home for the Strehlow Research Foundation and then helped Mr. Coulter and the then federal Minister of Aboriginal Affairs, Clyde Holding, secure the collection for the Northern Territory Government in negotiations with Mrs. Strehlow while she was enrolled in the M.A. programme here in Toronto. Impetus to these negotiations was the fact that during her stay here, the collection had apparently been spirited out of Australia for "safekeeping" by officials of the Strehlow Research Foundation, anticipating the application of federal heritage legislation by the federal government to the collection to keep it intact in the country.

This is a very controversial tale involving *Aborigines, Artifacts and Anguish,* as Ward McNally aptly entitled his book on the subject and I will not go into it here. Suffice it to say that everyone wanted access to the collection and all for different reasons: Aborigines to rediscover their culture and justify land claims, mining companies to deny these claims, anthropologists to pursue an understanding of Central Australian Aboriginal culture, collectors to sell these priceless objects on the art market. Suffice it to say that the collection was eventually turned over to the Northern Territory Government and is presently being housed in a research facility in Alice Springs (or at least most of it, as we are all uncertain as to just bow much was on display in the Strehlow home and how much of it was not was actually turned over).

My point here is that during the events leading up to this conclusion, Barry Coulter asked if I would undertake an assessment of Aboriginal policy in the Northern Territory, in particular on the issue of local government for Aboriginal people and for the Territory generally. The politics of Aboriginal affairs being what they are, only an "outsider" could do the job, he said. Apart from this unique opportunity to actually apply some of my ideas on how to handle "race relations" it would also give me the chance to return to Groote Eylaodt. I agreed.

I won't go into the details of my consultancy at this point. Suffice it to say that it did give me the chance to do something practical for the benefit of Aboriginal people, not to mention survey most of the Northern Territory anthropologically. The results are outlined in my report to the N.T. Government entitled *Transformation and Tradition: A Report on Aboriginal Develop-*

ment in/on the Northern Territory of Australia. The main title is a deliberate reversal of that of my 1974 monograph on the people of the Groote Eylandt area where the emphasis was on where the Aborigines were coming from, not where they were going to. As well, the consultancy gave a very good excuse for traveling to Groote Eylandt. Angurugu had been one of the first Aboriginal communities to adopt Community Government, a unique form of local government which allowed for aboriginal principles of representation and jurisdiction. The Community Government programme in general was what I was there to evaluate.

I was worried that the Aborigines might have forgotten us by now. After all, it had been 12 years. Then one day as I was coming in to work at my government office in the Paspalis building in Rundle Mall in Darwin I noticed someone who seemed familiar coming my way down the street. At first he didn't see me. When he finally did he paused and stared, then broke into a big smile and rushed toward me. Before I could say anything at all he had grasped me by the shoulders and kissed me on both sides of my neck. Then he wept. It was George Djawaranga of the Wurramara "clan", also my wife's. I had last seen him at Angurugu in 1974. I had never seen an Aboriginal man express emotion like this before. Nor, judging by their reaction, had the white people around us. Their looks were somewhere between bemusement and disgust.

In contrast to 1974, this time I knew what I was getting myself into by going back and was mature enough to deal with it. A 1985 report by David Biles of the Australian Institute of Criminology entitled *Groote Eylandt Prisoners: A Research Report*, pointed out that Groote Eylandt had the highest imprisonment rate of any single place in Australia. It was seven to eight times the Northern Territory rate which, in turn, was three times the national rate. Most of the offenders were young men who originated at Umbakumba. Most of the crime was directed at the property of the mining company and its employees at Alyangula. The problem was compounded by excessive drinking in the parental generation and petrol sniffing amongst the young. These problems had received nation-wide publicity and the Groote Eylandters were not amused.

In response to the Biles Report the Federal Government appointed a Task Force to investigate the matter. It contained no Groote Eylandters and but one Aboriginal member. In response to the Federal Government initiative the Angurugu Community Government Council revoked entry permits for all but incoming public servants and then for all non-Aborigines and invited Minister Holding to a meeting on Groote. What the Groote Eylandters wanted was an all-Aboriginal Task Force, most of them from Groote. As the minutes of that meeting show, the Groote Eylandters already knew what the problem was and how to arrest, if not solve, it:

> Some young people like going to gaol because they get good food, plenty of television, plenty of sport, and they have a real good time. Plenty of mates go with them and they have a real good holiday at taxpayers' expense. He [another Aboriginal] said that if gaol was hard, with only one ordinary sort of meal a day, no bed to sleep on, no TV and no sport, they would hate it and not want to go back and this would help our problem...
>
> I see this crime rate is really a warning to this community. It is a warning that is asking you to stop and think where you are going. Parents are drinking and they do not care for their children. It gets right back to the mothers and fathers. Mothers and fathers and the whole community must stop and think because they have had this clear warning that there is a big problem.

Not only were the parents drinking but the young people were getting off sniffing petrol. As a result of the meeting with Mr. Holding the Task Force was reconstituted with a majority of Groote Eylandters.

Not so well publicized was the occurrence on Groote Eylandt of a rare neurological degenerative disease, colloquially known as "the wasting disease", whose victims are called "bird people" by the Groote Eylandters because of their high stepping gait. A 1980 article in the Journal of Neurology, Neurosurgery, and Psychiatry by Kiloh et al. said that thirteen, and possibly sixteen, cases had been located in the area: "There were two relatively distinct clinical pictures: one coming on in childhood involved the motor system, the patients having remarkably lax ligaments; and the other, generally of later onset, comprising cerebellar, upper motor neurone and sometimes supranuclear opthalmoplegic features." In laymen's terms, the body wastes painfully away while the mind remains intact. This girl was born in 1968:

> She had a normal infancy but her gait was noted to be abnormal when two years old. She now walks in a stilted and slightly broad based fashion on her toes with knees bent and her left leg internally rotated. She has an obvious *pes planus*. Examination showed slight wasting of

the intrinsic hand muscles but she retained good power. The arms were hypotonic with lax ligaments and the deep reflexes reduced. There was marked wasting below the knees with weakness of hip flexion of the ankles. Spasticity was evident at the knees with increased knee jerks but her ankles were hypotonic with hyporeflexia.

The authors admit that "No causal factors were identified but there were indications that the disorder might be genetically determined." The "evidence" is from my own work on Groote Eylandt, namely my 1969 finding that a change in the traditional marriage system had occurred which allowed a man and a woman to marry so long as their parents were not real siblings. The traditional rule had prohibited marriage between any two people whose parents had originated in the same "clan" (called warnigarangbidja). The occurrence of these close marriages coincided with an increase in the reported instance of the disease. However, there was no mention whether any of the afflicted patients had been born of marriages of this type. Moreover, there is a serious methodological problem, also not mentioned, involved in equating even this degree of closeness in marriage with genetic closeness.

According to the Aboriginal theory, it takes two to three months' prolonged sexual intercourse with a woman to open up a path through which the Spirit of the child is able to enter her. Extra-marital affairs are frequent and in our terms there is no guarantee that the husband is the father. The woman may have a relationship not only with other men in her husband's "clan", but also in a "clan" "totemically"-linked to his, or even in one unlinked but in the same moiety.

But the authors put forward another possibility: the disease may have originated on Bickerton Island and was imported into Groote through intermarriage between the two peoples. The disease occurs more frequently at Angurugu where the Bickerton people now live than at Umbakumba, the home of the Groote people proper. At Angurugu most cases are in two Bickerton "clans". The authors speculate on the possibility of a "gene mutation" on Bickerton transmitted as "Mendelian dominant". Again, however, the paternity question arises to complicate the issue.

A third possibility is also offered: environmental factors may act as a sufficient cause, triggering off the disease in "genetically susceptible" individuals. One of the suspected triggers is manganese; another is cycad. Cycad angulata, or burrawang, the food for which Murabuda Wurramarrba came to Groote when he suffered his first experience of the missionaries. However, burrawang has not been used as a staple food here since the early Mission period. Manganese, though always present under the ground and used as a pigment in bark painting, has more recently been released to the atmosphere in the form of dust with the commencement of open-pit mining in the mid-1960s.

Two new events, then, coincide with the increased frequency of the wasting disease: close, *warnigarangbidja* marriages and open-pit manganese mining. There would have been occasional exposure to manganese traditionally as there would have been occasional *warnigarangbidja* marriages. These factors would account for alleged earlier manifestations of the disease. However, the frequency of Bickerton Groote intermarriage has not increased over the same period which at least seems to let the Bickerton Islanders off the hook. What I didn't know was whether any of those contracting the disease were a product of a close *warnigarangbidja* marriage. I couldn't know because I didn't know who had the disease.

As if the presence of this disease wasn't enough, the same article also spoke of psychiatric disorders showing acutely excited states, inattentiveness and unresponsiveness and a high incidence of heart, lung, skeleton and skin abnormalities as well as anemia. To be quite frank, I can't recall having noticed any of this in 1969.

* * * *

On January the 13th I arrived back on Groote. I wasn't there to make inquiries into the traditional culture. I was there to look at their Community Government Scheme. However, a side trip to Bickerton Island was too good a prospect to pass up.

By our standards there was no doubt that the Angurugu Community Government Council was working. In 1985 it had a total income of almost 1.2 million dollars. Its assets totaled $353,000. The main money-maker was the shop, with gross profits of $450,000 and a net profit of $158,000. Contract work and plant hire by the Council generated another $272,000, service fees and rents another $100,000. The Council also operated an outstation centre to service Aboriginal people living elsewhere on the island and ran a Library, a Print Shop, a Garage and built houses. The Council paid out over half a million dollars in salaries most of which stayed in the area.

One of the reasons the Angurugu Council was working was 40 years of Mission tutelage and a dedicated non-Aboriginal Town Clerk in the person of Lance Tremlett. Another was Angurugu's proximity to Alyanggula, the mining Township, where wage labour and contract work were available and whose European residents patronized the Angurugu store. Another reason the Council worked was the presence of the Bickerton Island people, traditional go-betweens linking the Groote Eylandters and the mainland Nunggubuyu, who simply transferred their diplomatic skills to dealing with Europeans.

But the major reason why the Angurugu Council worked was because it had included traditional principles of representation within its Community Government Scheme. Indeed, it was the only Aboriginal Council to date in the Northern Territory that had "got away" with it. I say this because, although Part XX (now Part VIII) of the Local Government Act permitted a Council to set its own criteria of eligibility both for membership in the jurisdiction and on the Council as well as the right to vote, in practice Aboriginal communities were "encouraged" to follow the conventional Australian model. This was basically simple residence within the jurisdiction as a criterion of membership and voting rights. But the Groote Eylandters, with the backing of Lance Tremlett, had insisted on exercising their rights under the Act.

What they did was establish "clan groupings" as the units of representation in the Scheme. These were 10 in all and this included all those indigenous to Groote Eylandt and Bickerton Island. In addition, some mainland Nunggubuyu "clans" were included (*) as well as one from north-east Arnhem Land (the Wanambi). The so-called "clan" groupings are listed below:

1. Lalara Ngalmi*	2. Amagula Mamariga	3. Wurramara Nundirribala*
4. Wurramarrba Amagadjeragba	5. Wurrabadelamba Djaragba	6. Mirniyawan Nungumadjbarr*
7. Murungun Manggura*	8. Wurragwagwa Yandarranga	9. Wurrawilya Maminyamandja
	10. Bara Bara Durila Wanambi	

There are 10 seats on Council, one for each "clan grouping". For the most part, the "clans" within each grouping are in the closest possible relationship without actually being the same: they are directly linked together by the travels of the same "totemic" beings. The exception here are those in grouping 9: the Wurrawilya are not, in fact, "totemically" linked to anyone, a peculiarity that takes some explaining, but not at this point in the story. So does the relationship of the two mainland "clans" in grouping 6 (the Wanambi in #10 are Durila who have reaffirmed their mainland origins).

Each of the "clans" is land-based in the sense of holding abstract, eternal jurisdiction over a stretch of country in the area. In this sense, all "interests" in the area are represented, irrespective of differences in population. Because of this, no one block is able to exert undue influence over the others or gain control over the Council. This is why it works. Furthermore, because of the "clan" representation principle outsiders are unable to move in despite a rule which says that anyone 18 years old and "ordinarily resident" in the "Council area" for six months may stand for office and anyone simply in the area may vote. Inclusion of the residential provision was the Aborigines' "concession" to the Government's own preference. Thus the Government missed the implications of the "clan" representation principle, at least at the time.

As interesting is the office of President. The President is elected separately by the voters at large from nominees by any of the "clan groupings". The Presidency is seen not so much to be a representative of the "clan groupings" as of the "clans" as a whole in dealings with Europeans.

The three elected to date each have a connection to one aspect of the dominant white society – Djambana Lalara to the Mining Company, Nandjiwarra Amagula to the Government and the incumbent during my visit, Murabuda Wurrarnarrba to the Mission. In keeping with this philosophy, the Aborigines permit non-Aboriginal residents of Angurugu to vote only for the office of President. Technically they could vote for Councillors but would do so on pain of their future on the island. These Aborigines also have land rights, that is, inalienable freehold title to their land, and can remove whites at will, plus make life pretty unpleasant for those who stay.

The problem with the Angurugu Community Government Council, as I had anticipated and saw confirmed during my visit, was that it did not physically encompass the entire Aboriginal Land Trust area, that is, all the lands owned by the "clans" represented on Council, considered as a whole. The Council covered only the area of the Angurugu settlement itself and Nandjiwarra's Yenbakwa outstation on the south-west coast of Groote. Other outstations have been in and out of the Council's jurisdiction during its lifetime and the major one in the area, Milya:gburra on Bickerton Island, has steadfastly refused to be governed from Groote, representation on the Angurugu Council or no.

Milya:gburra was established by the Wurrarnara "clan" in their traditional territory in the central south part of Bickerton, partly as a pledge to one of their old men, "Old Bill", who had lived most of his life there and with whom I had worked in 1969, and partly to provide an alternative to Angurugu which many of the Wurramara saw as too noisy, violent and disease-prone a place. The Wurramara refuse to allow other "clanspeople" to stay at their outstation, except those who have married in, nor will they let their outstation become a service centre for other Bickerton "clans" wishing to return to their own homelands. At Milya:gburra they allow no alcohol or dogs. The manager is Fritz, the European I mentioned earlier as having married Emily Wurramara and who was banished from Groote. Irrespective of my ethnographic interest in Bickerton Island, Milya:gburra certainly deserved a visit. It was both cause and consequence of the Aborigines' inability to establish their Government over the whole area. The other problem in this respect was Umbakumba on the other side of the island and home of the Groote Eylandt people proper.

As we saw in 1974 when I had last visited, Umbakumba was in collapse. I must admit things had not improved much by January of 1986. The place was a rubbish tip. The few old men and women who were there in 1974 were now dead. People seemed to be drunk or recovering from drink most of the day and night. My heart sagged when I saw this and my response was obvious to one of the men I had come to visit – Paul Bara, the new Umbakumba Council President. He lowered his head and muttered something about his first job being to clean the place up. We said nothing for some time. Then he offered this ray of hope:

"We've just put five women on Council. Now it's half and half. They'll get things going."

It came as a shock to learn that the women in question were part of the "Christian fellowship" group, and that they were under the tutelage of the new Anglican Minister at Umbakumba, my old friend Jock Nawaradidja Wurra:nggilyangba. When I was here in 1969 Jock was living at Angurugu and being subsidized by the other Aboriginal "clans" to learn the law from his father, not only as the last of his line but also as boss of the region's major sacred ceremony, Mardaiya:n. By 1971 he had moved to Umbakumba and was still there in 1974. By then his stature as a religious leader in his own culture had grown. His father was now dead and he had assumed his role. What had happened since then to change all this? I asked him.

The collapse of the mid-'70s had affected him much more than it had affected me. After all, he was part of the culture, and not just an innocent bystander who could leave at will. He had come to the conclusion that the fighting and the drinking and the running after women reflected a defect in the *Aboriginal* culture, and so he had decided to abandon it. He had "gone over to Jesus" and become a Minister. This had disturbed his fellow Aborigines no end, but eventually they decided to support him on the grounds that it was better to have a master in two religions than no master at all. He wouldn't have to abandon his culture altogether. Rather, he could still participate as an observer. On his ordination, in an elaborate ceremony, they handed him over to the Church in much the same manner as the young boys were handed over by the women to the men for circumcision, the first stage of initiation.

I didn't agree with him about his analysis of the situation but this was not the time to talk about it. What was more important was to encourage him and Paul and the new Council in their determination to clean up the community in a moral, as well as a physical, sense. We talked instead about Umbakumba combining with the Angurugu Council to deal with matters of an island-wide nature, such as relations with the Mining Company, road maintenance, contracts and so on. What I didn't realize at the time was that this move on my part caused some resentment amongst the still traditionally-oriented Aborigines at Umbakumba. Drink and fight and chase women they might but there was no way they were going to become "Christian"!

What also puzzled me during this visit was that nobody seemed surprised that I was back. At first I thought that Djawaranga, with whom I had such an emotional reunion in Darwin, had forewarned them. But I was wrong. Nandjiwarra told me they had sung us back to help them out. We were here. So it must have worked. There was no point arguing. As on my last visits, now back I was overwhelmed with information virtually none of which I could assimilate. In the intervening 12 years not only had my ability in the language diminished as theirs in English had increased, but I had also forgotten most of the personal biographical details about people that are necessary to locate them and oneself in the relationship system.

Though I knew my own "clan" (Lalara), my mother's (Warnindilyaugwa), my father's mother's (Amagula) and my mother's mother's (Wamungwadarrbalangwa), I remembered virtually no one else's. And you cannot relate to someone unless you know how your "clan" affiliations intersect with theirs. "Husband/wife", NA:NINGYARRGA/dadingyarrga, for instance, is someone in your father's mother's "clan" in your own generation whose mother is in your mother's mother's "clan", whose mother's mothers are in your mother's "clan" and whose father's mothers are in your own "clan". Poor Gula spent a frustrating afternoon with me in front of the shop identifying passersby only to discover that while I recognized them I could work out relationships only in ideal terms. This you can do if you know only the other person's "clan" and that you should marry the same "clan" in alternate generations. I married Wurramara, so all the Wurramara in my generation should be NA:NINGYARRGA/dadingyarrga. In the generation above me they should be NARNGIYARRGA/darngiyarrga, in the generation below me NABERRAGA/daberraga, in the generation two above me NUMINDJARRGA/dumindjarrga, and in the generation two below NA:NINGABIDJARRGA/dadiabadjarrga. I could do this for other lines of relationships once J knew the person was in my mother's "clan" or my mother's mother's or, of course, in my own, or, by the way, in a "clan" "totemically" linked to one of these. A person in my father's mother's "clan" should be "wife".

Gula was at least pleased I could still do this much, but I realized I had a lot of work to do before returning again in a few months' time. The next day, however, I discovered that I wasn't the only one in danger of losing the culture. It happened down at the river where I had gone to pick up my son Graeme who was swimming with a group of adolescent Aboriginal boys.

I waved at Graeme and uttered a few words in the language for the benefit of the others. As I watched them play, two of the boys came over and stood beside me, speaking to me in the language.

"What is yoar clan?"

I said I was Lalara.

"What is your name?"

I answered, "Garuma" (which is what the Aborigines used to call me when I was first here; lit. "little old wise man", a diminutive of *wuraruma* or "proper old, wise man").

"Why did you come back?" one of them asked.

"To visit everyone again and show them my children," I replied.

"No", was the retort. "Why did you come back from the dead?"

After recovering my wits I quickly switched into English and tried to explain that I'd been here before and learned the language. But I sensed they weren't convinced. And I later learned from Graeme that he'd been questioned about where he'd come from too. "Over the sea" was not an answer that would disconfirm their belief. The gateway to the "Land of the Dead" was in the sea off North-East Island, Amburrgba. As I wrote in my notebook afterwards, "There is really something strange going on among the young ones here."

I repeated the episode to Murabuda the next day. He seemed rather annoyed that I'd discovered this, as if it was something they didn't want me to know. Some of their young people, he said, particularly the petrol sniffers, believe that if you behave like a white man when you live you come back as a white man when you die. You are white and speak the language. They think you're a Lalara who's come back from the dead.

Where were their minds? Why did they want to be like whites? Couldn't Murabuda and others have explained to them who we were in a way they would understand? Didn't the two generations talk to one another? What were the sniffers up to and why did they sniff? Was it simply boredom as most Europeans around the place seemed to think? All I learned about it on this trip was what questions I had to ask on the next one.

The next day I was off to Bickerton. This was the chance I'd been waiting for – the chance to pre-test my theory that "clan" territories were resource specific, the permanent water here, the yams there, and who knows what everyplace else.

Milya:gburra was indeed a model outstation: clean, quiet, well laid out in a grid pattern of neat little houses and humpies or tin huts – and very few Aborigines around to disturb the peace. Despite protestations to the contrary, when it came to actually living in the bush away from the evils of Angurugu, as distinct from talking about living in the bush, most preferred the evils of Angurugu. There were only about a dozen people here but twice as many dwellings. The ones who were here, however, were permanent and committed to life in the "bush": Joe, Andrew, Gilbert and sometimes Raymond Wurramara, as well as Gudigba Lalara. I had been close to Gudigba before and it was on him that I would pre-test my theory.

But I was here first and foremost as a consultant to the Government to hear about their concerns. They were putting in fiberglass septic systems (at an outstation?, I thought to myself) but the backhoe (the backhoe?) had broken down and they needed $4,000 to $5,000 to bring a mechanic over from the Mining Company to fix it. Commuting between Bickerton and Groote would be a lot easier if they had a community-owned jet boat (jet boat?). Twenty-six odd thousand would do. Well, it certainly wasn't 1969.

I promised I would see to the backhoe for them, but if they wanted a jet boat they had better see the Community Development representative at Gove (another mining Township up the coast). Now I could get down to my business.

Gudigba took me down to the generator and pump station (they had street lights!) and explained to me that here was the best supply of fresh water on the island. This is where Yabongwa the Rainbow Serpent(s) had surfaced when t(he)y emerged from the sea on the shores of Bickerton Island where t(he)y discovered t(he)y were too old to push on any further. So t(he)y began to cry. That was the source of the well here. It was Yabongwa's tears. The water supply was year-round, unlike most other sources on the island. Well, this wasn't the Wurramara water I had been told about and taken to be the only permanent source on the island – that was held in rock holes on the other side. But then Gudigba went on to say that you could get water in the dry season in other parts of Bickerton by digging at certain points on the beach, though it could be salty. Then there was that spring – really two of them – over in Wurra:nggilyangba country on the east coast. They were full year round. So much for my theory.

Yes, there were yams in Wurramarrba country but did I mean round yams or long yams? There were patches of both kinds in Warnungwadarrbalangwa country too. And in Wurramara, though not in great numbers. They had taken out the best patch when they put their airstrip in (yes, alas for the illusion of pristine isolation, they have an airstrip too). As for the wild apples which I'd supposed were found only in Wurra:nggilyangba country, they were "everywhere". It now dawned on me that I had indeed confused the natural with the "totemic" in my thinking – or my informants bad. The Wurramarrba sang both Long Yam and Short Yam and therefore were subject to certain prohibitions as regards eating them as food. The Wurra:nggilyangaba sung Wild Apples. What about Fresh Water? Gudigba said the Wurramara Sung about it but it was not *alawudawarra* such that prohibitions on its consumption applied. Damn it! What did I need to come back for? My research was over.

But I was learning much more than just what I was after in the course of this conversation. There was more than one Yabongwa. Rainbow Serpent. Apparently a second one had taken over from the one that emerged from the sea and continued on underground to the other side of the island. It surfaced along the way and there is another well of fresh water at that place too: "We call this [story] *alawudawarra*, it happened a long time ago." I knew *alawudawarra* meant something like "sacred", but I decided to push my luck and dig deeper.

"What's *alawudawarra*?" I said naively.

He puzzled for a moment for he knew I knew the word, then he appeared a little lost as if he knew another word was not what I wanted. Then he made a sweeping motion with his hand as if brushing away a fly: "that's *alawudawarra*". It wasn't the place as a static thing but the motion between the places he was communicating to me. It was Yabongwa's wake, what t(he)y left of themselves as t(he)y moved along. I hadn't really realized this before. This was something I should come back to later and explore.

That night Gudigba and Gumbuli went out and caught three turtles. They could have speared a dugong but she was with young so they left her alone. There was always fresh fish. Certainly there didn't seem to be any shortage of resources in nature. If there was deprivation of particular resources in a land it certainly was imposed.

I returned to Angurugu to conclude my investigations for my Government report. Nandjiwarra's big complaint was that Lance Tremlett was slow to hand over the Town Clerk's job to an Aboriginal. There were also too many whites – all C.M.S. affiliated – in the office. Lance's big complaint was Nandjiwarra. If they rushed it and put someone in the Town Clerk's job who couldn't work with everyone, all that they had built over the past five years would collapse. Lance had been training Bobby Nungumadjbarr for the job but Bobby was from Numbulwar on the mainland. While this meant he had a certain detachment and everyone would work with him, it also meant he might go home once Numbulwar became a Community Government Council and went looking for a Town Clerk. To turn over the office jobs to Aborigines at Angurugu there had to be Aborigines to turn them over to and there seemed to be a problem getting Aborigines to train on the job. That problem will end when the Town Clerk is an Aboriginal, said Nandjiwarra. Then Aborigines won't feel so out of place and isolated in the office.

Murabuda was worried about the young people and the lack of activities for them. They were wasting their lives petrol sniffing and getting into trouble with the authorities in Alyangula. They wanted to get caught and go to jail. There was another reason why the imprisonment rate was high: the police came down and simply asked who had done such and such a thing the night before and the guilty person(s) just stepped forward. Perhaps banishment to Bickerton in the care of an elder instead of jail in Darwin would do the trick. Traditional authority figures, like the mother's "clan brothers", though, were too busy drinking to care. It didn't seem there was much they could do about that so long as the club at Alyangula was open to Aborigines. And even if it wasn't they'd find some other way to get alcohol.

Djambana was upset because he wasn't getting contract work from the Angurugu and Umbakumba Councils or the Government after he had set himself up as a grading and hauling business, on the advice of the Government and the Council. Part of the reason was that he was always being outbid and outmaneuvered by the giant Henry and Walker, a contracting firm from Darwin. The other factor was that he kept getting caught in the middle of disputes between the Umbakumba and Angurugu Aboriginal Councils over their respective jurisdictions. Instead of working, Djambana was fishing to feed his wife and children. As for his trucks and equipment, be now rented them out to Henry and Walker. It was cheaper for them than bringing their own equipment from Darwin!

Paul Bara's problem was to see Umbakumba survive. Its population was declining because of the violence and subsequent migration to Angurugu. There seemed no prospects for employment and no interest even if there were.

Aboriginal employment at the Mining Company had dwindled from what it had been in the '70s despite a company policy to employ any Aboriginal who applied for work. But part of the reason employment there had been high was because it was a prerequisite for drinking at the club. Since then the Company had dropped the employment qualification and now just admitted anyone whose behaviour was acceptable. In any event, Aborigines seemed to feel more at ease working for their own kind at the Angurugu Council, or working independently like Djambana. It's just that there was not enough work at Angurugu to keep all able-bodied Aborigines at Angurugu employed. Nor was there really any motivation at all to work in our terms.

A Trust Fund of royalty payments from the Mining Company had been negotiated by the Church Missionary Society on behalf of the Aborigines in the mid-'60s. It now totaled seven million dollars. Each year the Aborigines spent a sum of the interest which would amount to some $20,000 per "clan". This went on items such as 4-wheel drive Toyotas, motorbikes, TVs, bicycles, Walkmen and so on. Other funds, though, went for travel to ceremonies and funerals. The Groote Eylandt Aborigines, it seems, were suffering from affluence. So what are you supposed to recommend? No royalties? Abandon the mining? Back to hunting and gathering? No. What I recommended was finding ways to deal with all this as it was, beginning on the political side with an expanded jurisdiction for the Community Government Council. As I said in my Report (p. 41):

> The major problem with Community Government on Groote Eylandt and Bickerton Island is that it doesn't apply to the region as a whole. In fact, its very success had transformed the difference between the people at Angurugu and the people at Umbakumba, the Bickerton people and the Groote Eylandt people, into a tension and source of conflict...
>
> A Community Government Council encompassing Groote and Bickerton Island, constituted as the Angurugu Council is constituted, would alleviate the tension caused by the colonial-settlement period. Furthennore, it would be entirely consistent with tradition. The area

was already divided into "Townships" ["clan" areas] before Europeans ever arrived. Totemic linkages and marriage ties are one means of establishing interdependence between these jurisdictions; "representation" is another. Angurugu and Umbakumba could be seen more as meeting places than as ends in themselves and thus alleviate some of the tension between the two communities. Such an institution could bridge the gap between Aboriginal and Euro-Australian cultures which the young people in particular are finding it so difficult to cross. The more farsighted of the Aborigines here, in particular Nandjiwarra Amagula of Yenbakwa, Murabuda Wurrarnarrba of Angurugu and Paul Wurrabadelamba of Umbakumba, see the future in these terms. But from where things stand now, that future seems a long way off. For the moment all efforts are geared merely to arresting the present.

Strange, but no-one had mentioned the "wasting disease" during my visit. But then I hadn't asked about it either, although I had noticed a change in Kevin Lalara's appearance. It struck me that I bad not seen him walking about since I had been on the island. Instead, he drove around in a truck all day. His face looked emaciated. When I finally stopped him to say "G'dday" and looked inside I found out why. His body was all shriveled up as if he were about to die of malnutrition. But his mind was as sharp as ever. No Groote Eylandt Community Government Council was going to solve his problem. Perhaps that's why the Aborigines never mentioned the disease or pointed out to me anyone who had it. Maybe they believed it was something totally beyond their own or anyone else's control.

When I returned to Darwin I raised the issue of Bickerton's broken backhoe. The money was made available. I don't know what it went into, though, because when I returned to Bickerton some months later the backhoe still wasn't working and the septic tanks were still standing out in the open up above ground. My faith in the persistence of Aboriginal tradition was renewed.

* * * *

There's no point discussing the rest of my recommendations to the Government at this point as the recommendations involved translating Aboriginal culture into Western terms so as to change the terms of Western culture, and we have not yet come to an understanding of Aboriginal culture in its own terms. There is no better way to learn about Aboriginal culture in its own terms, apart from actually participating in it directly yourself, than to come back with me to Groote Eylandt and over to Bickerton Island. And by learning about it in its own terms, you may also learn why we need to change the terms by which *we* live in an Aboriginal direction.

In May of 1986, my consultancy ended, I was, indeed, on my way back to Groote, this time with my family.

PART II

EDENS

IV

The More Things Change, The More Things Remain the Same

We arrived at Angurugu on the afternoon 'plane from Darwin. Aringari Wurramara met us at the airstrip and drove us to the settlement. His attention was riveted on the children. "When David was first here, these were all bark humpies," he said to Graeme, Michelle and Iain, pointing to the houses in front of us as we drove up from the new bridge which spanned the Angurugu River. By the tone of his voice it was difficult to tell if he was proud of the change or lamenting. Other changes were noticeable too. The long grass which had extended all the way from the river bank to the settlement and which had made our nightly trek across the river to our "staging house" such a dangerous prospect because of the deadly snakes it concealed (king browns, tiger snakes, death adders) had been cleared away and in some places covered with sand. (We were only to see one snake during this visit, a large but harmless python living under our house).

The physical gulf between the European sector of the settlement to the west and the Aboriginal sector to the east was still intact, though the latter had begun to curl around the European sector on its southern perimeter. At the juncture now though was a brand new brick and steel shop. The old wooden building behind us down by the river which had served this purpose when we were first here was now in disrepair and about to be torn down. The garage on the southern perimeter of town, now in front of us, seemed to have expanded exponentially and it was not hard to see why: in front of almost every house we passed was a car or a Toyota truck. The Mission administrative building, now the office of the Angurugu Community Government Council, and the Church, however, were as they had been before. And just behind the Council offices was the old bark dormitory building, now a storehouse, a reminder of an earlier era when the Mission had relocated here from the Emerald River to the south. It was in such buildings that the Mission kept its young Aboriginal female charges tucked safely away from the older, polygamous, men to whom many of them had been promised. I recalled with amusement the missionaries' dilemma. This was a letter from Mr. J. B. Montgommery, C.M.S. Sydney to a Mr. Hoffman, C.M.S. Angurugu, Nov. 25, 1953:

I note that you have decided that the Girl's Dormitory is to be made man-proof and that the door is to be locked from the inside as you all thought that it would be too dangerous to have it locked from the outside in case of fire. I note also your suggestions with regard to the fastening of the windows both inside and outside. I heartily endorse all your suggestions.

The interest in all the outside security, of course, was that the girls were trying to get out as much as the men were trying to get in! The dormitory idea was soon after abandoned as much out of exasperation as out of a change in principle or policy. In fairness, though, the men were fighting amongst themselves over claims to the young women, principally the single men who were without wives and wished at least one and the older men who already had a wife or wives and wished others – as was their right. In the settlement context a large number of single men had been placed in close proximity to a large number of young, and not-yet-married-though promised-to-be-married, females. More importantly, here at the Mission the older men were prevented from exercising the full weight of their authority in the face of European disapproval:

> Native Mick aged approx. 55 years insists on attempting to take from the dormitory a native girl Gudaguda originally "promised" to Mick's (older) brother Gulagula who was murdered here some three years or so ago. Mick already has four wives and has cast a fifth off as unwanted. I have personally sought to pacify him, offering him generous recompense in return for his forfeiting his tribal right to marry the girl in question. But he has consistently refused all this and has been the cause of several disturbances here. He has not actually committed any crime nor caused any serious injury. But I consider that his removal for a period of time would have a quietening influence on himself and we have evidence already (since he left on the "KURU" on the 8th inst.) of a similar restraining influence on another native who is inclined to be a disturbing element in the camp.

This was a letter from Mr. B. D. Short, C.M.S. Angurugu, to the Director of Native Affairs, Darwin, Oct. 11, 1949. On 8 November, 1949, the following communique passed between the Acting Director of Native Affairs and the Superintendent of Angurugu: "l wish to thank you for your assistance to Patrol Officer Ryan on this recent visit to apprehend Mick Noanoa."

We turned the corner and arrived at the accommodation the Council had arranged for us. Aringari helped us out with our suitcases. It was a far cry from 1969 when we lived in a tent and a simply constructed more or less empty staging house across the river from the main settlement. This time the Council had given us a modern three bedroom prefab house with a fridge am.I slove dose lo lht: Council offices (though technically it belonged to the Education Department). That evening, about 6:30, we all went for a walk. I hadn't noticed when I had been out here on my short visit a few months before, because it had been raining much of the time. But the road was covered with black dirt which raised like dust when disturbed by our steps. It was crushed manganese, the Mining Company's gift to the community in the interests of road maintenance and beautification.

As we neared the intersection this side of the shop we were approached by a group of six or seven young Aboriginal girls. Two of them had coke cans hung about their necks and as they neared us the smell of gasoline filtered through the air. They walked unsteadily. They were sniffers. One of them was without a can and she asked us if we had come from Darwin. Without thinking back to my previous visit and the episode with Graeme at the river I replied in Anindilyaugwa that I had been on Groote Eylandt a long time ago. She turned to the others and nodded knowingly before moving off with them down the road. I vowed henceforth to keep my mouth shut about my origins.

The next day I began my work. The terms of this had changed too. I was no longer to be situated at the centre of Aboriginal life in the community in full view of everyday events, able to follow them up immediately with on the-spot interviews. Instead I was to have an "office" and I would let the Council know in advance just whom I wished to talk to and about what. As it happened, I had a definite list of questions and clarifications I wished answered and knew precisely who to go to for the answers – based on the hints in my notebooks I mentioned in the introduction. The arrangement suited me fine. But had it been 1969 when we had learned so much and in such a short space of time by living in the community, the arrangement would have been disastrous. Another disadvantage was that in the Council offices where I was to be located, even the Aborigines spoke English to each other and never talked about "tribal" (as the Europeans called them) matters. On the other hand, the Aboriginal men gathered together every day in front of the Council buildings to discuss current events and, as it was on my route to work, I had an excuse to stop and catch up with them. The meeting always broke up about ten when the shuttle bus arrived to take those of them on the "morning shift" up to drink at the club in Alyangula.

The next morning on my way to work Richard Bara (of the Wurrabadelamba "clan" (Bara meaning West Wind) stopped me on the road and from his Toyota asked me if the boy he had seen me with was my son. When I said "yes", he reached out and squeezed my shoulder and upper arm muscle, smiled affectionately, and without saying a word, drove off. In their terms, your child comes from your shoulder (you) and your womb (your sister) which is another way of saying it comes, not from you as an individual, a father, or from "you" as a "couple", a father and a mother, but from you and your "sister" (really you and your "brothers" and "sisters") – that is, a "clan" of men and women. "Clanness" is passed on through the father through the act of procreation with a woman of another "clan". But "clanness" really has nothing to do with kinship; what it *has* to do with, as we'll see, is the reason why we will soon have to stop referring to these Aborigines as living in "clans".

Two persons who come from the *same* shoulder and womb, such as the son of a man and the daughter of a woman who are from the same "clan" (i.e., a boy and his father's sister's daughter), are too close to marry. Theirs is that *warnigarangbidja* relationship we encountered earlier.

My main aim at Angurugu was to replicate the study of the so-called "kinship and marriage" system I had carried out in 1969. I was interested in the basis on which relationships were formed and whether or not this basis had changed over time. What I had discovered in my 1969 work was that relationships were conceived three-dimensionally, that is, in terms of genealogical connection within the Aboriginal theory of procreation, in terms of "clan" membership and in terms of generation. A fourth dimension emerges once it is realized that Spirituality is at the core of "clan" identity not to mention the Aboriginal theory of procreation.

It is easy for a non-Aboriginal to understand that an Aboriginal believes thats/he inherits semen or *amena* from the father and blood or *ma:rra* from the mother; but it is much more difficult for us to decipher how this is related to the process of conception. In the first place, it takes many acts of intercourse to make a child, in fact two to three months' worth, which means that in our terms, though not in theirs, as I have pointed out, the husband may not necessarily be the actual father of the child. But even if we get that sorted out, there is still the vexing question of just what in the semen and what in the blood are inherited to constitute the child's identity. The answer, I found out, was "nothing". *Amena* mixes with *ma:rra* all right, but only to make a seed or *mamungwara*. The seed grows the child, not the substances that gave the seed birtth. The child's identity emanates from the belief/fact that through prolonged intercourse the husband, the only person in a position to enjoy intercourse with the wife on a prolonged basis, opens up a pathway for the entry of the Spirit from his country into the mother to animate the fetus. This happens quite close to the time of the child's actual birth. More often than not, the identity of the Spirit – that is, the particular aspect of the particular Creative Being it represents – will be revealed to someone beforehand in a dream (*agulyangbararrga*).

In 1969 my closest friend, Na:nindilyaragwagwa (Johnny) Lalara, and his wife Lelina Wurramara were going to have a baby (technically in this connection, Wurramara should be written Damara, she-in-the-singular of the Wurramara "clan", but the pluralized version has become the "clan surname"). A short time before the child was born Johnny told me that Lulungu of the Murungun, the "clan" to which his mother had gone in marriage on the death of his father, had dreamed that a boy was coming from Arnbali, a Lalara place on the mainland. Another woman, Dangwunda, Johnny's father's brother's wife, however, dreamed it was a girl associated with a particular waterhole in the same place. Johnny was impressed that although Dangwunda had never been to that place she could describe the waterhole in detail. "I didn't feel happy about the first one," he said, "but I did about the second." The child was a girl and it was named on the waterhole. Johnny told of another occasion when he went to Darwin leaving his pregnant wife at Angurugu. One night he had a dream that a son had been born to him. Three days later he found out that his wife bad, in fact, been blessed with a son. "If I had dreamed a girl it would have been a girl," he said. By the time he found out, Djawaranga of the Wurramara, a man in his wife's "clan", had already dreamed the child's name on a mainland place in Lalara country.

On other occasions a child may be born and its identity dreamed after the fact. This was the case with Nandjiwarra Amagula's son in 1969. The people at Umbakumba on the other side of Groote Eylandt reckoned he had been at Umbakumba with the Spirits of some of hls "clanspeople" before he was born, having come there in spiritForm from Amagula country on the south coast. Someone at Umbakumba had reported seeing a baby pheasant flying around their house. Yugba, pheasant, is an important Amagula Creative Being associated with the sacred Mardaiya:n ceremony. When the child was ready to be born he appeared in a dream to his *dungwiyarrga* (father's sister) at Umbakumba and said, "I'm leaving you. I'm going to my father and mother (at Angurugu)". The people at Umbakumba knew he had been born because the wind and the rain there had suddenly stopped. This impressed those at Angurugu no end. The child was named on Yugba.

Before the missionaries came, I was told, the men used to sing the Spirit of the child from its country to the mother, picking the child's name out of the Song at some point in the journey. They don't trace a path like this out any more but they do still pick the name out of a Song. Even the dreamed names so originate. In addition to the name revealed in a dream others handed down from the past and still available in the present are also assigned to a child. The first born (*nelyenmanama*) in each generation receives a special name which has come down in this fashion through the generations. A "big name" (*alara*) in Nandjiwarra's line, for instance, is Geraidua which means "big store house" and was the name of a Macassan "boss" or "*bunggoa*" who used to visit Nandjiwarra's country and sometimes even stay there. A big name in Murabuda-of-the-Wurramarrba's line is also of Macassan origin: Djumedjumugwa, meaning "smoking trepang".

If the first-born of a first-born father is a girl she keeps the name in question until her father dies on which occasion she passes it on to the first born male in her "clan" and generation. This could be to someone other than her own brother. The first-born male is regarded as the leader of his "clan" unless nature has conspired to deny him the requisite attributes of mental and physical prowess.

Ordinary names can also be assigned to a child by the father or his "clan" brothers, the only requirement being that they be in the same Songstream as the father, that is that they have the right to sing of the travels of the same Creative Beings. The name of the Creative Being cannot itself be adopted as a personal name. Only an attribute of the Being is eligible, an attribute that will be associated with a particular place along its journey.

My friend Na:nindilyaragwagwa, for instance, is named on Silt, or rather the Silt churned up by the Tide, specifically the Silt churned up by the Tide where the fresh water flows from a creek at Arrnadadi on the mainland and mixes with the sea and is gone forever, never turning back. Silt is associated too with the travels of the Stingrays as they moved across to Bickerton and Groote, churning it up with their bodies as they glide through the water. Morris Lalara, whom I had also been close to and whom I learned on my return had been killed senselessly by his son who was drunk at the time, was named on Ya:aredungwa or King Brown Snake. One of his names was Nalunggwibanga or "superficial snake bite"; the other was Nalungbayibonga or "deeper snake bite" – both wounds which King Brown had inflicted on other Beings as he traveled about Lalara country on the mainland in the Creation period. Morris had primary jurisdiction over the places where this happened. Morris' son had the name Nalambiyaga. Yaga means "it's here!", and in the context of a Song about this Snake, refers to a particular place where a particular incident took place. "Lalara", the surname chosen by the "clan" when pressured to do so years ago by Mission officials for identification and bookkeeping purposes, means "dangerous snakes" which includes king browns as well as tiger snakes and death adders.

To call someone by the name of the Creative Being as such would imply that the person in question had primary jurisdiction over all the country traveled by that Being, an implication the Aborigines are at pains to avoid. "Share jurisdiction with those following the same Creative Being, each in his or her own small corner," yes; but overarching jurisdiction by one person or a sector of the "clan", no. It goes without saying that no-one can be named "on" a Creative Being which traversed the whole "clan" territory because there are no Creative Beings that travelled a "clan's" territory as a whole. Each person identifies with part of a Being in turn connected to a part of a whole which is defined by the relative closeness of the relationship between the parts of the whole in question. Such "name-lines" flow from grandfather to grandson though occasionally shifting back and forth across the lines as first-borns of the "clan" as a whole in one line relinquish their names to first-borns of the "clan" as a whole m other lines in succeeding generations.

Gula, the first-born and elder statesman of the Lalara, had summarized where the names "were at" in his own "clan" in 1969:

Admiral [his brother] is going by land [on Yandarranga. Central Hill] for his children's names; mine are all on Alumera [the Silt churned up by the Stingray]. The rest of them [the Lalara "clan"] are copying behind me. They have plenty of room on Yua:ba [Meat Ant] and Yandarranga but they're not near them – they're following me [on Stingray]. We pick the name out of the Song and then change it to make it a boy's or girl's name [this is accomplished by adding an *n* for a male or a *d* for a female to the root, as in the Damara example above].

There used to be many names and few people, he went on, but "Now there are too many children so we have to give each of them fewer names". One of the solutions, even in 1969, was to fill the gap by giving children additional English names. Of course they had no Spiritual implications, but they did tend to be names of some significance in the community. For instance, it might be the name of a European who had endeared him or herself to Aboriginal people. Or it might be a name given by a European of some significance. I had the honour of bestowing an English name on Gula's newborn son just before I left Angurugu in 1969. The name I chose was "Roger", the name of my brother who had passed away in 1970. Unfortunately the baby died, but Gula passed the name on to another son born later.

The Spirit that enters the child at birth seems to be differentiated into two parts or have two aspects. One is still partly attached to the dimension from which it has come and is forever fixed, the other is encased within the material world of the body and is released when the body dies. Both are called *awarrawalya* but they are different. When they become different, *awarrawalya*-released is called *amugwa*. *Awarrawalya* is also the name for the shadow cast by a person as well as the shelter built to house each "clan" or Company of "clans" in the Mardaiya:n sacred ceremony. *Amugwa* is also the word for the "gushingness" of a spring, for the "glowingness" of hot coals.

When you die, the encapsulated (part of the) Spirit is released and transported to the Land of the Dead, really the gateway to the world of the fifth dimension as such – one's "country" in transcendent form. The "other" (part of the) Spirit seems to remain where it is, perhaps a potential warp through to the fifth dimension which allows for reincarnation and/or re-embodiment in a material form. Interestingly, it is the liberated (part of the) Spirit that they are afraid of after a person dies, and not the seemingly fixed one.

There is even more to it than this: Spirit as *awarrawalya* is distinguished from Spirit as Amawurrena; or rather Spirit as *awarrawalya* is Spirit as Amawurrena transformed in the process of incarnation as human. But more on this later.

The crucial point for purposes of this discussion is that Spirit is no more incorporated into the body than individuals are incorporated as a unity into a "clan". Spirit is rather "affiliated" with a body as it journeys from and to the fifth dimension – from a state where its primary affiliation is Creative to a state where its primary affiliation is human. Perhaps we should think of Spirit as a rnbber band, one end fixed, the other stretching along the top strand through a transparent wall of water, eventually pulling the bottom strand and finally the other end behind it, then stretching back again in the other direction.

In 1969 the old men told me that the point of life on "this side" of existence was to understand life on the "other side" in relation to life as a whole. If a Spirit did not make it through to this understanding in the world of the body on the first try, it would return to its country and try again.

When a child died, then, its Spirit was not so much sung away as Sung back to its country. Its bones, a lock of hair, a wallaby (*yiberada*) jaw, a few parrot (*wurruwa:ba*) feathers and perhaps a piece of its clothing were placed in a bark container about a foot and a half long by a foot wide called a *warnamaleda*. This the mother carried around with her until she had a new baby. The new baby was regarded as an incarnation of the same Spirit as the deceased. If she remained childless the *warnamaleda* could be handed over to another woman of the same "clan" and her next child would be regarded as identical in Spirit to the original. It didn't matter if the first child had been one gender, the second another. Spirit is neutral until manifested in body. In other words, the body is sexed, not the Spirit. Sexual differentiation is only important as far as Spirit is concerned insofar as it enables Spirit to travel in an exclusive line – through males – over time which in tum allows it to group people in a coherent manner in physical space. It is only males who can open up a path for a Spirit from their country to enter the material world (though there is no reason in principle why Spirit could not travel through the female body-line to produce the same result; indeed, in some parts of Australia, notably amongst the Tiwi of Melville and Bathurst Island, it did). Amongst the Aborigines of the Groote Eylandt and Bickerton Island area, then, there is a sense in which the mother is not really the mother of the child she bears. She is more the receptacle within which the child is formed. By the same token, in parts of Australia where the principle of transmission is matrilineal, the father is not really the father of the child either.

However – and I have never been able to get to the bottom of this – even on Groote Eylandt and Bickerton Island there is something of the mother's own Spiritual being or identity (always the same as her father's of course) that does seem to "spill down" into the child. For that matter, what spills down is not only something of the mother's but also something of the mother's mother's and the father's mother's Spirits. With the child situated in the womb in such close proximity to the mother, with Spirit as "active" as it is, some "permeation" of one by the other seems to occur. The Spirit of the father's mother would have permeated that of the father and so slightly qualified his identity as well as that of his child; the Spirit of the mother's mother would have permeated that of the mother and so also of her child, though to a lesser degree. Indeed, this is the way Aborigines actually conceive the strength of these influences beginning with the Spiritual relation of father to child and ending with that between child and mother's mother. Another way of putting it is, <<father's country closer than mother's country closer than father's mother's country closer than mother's mother's country>>.

Yinigarnga is "mother's country" (that is, the country of her father) which is also the name of the dwelling or shelter you "come out of" in the sacred Mardaiya:n ceremony. It is also the name of the "playground" of the Mardaiya:n ceremony where the dances take place, indicating that the tie to mother's country is, Spiritually, very close indeed.

To say that when a child died it was sung back to its country to be reincarnated in the next-born is somewhat misleading. In his unpublished study of the Groote Eylandt Aborigines Peter Worsley (1954: 168) notes that a *warnamaleda* was made, and hence the Spirit returned to its country, if the deceased was up to 30 years of age! When a second child was born to the same woman, the *warnamaleda* containing the remains of the first was handed over to an old woman for safekeeping and could be used again if the second child also died before its proper time. "It's proper time", I found, was after its body, so to speak, had passed through all the stages of initiation or instruction to become fully knowledgeable, that is, fully human.

By 1969 the custom of making *warnamaleda* had been abandoned – and had been since about the time Worsley was on the island. Small replicas were still being made as children's dolls, as also had been the custom. In 1969 the Spirits of some small children were still being sung back to their countries of origin to be born again, though the practice was being carried on only by the very old men. Younger songmen had abandoned this custom altogether, having first reduced the requisite stage of initiation relevant to the practice to circumcision. Change was proceeding more rapidly at Angurugu, the site of the Mission, with its Christian notions of lineal time and irreversible progress to Heaven (with perhaps a detour to Hell), than it was at Umbakumba.

If a Spirit can be sent back to its country after it is made manifest, it can also be prevented from becoming manifest by the practice of contraception and abortion. Cunlra1,;eption techniques, according to Dulcie Levitt in her book *Plants and People: Aboriginal Uses of Plants on Groote Eylandt* (p. 62), prevented conception for all time and involved drinking the juice of fruit from the quinine bush (*Petalostigma pubescens*) or the mistletoe tree (*Exocatpos latifolius*) as well as of rainwater running down a tree during a rainstorm, though the connection here was unspecified. This latter technique, though, may be related to a method my wife learned of in 1969.

You take some of the bark of an *alabera* or stringybark tree, or of a *yimendungwa* or cypress pine after it has been hit by lightning, and soak it in the juices of *amunggwulya*, poison pea (*Gulactia tenuiflora*, though the word also refers to the edible yellow flowered-bean: *Vigna lanceolata* var. *filiformis*). This makes a red drink which prevents babies. But you have to shut your eyes when drinking it so as not to see the poison. Ruth also learned that there were substances a woman could ingest to induce an abortion but was unable to acquire the details. They were apparently being used to rid young single women of babies suspected of being "half- caste". She thought that because of the purpose and because she was white, the women were embarrassed to talk to her about the methods. Ruth was also told that some men had the power to sing and prevent babies. Djowila of the Wurramara was such a person. I didn't follow it up then and couldn't now – he had died in the interim and no-one else is left who can do this (or so I am told).

More modern methods of contraception are the swallowing of rusty iron filings and the pill, though Ruth had some time explaining to the women in 1969 that you didn't dole the pills out to other people as you normally doled out food if you wished to achieve the desired result!

At the complete other end of the spectrum, Ruth also found out that there were techniques to make you "grow a seed" and have a child. It had something to do with plants and stones in the place called Arumandja in Wurramara country on Bickerton Island – something to do with religion and ritual as well as medicine. I didn't follow it up then but would be able to now. The Wurramara it seemed, if Djowila was any indication, had the power to give life as well as the power to prevent it, if not take it away.

Once it is realized that Spirituality is at the basis of "clan" identity it becomes impossible henceforth to speak of "clans" at all, even in quotes. Aborigines do not classify, differentiate or group on the basis of kinship, though there is an element of kinship or genealogy in the way they differentiate or group. But even this must be qualified by stating that we are proceeding from a definition of reproduction which does not recognize a genetic connection between parents and children. In fact, it does not recognize the relationship "parents and children" at all. "Father" is differentiated from "mother" absolutely; "children" are the progeny of the father considered in his Spiritual dimension which he shares in a differentiated but interrelated way with others of his … what? Not clan. I prefer "Promised Land" for reasons which will become apparent in the next chapter. For now let us just say that Promised Land membership is based on Spiritual identity and is transmitted in like manner.

There is another dimension to interpersonal relationships in the Groote Eylandt and Bickerton Island area that needs to be explored and this is "generation level". This one had me stumped for many years until I realized that its significance lay in what it was not: "generation" was not expressed institutionally. That is, it bore no relation to Spiritual existence. "Generation", as the Australian Anthropologist Les Hiatt had tried to point out to me some 14 years ago, was something I had imposed on the culture in order to arrange people for analysis. And yet being from the same father, from fathers who were brothers (from a common grandfather, from grandfathers who were brothers) did seem to make a difference to the way people related to each other. People seemed to classify one another, at least in part, according to whether they were on the same "generation" in these terms or not. I thought that there was some way that "brothers" in one Promised Land could calculate whether or not they were descended through the same number of generations as "brothers" in another Promised Land and that the answer to this question made a difference to the way people classified and related to each other.

It wasn't until I began playing with the "system" on a computer that I began to realize that "generation" was, in fact, the "unabstract, uneternal factor" that permitted Aborigines to adjust relationships to the circumstances of the day while leaving the basic parameters of the abstract and the eternal more or less intact. To explain:

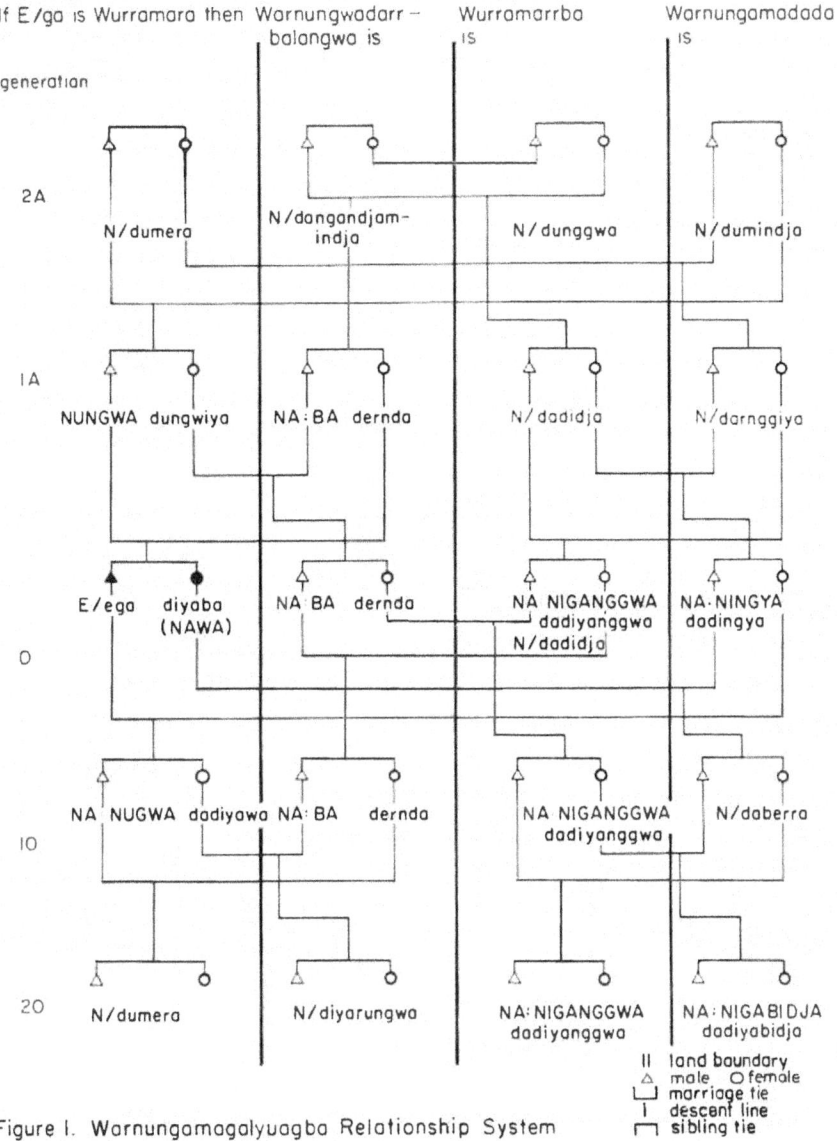

Figure 1. Warnungamagalyuagba Relationship System

The Terms of Relationships

Each term in the relationship system refers to a particular conjunction of Promised Lands as manifested in one's cognates affiliations with one's own and others' in the ascending levels. This is the Promised Land affiliations of one's father(= yours), one's mother, one's father's mother and one's mother's mother. The conjunction in question is established through marriage.

"Wife", then, is "someone in my father's mother's Land in my own generation whose mothers are in my mother's mother's Land, whose mother's mothers are in my mother's Land, and whose father's mothers are in my Land". The Aboriginal term for a person in this kind of relationship is NA:NINGYA (for males) and *dadingya* (for females). It is also the term for "husband". The critical feature is that the person is someone in one's father's mother's Land, that is, someone from a Land that entered into a marriage relationship with your own two generations ago. This is the Land you should marry in your generation.

Another term, NABERRA/daberra, designates people in one's father's mother's Land in the next generation whose cognates are in a different alignment to your own because of the marry-same-Land-in-alternate generations rule. NABERRA/daberra, then, is "people in my father's mother's Land in the first descending generation whose mothers are in my Land, whose mother's mothers are in my mother's Land and whose father's mothers are in my mother's mother's Land". They are people whose mothers are in one's own Land because in one's own generation their Land will have taken a wife from one's own. It will be easier to understand by consulting Figure I (p. 67) where l represent the system diagrammatically:

In the diagram, NA:NINGYA/dadingya is the tenn applied to people in relationship #7, NABERRA/daberra the term applied to people in relationship #8. The full range of terms and the relationships they designate are as follows:

Table 1. Wamungamagalyuagba Relationship Terms.

1. **NUM'ERA/dumera**: people in my Land in the second ascending and second descending generations whose mothers are in my mother's Land, whose mother's mothers are in my mother's mother's Land, and whose father's mothers are in my father's mother's Land.

2. **NUNGWA/dungwiya**: people in my Land in the first ascending generation whose mothers are in my father's mother's Land, whose mother's mothers are in my mother's mother's Land and whose father's mothers are in my mother's Land.

3. **NAWA/diyaba**: people in my Land in my generation older than I am, whose mothers are in my mother's Land, whose mother's mothers are in my mother's mother's Land and whose father's mothers are in my father's mother's Land.

4. **NA:NUGWA/dadiyawa**: people in my Land in the first descending generation whose mothers are in my father's mother's Land, whose mother's mothers are in my mother's mother's Land and whose father's mothers are in my mother's Land.

5. **NUMINDJA/dumindja**: people in my father's mother's Land in the second ascending generation, whose mothers are in my mother's mother's Land, whose mother's mothers are in my mother's Land and whose father's mothers are in my Land.

6. **NARNGIYA/darngiya**: people in my father's mother's Land in the first ascending generation, whose mothers are in my Land, whose mother's mothers are in my mother's Land and whose father's mothers are in my mother's mother's Land.

7. **NA:NINGYA/dadingya**: (as on p. 68)

8. **NABERRA/daberra**: (as on p. 68)

9. **NA:NIGABIDJA/dadiabidja**: people in my father's mother's Land in the second descending generation, whose mothers are in my mother's mother's Land, whose mother's mothers are in my mother's Land, and whose father's mothers are in my Land.

10. **NUNGGWA/dunggwa**: people in my mother's mother's Land in the second ascending generation whose moUlers are in my father's mother's Land, whose mother's mothers are in my own Land and whose father's mothers are in my mother's Land.

11. **NADIDJA/dadidja**: people in my mother's mother's Land in the first ascending generation whose mothers are in my mother's Land, whose mother's mothers are in my own Land and whose father's mothers are in my father's mother's Land.

12. **NA:NIGANGGWA/dadiyanggwa**: people in my mother's mother's Land in the present and second descending generations whose mothers are in my father's mother's Land, whose mother's mothers are in my Land and whose father's mothers are in my mother's Land; also, people in the first descending generation whose mothers are in my mother's Land, whose mother's mothers are in my Land and whose father's mothers are in my father's mother's Land.

13. **NANGANDJAMINDJA/dangandjamindja**: people in my mother's Land in the second ascending generation whose mothers are in my Land, whose mother's mothers are in my father's mother's Land and whose father's mothers are in my mother's mother's Land.

14. **NA:BA/dernda**: people in my mother's Land in the first ascending and first descending generation whose mothers are in my mother's mother's Land, whose mother's mothers are in my father's mother's Land and whose father's mothers are in my Land; also, those in the present generation whose mothers are in my Land, whose mother's mothers are in my father's mother's Land and whose father's mothers are in my mother's mother's Land.

15. **NIYARANGWA/diyarangwa**: people in my mother's Land in the second descending generation whose mothers are in my Land, whose mother's mothers are in my father's mother's Land, whose mother's mothers are in my father's mother's Land and whose father's mothers are in my mother's mother's Land.

The term NARNGIYNdarngiya is archaic in meaning and in 1969 was used to designate "wife's father" as such, independently of the actual interrelations of those involved.

Unfortunately for the reader, the situation is nowhere near as simple as my diagram and definitions imply. The question of direct and indirect Songstream linkages between what I have now come to regard as Promised Lands also applies. Basically, where there is no direct intersection of one's own and relatives' cognates' Promised Lands (that is, neither of you have a cognate in the same Promised Land), the principle of direct and indirect Songstream Linkage comes into play. A direct linkage is a connection through the travels of the same Creative Being: an indirect linkage is where one Promised Land is linked to another by one Being which is in turn linked to a third by another, thereby linking the first to the third.

Recall the way Promised Lands were aligned for purposes of representation on the Angurugu Community Government Council. With a few exceptions, each grouping there represents a direct linkage between the Promised Lands in question. Basically, direct and indirect Songstream linkages form Promised Lands in the Groote Eylandt area into four distinct groupings or "Companies" as the Aborigines call them in English (there is no word for them in the language). They are akin to the so-called "semi-moieties" of south-east Arnhem Land we encountered in Chapter II, though here they are not named. These Companies are as follows:

Table 2. Songstream Companies of the Western Gulf.

Songstream Company 1: Wamindilyaugwa (Mamariga and Amagula) and Wamungrnurugulya (now extinct), both of Groote Eylandt, linked by Hawk, Lightening and Rainbow Snake (among others) to the Wurramara of Bickerton and the Wamindilibala and Nungumadjbarr of the adjacent mainland.

Songstream Company 2: Warnungwamalangwa (Bara Bara). Durila and Warnungamagadjeragba of Groote linked by Dove, Ship and Tiger Shark (among others) to the Wurramarrba of Bickerton and the Warnunggargala (Mimiyawan) of the adjacent mainland.

Songstream Company 3: Wamungwudjaragba of Groote linked by Log Coffin and West Wind (among others) to the Wamungwadarrbalangwa of Groote and the Murungun and Manggamanggaraiya of the adjacent mainland, though Wurrawilya of Groote sometimes counted in here too.

Songstream Company 4: Wurramaminyamandja and Wamungangwurngwerigba (Yandarranga) of Groote linked by Shark Ray. Sawfish and Central Hill (among others) to the Warnungamadada and Wurra:nggilyangba of Bickerton and the Ngalmi and Nemamurdudi of the adjacent mainland.

Without delving further into the details of the direct and indirect linkages involved in each Company of Lands at this point, let me merely point out that if a correspondence in Promised Lands cannot be located when two persons cognates' affiliations are compared, then the Aborigines look to a conespondence in directly-linked terms to fix their relationship. For instance, a person may be called "wife" because she is someone in a Promised Land directly linked to my father's mother's. If no such correspondence can be located in direct terms then the people in question look for one in indirect terms. If there is at any point a conflict such that more than one term defines some aspect of their relationship, then the correspondence expressing the *closest* relationship fixes the term.

For instance, if the person is both in a Promised Land directly linked to your father's mother's but has a mother in your Promised Land, then the term chosen would be *dernda* over *dadingya*. This means she would be ineligible rather than eligible for marriage. This would hold even if the person in question was actually in your father's mother's Promised Land (at least the principle held in 1969). Father's Promised Land, as I pointed out earlier, is closer than mother's is closer than father's mother's is closer than mother's mother's; a direct Songstream Linkage is closer than an indirect one. Basically, then, to calculate how you are related to anyone in the society, you have to know the identities of your respective cognates (in Promised Land as well as in personal terms), the Songstream linkages between the Promised Lands, the meanings of the relationship terms as outlined above and the logic of their application involving degrees of closeness, not to mention that ubiquitous "generation level".

It took me about eight months in 1969 to work all this out and even then I had to have a pencil and paper handy to calculate just how I would relate to any particular individual. It was my own relationships to the Aboriginal people around me that I focused on because it was through my relationships to others that I had been taught.

Almost every day, when I was not out in the bush, I would sit for a time with the middle-aged men at the old widows' place, a nexus of activity in the village, situated as it was on the way to and from the administrative offices, and almost every day they would ask me, whenever someone walked by, "What do you call him/her?" (*Giyamarrgena nagina/dagina*?). At first my answers spanned the range of terms available in a random fashion much to the amusement of my "teachers", a confirmation of their belief that no European, no matter how intelligent and motivated, no matter how much time they spent teaching him/her, would ever be able to learn how to do it correctly. But over time, I began to notice a pattern: the correct term seemed to fall within a certain range of terms which somehow depended on mine and the other person's Land membership.

I began to impress my teachers when I was able to reply with the correct term I *should* apply to a particular person. By now I had learned that the Lands ought to be aligned in a particular way for marriage purposes and therefore their members ought to refer to one another only by the proper line of terms (as outlined in Figure 1). Of course, I always had to ask that person's Land (*angalya*) or Song (*ama:ba*) before I could proceed, but this kind of detailed biographical information they didn't expect me to know. Having told me once, however, they expected me to remember. I began to impress even more when I was able to rattle off a list of the probable terms I might call any given person independently of the ideal. By now I was engaged in soliciting not only the other person's Land identity but also the Land identities of their cognates. I also knew the relevance of my own assigned cognate's Lands to the calculation. Finally, when I started getting it right (what I judged to be) most of the time, they stopped asking me to identify people by my relationship to them. Now when I was wrong it was because of arbitrary alterations in the past which had caused people to be related in terms other than those defined by the intersection of their respective cognates' Lands and these they did not expect me to know. But they explained them to me so that I learned even more.

The relationship terms and their meanings, I found, were an ideal model to be emulated in practice. The logic of their assignment was a means of constantly adjusting practice in the direction of the ideal. If people were not related as they should be, then a term would be assigned which pointed this out – the example of the person who is in your father's mother's Land but who also has a mother in your own Land is a case in point. There is stigma attached to you and everyone else knowing that you would have been eligible for marriage to a particular person but since someone in your Land made a mistake in the previous generation, you aren't.

But "knowing" the way the system worked was one thing; proving it scientifically was quite another. The prevailing opinion in Aboriginal studies when I was doing this work was that relationships in Aboriginal societies were genealogically or kinship-based. I had found they were not, but would anyone believe my "opinion"? The answer surely must be, <<only if I met T. G. H. Strehlow's requirement>>. As Strehlow had put it in *Songs of Central Australia* (p. xvii):

> I do not for a moment believe that all of our present-day psychological or sociological explanations about the aboriginal Australians and their institutions are *sufficiently well-attested or statistically validated* [ital-

ics mine] to survive the criticisms of later generations ... we should at least do all within our power to ensure absolute accuracy in whatever documents we are accumulating now for future research.

When I returned to Canada after my (then) last visit in 1974, I vowed to put my ideas and my data to the test. Fortunately I happened to meet Dan Hoey, then a graduate student at the University of Manitoba who was a bit of a whiz at computer programming. After reading my book *Tradition and Transformation* on the subject, he said he thought he could duplicate the operations by which relationship terms were assigned by translating them into computer language, at this point the language of Fortran, and with more quantitative data exhaustively test my model. In an Appendix to my book I had set about predicting how one person related to 74 others in terms of this model and had been correct on 50 occasions. All but six of the exceptions I could account for by pragmatic factors. Now I would be in a position to test my (their) model on a 74 by 74 sample – over 5,000 individual cases.

Fortunately I had followed Fred Rose's method of collecting data without reference to genealogical relationship and heeded Peter Worsley's advice that the "clan" was critical in determining the way people related to one another. As a result I recorded Promised Land histories tracing the present generation of each Land as far back as they could remember along with the people they and their forbears had married. I also drew up a list of informants, 75 in all, and asked each what relationship terms s/he actually, as distinct from ideally, applied to every other person on the list. It was these data, together with biographical information on each of the 75 people interviewed, on which I based a testing of the model (adding informant #9 who had inadvertently been omitted from my original list). Then I compared my results with a sample of cases from Rose's 1941 data and Worsley's from 1953, eliminating any informants we had in common.

The preliminary results were published in Gisèle de Meur's book *New Trends in Mathematical Anthropology* in 1986. The model seemed to be confirmed. Of 2,878 predictions made, some 1,898 were correct, or 66%, the random chance of making a correct prediction being one in four ($z = 50.73$). More surprising was the fact that the 1969 results differed little from those of 1941/53 (collapsed because I was primarily interested in testing the validity of the model not in measuring the extent of change over the three periods). In the earlier period, of 1,039 predictions made, 726 were correct, or 70%.

However, there was a methodological problem with the concept of "generation level" in the computer programme which brought into question the statistical validity of the model. I'll let Ron Hughes, who later modified the programme to correct for the problem, explain by way of the Report he wrote for the University of Toronto who funded the project:

> During the translation process it became necessary to understand the purpose of the programme – i.e., it could not be a detached mathematical exercise. David Turner explained the details of his thesis to me and I also read his book, "Tradition and Transformation". From my understanding, it seemed that the programme did not produce an accurate summary of the data.
>
> The purpose of the programme was to (a) find the closest possible affiliation of Land for E/ego and Relative, (b) determine what term would be applied if the ideal model was followed, (c) compare this terem with the actual term applied.
>
> However, the existing programme began by using generation level as the main criterion in the analysis of the data. If the generation level did not match the one required in order for the ideal term to be possibly applied, then that item of data was not included in the results. This produced an inflated view of the degree to which people followed the ideal model.
>
> In order to help decide if generation level was a major source of error, it was necessary to revise the programme considerably.
>
> Basically, it was necessary to list the results of all 5,700 of the Ego/Relative comparisons and the tem1 that was applied to that comparison. Logically, one should make the comparisons only once, and store the results using some type of coding system. The code would need to record these factors: (I) which of Relatives cognates "clans" was responsible for the match, (2) which of E/ego's cognates' "clans" was responsible for the match, (3) generation level, (4) the term that was applied. For example the code "132" means <<Relative's father's "clan" (1) matched my father's mother's "clan" (2) and generation level (3) >>.
>
> Accordingly, a programme was written which made the 5,700-odd comparisons and stored the coded results in a text file. An Assembler language programme was written to read this file and sort the results

by term number. A third programme read the sorted file. analyzed and printed the entire set of data, and gave a summary of the results.

The results showed that, overall, the ideal model term was applied by people about 33% of the time. Either an error in the generation level data or an ignoring of generation level by the people could be the rationale for the incorrect term occurring in approximately 33% more cases.

In the summer of 1985 a single programme was written which does the following: (a) compare E/ego's and Relative's Land to find the closest possible match, (b) code the resulting match, (c) compares this code with the code used for the term applied at other generation levels (e) records results term by term.

The adjustment for generation level doubles the percentage correct. However, this adjustment is not justified unless it can be verified in Lhc field that either the generation data are extremely unreliable or that the people do ignore generation in order to justify a term they decide to apply.

The programme was run for both the data of Rose (1941/53) and Turner (1969). The two sets of data produced similar overall results (a 2% difference in % correct).

With the revised programme the model was confirmed, with a slightly higher number of correct predictions in the earlier 1941/53 period (68%) than in the later 1969 period (66%). And so in 1986 I had headed back to Groote armed with my new programme to collect another generation of data.

On the way I chanced to meet someone who had done his own independent testing of my model while on visits to the island in the late 1970s. After concluding a talk at the Darwin Institute of Technology one of the staff, a John Harris, introduced himself. His father had been the minister in charge of the Mission for about four years. John had been born on the island and nursed by Didjidi of the Wurramarrba. He had returned to Angurugu in the 1970s to serve as headmaster at the school for three years. He had always wondered how the "kinship system" worked and when my book came out read it and used it to calculate his relationship to Aborigines he knew on Groote. His own point of reference was the Warnindilyaugwa People/Land, the "clan" with whjch he had been affiliated. He said my model predicted correctly in 80% of the cases he tested. He had simply ignored generation and gone on to the "clan" intersections of his own and the other person's cognates. Admittedly most of the people he had tried it out on were on his own generation, but it was an independent testing. And it worked.

In my 1986 study I selected a random sample of 141 Aboriginal people, including children, put them on a list with space for a term beside each and then went about soliciting terms for these people from whomever was available at the time. I knew that it would have been impossible to proceed as I had in 1969 by drawing up a list of people and then asking each one on the list what term s/he called everyone else on the list. People were less accessible now than they were before and I had no means of transport. Eventually some 141 people were interviewed, 77 males and 64 females. Complementing this work, "clan histories" were updated with informants from each of the Promised Lands in question (the English "clan", unfortunately, was by now firmly entrenched in the Aborigines' own vocabulary). This task the Aborigines themselves were extremely keen to see completed as they wished copies of these "histories" for themselves for their own purposes, one of which was to teach their young people about past alignments and forgotten ancestors and ancestresses. Unlike the "roll" compiled by Mission and Government officials, my histories could be accessed visually, which the Aborigines appreciated. Each People/Land was depicted on a scroll which could be unwound to locate a particular person and his or her forbears as well as the person(s) they married. Only the offspring of male members of the People/Land were, of course, recorded on that "Land's" scroll. For the children of women of the Land one had to turn to her husband's scroll.

The results of the 1986 survey of terminological relationships as predicted from my model were as follows: The total number of predictions made was 4,265. Of these, 1,544 were correct, or 36% of the total. The number of those predicted correctly on the basis of a one-to-one correspondence between E/ego's Land affiliation and those of his or her relative's cognates was 1,119 (72%). Those predicted correctly on the basis of a direct Songstream linkage was 412 (27%) and on the basis of an indirect link it was 13 (1%). The number of additional predictions, discounting generation, was 1,270 or 30% of the total. The overall success rate, apart from the question of generation, then, was 66%. With or without generation included the result was statistically significant.

In the 1969 period the number of predictions made was 5,649. Of these

2,035 or 36% were correct, as in 1986. The number predicted correctly on the basis of a one-to-one correspondence was 1,442 or 62%, on the basis of a direct Songstream linkage 553 or 26%, and on the basis of an indirect linkage 40 or 2%. The number of additional correct predictions, discounting generation, was 1,683 or 30% or the total as in 1986, giving an overall success rate, as before, of 66%.

In the 1941/53 period the number of predictions made was 2,127. The number correct was 802 or 38%. The number predicted correctly on the basis of a one-to-one correspondence was 674 or 84%. On the basis of a direct Songstream linkage the number was 126 (16%) and on the basis of an indirect linkage 2. The number of additional correct predictions, discounting generation, was 640 or 30% of the total, yielding an overall success rate, apart from the question of generation, of 68%.

In conclusion, not only had some things not changed significantly between 1941/53 and 1969, as my earlier testing had anticipated, but they had not changed by 1986 either! What this meant, given the criteria on which relationships were predicted, was that the Promised Land–Songstream arrangement was basically unchanged from pre-contact times.

While this news may not startle many readers at this point, it might once they learn that the, so-called, economic "base" of this society has changed fundamentally since 1941. Theory, whether on the Left or the Right, holds that "culture" and "social relations" are predicated on an economic base. When that base, which includes the technological means of production as well as the social relations of production, distribution and consumption, changes, "culture" and "social organization" change in response. Or so the theory goes. In this case, they hadn't. In fact, in some ways there had been a strengthening of tradition.

Ron Hughes had rewritten the programme so that results could be broken down on a term-by-term basis. As expected, predictions were highest where a term spanned more than one generation, namely NA:BA/dernda and NA:NIGANGGWA/dadiyanggwa. Predictions for other terms were more or less uniform. The interesting difference was in the comparison of the 1941/53, the 1969 and the 1986, situation with regard to the two terms most closely related to marriage, that is NADIDJA/dadidja, the "mother-in-law" term, and NA:NINGYA/dadingya, the term for "wife". The Land intersection appropriate to this term, whether one-to-one direct or indirect Songstream linkage, predicted the correct term 61% of the time using the 1941/53 data and discounting the "generation" issue. Predictions on the same basis were, then, incorrect 39% of the time. By 1969 the percentage of incorrect predictions had risen to 41%, the percentage of correct to 59%. In 1986, however, the number of incorrect predictions actually lowered to 29%, the percentage of correct predictions rising to 73%.

In the case of NA:NJNGYA/dadingya, the appropriate Land intersection predicted the term correctly in 71% of cases in 1941/53, while in 29% of cases the requisite intersection was there and failed to predict. In 1969 the percentage of correct predictions had fallen to 53%, the number of incorrect rising to 47%. In 1986 the percentage of correct predictions had stabilized at 52%, the number of incorrect at 48%.

Here was a statistical basis for what my Aboriginal informants had told me in 1969, namely that the marriage system was in the process of breaking down but that they were now taking steps to prevent it. We had been in the midst of a revitalization movement in 1969 which, however, did not bear fruit until much later. The pessimism I felt in 1974 about their culture was not justified. At the same time as things were "coming apart" steps were being taken to put them back together again. Conditions had now stabilized. Commenting on change in my book *Tradition and Transformation* in 1969 I noted that

> Even though transformation has occurred in some aspects of the social life of the Groote Eylandt area Aborigines because of Western contact – particularly in the economic and religious spheres – much has persisted from the past, or has changed within the bounds of tradition, primarily because the alien elements did not 'oppose' indigenous ones in the areas in question.
>
> Thus, traditional assumptions underlying patterns of kinship, totemism and marriage (although questioned for a brief period by the Warnungamagalyuagba) have remained intact. Although kinship in its contemporary context was shown to involve a constant examination and re-examination of how different people and groups should and do relate to one another – particularly as concerns those alliances which produce new members of the community – and alterations were made and realignments effected in the course of day-to-day existence, this was evidently also a feature of traditional life. Still underlying this

process today are the same principles of classification and definitions of kin with their sociological, as well as genealogical [and cosmological] dimensions... (p. 194)

In the Groote Eylandt area the impact (of European contact) has not been so fatal. but still these Aborigines have come under the influence of Whites who are, with varying degrees of commitment. bent on remaining in prolonged contact with them and changing them into a stereotyped image of 'western' man. *If the power and ideology of these Whites remain intact,* they may more or less determine the future direction of change in Groote Eylandt area society. (p. 197)

I have added the italics to emphasize the qualification. Something critical did occur between 1969–74 and 1986 which to a degree altered the power and ideology of "these Whites" by which I meant Government and Mission officials as well as those connected with the Mining Company. Aboriginal land rights were granted in 1976. People on Reserve Land were granted them automatically without application. Groote Eylandt and Bickerton Island was Reserve Land. Not that this eliminated assimilationist forces and reversed recent historical trends; but it seems to have helped stabilize the situation I encountered in 1969. My 1986 data on relationship formation, in comparison with the 1941/53 period, indicate general overall stability in the basic foundations – the significance of Land – of society over the period. My analysis of marriages as such later confirmed this impression.

By the end of my follow-up re-visit in 1987 I had recorded some 195 marriages contracted since 1 969. Of these 22, or 12%, were of the *warnigarangbidja* variety, that is, the wife's mother was from the same Promised Land as the husband's father. Between about 1945 and 1967 six marriages of this type had been allowed to occur, partly because Aborigines were questioning their concept of closeness in marriage and partly because of pressure to find single women for single men. As I said earlier, Europeans were insisting that any two persons could marry so long as their parents were not actual brother and sister and Aborigines could see that European children were (physically at least) normal. Their own ideology had told them that close marriages produced deformed offspring (though they conceived closeness in Spiritual rather than genetic terms). However, one of the six marriages they allowed did, in fact, produce a number of stillbirths and deformities and this was sufficient to persuade them to reconfirm their rules. None of the 10 marriages contracted between 1967 and 1969 fell into the prohibited category.

Now, in 1987, I found out that more marriages of a *warnigarangbidja* type had been permitted but none of them were so close that the mother of the wife and the father of the husband were actual brother and sister. (I should mention that the "mother" and "father" at issue here are considered close because they share the same marriage histories – have cognates with exactly the same Promised Land affiliations – not because they are close in kinship or genealogical terms. That is also why an actual brother and sister are the preferred unit on both sides of a marriage exchange between Promised Lands.)

Polygamy – the practice of a man having more than one wife – was in decline at Angurugu in 1969, more so at Angurugu than at Umbakumba. In 1969 at Angurugu, of 55 married Bickerton men there 5 were openly polygamous, four with two wives and one with three. We have already encountered the role of European law in enforcing this, including the partly indigenous, partly Mission-inspired move to provide single men with wives and so alleviate the tension present at Angurugu. Today the 90% 1969 figure for married Bickerton men living monogamously instead of polygamously now applies to the island population as a whole. The promise system – the practice of arranged marriages from a very early age if not before birth itself – however, was and is still in force.

In 1969 promises were being made but the man given the choice of opting out of the arrangement if he so wished (as it was his choice to opt in or out of polygamy). This itself was a significant concession to tradition which relied on promises to maintain the proper relationship between Promised Lands such that one would marry another in alternate generations. By 1987 it was the woman who had been given the choice of opting out of a promise (as well as of opting in to a polygamous relationship). She should love her promise, it was said. The reality was that the promised woman, if she did not "love" the man she was promised to, could simply pack up and leave the island if she so wished and would be protected in doing so by European law. Some had. By the same token, some Aboriginal women who could not be found a "straight line" husband or even one not so "straight" were being encouraged to leave the island by the Aboriginal elders in charge – or at least encouraged to find a husband from elsewhere.

Of the 185 marriages contracted between 1969 and 1987, 53 or 29% were promises. Only 5 of the 53 were not "straight", that is, were not of a kind where the partners called each other NA:NINGYA/dadingya before marriage.

Of the total of 185 marriages, 92, or half, were "straight". This is up from 1969 when only 38% were straight (though I based my analysis only on Bickerton Island people then). In 1969 about 66% of marriages involved an exchange between Promised Lands; in 1987 the figure was down to about 50%.

In general, these data confirm the computer analysis conclusion that there has been a stabilizing of tradition following a period of potential disruption in the basic ordering principles of the society. This said, a number of factors should be pointed out regarding future directions of change. In the first place, I came across 17 cases of people who had a relative in their father's mother's Land, with no closer correspondence to eliminate this criterion, who did not call that person NA:NINGYA/dadingya. Interviews indicated that there was some change going on in the definition of "ideal spouse" despite the strengthening of the traditional concept of "husband/wife" from 1969 as "a person in one's father's mother's Land etc". And in only 17 of 92 NA:NINGYA/dadingya marriages did a one-to-one correspondence in Land affiliation at the father's mother's level predict the relationship. But in 61 of 92 cases a direct Songstream linkage between Lands predicted the NA:NINGYA/dadingya relationship. Although 85% were defined according to the criteria set down in my definition, there seemed to have been a broadening out of the category "straight" or "close" NA:NINGYA/dadingya to include people linked in other than one-to-one correspondence terms.

In my 1974 book I speculated that the Aborigines of the Groote Eylandt area might be tempted to simplify theis situation by considering all people linked on the same Songstream as a single category for purposes of classification and marriage. Indeed, before I left in 1969 I had suggested this to some of the elders myself as a way out of the problem of adjusting the complexities of the present to the ideal model of the past. The men present nodded absentmindedly and then went about their business as usual. I had hypothesized that this was the way the Mara people on the mainland to the south organized themselves (1974: 100) and then discovered when I went to Roper River to investigate this that I had been incorrect, as we saw in Chapter II. Their "semi-moieties" were not crucial in this regard – the "clan" remained critical.

But given the above statistical findings on merging in the meaning of some terms, I am now faced with the ironic possibility that the Groote Eylandters are in the process of following my former advice and inventing the very system I was wrong about and which didn't exist to the south...

In 1986 I also came across a new category I had not encountered before that I thought might be related to changes in the concept of "spouse" – that of the "straight *dungwiyarrga langwa*" marriage. In a straight *dungwiyarrga langwa* marriage the husband calls the mother of his wife *dungwiyarrga* before marriage. This is also the case in a *warnigarangbidja* or prohibited marriage relationship. It is, potentially, marriage with someone whose mother is in the same Land as your father. My marriage survey revealed four "*dungwiyarrga langwa*" marriages (wife born from a woman that the husband called *dungwiyarrga*) which the Aborigines nevertheless regarded as equivalent to NA:NINGYA/dadingya marriages. But closer inspection revealed that in each instance the wife was a person in the husband's father's mother's Land. In other words, Land intersection, implying "marriageability" took precedence over the terminological relationship, implying unmarriageability. As I had pointed out in my 1974 book, by 1969 the logic of terminological assignment on terminological grounds (e.g., the son and daughter of a Namggiya and a *dadidja* should always be NA:NINGYA/dadingya or "husband/wife") was out of kilter with people's cognates' respective Land intersections. Aborigines were having a great deal of difficulty adjusting one logic to the other due to the frequency of non-ideal marriages, fewer promises and a growing pragmatism in marriage negotiations and promise-keeping. "Straight *dungwiyarrga langwa*" marriage was one outcome.

One alternate marriage that was still allowed in 1987 from 1969 was marriage with the mother's Land so long as your own Land had not given a woman to that Land the previous generation. If your Land had, of course, you would be marrying a woman whose mother was in your own Land, i.e., *warnigarangbidja*. The permitted form was "*awilyaga:rra dernderrga langwa*", or "from far away dernderrga". Thirty-five of 185 marriages were of this form and 15 of these involved marriage into mother's Land as such. The rest were even "further away" *dernderrga*, that is, in Lands on the same Songstream as mother's or were simply from terminological *dernderrga*.

[I might interject at this point to say that you may be completely lost if you have been thinking that marriage is prohibited with the mother's Land. This would seem to be the negative implication of the positive preference for mariage with the same Land i.n alternate generations. But this is to think one-dimensionally in terms of "group", a complement to thinking one dimensionally in terms of "genealogy". What is (was), in fact, prohibited is marriage with someone whose *mother* is in your Land. What is preferred is someone whose father's mother is in your Land. This is a different thing entirely. In my view most of the problems in Australian Aboriginal Anthropology are related to thinking one dimensionally about Aboriginal societies in individual or group terms in an attempt to force them into a "descent" or an "alliance" mould. It is more that group*ness* is passed down individual descent lines to define relations such that you have different levels of relationship.]

John Harris was right to leave "generation" out of his calculations of relationships and base them, first and foremost, on how his cognates' Promised Lands intersected with those of his relative's cognates. A person's "generation" can be adjusted upward or downward to fit the requirements of a term that defines his or her relation to another in the way their respective cognates' Promised Lands intersect. "Generation" here is not institutionally enclosed. There are no generation categories to relate people systematically to one another within their own or across Promised Lands as there are in other parts of Australia.

In other parts of Australia, as we saw in Chapter II, named generation divisions cross-cut Promised Lands and combine those in alternate generations in the same Promised Land into the same category (e.g., grandfather, E/ ego and grandson into one "section"; father and EGO's/sister's son into another). Another way of putting it, more in line with Aboriginal logic, would be to say that a part of one is separated out from another in the same People/ Land and then recombined into a new category. In the absence of such institutions there is no institutional means of linking older people to younger within the Promised Land apart from common Promised Land membership itself (which, as we have seen, does not imply unity amongst its members). No institutional context is present which would imply an obligation on the part of the old to the young (and vice versa). In consequence, Aboriginal society in the Groote Eylandt area suffered from what can only be termed a "class" tendency – a gerontocratic tendency – a tendency for older men to act autonomously with respect to those beneath them and use their knowledge and power to monopolize the young women as wives. This aspect of Groote Eylandt culture was first noted and explored by Fred Rose in 1941.

Fred Rose was first on Groote Eylandt in 1938 as a meteorologist at a Flying Boat Base near Umbakumba on the north-east part of the island, established that year as a refueling depot on the north-west/south-east route to Darwin. Umbakumba settlement was developing about Fred Gray, a pearler who had decided to settle down in the area. He was well known to the local

Aborigines and they allowed him to do so. Rose reports that in 1941 there were but a dozen European personnel at the Base, to which they remained confined. Other Europeans on the island at that time were Fred Gray and two "half-castes" at Umbakumba and three European staff and two "half-castes" at the Old Mission on the other side of the island. Intrigued by the Aborigines he encountered in the vicinity of the Base (he was, he says, the only staff member given permission to visit what was then an Aboriginal Reserve), Fred Rose returned in 1941 to undertake anthropological investigations.

In his 1960 book based on these studies he tells us that "Girls are normally promised as wife to men 20 or 30 years their senior before birth" (p. 17). Once married an older man normally accumulated women thereafter, beginning with the younger full sisters of his first wife. At contact some men had as many as eight wives and many four or five. As I was to discover in 1969, however, this was not entirely due to the exercise of power on a man's part. Marriage was rule-governed; an exchange between Promised Lands was sought, the preferred partners being a man from one Land and women from another with the same Promised Land marriage histories, that is, cognates with the same Promised Land affiliations. Full sisters always met this requirement hence were the preferred partners in an exchange. When the husband died, the wives would go to a younger full brother, that is, someone who shared the same marriage history as himself and who could maintain the original exchange relation intact. If the women went to another man in another Promised Land, it should be someone sharing the same marriage history as the first husband. These are the rules and the men are as bound by them as the women.

This said, Rose's 1941 data show 45 cases of a woman changing husbands inside the Land, 36 outside. "When a death occurs," he reports, "there is a marked tendency for the wife to be inherited within the clan, which occurred in 22 cases compared with 5 cases outside the clan" (p. 77). But, as Rose points out, there are reasons other than the death of their husbands as to why women change men. They are also stolen and elope. Rose's data show 27 cases of women changing hands peacefully on the death of their husbands, but 36 changed hands by stealing or elopement. Another four he lists as "gifts" from one man to another, which I take to be in the rule-governed category.

The question, though, is not just obedience to a set of rules applicable to all, but who originated the rules and why – that is, are the rules just? If it were strictly a case of exchange-relations between Promised Lands and the obligation to see them properly maintained, then an old woman would count for just as much as a young one. She might start off as a young woman with an older man but end up as an old woman with a young man. Be that as it may, "The writer's observation", Rose says, "was that it was not so much the old men as the old women who did not have spouses" (p. 79). Even though men stood in the correct marriage relationship to them, when they became available for re-marriage they were not prepared to take them on. The men already had multiple younger wives. In consequence, the older women moved in with a son and his wife or lodged on their own.

Aboriginal men with no wives noted such inconsistencies in my time and I'm sure they did in Rose's. And older man enjoyed the benefits of young women as sexual partners and economic producers and it was little consolation to young men to be told that someday they too would enjoy such a monopoly because of the way the system worked when they could see it did not always work the way the older men said it should work. There was conformity – in a sense the rules were universal and just when judged in the context of a lifetime – but there was also tension and when the tension built up to frustration level there was trouble. Hence the conspiracy amongst the older men to control and indoctrinate the younger to "the rules", that is, to their own immediate interests. Norman Tindale, one of the first Europeans to set foot on Groote describes the situation (1925/26: 70–71 and quoted in Rose 1960: 19–20):

> One of the outstanding differences in social customs in comparison with the adjacent mainland natives is the general and strict enforcement of seclusion of the women of the tribe. No native from the time of his initiation until he is of the age to marry, and no strangers, are allowed to approach the women, who are compelled to live apart in camps guarded by old men, but they are visited secretly by those entitled to the privilege. The women are in the minority, and are monopolized by the older men, who each have two or more if possible. The rest of ihe men iherefore live together in open camps with some of the old men, collecting the greater part of their own food themselves, but the older ones frequently receive parcels of yams and burrawang cakes from the women-folk. The younger men are not allowed near places where the women are likely to be yam digging or burrawang-nut gathering, or to look at them under penalty of spearing. Should a young native accidentally come upon them he must turn away and give warning of his presence.

Groote Eylandt women wore hinged bark sheets when in the presence of men other than their husbands, a practice which seems to extend at least as far back as the Macassan era when visitors from Indonesia plied their shore on a seasonal basis. These Aborigines, then, had "dormitories" of their own even before the Mission arrived, though their purpose was to group the young men away from young women to the benefit of the older men, the reverse of the Mission purpose.

Control by the older over the younger men was also exercised through the guardianship relation by which a young boy went to live with an older man, likely someone from his prospective wife's or his mother's Promised Land. The relationship was instituted from the age of circumcision (7 years or so) until his late teens when a cicatrice was cut across his chest by his guardian, the first official recognition of approaching manhood. In most Australian societies the young men are strictly controlled in secret ceremonies where the "law" in question is imparted. But until they were introduced from the mainland in historic times, the Groote Eylandt and Bickerton Islanders appear to have had no major ceremonies, or at least no secret-sacred ceremonies. The older men sang the Spirit of a dead person through to the fifth dimension, as I have noted, and in the process taught the younger men their Songs, and through the Songs, the law. But this was done in public in full view of the women and with a very solicitous attitude to the young men under instruction. As we'll see later, there are situations that transcend class and the battles of the sexes and this is one of them. In the context of singing the Spirit, such differences are reconciled rather than exacerbated.

Though polygamy was on the decline at Angurugu in 1969, many men were trying to be polygamous but for a variety of reasons were having a great deal of difficulty doing so. The first wife might strongly object – or the prospective second; another man may be laying claim to the woman in question; or a single woman might simply be playing havoc with a married man, leading him on until all hell broke loose and then rejecting him herself. In response, the men in question simply refused to relinquish the women to other men, as was their right if they had already been promised to them. Some 55 men at Angurugu, in fact, refused to release some 19 of 28 "single" women to marry other men. And all hell did break loose.

* * * *

Ruth says I should never underestimate the role of women in fomenting trouble between the sexes in this Aboriginal society. Though she was not formally studying the culture in 1969 she learned much, mainly because she was with the women on a day-to-day basis and they would not speak to her until she learned to communicate in the language. Though she didn't make many notes, those she did were revealing of women's place in society, albeit in a society in which their role as food procurers was by now much diminished. On weekends, though, many if not most "went bush" in the vicinity of Angurugu or down on the beach at the mouth of the Angurugu River. This was in the days before the Toyota explosion when truckloads of people would be able to reach virtually any part of the island within the space of a day. On weekdays, on the other hand, as today, the women just sat, though more likely than not with babes at their breasts and often not their own babes, if that concept has any meaning at all in Aboriginal society. Ruth sets the scene in the June 1st entry of her notebook:

> The women seem to sit and not do much. In Djambidjira's camp. Dangwunda will do washing or cook food. Mary will just sit, fuss over Roseanne. Single girls come and go. People sleep. When Gaiyangwa's there, they may mention a bit of the latest gossip.
>
> Considering they live so close together [it is strange that they should] sit together almost every day. What is there to talk about? When stories are recounted they are told with all the "whoops" and "chug chugs" and calls and noises to illustrate a point. Storytelling is a real show – especially by some. In normal speech there is no noticeable use of hands except a few gestures.

Later, by June 12th, she had found out what they talked about most:

> Seems like the only thing that concerns women is *amongmonga* [sex]. At least single girls. It's the only activity and interest . . . [what follows are the names of those most active and interested]... What else the women do or talk about I don't know.

Of course she did. They talked about many other things. The point is that the women were well aware of the power of sex and talked about it openly in order to control its power. This comment follows the above June 1st entry:

When the women have asked where David is [which they do constantly] and when I have answered *"ninga:ningbala"* [I don't know] – the muttering all around is *"na:niyarriya"* [I'm sorry for her].

It seems one should know every move of one's husband. If I don't know they'll ask around or send a child to look.

I was asked the same questions about Ruth's whereabouts from the men. When I said I didn't know where she was they would pucker up their lips and point them in a particular direction, and say *"Dangaba"* ("she's over there"). Only the women weren't so much worried about their husband's whereabouts as of the whereabouts of the women who were usually with them. More likely than not they would be the ones most eligible to their husbands, namely their own "sisters". If the husband was missing, which one of them was also missing? The same principle applied to a man in a group of men keeping track of the whereabouts of his wife. Letting everyone know everyone was watching kept people close to home and out of the way of potential trouble.

One of the few public occasions where men and women who are eligible to have sex and marry are permitted to be together is during card playing. Flirtations consists of women sitting directly across from the men they are interested in, legs crossed in front of them, dress pulled down between their thighs and under their buttocks and nothing on beneath. When a woman wanted to let a man know she was interested in sex she gave him a little peek during card playing. (Ruth [Sept. 2nd diary entry] knew that she was accepted by the woman when they would "sit with their legs apart, no horror at not wearing pants when I'm around".) The possibility of this experience is what Morris Lalara meant when he told me one day: I'm going to play cards to have fun with the girls – to make me feel good". Morris also told me: "If you're a married man you let the girl come to you. If single you go out and get her".

If the single girls come to you and you're white, however, you had better turn right around and march into the community and complain to the first elder you meet that they are trying to get you into trouble with the Aboriginal men. Because if you don't you soon will be!

It was the women who raised the young boys to about the age of seven when they were circumcised. They preferred to give birth to girls, however, not just because they preferred the company of their own kind, but by 1969 at least, because they got more money for them from social benefits. When the women sat together with their infants they spent considerable time playing with the little boys' genitals, or as Ruth put it, "by blowing on them and roughing them up with the mouth". You have to remember that these aren't "their" sons in our sense. They're the sons of their husband and his Promised Land. By associating women with pleasure at this stage, the "mothers" are simply setting them up to be eventual pawns at the hands of women in Promised Lands not their own...

In 1969, then, the women didn't just sit; they sat and plotted the fates of men.

In the course of our 1986 survey of relationships and their basis, I noticed the reluctance, indeed the unwillingness, of a woman to say the term Na:ningya to someone on my list of the opposite sex whom she actually referred to by that term in the presence of her husband. This is, of course, the term for "husband"/"wife". A few knowing glances would pass between the couple, then some snickering, a signal to me that I could write down the appropriate term without it being said. I had not realized the sexual significance of the term before, but had seen it mainly in formal, alliance terms.

At Umbakurnba I saw something of the deeper significance of this term when 1 came to one of Nyabana Mamariga's wives on my list and asked him by what term he referred to her. The look of love in his eyes told me what words did not need to speak.

During the course of the survey I also noted something closely related to the husband and wife relationship: at Angurugu, at least, sister and mother in-law avoidance relationships were continuing. In other contexts your behaviour towards your sister is "normal". But when she brings you food or drink or whatever she must turn away and put it down beside you. You may not even come near your mother-in-law, let alone talk to her. I know these customs are still in place at Angurngu because I have learned to follow them myself. But at Umbakumba the sister-avoidance rule at least was not followed. Brothers and sisters (those from the same Promised Land with the same marriage histories) sat together and handed each other things. People at Angurugu remarked on this disapprovingly. Why the custom is being breached I don't know. Why customs such as these were observed traditionally I suspect has something to do with women in these relationships being the-most-by-proximity/least-by-law, accessible as potential sexual partners. In traditional times on Groote, men were normally about the same ages as their mother's-in-law whose daughters they knew they would be marrying even before they were born.

The survey, however, revealed something I was far more unprepared for than this. Single women with children listed the children as members of their own Promised Land. This seemed completely outside the bounds of tradition. Children were always in the same Land as their father. Only in this instance the fathers weren't Aboriginal; they were white. As I have noted, in 1969 through to 1974 the first part-Aboriginal children had been assigned the Land of the man that the woman should have married. This, apparently, had proven unacceptable to people in the Lands concerned, some of whom never did receive the woman in question or who were rejected by the woman in turn. So the women had begun this practice on their own. It had the desired effect. The fact that, as Murabuda of the Wurramarrba put it, "it just couldn't be this way", didn't prevent them from meeting to sort it out anyway.

V

The Promised Lands

Pilgrimage to Arumandja

It was the beginning of July and we were finally off to Amagalyuagba, Bickerton Island. I must admit I had been getting a bit tired of life in my "office" at Angurugu and so, I sensed, was Murabuda who as Council President passed by me on the way to his own office each morning and thus was the first to fall victim to my never-ending stream of questions. But I had learned much from these daily encounters, particularly of his country on Bickerton, and I was eager to see it for myself. I had, as I said, circumnavigated the island in 1969, mapping coastal place names and noting the boundaries which separated the various Promised Lands. But I had not gone far inland and the sites there needed mapping too. In particular I had not been able to visit the place where Nambirrirrma had sat down. Now I would be able to do so. In fact, the Wurramara, in whose country the place was situated, seemed quite keen that I should do so. It surprised me that they seemed quite surprised that I was still interested.

Nambirrirrma was the man who had come down from a cloud on the rain at Arumandja and, by reaffirming, established the law to the Aboriginal Peoples of the island. I had based my analysis of their culture as well as organized my book *Tradition and Transformation* around this tale. The book opened by recounting the story itself, then derived a model (Figure 1) of Aboriginal society from the substance of the story, traced the connections inherent in the model eastward from Bickerton to Groote Eylandt and westward to the adjacent mainland, afterwards showing something of the philosophic-religious underpinnings of the model in the Songs performed by the local Aborigines in mortuary rites. From here I went on to show how the model and its practice had been modified by Mission contact, examining in particular the role of the missionaries in persuading some Aborigines to question traditional notions of life, death, social organization and so on. I am essentially following the same plan here in this part of the book, though with a deeper understanding of the way of life in mind.

We pitched our tent at Milya:gburra, the outstation founded by Joe of the Wurramara to fulfill the promise he had made to his father. Joe's real name was Milumdum, a name on Duwa:dirra or White Cockatoo and on Widjmarlamarl, a place on the mainland in the vicinity of Harris Creek. I should rather have said "names": he was also called Marlambardi on Munenga, Burrawang, associated with a place called Waldar on the mainland. His third name was Nenuwabilya, associated with Malurba or the crown of Rrugbulya outcropping between Mungwurridjirra and Arumandja, the place where Nambinirrma had landed on Bickerton. This name bad been given him by Gandiya Wurramara, older brother of Ba:da, in a different line from his own father, Nyangwudura, or Old Bill. I give the details because it is important to him. I was corrected as soon as I reached the outstation and called him "Joe". Here he was "Milurndum".

At the outstation be also revealed to me that he was really of the Mimiyawan People/Land, that is, really a mainland Nunggubuyu man and not Wurramara, or a Bickerton Islander, as I had always thought. Hence the two out of three names of mainland origin. Nyangwudura had taken his mother from his father in a fight just before he was born. Later his mainland father had given Nyangwudura permission to bring him up. Hence his Wurramara name had come from outside Nyangwudura's line. He had been affiliated, not incorporated. It was in an affiliated capacity, then, not as an "owner" of the site, that Milurndum took me to Arumandja. But then "owners didn't "own", not in our sense at least

Milurndurn said that he couldn't go to the site without a *djunggwaiya:* or "boss" of his Land, but since I was counted Lalara and "married" to a Wurramara, it would be all right. I called Milumdum Na:ningyarrga. A "boss" is someone closely related to your Land by marriage such as a person in your mother's or father's mother's Land. One of his jobs is to prepare the way for you as you approach a particularly important place in your own country. He does this by lighting fire to the grass before you. This is to create smoke so as temporarily to remove the Spirits of the place from the place and thus decrease the chances that your own Spirit (one or the other or both) will be drawn into the site. Milumdurn could have visited the site without burning the smoke, but he would have been *angwabugwaba*, or taboo, and unable to feed himself but would have to be fed by others until such time as he was himself "smoked" in order that the Spirit-matter with which he had been "contaminated" had been carried off.

We can discuss the consequences of burning off the land in this manner for land management and conclude that it has a regenerative effect on the environment. But that is not why I burned the grass on this trip. It was to save Milumdurn's soul (though he did mention that the fire would drive away any snakes in our path).

We set out from Milya:gburra and headed south-west for a kilometer or so until we crossed the log pole bridge at Amagadabuda. This place is the tidal mangrove swamp where Yabongwa, the Rainbow Serpent(s), left South Bay and entered Bickerton proper. Or perhaps it would be more accurate to say this is where a second Yabongwa, Rainbow Serpent, began its journey to Bickerton after the first one reached this place from the bay. This much I had learned from Gudigba on my previous visit. But now, talking with Milurndurn, I learned that there was yet another place on the other side of the bay, a creek where a third Yabongwa made its way on to Bickerton. Or was it a fourth? There seemed to be still another Yabongwa in a sector behind the "third" in the bay. Not only that, some manifestations appeared to be male and others female. Yabongwa at Amagadabuda was also called Duwurrawilya, the Snake in female form (technically the Rainbow reflected by Snake). And this was just "one" Creative Being in "one" Promised Land!

Crossing the bridge and moving up the sandy hill beyond, we looked out onto the south bay of Bickerton which the Aborigines refer to by the general term *mulgwa* or womb, in common with many other bays in the area. As far as I could ascertain there is no name for this bay in particular. The foot of the bay, however, can also be referred to as "Arumandja", also the name of the place on the shore where Nambirrirrma landed. We were now in Amamagulyara, a name on Nambirrirrma whose country lay just before us. It was at Amamagulyara that I started to burn the grass. The whole landscape suddenly seemed to come alive.

On Milurndurn's instructions I burned again at the point where we crossed over into Arumandja. Then again down by the beach and again up on the dunes. We were surrounding the site with smoke. On the beach Milumdum pointed to the rocky shoal reaching out into the shallow water: "If you smash the rocks here in Arumandja, you will have a baby…" he said. Anticipating the clarification I would require he quickly added: "man or woman", referring to the "you" in his comment.

"We call this *waridjirra wurralawudawara* (Baby Dreaming)", he went on. "You can also break off a twig from *mabalba*" (peanut tree: *Sterculia quadrifida*), he said, pointing to a bush just back of the beach, "and send it to the woman and she will have a baby. This country is Good Baby Dreaming", he went on. "On the other side is Bad Baby Dreaming", he said, pointing down to the end of the beach where the bay turns south and begins its journey to the mouth. The place he was pointing to was Amalyuwa which began at the creek where Yabongwa also made its way on(to) Bickerton.

We moved directly back from the beach, just ahead of where I had last burned the grass. At first I didn't see it. But there was a depression in the sand, almost imperceptible among the dunes, but a defined space nonetheless once you examined it closely. In it were hundreds of small shells and a few "baler shells" (*mungarnunggwerna*, spider shell: *Lambis truncata*). The smaller shells, said Milurndurn, were remnants of food collected for Nambirrirrma. The "baler shells" were his drinking vessels. This was where Nambirrirrma sat down (another name for him is Nanarrbarrenga or "he who sat down") and was later buried. And, he added, telling me something I had not known before, this was where his son, Badjuini, was also buried. The burial platform wouJd have stood just back of the depression, he said. Their bones were buried in bark containers beneath the ground here. This site was their "country", then, and the Aborigines were following the traditional practice of returning bones and presumably a lock of hair there when they died.

Milurndurn could not enter the depression, but I as *djunggwaiya:* could, though he cautioned me not to disturb anything. Women could look at the site but were also not allowed to enter the depression no matter what Land they belonged to. However, to be on the safe side – to ensure there was no transgression – women usually kept to the beach or to the bush running along the base of the ridge on the island side.

We returned, but not to Milya:gburra outstation. Instead we beaded north to the big bay on the north side of the island. I lit fires as we moved away from Arumandja and assumed that was the end of it. But no. Milurndurn instructed me to keep on burning as we turned north into the bush. This time he joined me. It wasn't to keep the Spirits away. He said explicitly that it was to rid the land of its dead matter so that it could better rejuvenate itself.

It was also on this trip that I straightened out the location of the places in the bay. My previous attempt in 1969 had been from its mouth and I had made some mistakes. Either that or old Galiyawa had deliberately misled me as to the location of Arumandja. But I had never known Galiyawa to lie and I had skewed all of the places in the bay over to the west as well as missed some in between, including Milya:gburra. Since Arumandja was a name that could refer to the whole bay, including all the land behind it right back to the ridge, it is easy to see how I could have misled my informants when asking them for the location of the place in particular. In any event, this was the first of a number of trips along the beach and inland both to check my original mapping and to add in the inland areas. Each trip added a new dimension to my original understanding.

As I said, my original understanding of the culture rested primarily on the Nambirrirrma tale. I will recount it again, adding in what I have since learned about the ending:

Nambirrirrma Nana:gbarrenga

| Wurramarrba nalegarn | augwalyuwa angaluba | hunting augwalya |
| he was going | fishing | from this way |

| Wurramarrba | nawalegarna | Yingelanggwaberangamandja. | Nelari |
| | he kept on going (to) | (Map 3, no. 92) | rain |

| ya:lyugwa. | Nelari ya:lyugwa. | Nawalegarna | wurragina wi: |
| was falling | rain was falling | he kept on going | that man |

| Nalegarnagarna | Wurramarrba bi: Arrilya. | Aiyugudjiya | ngalaidja |
| he went on and on | (Map 3, no. 91) | small | it |

| angubina | nelarrina | ya:lyugwa. | Nawalegarnuwawurragina bi: |
| clouds | it was falling | rain | He kept on going that man |

| Anadja | aragba | Nanarrbarrenga | nambarrenga | aragba, | nardjiyinga. |
| the man | then | (Nambirrirrma) | he landed | then | he stood. |

| Nambarrenga | aragba | Nanarrbarrenga | Nambarrenga aragba. |
| he sat down | then | (Nambirrirrma) | he sat down then |

| Nawalegarna | biya | amagadabuda | nadjardanga, |
| he (Wurramarrba man) | then (at) | the point | he came |

nadjardang 'agina augwalyamandja.   Nandaiya hunting augwalya,
                to fish.   he looked for   fish

nandaiya.   Nemarrengga.   nara genandaiya a: rribarribawa.
he looked   he looked at it (the ocean)   he didn't look   into the bush

Nalelegarnuwa ngawa   nalelgarna ngawa bi: hunting a:rribarribawa
he went on   still   went on   still and on   to the bush

negugwardja:ya.   "Ngambulangwa   warnamamalya   warna?"
he stood   where is he from? the Aboriginal man that one

Ambaga nardjinga   ngawa. Anadja? "Warnungwadarrbalangwa?"
wait   he is standing still him   (is he from this this People/Land)

Aba nelegarna Amalyuwa   angalyuwa   Amalyuwa nelegarna anadja
Now he went   (Map 3, no. 83) to the place   he went him

Warnungwadarrbalangwa   anadja hunting augwalya yandjarragina.
from the country of People/Land) him   fish   that way

Nelegarnaangaluba Adiminimburra   langwa.
he came from this way (Map 3, no. 111) from

The Wurramarrba man: "Anggaberra warnamamalya warna?
                      who   the man   this one

Ridjirebe langwa? dangaba langwa? enda mainland-langwa? Nara," niyama.
from Rose River from over there or from the mainland no   he said

"Enda angaluba   Barlamuma?"
or   from this way   Aboriginal people of north-east Arnhem Land

Nanirrabarrengga   enda   different warnamamalya warna da!
he stared at him   but the man   this one

"Wurrengga warnamamalya waga da warnamamalya warna da!"
look at   the man   different   kind of man   this one

Nalelegarna mangaba   mangwa   ya:laugwa nardjina.
they went   over there to the mangrove*   there   they stood

Wurramarrba man: "Anggaberra garnemamalya geragina nungurruwa?"
                    who are   you person   you   you

Stranger: "Naiyuwa na? A:na:n' angalya nganyangwa a:na:na da.
              who, me   this   country mine   this one

Wurramara ningarna da!" niya:ma.
          me   he said

Wurramarrba man: "Anggabera   a:girra?"
                    what is (your) name

Stranger: "Nanarrbarrenga Nambirrirrma."
              (personal names)

Wurramarrba man: "Yau. Wurrangaba warnamamalya nawalegadjamerra
                    yes   over there that man   he is gong along

na:ningyarrga.   Warnungwadarrbalangwa," niya:ma. Nalegarna,
my (NA:NINGYA)   (People/Land)   he said he came

naugudangwuda. "Wai! Wai! Naningyau!   warnamamalya
he came closer heh heh (vocative form of NA:NINGYA)   the man

warna dagwa! Yaungurrangwa wurrarenggina warna warnamamalya!
this one   come this way look at   this man

Nengganingma warnamamalya warna   nugguwa?"
do you know the man   this one you

Warnungwadarrbalangwa man: "Nara! Nara naiyuwa ninga:ningbala."
                              no   no   me   I don't know

niya:ma. Niya:mina Wurramarrba niya:ma. "Nara   naiyuwa ninganingbala
he said   he said   he said   not   mine   I don't know

ngaindjugwaba. Dugwa warna   warnamamalya angaluba   naya:mina
me either   perhaps this one   man   from this way   he moved

nalarra wurragina God dugwa   miya:mba:na nalarrimerra."
he fell that one   perhaps what   he fell

Warnungwadarrbalangwa man: "Emba a:na:n' ayaugwa?"
                                but   his   language

Wurramarrba man: "A:na:n' ayaugwa? Niya:ngbinama warna   nara
                     his   language he speaks   this one not

different   ayaugwa nara-a:na:n ayaugwa ngaugwurralangwa."
            language not this   language ours

Nambirrirrma: "Yau, mm. Wurrangamba   wurramina:na
                  yes   where are the people   people belonging to

analya   Wurramara?"
this place

Warnungwadarrbalangwa man: "Yau embalgaindja,"
                                yes and me

Warnungwadarrbalangwa niya:ma, 'Ngaindja angab'   angalya.
                      he said   me   over there   place

Nambirrirrma: "Emba a:nga:mba nganyangwa?" niya:ma Wurramara.
                  but   place   mine   he said

Wurramarrba man: "Angaba   angalya nunguwa. Naiyuwa. Angaba pointing
                     over there place   you   mine   over there

aragba ambilyuma agina   ingga   pointing 'nganyangwa angalya,"
then   two   those   different   my country

naya:ma Wurramarrba.
he said

Nambirrirrma: "Yau.   Gambira   nadidja
              yes   then   (you call then you him NADIDJA)

gamba nenggagina?" niya:ma.   Nanarrbarrenga.
then   you   he said   (personal name)

Wurramarrba man: "Yauwa! A:nan' angalya   yaugwulangwa, nayinamerra
              yes   these   countries ours   like

wurragina   gamba da nayinama angalya   aba   augwa   gamba I call him
that man   then   like   countries the   one   then

nadidja.   Emba nangaba   na:ningyarrga."
NADIDJA then him over there   my NA:NINGYA

Nambirrirrma "Na:ningya?"

Wurramarrba man: "Nangaba Warnungwadarrbalangwa na:ningyarrga,"
                 over there   my NA:NINGYA

niya: ma Wurramarrba niya: ma, "Na: ningyarrga   nagaba?"
he said   my NA:NINGYA   over there

Nambirrirrma: "Yau! nagina   gamban agina   naberrarrga da!" niya:ma.
                Yes that man   then   that man   my NABERRA he said

Nanarrbarrenga, niya: ma. "Gamba nganyangwa   naberrarrga da."
                he said   then   my   NABERRA

Wurramarrba man: "Ah, yau, um gamba   nunggelegadja
                     yes   then   are you going

Wurragwagwuwa   anga:riba?"
to the Wurragwagwa People/Land   over there

arra:gbamandja, "   niya:ma. "Gwa. Wurrarrenggena Wurramara country
in the open country   he said   come look at him

abin'aberralangwa." Nalelegarna nalelegarna (awilyaga:rra wiya mm)
this theirs   they went on and on   (a long way)

ya:laugwa   mangaba   manggwa   numulgaiyinga
there   over there   the mangroves   are standing

A Wurramara man: "Nungamiya:mba:na nunggagina, nungganina?"
                    who are you   you

Nambirrirrma: "Naiyuwa, na? Wurramara naiyuwa da!"

A Wurramara man: "Ah, ngaindjugwaba Wurramara da!" niya:ma Wurramara
                    me too   he said

Nambirrirrma: "Yau (yadiyarumandja).   Gamba nawa wanalerragagina da."
                 yes we call each other   then NAWA/ those two men
                 NAWA/NA:NINGUMA   NA:NIGUMA

A Wurramara man: "Ah, yauwa. mm." Angaba   midjiyalyamandja
                     yes   over there   on the beach

malgadabuda   Ngamandja ngaladja nuwambilyuma da, angab'
at the end of the beach where   he   he is staying   over there

aberradju anadja nabilya.   Nawalelambarrina Warnungwadarrbalangwa
there him   he is staying   they made camp

nawalelambarrina   agubina.
they were camping   close by

Namunggul. Namunggul. Namunggul. . .Wurramarrbalalyimbugwaiyina.
three nights they slept   they were talking about each other

    Bystander: "Agiyamarrgena?
                   what's happening

old man, warniyarrangga. "Gurruwa! warnamamalya wurrangaba
    old men   you   over there

nayardemerra."
he arrived

Wurramara and Wurragwagwa old men: "Ngamandja?"

Wurramarrba man: "Wurrangaba Arumandja."
                        over there (Map 3, no. 85)

Old men: "Warna   ngambulangwa?
            this man   where did he come from?

Wurramarrba man: "Naya:mamerra angaluba   abalgaiya agina
                        he said   from this way above   that

Wurramara wurragina Warnungaunggeragba wurragina, Nenarrbarenga,"
       that man (a sector of the Wurramara)   that one

na:yamina Nambirrirrma niya:mina.
he said

Old men: "Yau. Aduaba?"

Wurramarrba man: "Aduaba nalegadja. Aberradjugwaba Yau.
                  today   he came they too   yes

Warnungwadarrbalangwa aduabagina yaungurrangwa." Nawambilya
           today   going to there   they stayed

namerndagina. Mangaba   mamawura. Nadjardanga. Mangaba mamawura.
all of them   over there the sun   it's gone down over there the sun

Nadjardanga. "Wurrangaba   wurragina   wurrangaba
it's gone down   over there there they are   over there

arra:gbamandja, " niya:ma. "Gwa. Wurrarrenggena Wurramara country
in the open country he said come look at him

abin'aberralangwa." Nalelegarna nalelegarna (awilyaga:rra wiya mm)
this theirs they went on and on (a long way)

ya:laugwa mangaba manggwa numulgaiyinga
there over there the mangroves are standing

A Wurramara man: "Nungamiya:mba:na nunggagina, nungganina?"
who are you you

Nambirrirrma: "Naiyuwa, na? Wurramara naiyuwa da!"

A Wurramara man: "Ah, ngaindjugwaba Wurramara da!" niya:ma Wurramara
me too he said

Nambirrirrma: "Yau (yadiyarumandja). Gamba nawa wanalerragagina da."
yes we call each other then NAWA/ those two men
NAWA/NA:NINGUMA NA:NIGUMA

A Wurramara man: "Ah, yauwa. mm." Angaba midjiyalyamandja
yes over there on the beach

malgadabuda Ngamandja ngaladja nuwambilyuma da, angab'
at the end of the beach where he he is staying over there

aberradju anadja nabilya. Nawalelambarrina Warnungwadarrbalangwa
there him he is staying they made camp

nawalelambarrina agubina.
they were camping close by

Namunggul. Namunggul. Namunggul. . .Wurramarrbalalyimbugwaiyina.
three nights they slept they were talking about each other

Bystander: "Agiyamarrgena?
what's happening

Nambirrirrma: "Nganuguna wurradarrengga nagina nadidjarrga."
             he's giving me some women that man my NADIDJA

Bystander: "Ah. Nara wurradarrengga wurribina da. Naga da
             no women any that man

nganugunana?"
he giving you

Wurramarrba man: "Ah, ngaiyuwa nenungunamerra
             me I am giving him

nanagberangandjamerragiya wunalagina ngawa. Ngaiyuwa
I am making the two of them meet each other those two still I

nenugunamerra daberrarrga nganyangwa daberrarrga."
I am giving him my daberra my

Nambirrirrma to Bystander: "Ah. Nganuguna nagina nadidjarrga
             he's giving that man my NADIDJA

naberra:na."
your NABERRA

Bystander: "Duwilyaba"?
             one

Wurramarrba man: "Duwilyaba daruma augwa wurriyugudjiya waridjura.
             one grown woman with small child

Duwilyaba augwa wurriyugudjiya waridjura."

Nambirrirrma: "Nara angaiyinduma wurragina wurradarrengga wurragina.
             no I don't want that woman that

wurraruma."
grown one

Wurramarrba man: "Wurraruma wurradarrengga? Wurrambilyuma?
                 grown   woman   two

Wurrabiyagarbiya, na?"
three

Nambirrirrma: "Nara wurrawilyaba."
              no only one

Wurramarrba man: "Liligila?"
                  little girl

Nambirrirrma: "Yau, liligila!   Get um pickaninny   nara angaiyinduma."
               yes   little girl   I don't want

Nambambilyuma. Aragba nanilyunga   narrangilyunga dagina
                      then   they took him   they took her   that (girl)

nenugwa.   Nanilyunggwa nenugwa   narrangalyunggwaiyina
(they gave) him   they painted   him   they gave him they painted her up

aleda anadjugwaba   nalyunggwa:yina   aragba.   Aragbaniyardena
(with him too clay)   they painted each other up   then   they slept together

aragba nagina niyardena   aragba paint-a nilyunggwa:yina gaidjungwa
then   him   they slept together   then   they painted each other   so that

ga:niya:miyada   gambira wunelagina   ga:niya:miyada
they can live together   then   those two   they can live

ga:niya:miyada ga:niya:miyada. Awilya:garra awilya:garra nambaribaba.
they can live together   for a long time   they lived together

Niyamdjama   got um pickaninny   nagina
(time passed)   they had a baby   him

Nanarrbarrenga wurruwilyaba Nayangbarrenga nagina a:gira
    one (child)   (personal name) him   name

Nayangbarrenga pickaninny. Nidjungwa. Ngawa bina da. Naw' aragba da!
    child   he dies   finished   That's all now

It is a long and complicated tale, though not to an Aboriginal. Those listening to Galiyawa as he told it sat with rapt fascination, following every nuance of the story, laughing and the apparent confusion of the Islanders as to their proper interrelationships and sighing with relief when they worked them out. The tale is about the Law – how People from the various Lands on Bickerton should intermarry and by what terms they should refer to one another (which, in the Aboriginal mind, amounts to the same thing). Knowing the real situation in the present, there are all sorts of implications for inter-personal and inter-Land relationships. There is also information about old ways no longer in vogue, such as the description of the marriage ceremony (if you can call it that, considering the couple will usually have been married/promised before they were born). People are no longer painted up with white clay when they start living together, nor were they in 1969, though the term they now use for marriage in our sense is still *ga:niya:miyada* or, simply, "living together". It has also been a long time since there were only four People/Lands on Bickerton. Most people now associate the Warnungamadada, or Lalara, with Bickerton whereas they really originated on the mainland. Most now associate the Wamungwadarrbalangwa with Groote Eylandt (as the Wurrabadelamba) whereas they originated on Bickerton. But no-one is puzzled that no mention is made in the tale of Groote Eylandt and mainland Peoples who have bits and pieces of country on Bickerton (Maps 2 and 3). These countries do not have the same significance as the Main Lands.

The relationships between the characters and their Lands established in the tale will be confusing if you have forgotten just what the relationship terms mean. I'll refresh your memory with a few short-hand definitions of the critical ones:

NA:NINGY A/dadingya: a person in father's mother's Land in my generation – this is the person you marry.

NABERRA/daberra: a person in father's mother's Land in the succeeding generation – this is a person in the Land your own marries but not in the generation following yours. It's the one to which yours has given a woman in your generation and is therefore too close for your own (Land's) offspring to marry.

NADIDJA/dadidja: a person in your mother's mother's Land in the previous generation – this is a person in the Land out of which your wife is born, that is, the mother-in-law's Land.

NAWA/NA:NINGUMA and diyaba/dadiyawa: an older/younger man/woman in your Land and generation.

Now I am in a position to render a general translation of the tale:

One day a man from the Wurramarrba People/Land went fishing on Bickerton Island in the country of the neighbouring Wurramara. At the same time, a man called Nambirrirrma descended from a cloud on the rain to a place in Wurramara country. When the Wurramarrba man arrived at his destination he saw this stranger and wondered where he could have come from. He was a different kind of (Aboriginal) person. Nambirrirrma told him that he belonged to this particular place, but before they could talk further, the Wurramarrba man sighted his own NA:NINGYA, a man of the Wamungwadarrbalangwa Land, coming toward them. He called his NA:NINGYA over and asked him if he knew this stranger. He replied he did not but suggested he may have come from "God". Both men found it odd that this man, being a stranger, should speak their language. Nambirrirrma then asked them the whereabouts of the people who belonged to the country they were in. The Wurramarrba man answered that they, the Wurramara, were presently on the other side of the island in Wurragwagwa or Wurra:nggiJyangba country (which, the storyteller explained later, was their mother's country). Pointing out the boundaries of Wurramara country to Nambirrirrma, the two men now showed him the location of their own respective countries. From the information now available to him, Nambirrirrma was able to deduce that he called the Wurramarrba man by the term

NADIDJA (that is, of the People/Land out of which his own wife should be born) and the Warnungwadarrbalangwa, NABERRA (that is, someone in the Land his own married but a generation below him).

While Nambirrirrma remained behind, at his own insistence the Wurramarrba man went away to fetch the Wurramara People from Wurragwagwa country. The Warnungwadarrbalangwa man went away to fetch his own People. When the Wurramara arrived back in their own country they asked Nambirrirrma who he was, and ambirrirrma replied he was also Wurramara and therefore they should call each other by the term NAWA/NA:NIGUMA. After holding a meeting, Nambirrirrma's NADIDJA, the Wurramarrba man, arranged that he be given his (the Wurramarrba man's) *daberra*, a woman in the Warnungwadarrbalangwa People/Land, as wife, providing him with a choice between two or three adult women with children and one young girl without. Nambirrirrma picked the young girl and they were married, eventually having one child. Finally Nambirrirrma died.

Even when Galiyawa was telling the story in 1969, Old Borneo of the Lalara who was there at the time was puzzled as to why Nambirrirrma would choose one single girl over two or three who were already married. Galiyawa shrugged off the question as if to say, "That's just the way the story goes". At first I thought it might be due to Mission influence regarding the virtues of monogamy. But then in 1986 when visiting Nambirrirrma's landing place at Arumandja, I not only learned that Nambirrirrma's son by this marriage was called Badjuini but that Badjuini also married before he died. Whatever Nambirrirrma represented – and it was by no means Wurramara-ness, as Nambirrirrma's own query "Who me?" whenever addressed as Wurramara, indicates – it was important that it continue. In Aboriginal terms it could only continue if he had his "own" children. However, the answer to this puzzle only raised a new one. Badjuini also married the Warnungwadarrbalangwa as his father had. Granted it was not a Land to which his father's generation had given a "sister", that is, it was not a *warnigarangbidja* marriage, but it was, nevertheless "close". And this the son of a father who had laid down the Law (or persuaded the Aborigines he met to reaffirm their own Law)! Surely it was not the "deviation" but the "law" that the Aborigines wanted passed on. And yet the son was buried at the same "sacred site" as the father, indicating his co-importance. We'll come back to this puzzle later.

From the story we learn there are four People/Lands on Bickerton, that they are differentiated one from the other and that Wurramara marries Warnungwadarrbalangwa in one generation and Wurramarrba marries the latter in the next. When the Wurramarrba are not marrying the Wamungwadarrbalangwa the Wurramara marry the Wurragwagwa. When they are not marrying the Warnungwadarrbalangwa so do they. Hence, each marries the other in alternate generations and neither the Wurramarrba and the Wurramara on the one side, nor the Warnungwadarrbalangwa and the Wurragwagwa on the other, marry each other.

What we don't know from the story is precisely where each of the Lands in question is located, though they are *pointed* out during the course of the tale. The Aboriginal listener would gain his or her bearings from the actual places mentioned and be able to plot the locations of the Lands in question. But I could not, hence you can not. I would have traveled the inland areas and mapped them had I stayed for a longer time in 1974. Now that I was back in 1986, it was now one of the jobs I intended to complete.

Besides the trip with Milumdurn to Arumandja, three more with other Aborigines were particularly instructive. By taking you along with me on those journeys you will see just how much there was to learn (and how much there still is to learn) about "country" on Bickerton (not to mention elsewhere in Australia).

Surveying, Aboriginal Style
Gudigba was one of the few Aboriginal men of whom I could say hadn't visibly changed in the past 12 years. He was still a solidly built, powerful man with the highly developed neck and shoulder muscles of a professional hockey player. This is an Aborigine who is good with a spear and fearsome in a fight. However, that's not Gudigba's disposition. He stays out of trouble by staying on Bickerton and trouble stays out of him because he does not drink – or only rarely when on "holidays" on the mainland or after someone close has died. And he's not married – never has been. He lives mainly on bush foods on Bickerton – fish, turtle, wild yams, supplemented with introduced flour-made damper and tea. Gudigba is my *nawarrga*, or elder fellow-Promised Land and generation mate. He must be in his early 50s. Because of his chosen life-style he is bush-smart and in Aboriginal terms this means knowing the Songstreams as well as the physical lay-out of the Land. More to my own interests, his own Land is on Bickerton and he is named on a section of it along the north coast.

"Gudigba" denotes the area of Bickerton where Yandarranga, Central Hill, left the sea and moved on to land (Map 3, #55).

The first question I asked Gudigba, then, was one that I had neglected to ask anyone before: "What are the names and locations of the inland Bickerton places traveled by Central Hill as be made his way across Bickerton to the large bay on the east coast?" (see Maps 2 and 3). His answer was not unsurprising. He gave me a list of place names in a line one after the other. This was normal when you asked for a Songstream; but you didn't expect the places actually to appear in a straight line when you transferred them to a map. Usually they were scattered. But with Gudigba's it was different. They did. I wasn't sure whether this was due to Gudigba's inability to read a topographical map as we do, or whether the places actually fell into line in actual as distinct from abstract, eternal, space. I would find out the answer by actually traveling to the sites.

I learned to my disappointment that this was impossible. The places were in a remote part of the island and some of the land there was still too soft from the rains to be traveled by Toyota. Nobody really wanted to walk. Neither Gudigba nor anybody else bad been there for a long time as there was little to go there for; "why else would the names of the inland places go to dogs?" Gudigba had said. We could, however, drive down the eastern shore of South Bay along the beach and return by an inland track which was dry and which almost touched on the last place visited by Central Hill before he left Bickerton and re-entered the sea.

I checked my coastal place names as we made our way south from Milya:gburra and noted some discrepancies with my original maps. These I would check out later. Eventually we arrived at Mada (#94), which I had not differentiated from Murugulya on my original map, and turned inland along the dirt track cut by surveyors from the Mining Company who had once traveled this palt of the island looking for possible manganese deposits. Fortunately they hadn't found any. The Company had established a barge site just beyond Mada at Laugulalya, though it was no longer in evidence.

As we began to turn north along the track Gudigba said something to me that I found quite remarkable: "Wurramara country meets Nimbarela (#9) here," he said. "You line up Nimbarela with the place where Central Hill came on to Bickerton and this side (the east side) is ours (Warnungamadada and Wurra:nggilyangba or Wurragwagwa), and that side (the west side) is theirs (Wurramara)."

It was either side of the track we were traveling on in the Toyota that he was pointing to. There were no place names on this "line". My problem was that I could grasp no point of reference which told him where Nimbarela was or where the Central Hill place should be. But he knew precisely where they were and, from this, where we were.

Yingelanggwaberangamandja (#92) in Murugulya/Wurramara country was on our left and extended back from the beach to here; Nimbarela at the border of Wurra:nggilyangba country was on our right, extending back towards us from the east coast. Behind us was the inland place Amadja (#146) belonging to the Wurramarrba People.

At first I thought that Gudigba might be using the road as a convenient dividing line and that a "boundary" did not really exist. If so, the boundaries were a European-determined invention. I asked Gudigba about this. No, the road really did separate Wurramara on one side from Wurra:nggilyangba on the other and it was surveyed not by Europeans but by four Aborigines – Djurrba Wurramara, Alex Wurramarrba, Djambana Lalara and Hindu Mimiyawan. Europeans had merely wanted an inland route through Bickerton and this was the route the Aborigines had plotted for them. They had followed the pre-existing line. Or had they merely chosen the most convenient path through the bush which had then become a boundary? I still wasn't sure. Gudigba said that long before Europeans arrived the old men had made a footpath along the road in question: from Nimbarela north to Mulgurramadja (#61). And they had made another one from Arawura (#20) where Central Hill had left Bickerton to the same place. This traced the line of places he had given me as the inland countries of Central Hill!

To make sure, though, I would ask the old men. Those who had surveyed the road for the Mining Company were Gudigba's contemporaries. How would the old men interpret a journey along the same route? Unfortunately there was but one old Bickerton man left – that is, one born in the bush and unable to speak English. Fortunately he was at Milya:gburra during my visit and he agreed to accompany me.

I retraced my steps from Milya:gburra south to Mada with Naugunga, correcting the coastal place names on my map as we went. I had thought that Mada marked the division between Wurramara country now behind us and Wurramarrba, now in front. I had asked Naugunga to take me to the boundary; but he kept on going until we reached LauguJalya (#95). We were adjacent to a rocky shoal jutting out into the water. Naugunga ordered the vehicle stopped and got out. "Right here. This side Wurramara, that side Wurramarrba," he said, pointing first behind him in a sweeping motion and then ahead toward South Bay.

Then we headed over to the inland track I had driven before with Gudigba and we drove north. As we proceeded, Naugunga, like Gudigba before him, called out the names of the coastal place of the Wurra:nggilyangba to his right and the coastal places of the Wurramara to his left, the road again being the dividing line between the two main Lands. We were traveling north "on Arawura", he said. Arawura was the place ahead of us in the big bay in Wurra:nggilyangba country where Central Hill had left Bickerton for the sea. At the intersection of a dry creek bed and the road we turned north west. We were at the inland limit of Arawura, Naugunga said, not to mention the inland limit of a Rainbow Serpent place stretching toward us from the Wurramara side (#89).

Now we were "on Mungwurridjirra" (#69), said Naugunga, as we traveled to the north west. Mungwurridjirra, an old ceremony ground, was directly in front of us, though invisible to our gaze, some seven kilometers away on the coast of North Bay. Reaching another Rainbow Serpent's place (#97) we turned south "on Amagadabuda" (#86) where the Serpent(s) entered Bickerton. Of course we could not see this place in order to sight it, but you can see on the map that it is on a straight line from where we had turned at #97. In other words, through all this, we were following an invisible grid surveyed directionally on important Songstream places in the landScape: due north from a on b, north-west on c and south on d. This was not only how roads were traveled but bow they are constructed.

Directions are known in many ways: one of them is by the wind. Knowing the season, it can be predicted with some certainty from which direction the wind is blowing. At least eight different winds can be identified by the season in which, and direction from which, they blow (Figure 4). Places, then, can be lined up on the wind – as long as you know where you are now or have been before. Directions are also known by markers in the bush which "point you" in certain directions, again as long as you know where you are now or have been before. Knowing these "survey posts" is what it means to be "bush smart" or "find your way about" in the bush. I tried to find out how this was done once when two of us were in the middle of the bush on Groote. My Aboriginal companion had just told me that we were "on" a certain place on the coast.

"How do you know?" I asked. "It's on the other side of that big tree," he replied. I spent the next 10 minutes trying, unsuccessfully, to discover how he distinguished that "big tree" from the rest.

On another occasion I asked my companion how he knew we had just crossed over into someone else's country.

"You feel different when you reach another place. You just know where you are," he replied.

To return to my trip with Naugunga. It was in the aftermath of our journey that I learned how Aborigines handle boundary disputes. I took the opportunity of a trip to Angurugu for a mortuary ceremony to check the place names I had been given by Naugunga and Gudigba with Murabuda of the Wurramarrba. Mada, he said, was the last Wurramara place; Laugulalya was the first Wurramarrba place. Naugunga had given Laugulalya as Wurramara. Gudigba was unsure, neither being his country. When I returned to Bickerton I checked again with another Wurramara man, Nawurawinya. "Laugulalya is Wurramara," he reiterated. I then put the discrepancy to each of them independently, and each one replied seemingly without reflection, "Half is Wurramara and half is Wurramarrba." It was said so quickly on a matter that I defined as contradictory that I was taken aback. The possibility of conflict had been overwhelmed by the principle of conciliation: "differentiate and redistribute" was the result. Given the instinctive response, it was obviously a principle deep within the culture.

It was Nawurawinya, by the way, with whom I traveled to complete my survey of the inland places of Bickerton. This time we followed the western extension of the Mining Company's exploration road. We traveled north "on Malurba" (#101), due west "on Adarrbalangwa" (a general name for the west coast area), north "on Ngamaburra" (#110), then back the other way, south "on Midjiyanga" (also "on Yinbiya" (#129)), in Wurramarrba country. "On Midjiyanga", though, was qualified as, "as far as to Yigbudena" (#80). Yigbudena is the last Wurramara place going south along the bay. A line drawn inland in a strajght line from its southern boundary intersects with the projection of our road southward. Nawurawinya was pointing out that although we were traveling "on Midjiyanga" (or Yinbiya), these places are not in Wurramara country.

But the third journey I wish to detail before presenting the results of my survey of the whole island are the two flights I took around Bickerton by air with Murabuda and Djambana Lalara. I did this to check the location of sea places belonging to the various Bickerton People and situate them within the pattern of Songstreams in the area. My preliminary attempt at locating these on a topographical map with Murabuda's assistance was revealing. He was having trouble reading the map against whatever grid was in his own mind when all of a sudden something seemed to click. We had been trying to position a reef (*aiya:ba*) associated with Wild Apples (Yinemanenga) in the sea to the east of Bickerton. He took my ballpoint pen from my hand and began to draw dashes out from Adjeringmina (#29) in a curve around the point then in a straight line south toward the salt-water pool in Connexion Island. This complete, he then moved his pen to the boundary line between Yinemugwaba (#8) and Nimbarela (#9) on Bickerton and began to dash out another line directly east. When this line intersected with the first line coming down from the north he said, "Here it is." The second line, I found, had been drawn "on" the Channel between Winchelsea Island and Groote beyond Connexion to the east.

We flew out over the Gulf from Angurugu in search of the first place on my provisional map, Yigbalyigba (#147). Murabuda identified it as a large expanse of yellow water stretching from that number on my map back toward the small islands off the south-east coast of Bickerton (#1,2,3). It was Wurramarrba country associated with Midjiyanga, Macassan Ship. We flew on, turning to the south-west on Murabuda's instructions, in search of (from my point of view – Murabuda already knew) Mungwarugwa. Murabuda identified it as this end of a patch of milky water extending in a north-south direction (#148). There was a rock shaped like an "umbrella" under the water, he said, which caused the water to be milky like that. Mungwarugwa too was Wurramarrba, on Ship. Beyond was Walbalya (# 149), a Wurramarrba place on Yina:barranga, Cut-leaved Palm, and Derrarragurrgwa, Dove, marked by a large expanse of yellow water running in a north-south direction then turning toward the mainland. Under the water here, said Murabuda, was a sand bar.

And so we proceeded around Bickerton. Basically all the sea places we located were identified by a patch of milky sea or bubbly sea which my companions associated with a rock formation below the surface, by a patch of yellow sea which they associated with a sand bar, or by a reef above or just below the water causing waves or ripples. Most of these associations I confirmed by comparing the locations with a navigational map provided by the Mining Company. When I asked Murabuda how he knew about the underwater formations in question, he said "We can't see them. We know from the currents." Intriguing in this respect was the Wild Apples place in the sea off the north coast of Connexion Island that Murabuda had located on my map by Aboriginal surveying methods. "There's a reef under the sea there," he said. "When you approach it, it rises up and you can see it. It looks like a bunch of white things under the sea. But when you come closer it goes down. It's a living rock. We give it a miss when we're out that way in our boats".

Something else intriguing happened while we were on our flying trip. As we left Yigbalyigba and flew on to Mungwarugwa we had to fly over Yadalyurna or the Sea Channel cut by the Rainbow Snake(s), Yabongwa. Murabuda in particular became visibly agitated. I asked him about it and he said he was scared of the Yadalyuma. If we had been traveling by boat, he said, he would have struck the side of the vessel with his hand as we started over. The old men would have taken some sweat from under their armpits and rubbed it on the boat, but they didn't do this any more. But still they felt scared. Hitting the boat (like smoking a place or rubbing sweat on something) would protect them as they passed through.

But here we were feeling this a thousand feet above the sea and its Channel. It was not just land and sea places I was mapping but also those in the air. Perhaps it would be more accurate to say that the Amawurrena that was the Spirit of the place and defined its boundaries permeated the same slice of land, subterranean sea and air.

Before I trace out the Promised Landscape of Amagalyuagba in detail, let me first explain the so-called "clan" names of the Peoples there in terms of this 'Scape. The Wurramara are so called on the Head of the Rainbow Snake(s) Yabongwa which is also the name for Rock Soak which is also the name for the rain on a Rainbow reflecting Snake which is, by the way, the same rain on which Nambirrirrma descended. The "old Wurramara", the first Wurramara, though, are called Warnungaunggeragba, the root of which refers to country on the east side of the north-west to south-east diagonal that bisects "Wurramara" country as a whole. Their descendants hold jurisdiction on this side of the diagonal, the Wurramara proper on the western side.

The Wun·amarrba are named on the quiet, fresh, South-South-East Wind which blows at the time of year when the morning dew drips gently from the needles of the whistling pine, *muworraga*. Amarrba is also the spray that blows through rock holes near the sea. Another name for these People is

Wurralyilyanga, the root of which refers to the Seven Sisters Star Formation, Wurramarrba.

The Wurra:nggilyangba are named on the term for their country considered as a whole, A:nggilyangba. They are sometimes also referred to as the Wurragwagwa which refers to the People linked by Central Hill, Yandarranga, east from Bickerton. The Warnungwadarrbalangwa are named on their country running down the west coast of Bickerton but are now also known as the Wurrabadelamba, the country they assumed on Groote by the grace of the Warnungwudjaragba there. The Warnungamadada are also named on the term for their country as a whole – Armadadi on the mainland – from whence they originated. As I've said, they are also called Lalara, Dangerous Snakes.

Other People we will encounter in the Promised Landscape of Amagalyuagba are the Wurrawilya, a Groote Eylandt proper People as are the Warnungwamalangwa (alternatively, Bara Bara), and the now extinct Warnungmurugulya. The Warnungamagadjeragba are a Groote Eylandt People, the Murungun are on the adjacent mainland.

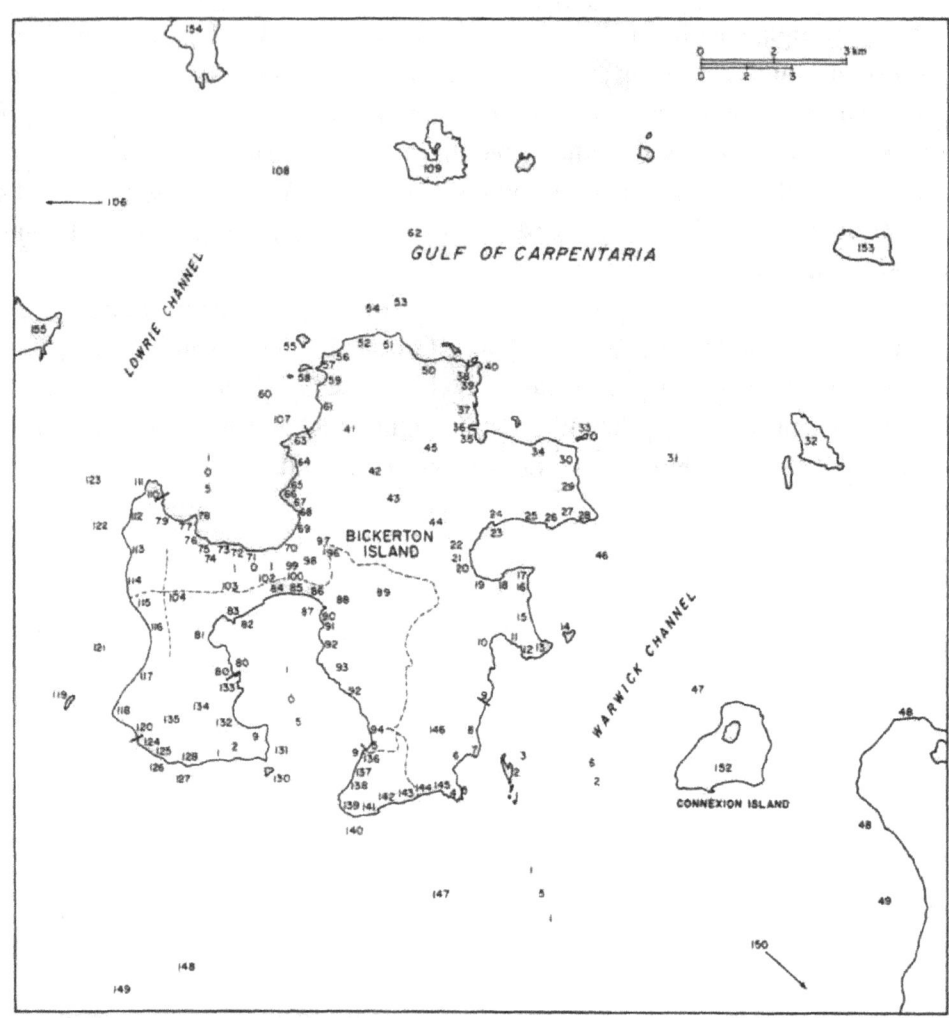

MAP 2. The Promised Landscape of Amagalyuagba: Place Names

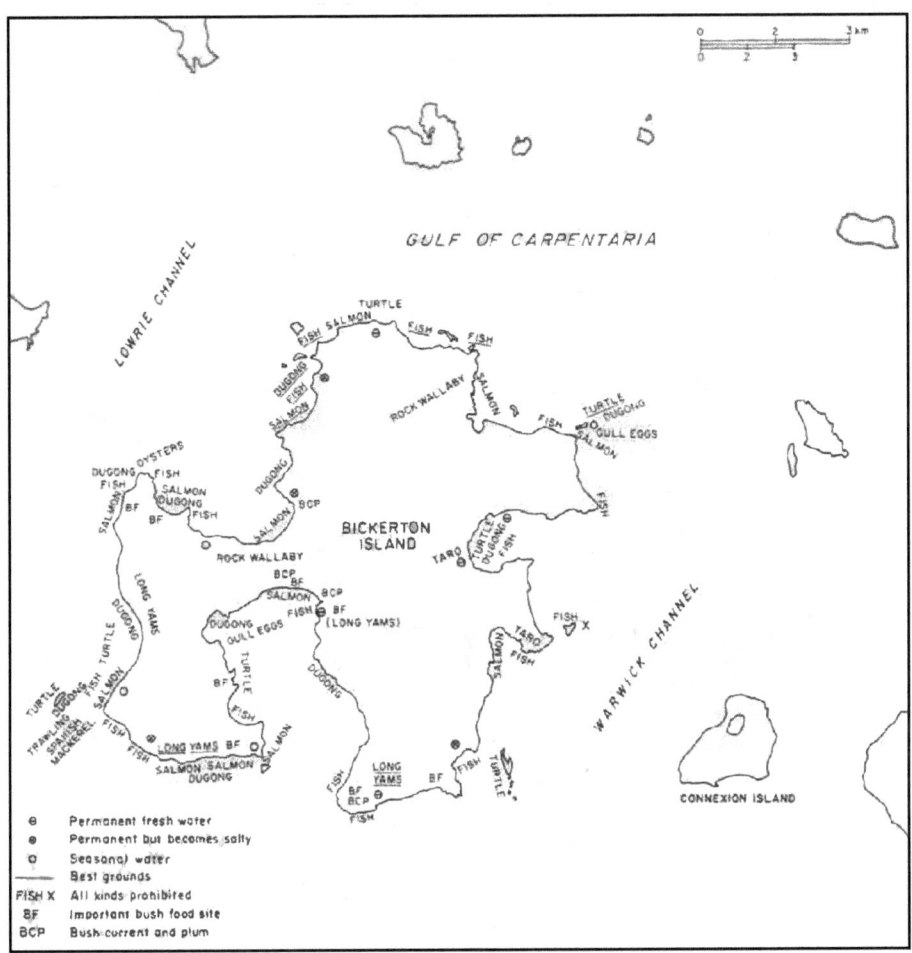

MAP 3. The Promised Landscape of Amagalyuagba: Resources

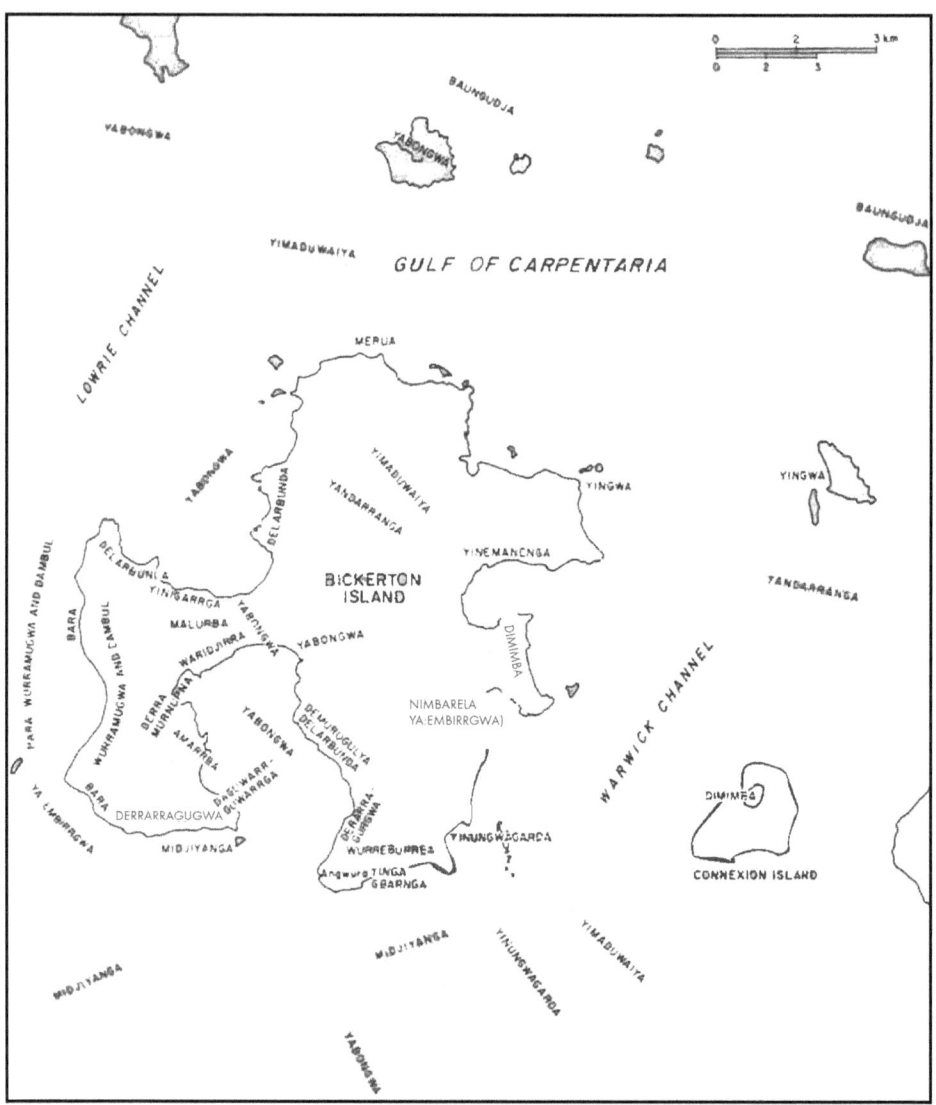

MAP 4. The Promised Landscape of Amagalyuagba: Songstreams

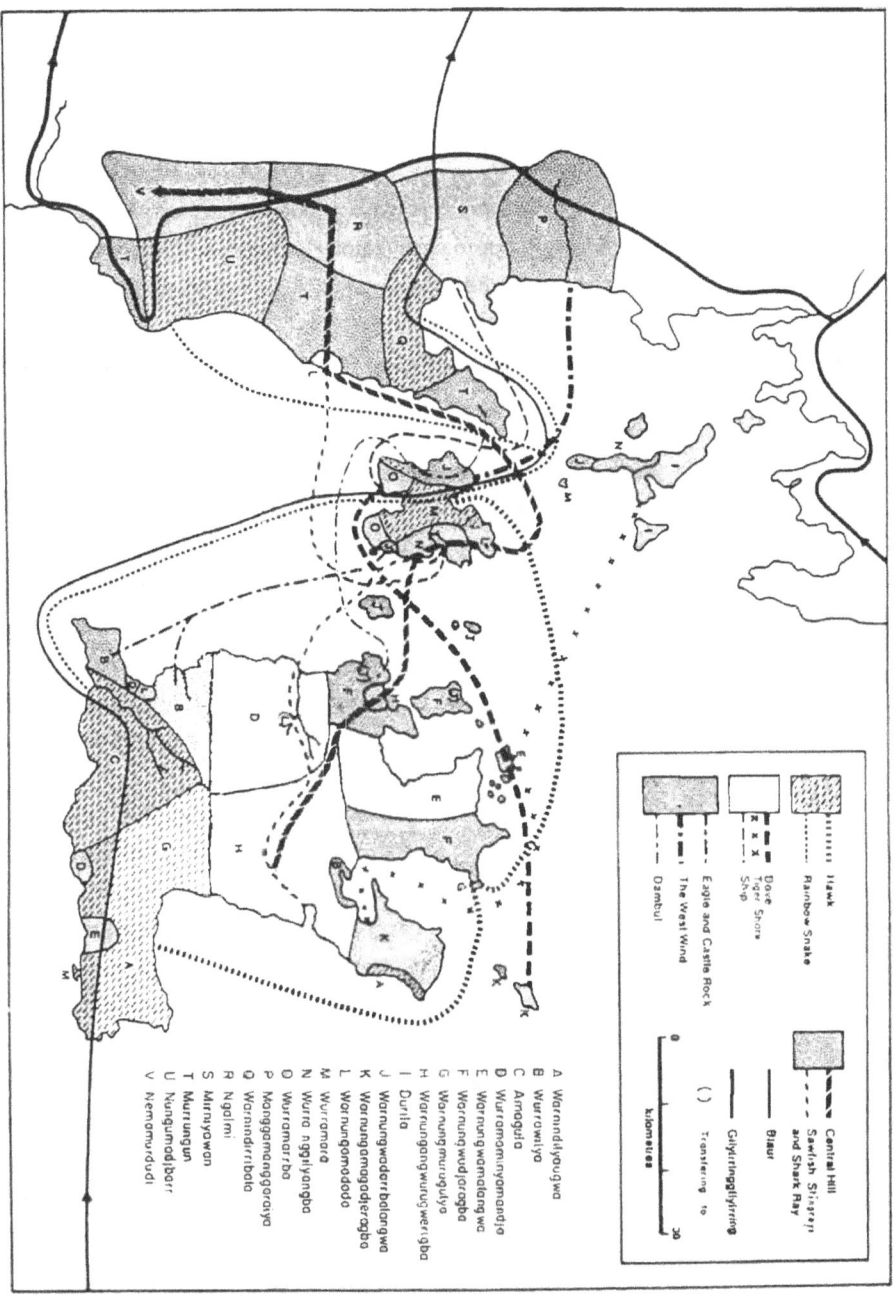

MAP 5. Songstreams of the Western Gulf, 1969–

Table 3. Key to the Promised Landscape of Amagalyuagba.

Number Name Meaning

Wurrawilya/Warnungwadarrbalangwa

1. **Yidjidjemadja:** a place belonging to Yinungwagarda, Sea Eagle.
2. **Marngarnemurumadja:** "Nightfall", associated with the Wurrawilya People.
3. **Abungarilyauwiya:** "Fog", associated with the Wurrawilya.
4. **Wurawabegba:** the place where Parrots, Wurruwa:ba, are buried.
5. **Yimerndamadja:** "place of the Fleas"; place where a twig was broken off a bush to poke the fleas off the body; Wurrawilya place.
6. **Nemabergunga merugura:** place where Sea Eagle and Osprey, Duwanggarrariya, cooked Long Tom, Marrugurra.

(They put the fish in a hole with the ashes of the fire and covered it up. After cooking it for a time, they took it out. Eagle saw that it was still raw. "Let's try it anyway," he said. Osprey agreed. "Raw fish is good," insisted Eagle. We don't have to cook any more. Instead we can catch fish and eat them raw. Eagle flew off to Yidjidjimadja [#1].)

7. **A:nemurremadja:** "here is the place", half belonging to Wurrawilya, half to Warnungwadarrbalangwa.
8. **Yinemugwaba:** Warnungwadarrbalangwa place made by Parrot Fish, Ya:embirrgwa.

Wurra:nggilyangba

9. **Nimbarela:** the home of a giant Wurra:nggilyangba Cannibal Man of the same name. Another (unrelated) Cannibal Man of the Warnungwamalangwa People lived on Anyera, Hawknest Island. He ate his sons but let his daughters live and kept them as wives.

(Older informants said that a long long time ago this area used to belong to the Warnungwudjaragba of Groote on "Parrot Fish".)

10. **Mulgwa:** "the bay". Named on Ngwulya the burial ground/island nearby. Also frequented by Nimbarela.
11. **Milyalyamurrumadja:** a place frequented by Nimbarela.

12. **Mangambawiya**: place associated with Nemarmbawiya, a man associated with the Blind Woman, Dimimba.
13. **Mardjerumadja**: as above.
14. **Ngwulya**: Wurra:nggilyangba burial ground.
15. **Lagelyamurumandja**: a creek associated with Blind Woman.
16. **Anugwunda**: a place associated with Swordfish, Yugurredangwa.
17. **Dimimbamandja**: place where the one-eyed Blind Woman is watching Badelamba Bay on Groote Eylandt and wondering if she could go there.
18. **Naranganarba**: a place near a gushing spring, *mamelagunda*, named on the Tide, Merua, and Mangrove, Anema.
19. **Abarra**: a name for the whole bay or for a place associated with Swordfish.
20. Stingrays (Yimaduwaiya) or Reef (A: berigba).
21. **Arawura**: "Big Place". A name for places deep in the bay or for the depression in a particular place where Central Hill, Yandarranga, sat down. From here he began to move into the sea but the water was too deep so he moved over to #19.
22. **A:nibaranba**: the place where Central Hill threw off the Parrots, then travelling in human form they turned to stone (henceforth referred to as Warnibaranba).
23. **Arnidjuwa**: another place, just inland behind another gushing spring, where Central Hill threw off some more Parrots (Warnidjuwa) and also some Meat Ants, Yuwa:ba.
24. **Mamalagunda**: a gushing, fresh water spring in the sea.
25. **Yimilymandja**: the place where Central Hill threw some Wild Apples, Yinemanenga. It was too muddy for him there so he left.
26. **Yirindjiramandja**: an Arawura place. Stony country through which Central Hill travelled and from which he first saw Trevally, Yirindjirra.
27. **Abilyarilyargwa**: another Arawura place. "We can see you clearly", referring to the glistening from the Stingrays.
28. **Niganggumandja**: Arawura place. "He goes into the sand and mud and stops," referring to Central Hill. Also associated with Stingrays.
29. **Yangbudemandja**: "Strong Tide place."
30. **Adjeringmina**/30. **Amagilya:djira**: Place belonging to Wurra:nggilyangba. This place belongs to the Warnungwadarrbalangwa, perhaps a long time ago to the Murungun of the adjacent mainland. Here, Crow, Yingwa, speared two Birds, Debuda:gbuda.
31. **Maugura**: channel cut by Crow's spear.
32. **Angwardenmadja**: from #30 to this island is Crow Songstream:

(Crow was a young man. Two old women dug a big hole and went to the toilet in it. Then they called Crow over and told him it was a bandicoot's nest. Crow jumped in with both feet first to catch the bandicoot. The two women finally pulled him out and, with Meat

Ant, dried him. Then Crow carved a fish out of wood and placed it in the Channel between #30 and #31. He told the women that if they checked the sea at low tide they would see a magical fish. When the tide went out Crow told them to sit on the beach touching leg-to-leg, shut their eyes, and he would go out and push the fish in to them. But instead he went out and threw a spear at them, catching them from the side and pilloring them leg-to-leg. He told them he would leave them there in the shallows until the tide came in and they would drown. The tide came up over the old ladies and Crow flew off to Angwardenmadja. But the tide took the old ladies there too.)

33. **Anggangmadja**: place on Crow, said one informant; place on Crane, Demarnda, said another. Crane is associated with the Wurramarrba and Warnungwamalangwa Peoples.
34. **Amarbiramandja**: as above
35. **Dumindamadja**: as above
36. **Damadilya**: place where the Coughing Lady of the same name caught the 'flu. Belongs to the Warnungmurugulya People, but Wurramara coming in too.
37. **Aiyargerra**: as above
38. **Derra:mernurna**: Crippled Lady place belonging to the Wurramara.
39. **Aragbura**: Wurra:nggilyangba or Warnungamadada place (informants not sure).
40. **Ma:gebarregumadja**: as above
41. **A:nebarrenba**, 42. **A:gwugwarna** > 43. **A:nuburda**, 44. **Milyilya**: these are all places along Central Hill's inland journey. You can see the trough he made coming through. The old men made a path along it. Dogs are given their names on these places. The Stingrays, the Parrots and the Meat Ants travelled behind him and turned into humans as they made their way across the land. When he left them behind they turned back into their Dreaming (*alawudawarra*) form.
45 **Yilarrba**: Liviston Palm place. Central Hill planted them in a circle when he rested here.
46 **Yinggelarramandja**: yellow-water sea place on Blind Woman.
47 **Aiya: ba**: Reef and yellow-water spots in sea on Wild Apples.
48 **Mera**: Dimimba's blood washing up on shore after she ritually cut herself when Central Hill "escaped" to Groote.
49. **Gurruramandja**: reef on Dimimba

Warnungamadada

50. **Yarraidja:** place on Stingrays, Parrots and Tide.
51. **Algumerramandja**: place where crabs, *miyalgwa*, found on low Tide.

52. **Marrbiya: nemadja**: place on Tide.
53. **Mungarniya:mdumadja**: as above.
54. **Wurrawardamandja**: place where the Dingo was swimming, trying to cross to the other islands, but couldn't.
55. **Nemauguwa**: place in Gudigba region where Central Hill landed on Bickerton.
56. **Anima:bunamadja**: as above
57. **Ngangugumadja**: as above
58. **Murrgwarrdungburramadja**: as above
59. **Aburrgmadja**: as above; the place was too muddy for Central Hill to land on so he moved down shore a bit.
60. **Melarrgumurumandja**; as above; island on Central Hill.
61. **Mulgurramadja**: as above: bay where Central Hill landed on Bickerton.
62. **Yadalyuma**: Stingrays' Channel. They swam north-west toward Blue Mud Bay but the Tide was too strong so they swam back into the Channel. Surfaced in bay at Arawura and swam to Angurugu River on Groote.

Wurramara

63. **Alyimbiyaugwamandja**: place where Frog, Delarbunda, made fresh water.
64. **Amuralya**: place where Frog camped and then left.
65. **Anabarunggwa**: Frog place.
66. **Amuma:na**: Frog made a little creek here.
67. **Amburderra**: Rainbow Snake, Dengarna, place where she looked up and said "my country is this way."
68. **Wandera:minamandja**: place where Dadegabongwa stopped because she couldn't walk. (Seems to be becoming a Crippled Lady Place.)
69. **Mungwurridjirra**: important ceremony ground belonging to Warnungaunggeragba. Its name was called out by Blaur, founder of the sacred Mardaiya:n ceremony.
70. **Miribamandja**: there was an Old Man named Nemadjidjibira who complained, "I can't go anywhere." So the Rock opened up and he went in and the Rock closed.
71. **Milyabilyamandja**: too many people were coming into this place so the Rock came down and crushed them. Their bones were there before but gone now.
72. **Namadarrumera** (Ma:nigarrga): a Man, Numurngariya, threw a spear at the Rock and made a cave. Hawk, Yinigarrga, came along and they fought together. The Big Rock, Malurba, told them to shut up and Numurngariya threw a spear at him.
73. **Mungwarramandja**: place where the old people killed a hammerhead shark, *mungwarra*, because they were hungry.
74. **Marngabongamadja**: this place was Dreamed by Old Bill, Milyurndurn's father.

(Old Bill Dreamed that people were living there in the Big Rock but only came out at night when the Rock opened up. They had a Rock canoe and travelled in it by night. At daybreak they went back in the Rock and it closed up. Old Bill "carved" the place out of the Big Rock. The beach in front was his and his wife's favourite campsite. His wife was Murungun and she could sit with him and look out beyond the bay to her own country at Windanga point on the mainland.)

75. **Aringgari**: very important place for the Wurramara. It is where Rainbow Serpent emerged on the north side of Bickerton. Place name called out by Blaur. To the east of here on south-west diagonal is Warnungaunggeragba country; to west on same diagonal is Wurramara.
76. **Lauwura** (Merragabarngwa): place and name that can be called out instead of Aringari to avoid saying it because of its importance.
77. **Miyandenumandja**: this used to be a Warnungwadarrbalangwa place but it was changed to Wurramara. This was because the place was rocky and rocky places connected to the Big Rock should be Wurramara.
78. **A:birigba**: Reef on Frog.
79. **Adangmadja**: Frog's Eggs in fresh water pools here. Also Yimbarela, Big Dog, place. Nobody gave him any food so he got mad and came here to steal some.
80. **Yigbudena**: Crippled Lady, Derra:mernurna, place. There is a big round Rock back from the beach. If you go there you will get crippled too.
81. **Agememalyamandja**: place on Crippled Lady.
82. **Agberrenga**: an old man named Nema:ndja:bina sits on this rock in the sea telling people, "This is my place and you go away."
83. **Amalyuwa**: to the south-west of this place is Bad Baby Dreaming where children will be born with big heads and small bodies. To the east they will be like us.
84. **Amamagulyara**: place on Nambirrirrma, later called by Blaur.
85. **Arumandja**: (A:rrirra:gba, Amiya:mba:na: "Why"): place where Nambirrirrma sat down.
86. **Amagadabuda**: Rainbow Serpent place; general area where t(he)y entered Bickerton.
87. **Aleriba**: Head of Rainbow/Serpent, Duwurrawilya, place.
88. **Liridera**: "Serpent's Water"; billabong where Rainbow Serpent swam and swallowed two Boys.
89. 89.**Dingarna**: Serpent's place where she swam inland along a creek before being blocked by Central Hill and Stingrays.
90. **Milya:gburra**: ceremony place for Wurramara in the Dreamtime; name called by Blaur before he called out Mungwurridjirra which makes the Wurramara line more

important than the Warnungaunggeragba in Mardaiya:n ceremony; place of Rainbow Serpent's tears.
91. **Arrilya**: bay
92. [[92. **Yingelanggwaberangamandja**: place on Lightening, Demurugulya: Belongs to Warnungmurugulya (now extinct)
93. **Duwurawilya**: head of Rainbow Serpent place.
94. **Mada**: place on Lightening and Eye of Frog. (#92-94 can be referred to collectively as Murugulya.)]]
95. **Laugulalya** (1 /2): "sounds like it's Wurramara", my informant said.
96. **Liridera**: "Serpent's Water" where Rainbow Serpent surfaced and was cut open and the Two Boys were (re)born and circumcised. The White Sand on the north side of the site is the meat and the fat of the Serpent.
97. Yarranganamuramandja: place on Leech, Yarrnga Yarrnga. Leech, along with Frog, is in the billabong where the water floods down from the Big Rock in the wet season.
98. **Ederra Miya:dja Mandja**: Cave on Canoe Paddle, Miya:dja, belonging to the Warnungwamalangwa.]
99. **Rrugbulya**: the crown of Arumandja on Malurba.

100. (This is the place of the Mermaids of Wurrangalya (lit. they of the place), men and women who emerge from the fresh water pools when no one is about. They go down the Flood waters with Frog and Leach. But they no longer appear because there are too many Europeans coming in and out (without permission via the beaches on North Bay).
101. **Nina:gba**: place where Rainbow Serpent burrowed down to make a fresh water pool at the base of Rrugbulya.
102. **Malurba**: Big Rock between North and South Bays of Bickerton.
103. **Malara Muwurariya**: Trouble Rock. He came from the direction of Rrarrarrarra (#139) (i.e., from the south-east) but was too heavy to move any further, so he stopped here and started fighting with whomever came along. If you think about this Rock you will go off and kill someone (Malara is manganese).
104. **Dilyanderamandja**: a water hole on Rainbow Serpent.
105. **Yilyunga**: Rainbow Serpent sat down here but didn't like it so kept on going. There used to be a spring here, but no longer.
106. **Madalyuma**: Rainbow Serpent(s)' Channel stretching back to the Amagula River and on past Bickerton to #106 in Blue Mud Bay and down into Nundirribala country on the mainland.

107. **Murrgurrmurrgwa**: place in Blue Mud Bay where Rainbow Serpent turned south to Nundirribala country.
108. **Nadjergala**: reef in Serpent(s)' Channel.
109. **Langara**: Sand Bar, Yiningilya, where Serpent turned west.
110. **Malgara**: Island where Serpent laid her eggs. She cut deep into the bay from the north side.

Warnungwadarrbalangwa

110. **Ngarnaburra;** (Ngarnaluru): place where the Ghosts, Wurramugwa, arrived on Bickerton pulling Dambul, but they didn't like it so they went back offshore to the shelf around the island where they stretched Dambul out.

(Dambul are the two posts decorated with feathers with string attached between them that are pulled along by the Ghosts. To the mainland Murungun People, the posts represent Hollow Log Coffins though this is not the tradition on Groote Eylandt. The Ghosts pulled Dambul over from Cape Barrow. At #121 one of the posts fell forward and landed at #123, breaking the string and creating a Sea Channel between Bickerton and the mainland. When they arrived at #123 the Ghosts put Dambul back together again.)

111. **Adiminimburra**: the place where Dambul is standing all the time.
112. **Ayuwurra**: low tide, so you can see the Reef, Aiya:ba, on West Wind, Bara.
113. **Yalyimadja**: flying fox, Yalyiya, place. ("Maybe belongs to Wurrawilya People, my informant said.)
114. **Ainana**: the impression of a footprint in the sand, on West Wind.
115. **Larragarainggingmandja**: "the place with the trees on it is far away." On West Wind.
116. **Marrimamerramandja**: a Big Tree called Marrima, on West Wind.
117. **Laugwa**: left and went away, on West Wind.
118. **Amagwaugwara**: place where nobody lives; West Wind is looking at it.
119. **Adrrunggurra**: the place where the Wind blows.
120. **Warnda**: place where West Wind left his walking stick.
121. **Yiningilya**: Sand Bar on Dambul.
122. **Aiyawura**: where Dambul is fishing Parrot Fish, Ya:embirrgwa.
123. **Yiningilya**: Sand Bar above the water on Dambul and on Tide-when-the-sea-is-choppy.

124. **Amunggrilyalyugwa**: the spray of the waves from the South-South-East Wind, Amarrba.
125. **Mirimurumandja**: foggy, smoky place where Dove, Derrarragurgwa, cooked the Yams Murndigrriya:ra/Murungwurra.
126. **Langgurra**: instead of relying on Spider, Daguwarrguwarrga (also Derrarragurgwa), Damarrba (Wurramarrba woman), made a web for herself. Langurra describes it as it is pulled out then breaks and the ends all recoil together.
127. **Midjiyanga**: Macassan Ship that sunk here (the story will be told later).
128. **Murunggwa**: Dove place; the ground is shaking as someone walks on it.
129. **Yinbiya**: Spider place, point of land, hard to see; place where Dove became a Bird.
130. **Barndebarnduwa**: coils of rope from the sunken Macassan Ship, also broken Spider string.
131. **Aiya: ba**: Reef under water on Dove.
132. **Yiridjira**: Spider standing with legs outstretched, getting reading to move.
133. **Abadurrunggwa**: the South-South-East Wind blowing sand in the air.
134. **Yininga**: Spider dug out a sand bar and moved it on to the land here.
135. **Murrunggwa**: place where Dove dug Yams.
136. **Laugulalya** (1/2): "bit of string" belonging to Dove and Spider.
137. **Warrenburemadja**: place where Spider web is spread out and being carried along in the air not attached to anything.
138. **Yinimbinimbawiya**: the Spider web was broken but is still hanging in place.
139. **Rrarrarrarra**: the burnt smell on the Wind after a fire -- where the First Fire was born. Place where the South-South-East Wind has blown leaves of plants and they are bending in the breeze. Place where Dove/Spider put the string back together again. (Place where Wurramarrba Songs intersect.)
140. **Mirrbarra**: place where the Spider web becomes detached but remains intact then tangles all up into a little ball as it is being blown away.
141. **Nunggwarrbamandja**: Wurramarrba Mermaid place; place where water bubbles up.
142. **Arngamarrba**: the place where the Wurramarrba people are. The place where the Land and Wind stick together.
143. **Walbalaleriyamuda**: place of the Wild Palm, Yingagbarrnga; also, sand bar on land.
144. **Alyama** (Alyilyama): place where the Wind rolls into the Land.

145. **Yalyugwamandja**: the spray is falling with sunshine in it over there away from this place. The Seven Sister Stars, Wurreburrba, are rising in the east over there away from this place. It is raining to the east, over there away from this place.

(#137 to #145 is a Seven Sisters "block" of places)

146. **Amadja**: Dove flew here from #139. But the land was too low so she made a track in the sand -- her mark -- and flew back. Then she went on to Amagadjeragba (north-east corner of Groote Eylandt).
147. **Yigbalyigba**: bits of the Ship that floated away as it sunk; canoes.
148. **Mungwarugwa**: coils of rope from the wreck of Ship; also rope or string of Dove/Spider.
149. **Walbalya**: on Yingagbarrnga, Cut-leaved Palm ("like Coconut", Galgwa).

Others' Places

150. **A:berigba**: Reef belonging to Wurramaminyamandja at the mouth of Angurugu river.
151. **Yadalyuma**: Wurrawilya Sea Channel between Bickerton and the south-west point of Groote, on Sea Eagle.
152. **Yirrgamera**: Connexion Island.
153. **Anyera**: Hawknest Island and the place on Woodah Island, A:rra:ra:gba, where Baungudja, Tiger Shark (also pointed-nosed sharks in general), travelled. Belongs to the Warnungamagadjeragba.
154. **Angwurra:rrigba**: Woodah Island.
155. **Windanga**: Murungun place on Mainland.

From the journey I took around and across Bickerton Island I gained a much clearer idea of the Aborigines' relation to land, sea and air than I had previously – indeed I learned that the combination of land sea and air was implicit within the definition of *angalya* or "country" as Aborigines called it in English. The land or ground as such was called *adjerengga* and could be referred to as *amerarrga* or "grandfather". So could *magarda* sea as such – as *mamerarrga*.

The eternal aspect of the connection to country by a line of people was illustrated by the places referred to collectively as "Murugulya" on the east side of South Bay (#92–#94) on Bickerton. Not only were there no Murugulya people left on Groote Eylandt where their main Land was situated, but this "Murugulya" was merely country within someone else's country – the Wurramara's – and one would have thought that it would have been merged with theirs by now. Not so.

The existence and persistence of this and other "countries within countries", however, raised doubts as to my original 1981 hypothesis that these smaller areas had been carved out from larger ones as Songstream Company linkages shifted, in particular those between "brother"/"sister" Lands. If the relation was no longer to be a "brother"/"sister" one but something else, I thought, it would make sense from an Aboriginal point of view to subdivide the territory to which *both* were connected and award one part to one People and its Creative Being and the other part to the other and its Creative Being. In other words, the "law of the Dreaming" would remain intact but the relationship between the two could be altered and what were closely linked countries would now become separate and distant. But Murugulya country within Wurramara was between "brother"/"sister" People/Lands.

On the other hand, there were countries within countries in which those in the smaller area were *not* "brother"/"sister" People/Lands, as I had hypothesized. "Yingwa", Crow, country of the Warnungwadarrbalangwa (#30–#33) in Wurra:nggilyangba country on the east coast of Bickerton is a case in point. The two Peoples are Nadidja/dadidja or "mother-in-law's brother/mother-in-law" to each other. Here my original hypothesis seemed to apply. But let us take a closer look at this area: it is not just a Crow area that has been carved out here; there also seems to be a Demarnda or Crane place (#33) belonging to the Warnungwamalangwa of Groote and Wurramarrba of Bickerton as well as a Coughing Lady, Damadilya, place (#36) belonging to the extinct Warnungmurugulya and Wurramara not to mention a Crippled Lady place, Derra:mernurna (#38), belonging to the Wurramara. Indeed, apart from the adjacent Wurra:nggilyangba, there is one People/Land in this area connected to each of the four Songstreams represented in the Groote Eylandt-adjacent mainland region as a whole. The same situation obtains in reference to the south-east corner of Bickerton.

Here we find that just below Wurra:nggilyangba country to the north, beside Wurramara country to the north-west and Wurramarrba to the west, are sandwiched a Warnungamadada/Wurra:nggilyangba place (#4), five Wurrawilya places and one, or one-and-a-half, Warnungwadarrbalangwa places. Though only two Companies of Peoples out of four are represented here, the other two are connected to the adjacent Wurramarrba and Wurramara Lands.

I emphasize this because I now think that what we are encountering here as well as in the case of Yingwa country to the north is a "stopover" point on a major traffic route where a dominant People/Land has partitioned a part of its country and distributed it amongst a sample of those from the other three Companies in order to provide them with a safe haven during their journeys. The status of the south-east corner as such a place is reflected in the contents of the rock art gallery there which emphasize sea craft from the present to the pre-historic past. (I published a full account of this site in 1973.) The nature of these havens is such that they remain safe despite the on-going political situation in the region. The two areas in question are also sheltered from the prevailing north-westerlies in the wet season and would have allowed travelers to rest up in preparation for the dangerous journey across open water to the mainland. In the old days it was a half-day's journey by bark canoe and paddle over open water from Groote to Bickerton alone. The cynical may wish to posit that People from a sample of other Lands forced those in such strategic locations to so partition but I would not so posit myself.

This theory would help us make sense of other, though not all, "countries within countries" in the region. For instance, smaller countries within larger wholes on the southern coast of Groote Eylandt belong to People/Lands at the outer, northern, edge of the Groote-Bickerton area from east to west along the southern Groote coast are places belonging to the Wurramara of central Bickerton, the Warnungwamalangwa and Warnungwudjaragba of northern Groote, and the Wurramaminyamandja of west coast Groote and the Warnungamadada of northern Bickerton. The Wurrawilya of South Point, Groote, in addition to having country on the south-east corner of Bickerton, also have some in the vicinity of Umbakumba on north-east Groote. All of these would be sort of "guest homes" for those from remote areas rather than "stopover" points on an international traffic route, but the principle remains the same.

I am distinguishing here, as the Aborigines distinguish, between foreign countries adjacent to larger host countries and places where a Creative Being from one Land merely touched on the Land of another to establish a relationship but did not carve out a country. Murugulya-in-Wurramara may very well fit into this category considering that only the beach area is "really Murugulya", the inland area being more strongly associated with Wurramara

Creative Beings. For a separate country to be delineated, the foreign Creative Being in question must actually Create something there. To pass through or even touch down is not enough. Such is Dove, Derrarragugwa, principally associated with the Wurramarrba of Bickerton but connecting them as "brother"/"sister" to Wamungamagadjeragba on the north-east corner of Groote. It is critical to know then just bow much Creativity a particular Being exercised at a particular site, before asserting claims to Land. With People now frequenting certain sites less, with the old men knowledgeable in the lore of these sites dying out, the time is ripe for disputes to emerge. And they have.

By way of introduction to what I will say later about the effect of land rights on the Aborigines of this area, recall the mess I got myself into in 1974 by having placed the number "4" on the south-east corner of my Bickerton map signifying it belonged to the Wamungwadarrbalangwa. I left thinking I had ceded the Land over to Wanaiya and his People despite knowing that part of the Land – as it turned out the major part of the Land – was really Wurrawilya. How presumptuous of me. In fact, my book had merely re-opened a debate about strength of association that had been going on for some time. Since then the Aborigines did what they did at Laugulalya when they disagreed over affiliation. They subdivided it, half of A:nemurremadja (#7, and points north) being given to the Warnungwadarrbalangwa and half (and points south) to the Wurrawilya. The islands remained Wurrawilya as they always had been.

If "forgetting" the Songs of a place may cause problems, "remembering" them again is sometimes a solution. I noticed that when an informant was unsure of the name for a place he would eventually give me the name of one adjacent, sort of filling in the blank in his mind with the nearest Spirit of the Land he could think of. However, when I eventually did get the proper name for the place the informant would quickly retract the Spirit and substitute the appropriate one. Apparently parts of Woodah Island to the north of Bickerton have gone blank and Aborigines are now competing to fill them in again. In 1969 I had sailed around the island with Galiyawa, Gudigba and Nanggadjaga believing that I had accurately mapped its sites; and I had, from a narrow point of view. I began to notice discrepancies when checking with Gegenda of the Durila in 1986.

In the distant past Angwurra:arrigba, Woodah Island, was inhabited by a number of Peoples known collectively as the Warnungwurra:arrigba who spoke the Anindilyaugwa language. However, they were all taken by a mysterious illness which my informants in 1969 termed "*burra burra*". I have had this translated as "measles" or "whooping cough" by Aborigines familiar with these diseases, but then I have also heard *burra burra* referred to as "sorcery". I have even been told that it was *burra burra* that claimed Nambirrirrma's life. Tradition has it that the Wurrawilya and Warnungamagula of Groote were also hard hit by the "disease". The same tradition holds that seven people from one Land died in one night. Whatever the details, it is obvious that something nearly catastrophic happened on these islands long before Europeans actually arrived in person; perhaps their diseases preceded them through the ceremonial and trade ties that the Groote Eylandt area people had with mainland Aborigines to the south. Perhaps they came with the Macassans. Who knows? In any event, Woodah was left without people and no one moved in to lay claim to it by right of Creation Being affiliation. There is no permanent fresh water there and the People of the region were already attached to more favourable habitations elsewhere.

In 1969 there were no recognized Songstreams between Bickerton and Woodah, though the path of Baungudja, Tiger Shark, did link it to Groote and the country of the Warnungamagadjeragba in the bay to the northeast of Umbakumba. Dove connected the Wurramarrba of Bickerton to the island of Yimburrurra off the east coast of Woodah, though in 1969 the island was regarded as belonging to the Durila People. The Durila had arrived on Groote from the Blue Mud Bay area of the mainland via Woodah Island before European contact and had been aligned with the Warnungamagadjeragba there. My informants said that the Durila had been living on Woodah with the permission of the Warnungarnagadjeragba but had no Songstream linkages to them. The association between the two was merely an informal one. Nevertheless my Durila companion on the voyage to Woodah in 1969 said that the northern part of Woodah belonged to the Durila. All thought that the central part of Woodah and the island to the west called Yiduwagba belonged to the Wurra:nggilyangba. The southern tip of Woodah was Warnungwadarrbalangwa. But the Warnungamagadjeragba (and even one old Durila man living on Groote) said that Durila country on Woodah was really Warnungamagadjeragba. The point is that because of the Durila's desire to establish permanent, by which I mean eternal, linkages in the area, their "mapping" of Woodah cannot be trusted.

In 1986 the Durila claimed places in the northern part of Woodah as their own independently of the Wamungamagadjeragba – for instance, those along the north-east coast. But then my informant went on to say that some of the places on the north-west coast were neither theirs nor the Amagadjeragba's but the Warnungwadarrbalangwa's!

The small island to the west of Woodah, Yiduwagba, which I had linked to the Wurra:nggilyangba, my Durila informant divided between them, the Wurrawilya and the Warnungwadarrbalangwa. With two water holes there, the island would certainly have been an attractive stop-over point on journeys between Groote, Bickerton and the mainland.

To be fair to the Durila, no one's mapping of Woodah can be trusted. In 1969 there were no Songstreams linking Bicketton People to either the south part of Woodah or the island to the west. The Wamungwadarrbalangwa, the Wurra:nggilyangba and the Wurrawilya, I was told in 1986, however, had been "singing up there" even during my initial visit, hoping eventually to stake a permanent, as distinct from a visiting, claim. The proper way to put it is this: Dugwururrgwa (Brolga), Wurramugwa (Ghosts), Ya:embirrgwa (Parrot Fish) – all Warnungwadarrbalangwa Songs; Yinemanenga (Wild Apples), Wurruwa:ba (Parrots) – both Wurra:nggilyangba Songs; and Yinungwagarda (Sea Eagle) – a Wurrawilya Song – are all "in there" and the Songmen are trying to find them...

To be fair to everyone, it was obvious from my mapping experiences that, over time, changes in jurisdiction did occur. The now Wurra:nggilyangba place on Bickerton, Nimbarela (#9), apparently had once belonged to the Warnungwudjaragba on Ya:embirrgwa, Parrot Fish. Within a Land, a new place would be carved out (#74), a new meaning would emerge (#68).

What my mapping experiences also taught me was that some places were deemed in greater need of demarcation than others – for instance, coastal as distinct from inland areas. Indeed it dawned on me that Bickerton Island was not considered an island at all, but rather a coastal fringe of the sea! In 1986 I had asked old Galiyawa of the Wurramarrba to draw me a map of Bickerton Island. What he drew was Figure 2. In other words he conceived the island in the form of an inverted horseshoe with the various Lands drawn as islands around. This to me was meaningless until I later realized that the Bay was the important aspect of the island, the land peripheral to it. As I discovered in 1986, general survey techniques were applied to demarcate inland boundaries such as between the Wurramara and the Wurra:nggilyangba (a line down the middle and we each take what's on either side), whereas more precise means were employed along the coast.

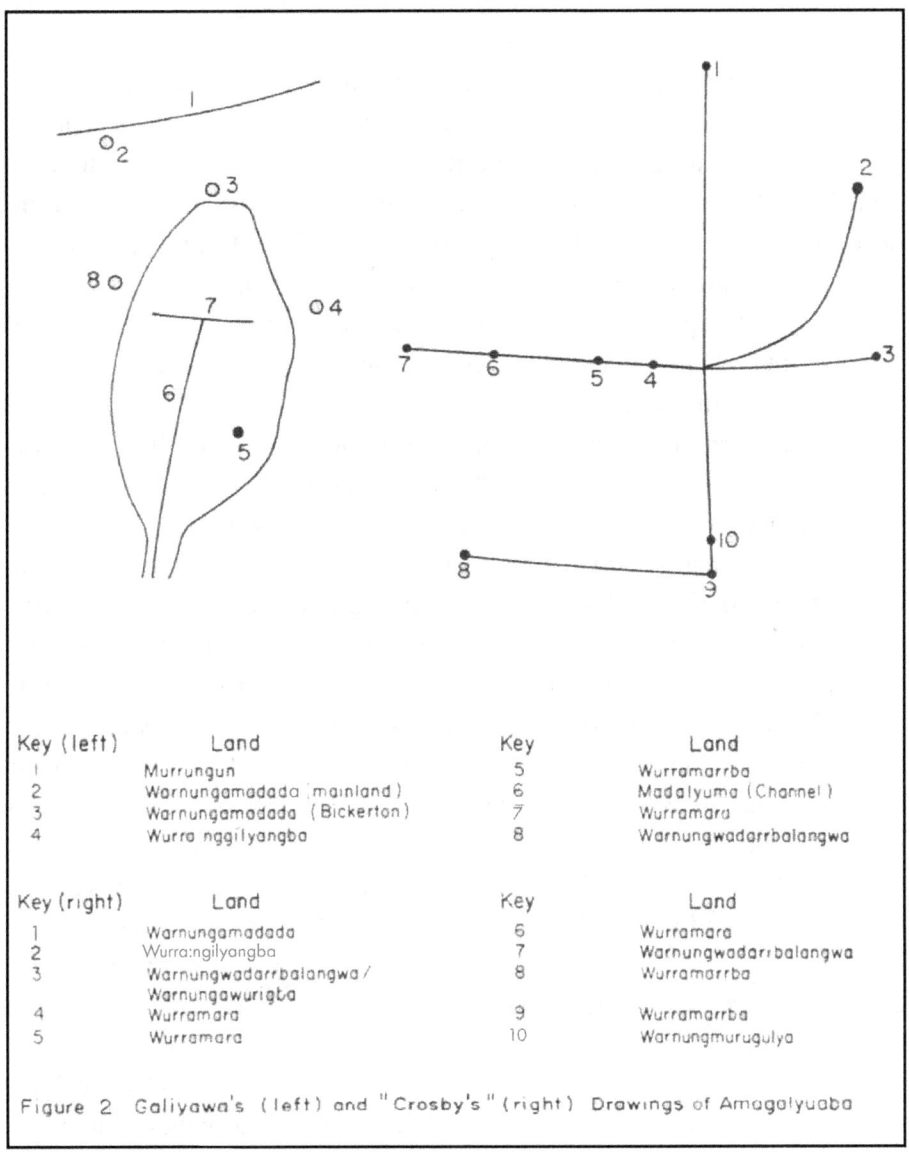

Key (left)	Land	Key	Land
1	Murrungun	5	Wurramarrba
2	Warnungamadada (mainland)	6	Madalyuma (Channel)
3	Warnungamadada (Bickerton)	7	Wurramara
4	Wurra nggilyangba	8	Warnungwadarrbalangwa

Key (right)	Land	Key	Land
1	Warnungamadada	6	Wurramara
2	Wurra:ngilyangba	7	Warnungwadarrbalangwa
3	Warnungwadarrbalangwa / Warnungawurigba	8	Wurramarrba
4	Wurramara	9	Wurramarrba
5	Wurramara	10	Warnungmurugulya

Figure 2 Galiyawa's (left) and "Crosby's" (right) Drawings of Amagalyuaba

For the most part, coastal boundaries between Lands are marked by the precise point at which a shoal begins or ends, by a dry creek bed, by the juncture of rock and land, by a point of land. Even where a disputed place is subdivided to create two new places, such as at Laugulalya between the Wurramara and Wurramarrba (#95,136), the subdivision tends to be at a visible marker. Locating the points of differentiation between places within the same Land, however, was for me a much more difficult task. Often only a site on a particular Being will be elicited and that will define the place as a whole, this place tending to merge imperceptibly into the next. "Duwurawilya" in Wurramara/Murugulya country on the east side of South Bay, for instance, is a rusty red outcropping which becomes Yingelanggwaberangmandja as it slopes down to the beach.

In other words, between different Peoples and Lands a firm line is drawn; within the same Land it isn't, even though sites have individual associations to particular People in the overall jurisdiction in question.

I also found that Land which is "bad" is even less well demarcated internally. Here, I think someone is, or was, trying to make a point about "culture". The place I have in mind is the Bad Dreaming country along the west side of South Bay. As you can see from Map 3, only three places are distinguished from the beginnings of Wurramara country in the south back into the heart of the Bay. Seven places are demarcated along a comparable section of the land across the Bay. Certainly the area is not much frequented, but not so much from barrenness as from fear. It is a dangerous place held in contrast to the east side of the Bay which is seen as positive and life-giving. Herein lies the significance of the "undifferentiation" of the Bad Dreaming side. It represents negative and life-taking forces: strange as it may sound to the Western ear, it represents the forces of unity as oneness. It is perhaps incorrect to employ the English term "boundary" in this and subsequent discussions as it carries the implication of "barrier", some sort of physical imposition to be overcome. Aboriginal boundaries, like the substances they bound, are rather transparent, permeable, allowing matter to flow between them, all the while transforming them in subtle ways to create interdependence between People(s) while preserving their respective integrity(ies) intact.

VI

The Economics of the Dreaming

It was June 6 at Angurugu before I was to travel over to Bickerton. I decided to check with Murabuda of the Wurramarrba about resource distributions on Bickerton on the off-chance – in the hope – that the information Gudigba had given me was incorrect. So certain was I that boundaries were drawn around exclusive resources to effect interdependence. Alas:

No, there's pennanent water in Wurramarrba country. There's a well at Nungwarrbamandja [#141]. That's the name of the place, "bubbling water"; it's never salty. There's also water in my country at Langgurra [#126) on the other side of the bay but it's salty. There are wells in Warnungwadarrbalangwa country, but the one in the southwest [#118) dries up at Marnariga [dry season] time and the one in the south-east is swampy. You can drink it though.

The Wurra:nggilyangba have fresh water around Arawura [#20) and there is fresh water in the sea at Mamalagunda [#23]. The old people used to tell the young people not to drink it because it was *alawudawarra* [a Dreaming site]. The old people really believed you shouldn't drink it. When they traveled near it, they would rub their sweat on the boat. But I went there with Gerry Blitner once and we put a hose down into the sea where it was and we drank it. It was really sweet fresh water. There is also water in Wurra:nggilyangba country around Yimilyamandja [#24] in some swampy country.

There's also water near Algumerramandja [#5 l] in Warnungama-dada country.

No, there's yams [*murndigrriya:rra*, long yam, *Dioscore iransversa*] all along the west coast in Warnungwadarrbalangwa country and on both points in my country. But there's none on the east side of the island. There's some in Wurrarnara country in Milya:gburra where the airstrip is. But now they have the airstrip they don't have them any more. There's other kinds of yarns [*murunggurra*, round yam, *Dioscorea bulbifera*], everywhere.

No, there's wild apples (*yinemanenga*, red wild apples, *Syzygium suborbiculare*] all over the island.

Well, this is not what I wanted to bear. Wild Apples were Sung by the Wurra:nggilyangba, and therefore prohibited as food to them, but they were not confined to their country. Same with the yams in relation to the Wurramarrba. But Murabuda's comments had raised other questions. I had wondered how "fresh water" could possibly be Sung if the implication was "therefore it is prohibited to drink". Yet here was a piece of fresh water, mamalagunda, that was Sung and so prohibited, albeit in Wurra:nggilyangba not Wurramara country. Could this imply that it was thereby permitted to the Wurramara who were prohibited from drinking their own fresh water stored in Malurba's pools? Different kinds of water were distinguished, some fresh all year 'round, some seasonal, some always brackish. Were some kinds Sung, others not? The "other kinds of yams" might be "everywhere" (which, of course, could not be literaUy true) but they, like the Long Yam, were also Sung by the Wurramarrba. Wasn't this a bit excessive, associating the staple vegetable food in both its forms with one People? The implication was that they couldn't eat it. I arrived on Bickerton with many new questions in mind.

I began my investigations with Djambana Lalara, my *nawarrga*. He was the most active sea hunter at Angurugu and knew Bickerton intimately. His People's Land was on the north part of the island. I asked him, as I would ask two other sea hunters, where were the good places to catch the two prized sea animals, *yimenda*, turtle, and *da:nunggelangwa*, dugong, as well as the much sought after fish, *yimerrarra*, "salmon" as the Aborigines translated it, but which is "milk fish" (*Chanos chanos*) to us. These fish are speared in the shallows from May into July. Then I asked him where were the best places to catch each of these species – that is, if you could go only to one place for each of them where would you go? I had some trouble with this as Djambana immediately replied "You mean where would I go first?" I anticipated that if I asked my question this way I would get places within his own country. So I repeated my original question, not knowing if he would take my meaning. In the Anindilyaugwa language "best" comes out as "a degree of better" no matter how you try and express it.

My fears seemed well founded when he located all the best dugong, salmon, and fishing-in-general places in his own country. The best turtle place was at ambiguous Anggangrnadja (#33) down the coast to the east to which be had access with impunity. "Good" places for each of these species, however, he pinpointed about the island (see Map 4).

However, when I repeated the exercise with Murabuda of the Wunamarrba he declined to locate the best places in his own country. Though he didn't pinpoint them for me he did insist that most of the species in question were found in greatest abundance along the north coast just as Djambana had said. Milumdurn of the Wurramara was more specific: not only were the best places not in his own country but his own country was one of the worst for turtle. There was no doubt that the best fishing grounds in general were along the north coast in Lalara country.

As to the good salmon/fishing, turtling and dugong hunting places there was considerable uniformity in the answers of the three men whom, by the way, I had questioned separately. Map 4, then, is really a consensus map of the better and best places around the island for the resources in question. They did caution me though that most of these species could be found just about anywhere and that to some extent their answers had to be seasonally adjusted. Of course I could not be sure that these really were the best places, but they were acting as if they really were and that amounted to much the same thing as far as I was concerned. It was their relationships to each other I was interested in.

Slowly my original hypothesis about resource areas and boundaries began to assume a more subtle, and realistic, form. It was the abundance of the resource in question that was bounded rather than the resource itself. This applied to fresh water as well as to fish, yams and wild apples. Sure they were "everywhere" but there was more of each in some countries than in others – or at least they *thought* as if there were more. There was a sense in which the Wurramara did have the fresh water, the Lalara the fish, the Wurramarrba the yams and Wurra:nggilyangba the wild apples and the Warnungwadarrbalangwa the ... ? Actually they didn't seem to have much of an abundance of anything at all except in the fishing grounds around Adrrunggurra (#119). This paucity of anything in abundance in Warnungwadarrbalangwa country perhaps explains how there could have been a famine here which did not also affect the surrounding Lands to the same degree and which caused the Warnungwadarrbalangwa to seek refuge on Groote on Land subdivided for them there by the Warnungwudjaragba.

The really interesting thing, though, was that what one had in abundance, one was prohibited from consuming. The Wurramarrba Sang both species of yams, the Wurra:nggilyangba wild apples and the Warnungwadarrbalangwa parrot fish (Ya:embirrgwa), one of the most frequently caught fish. The Wurramara Sang fresh water – or at least fresh water in the pools of Malurba, the most abundant source of fresh water on the island. There was, however, other fresh water in Wurramara country at Milyga:buna where Rainbow Serpent(s) had shed his/her tears and a well at Marngabongamadja (#74) in Old Bill's place.

Fresh water *could* be a prohibited resource – everyone had been forbidden to consume the waters of Mamalagunda (#23).

The Lalara did Sing all manner of Stingrays, including Diamond Stingray, Yimaduwaiya, and Shark Ray, Yilyanga, all edible fish but not ones regularly sought after. In other words, it would have made little difference whether they had them in abundance in their country or not. Yimerana, Salmon, which is in abundance in their country according to my informants, is Sung by the Warnungamagadjeragba of Groote. The Lalara situation on Bickerton is, I am sure, complicated by the fact that their country would have been "sliced off" from that of the Wurra:nggilyangba when they came to the island from the mainland in the recent past. Perhaps they were gearing up to developing some Fish Songs when European contact deflected them to Groote Eylandt! Who knows?

It was interesting that fishing as such could be prohibited, as around the burial island of Ngwulya except by those who were *djunggwaiya:* or bosses of the island (primarily those with Wurra:nggilyangba mothers.) But when I began to investigate the nature of these prohibitions and of prohibitions in general, again I was to see my initial expectations dashed. Murabuda was quite blunt: "Everyone can eat anything at all. With all this good bush tucker around we'd be silly not to eat it."

What prohibitions, I asked myself. But I'd seen them with my own eyes in 1969: once was on my trip to Bickerton. We had caught a stingray (*yimaduwaiya*) and while he was cooking it, Gudigba told me that he really shouldn't eat it but because there were no *djunggwaiya:* about "to make me pay", he'd have some. The "bosses" of his Land would exact a penalty from him if they'd seen him – or even known after the fact that he'd eaten his Song-species. Another instance of a similar food prohibition I recalled was likewise honoured in the breach. I was on a trip down the east coast of Groote Eylandt to see a gallery of cave paintings. We had shot some geese (*yingagiya*) and one of the men present from the Warnungangwurugwerigba Land made a point of telling everyone that he would not eat the bird because it was his Song-species. However, while he was cleaning some fish near to where the geese were cooking I saw him pop a few morsels into his mouth when he thought no one was looking.

I must admit I didn't pay a great deal of attention to the custom in 1969. I simply took at face value the older men's comments that a person shouldn't eat his or her Song-species and noted instances when this seemed not to be occurring. Maybe I had made a mistake: perhaps these were the rule rather than the exception.

This time I would be more observant. And who better to observe than Gula, the leading Songman of the islands. One Saturday, Ruth and I and the children joined him and his wives for a trip to the mouth of the Angurugu River to do some fishing with our wire-spears (*dengarrgwa*). These are wooden spears with three sharpened metal rods attached to one end. They are thrown with the aid of a spear-thrower (*yigarba* or *bandaga*, the rounded type, which is indigenous; *yimangala* the flat type was introduced from north-east Arnhem Land). The wire-spear is obviously post-contact, replacing the indigenous two-wooden-pronged fishing spear (*maugura*). This fishing spear is a hooked spear (*mamilyerigbira*) and is distinguished from the fighting hooked spears, *yalga*, barbed along one edge, *menggarrambilya*, barbed along two and *menarrgigba*, barbs both ways. These spears are ranked as to the degree of damage they can inflict, the barbs pointing back down the shaft being impossible to remove without tearing the flesh. If the spearing itself doesn't kill you then the ensuing infection will. The killing spear, *lama*, is fashioned from a piece of metal and honed until it is razor sharp. The wounding spear, *mamanugwa*, has no barbs and replaced the indigenous stone-headed spear, *miya:rnawa*.

On the walk down to the river's mouth I asked Gula about eating his Song-species. Yes he could eat it, he said, repeating more or less what Murabuda had already told me. When we arrived at the beach, Ruth, Gaiyongwa and Damaiyinggilyaba gathered wood for fire while Gula and I went out into the shallows to fish. Gula warned me to keep an eye out for bubbles moving behind us in the water. There were salt water crocodiles (*dingarrbiya*) around and we would have to be careful. As a result of this comment, he fished, I watched.

We returned with a few fish and a small stingray, *yimaduwaiya*, his Song-species. These the women cooked over the open fire. Except for the stingray. Gula picked it up himself and sang to it as he put it on the coals. I couldn't make out the words. When it was cooked he simply took it out of the fire and laid it to one side. It remained there uneaten until we left.

On the way back I asked him about the Song he had sung. He was apologizing, he said, for having killed and cooked it. Why didn't he eat it? I asked. He could eat it if he cut its head off and gave it to a *djunggwaiya:*, he said. There were no *djunggwaiya:* around. Anyway, it was too small.

I recalled something else I'd observed in 1969: the men often used to sing a few bars of a Song on arriving at a particular fishing place or when they caught a fish. They too had been apologizing for disturbing the Spirit of the Place/Species in question.

So I went back to Murabuda and questioned him about his remark that everyone could eat everything. But I'd be specific: what about his eating yams? Both varieties, the long and the round, were his Song-species. Well, he said, he really shouldn't eat the long yam, the *murndigrriya:rra*: "I have to give it to my *djunggwaiya:*. But that law is going down, down down." But was it? When one of a group of women Ruth had been sitting with mentioned she had been looking for long yams, Ruth remarked, "But you are Damarrba," implying to Ruth at least, that she shouldn't eat it because she was of the Wurramarrba People. The woman grimaced and put her head down.

I mentioned to Murabuda how definite the old men had been about not eating your Song-species when I had been here before. And then it came out. But wasn't it silly not to eat all that good tucker in the bush? Wurrabalanda (Europeans) did. To this I said, "If you can't eat your song species it means that someone else can, doesn't it? It's like the 'forbidden fruit' in the Bible. Remember what you told me was the thing you disliked most about Wurrabalanda?" Of course he did. It was their greed, taking whatever they wanted wherever they went. Aborigines weren't this way.

I wasn't sure if I was putting thoughts into Murabuda's mind or if I was causing him to rethink some changes of mind he'd already made. But we talked about this for a very long time until at last he nodded thoughtfully and excused himself. After that I had no problem eliciting information on Song-species prohibitions. Everyone was talking about them.

My original thesis was too simplistic. The major prohibitions were on those species "performed" in the sacred Mardaiya:n ceremony. This is a "remembrance" for the ancestors and their Song-species. Each People/Land has a corpus of Species whose Creative activities are imitated there and these are prohibited as food. An example is goose, Yingagiya, which is associated with the Warnungangwurugwerigba and which I observed in the breach, above, in 1969. I cannot produce a full list of these without going beyond the bounds of permissibility, so this example will have to suffice, except to say that these Song-species are singled out as a class and called *mudelarre-darr*. In the Lalara's or Warnungamadada's list one of them is *not* Stingray, yet Gula avoided it. Neither, to my knowledge, is Parrot Fish a Mardaiya:n Song-species, yet I saw it avoided during our stay on Bickerton in 1986.

One day we went in the Toyota with Gilbert and Nawurrawinya, their wives and children, to pick rock oysters (*yinungwalya, Hyotissa hyotis*) at Ngarnaburra (#110) on the north-west corner of Bickerton. Ourselves gorged and our billycans full we returned to the fire where Raymond was cooking some parrot fish. He said to his wife who was Warnungwadarrbalangwa, the People who sung this fish, "These are your countrymen. If you eat them you have to pay." Of the *yinungwalya* in my billycan he said, "You are *djunggwaiya:* for this. If they eat this they have to pay you." I was too embarrassed to ask who the "you" was he was referring to because up until this point I had not even known Yinungwalya was sung, let alone sung by someone to whom I was theoretically connected. Nor was I able to sort this out subsequently.

But by far the most interesting example of a Song-species food prohibition was another experience with Stingray, this time a Shark Ray, Yilyanga. Ruth had been fishing with the women this side of Miribamandja (#70) and hooked him from the shore. After a long struggle she finally hauled him in. This one was big enough to require special cooking which takes time so she brought it back to Milya:gburra. Fish like stingrays and sharks are cooked by cutting them up into sections and boiling or roasting them after removing the lungs. The lungs are cooked separately in their own fat in a billycan. After boiling or roasting, the meat is pared from the bones and kneaded until the water has been removed. Then it is rolled into balls and dipped in the hot fat from the lungs. It's absolutely delicious and tastes like buttered crab meat.

When we returned to Milya:gburra I suggested we give the Shark Ray to Milurndurn as a gift. I handed it to him and he said I should take it over to Old Lulungu for cooking. She called the fish *dunggwadugba:* (her "mother's mother") and it was all right for her to cook and eat it. His face beamed when I asked him if there were any *djunggwaiya:* around to stop me from having a bit. He replied that the fish was me and I couldn't eat it. But the nicest touch came the next morning after the ray had been roasting in the coals all night. Little Iain, my son, who was three, came over with me to see Lulungu moulding the flesh into balls. She beckoned him over and went to hand him some to eat. But he shook his head and said, "*Nara* (no), *ngaiyuwa* (I am)

Lalara'. Lulungu's face shone as she drew him nearer and gave him a great big hug. Later, when the two of them were alone, I saw her giving him some and he ate it.

The women would never admit to food prohibitions to a white woman and were still reluctant to do so to Ruth even though they knew she knew. The men opened up on the subject when I cited the evidence of the old men in 1969. They had the idea that it was a "silly custom" from their experience with whites – who thought their marriage and relationship rules were silly too (if they understood them at all, which they didn't). Well, here was one white who didn't think that way and I had no compunctions about convincing the Aborigines of my point of view. Perhaps, though, there was little need. When my eldest son Graeme told a group of Aboriginal boys at Angurugu that he was about to leave for Bickerton, one of them replied, "If you are Lalara and you go to Bickerton and you eat a Parrot you'll sound like a Parrot." That there was a penalty to be paid for eating one's Song-species was still being inculcated into the young early in life.

"Fresh water from the pools of Malurba", I found, could be drunk by the Wurramara after all. The Wurramara, it seems, didn't so much sing Fresh Water as sing "on" fresh water (*augwungwa mandja*), that is sing species organically or logically connected to fresh water – such as Frog, Leach, Mermaid.

In clarifying the situation, in deepening my understanding, I did discover that the original principle I had deduced as behind Song-species prohibitions (not to mention behind the forbidden fruit in the book of Genesis), still held: what one has (in abundance) is denied to you thereby making it available to someone else. The Wurramara's water supply was available to all who attended ceremonies at Mungwurridjirra – and in the old days this would have included People from Groote Eylandt and the adjacent mainland as well as Bickerton. Indeed, if the Wurramara had wanted a monopoly on water, then why allow the ceremonies to be held there? It is why, when they were later held on Groote Eylandt, that they were and still are staged beside the Angurugu River.

But the real confirmation of the principle lay in the fact that it also explained the apparent exception to the Song-species food prohibition rule. You paid the *djunggwaiya:*, or "boss" of your Land – normally someone in your mother's, father's mother's or spouse's Land – as compensation to those who would have consumed your "surplus" had you not done so yourself. In the old days this would have been food, now it is money.

I had recorded evidence of this principle of "self-denial leads to relationship" (it can hardly be called "exchange") in 1969 but missed its significance entirely:

Sunday, February 23. Morris Lalara: My *na:ningyerrga* (wife's brother) gave some fish to Mamaraiya. He's got a refrigerator. He gave some to Dagiyuwa, his *dernda:na* (in his mother's Land). Some men don't go fishing all day. I give it to them. Not to my brothers. They go fishing and get a lot of fish.

I was puzzled as to why I could discover no consistent pattern in the way food was distributed, expecting it to be on a "degree of kinship" basis. Sometimes it went to (in simple translation) "my *diyaba* (sister)", sometimes to "my *nawawa* (brother)", sometimes to my "*dungwiya* (father's sister)", at others to "my *dadingya* (wife)", to "my *dernderrga* (mother)" and even to persons like "Rupert who married a Groote Eylandt woman". Certainly you were more likely to give to those without who were closer in relationship to yourself, but that wasn't the basis of the giving. Nor did you expect a return – unless you were without and then it could come from anyone (barring a mother-in-law!). Ruth had recorded this incident in her 1969 notebook:

October the 25th. The children demand food and the parents will portion out the meat, usually to the young children. They will guard it usually until they are full, or tire of it – then they put it down, hand it to mother etc. At that point the women will take a bit, and if this doesn't invoke wrath, they will get their portion. Pieces are broken off the chunks the children have as they eat it. Though they are all indulged on demand, they learn early to share their parts.

Jeffrey demanded raisins desperately, but as soon as he received them he turned about and offered them to all the other children. This seems consistent with training in other things. Becky grabs marble from Fred. Mother demands she give it back but she won't, screaming and kicking Fred etc. Within five minutes time, Fred is still whimpering, Becky has forgotten this display of temper and Dangawala says give the marble to Fred and she does without a murmur. Fred is happy again.

It's not "sharing" they are learning at an early age but the principle of "receiving from someone who has something when you have nothing". It was not so much that Fred had a marble and Becky wanted him to share it, as Becky had no marble and Fred did. She had a right to it. Once Fred had no marble she gladly gave it back – though she really didn't give it "back". It was now hers but he was without one. He now had a right to it.

When I went through the second stage of initiation, an event I will recount in the next chapter, I was told the next day when I asked what it all meant for me personally that "You have nothing now. What we have is yours."

My point is that this isn't communalism, sharing, or even co-operation. Those terms are more appropriately applied to people who regard their property as held in common which these people do not. Rather, these Aboriginal People regard property as circulating from those who have it to those who don't. That's also the way they play cards – continuing on until one person has won everyone else's money who then must put it all back in the pot again the next day having taken out just enough for the food for him"self" or her"self".

These Aboriginal people are in another economic world – somewhere in between, or over and above, communalism and personal possession.

My original hypothesis before I returned in 1986 was that Land boundaries were drawn around exclusive resources so that no one People/Land could be self-sufficient. Now I had found out that where exclusive surpluses were bounded, they were also to some extent forbidden as food to those whose boundary it was. It was almost as if these people were imposing scarcity on a reasonably abundant environment so that social relationships of an interdependent kind would follow. In denial, in "nothing", was relationship to be established.

At first glance Bickerton may not appear as an abundant resource area. Only four land animals of any food value are found there: *dirangga*, spotted tree goanna (*Varanus timorensis scalaris*), *dugululuwawa*, frilled lizard (*Chlamydosaurus kingii*), *dilanda*, rock wallaby (*Petrogale brachyotis longmani*) and *warnungwenimbaluba*, dingo (*Canis familiaris dingo*) or wild dog. One of these, the dingo, is not eaten (the prefix *warnung-* indicates its ambivalent status between animals and man) and the other two are not even important enough not to be prohibited to some so as to be available to others – neither are sung. And outside of these animals, "all the rest is snakes", as one of my informants described Bickerton.

But the island is rich in sea food. Indeed, as I have already shown, the old men actually conceived of Bickerton not so much as an island as a stretch or band of sea fronting on land. When Ruth asked the women camped on Bickerton to list the important (*amagwulyamuda*) bush foods (*anenga* and *augwalya* non-fleshy and fleshy foods) of the island, as Table 4 shows they listed the three land animals mentioned above (minus the dingo), plus 19 other land-based foods, which together constituted just less than half the total. Twelve of the 45 were beach or shallows-situated foods, mainly shell fish; five – six counting flying foxes – were airborn; and five were sea-based, including turtles and dugong. However, here only the highly prized fish "salmon", turrum and Spanish mackerel were singled out. Include the smaller but most frequently fished species like the parrot fish, and the land-based foods would shrink to very small proportion of the total indeed.

The immediate qualification that comes to mind is, yes but ... weren't fish only speared traditionally and therefore these smaller species were of far less importance than in the post-contact period. My own information from the old men was that, in fact, fish were hooked with line and bait even before the Macassans came from Indonesia. They used the claws from the sea eagle, *yinungwagarda*, and osprey, *duwanggarrariya* as hooks and rolled threads of bark from the *manyungwunya*, sand fig tree (*Ficus superba var. henneana*) and *mabalba*, peanut tree (*Sterculia quadrifida*), for line. The last to use only this technology was Maradjui of the Murungun who was at Angurugu when 1 was first on Groote in 1969. He would have been a man of about 55. His son told me be didn't trust European technology. The last man to use only a stone axe, *marnunggwaiya*, by the way, was Wurrugumindja or Bowargurda of the Wurramarrba who died just before World War II.

Table 4. Important Food Resources of Amagalyuagba

Species or Resource	Translation	Scientific Name	Sung First By
Land-based			
dugululuwawa	frilly lizard	*Chlamydosaurus kingii*	mentioned in road to Land of Dead, anybody can sing

Species or Resource	Translation	Scientific Name	Sung First By
dirangga	spotted tree goanna/monitor	*Varanus timorensis scalaris*	nobody
dilanda	rock wallaby	*Varanus timorensis longmani*	nobody
yilyaugwa	sugar bag	from: *Trigona (Tetragona) hockingsi*	two kinds: one sung by Ngalmi, the other by Mirni yawan
murndigrriya:rra	long yam	*Dioscore transversa*	Wurramarrba
murunggurra	round yam	*Discorea bulbigera*	Wurramarrba
adamiya	hairy leafed convulvulus	*Ipeomoea abrupta, flobody velutina*	nobody
ariyuma	type of root vegetable	*Cayratia trifolia*	Murungun and Warnungwadarr-balangwa
amerndangir ungurra	grass potato	*Curculigo ensifolia*	nobody
ard	type of root vegetable	*Cartonema parviflorum*	nobody
ma:mirrgwura	potato bean	*Phaseolus dnanthus*	nobody
munenga	burrawang	*Cyca angulata*	sacred: in Mardaiya: n
(not found on Bickerton, but imported from Groote)			
manggarrgba	wild plum	*Buchanania obovata*	Nungumadjbarr

Species or Resource	Translation	Scientific Name	Sung First By
marringmerda	bush current	*Vitex glabrata*	nobody
mungarnarra	mauve convulvus	*pomoea* sp. aff. *gracilis*	nobody
magbiya	eat berries of	*Grewia orientalis*	nobody
midirridirra	custard finger	*Uvaria* sp.	nobody
mamulyilya:na	taro	*Colocasia esculenta*	nobody
alumilya	bloodwood	*Eucalyptus polycarpa*	nobody
mabalba	peanut tree	*Sterculia quadrifida*	nobody

Beach- or Shore-Based

yilarda	triton shell	*Gyrenium pusillum*	nobody
yuwalgura	Cyrene (shell)	*Geloina coaxans*	nobody
angwala	mud crab	*Scylla serrata*	Mirniyawan
yinungmugwa:na	venus shell	*Marcia hiantina Tapes veriegata*	nobody
ararugwura	mangrove oyster	*Ostrea* sp. *Sccostrea amasa*	nobody
yilyangmurra	ark shell	*Anadara antiquata*	nobody

Species or Resource	Translation	Scientific Name	Sung First By
yinungwalya	rock oyster	*Hyotissa hyotis*	nobody (?)
yinumabugwala	toothed pearl shell	*Sognomon ephippium*	nobody
yinungwambaga	giant clam shell	*Tridacna sgamosa* *Hippopus hippopus*	nobody
mungindjerrugwa (mungugwa)	top shell	*Monodonta diminuta Prothalotia* sp. *Techtus fenestratus Trocus hanleyanus Trochus niloticus Trochus pyramis*	nobody
yugwurna	baler shell	*Melo amphora*	Warnungwama-langwa
yinimamuwa	turtle eggs		nobody

Airborn

ya:lyiya	little red flying fox	*Pteropus scapulatus*	Wurrawilya
dugurrurrgwa	brolga	*Grus rubicundus*	Ngalmi and in on Warnungwadarr-balangwa
derrarragugwa	dove, peaceful bar-shouldered diamond	*Geopelia striata Geopelia humeralis Geopelia cuneata*	Wurramarrba
yidjarra	tern, common lesser crested roseate black-naped gull-billed	*Sterna hirundo Sterna bengalensis Sterna dougalli Sterna sumatrana Gelochelidon nilotica*	Nemamurdudi (mainland)

Species or Resource	Translation	Scientific Name	Sung First By
yurumba	silver gull	*Larus novae hollandia*	Warnungamagula/ Mamariga
dimirr	Torres Strait pigeon	*Duculus spilorrhoa*	nobody
Sea-based			
yimerrarra	milk fish	*Chanos chano*	Warnungamagad-jeragba
gungurn	turrum	*Carangoides fulvoguttatus*	Warnungwudja-ragba Warnungwadarrbalangwa and Murungun
mungindjaba:na	mackerel, narrow-barred	*Scomberomorus commersoni*	(?)
	Queensland school	*Scomberomorus Queenslandicus*	
	broad-barred	*Scomberomorus emifasciatum*	
	spotted	*Scomberomorus munroi*	
	shark	*Grammatorcynus bicarinatus*	
yima:nda	turtle—any kind including billed:	*Chelonia myda*	as Yimowuraga (green) and Dengalua (spoon-billed) by Mamariga People
yingmungmurn-da	snake-necked:	*Chelonia rugosa*	in mardaiya:n
a:nuwa	flatbacked:	*Chelonia depressa*	(?)

Species or Resource	Translation	Scientific Name	Sung First By
da:nunggulangwa	dugong	*Dugong dugong*	Warnungwadarr-balngwa

The situation on Bickerton accords generally with what my predecessors Fred Rose and Peter Worsley found for Groote Eylandt proper. On Groote, writes Rose in his 1960 book (pp. 14–15), 44% of the edible foods consumed by the Aborigines were fish, shellfish and sea animals while 24% were plants and 8% land animals. As on Groote, this is not to say that on Bickerton bush foods were not there in abundance. It is more, as Rose and Worsley put it in relation to Groote, that although the island was rich in bush foods traditional economic activity was nevertheless oriented toward the sea.

While we were there, the women at Milya:gburra on Bickerton would go bush at least two or three times weekly to collect vegetable foods (they would go fishing almost every day), though mainly in the vicinity of Milya:gburra. The following is an account of a typical expedition undertaken by some of the women as recorded by Ruth:

Sunday, July 27th: Went to Mungwurridjirra (#69). En route where we stopped I asked Lulungu the name of the place and she said Arumandja (#85, a general name for whole bay area). At Mungwurridjirra Lulungu stayed behind and Djamami and Darawura and I went for firewood and ended up looking for yilyaugwa (wild honey). We saw some in a new tree but it was too thick to push down so we will come back later. Then we went fishing along the beach west toward the rock face – the tide is out. Djamami is mad at me for asking so many questions (especially why they are shy of David), and Iain (our son) would not walk and was whiny so I turned around and went back to see Lulungu. I fished for a bit on the shore and then went back to her. She wanted to go for wild honey. But first she pointed out the places around the bay by marking lines in the sand like this: ||||| . Each time she added a line she called out a place name. First she called the Warnungwadarrbalangwa places ("our" places – she is Murungun), the Wurra:nggilyangba places (Gadjarua's), and then went on about "their" places, Yinbiya (#129) (the Wurramarrba's) and so on.

Then we went for wild honey. We went back into the mangroves and circled the whole lot. She could point to trees that she had previously cut. We went right back to the cliff. Called area "Arumandja" again. (How they look for wild honey: the sign is the bees – holes in tree and if bees are entering. If they think it's there they hit the trees and look for the bees to leave. They also listen to the tree for the noise of the bees.) Found three lots. The first Lulungu found and she hit the tree and I saw the bees escape. There was only a little in there, enough for one of the children to eat. Then, much later, I saw a hole with bees entering, high up in a tree. We cut it down and we got a lot. The cone part is thrown out and the darker part with the honey in it is eaten.

I found a third in the crotch of an old tree. Then we circled back to the beach. Iain found some *alumilya* (bloodwood). Lulungu said it was good food. On our return I asked Djamarni what it was. She said she didn't know – or was she still mad about asking too many questions. Darawura said they used to eat it when they were children and gave me the name. Lulungu knocked it with an ax and inside there was a hollow area with some small, pink shreds inside – rather like fine coconut. It had a bland taste. Then we went fishing.

Michelle (our daughter) caught a small fish and we used half of it for bait. Just as the rain started to fall I hooked a large fish. Eventually I pulled in a three-foot *yilyanga* (shark ray). Drenched, everyone was under the trees and Lulungu tried to stir up the fire to warm us. Then the Toyota came. On the way back Djamarni and Darawura counted five *dugululuwawa* (frilly lizards), but we didn't stop to catch them. I said name of *yilyanga* and said "Lalara *langwa*?" (sung by Lalara?). "Yau" (yes), was the reply.

"Can David eat it?" "Lalara *nagina*, Lalara *baba nara*" (he's Lalara, so no). She laughed. I asked repeatedly and she said no, "*Nar'alybaruma nara*" (He can't eat).

On the way back we saw that the grass had been burned. Djamami asked who had lit the fires.

"Joe had," said Darawura. She pointed in the direction of Nambirrirrma's place and said something about *warnunggwarba* (men). I asked, "Joe *augwa* (and) *nagina*?", pointing to David in the front seat. They agreed. Joe must have told them where he and David had been . . . they knew about why and wherefore.

The women were knowledgeable of resource bases all over the island and could be very specific about where they would go for certain species of plant food. Resources numbered 5 to 10 on the above list, they said – and experience bore this out – were found together (as part of the same ecosystem). The women singled out a number of places on Bickerton where they were to be found in abundance. These I have marked on the resource map (as BF). Two other foods, the wild plum and the bush current, are also found together and I have marked the best places in which to obtain these (as BCP).

It is interesting that the women would consider *munenga* or burrawang a Bickerton bush food when it is not indigenous to the island. It was imported from Groote Eylandt and had to be carefully treated by washing to remove a toxic substance before being ground into flour and used to make damper. The three sites where it was plentiful on Groote were Yedigba or the Emerald River, in Wurramaminyamandja country, Amalyigba just east of the present mining township of Alyangula along the coast in Warnungwadarrbalangwa country and the Amagula River down south in the country of the People of the same name. It is also interesting that burrawang alone of these plant foods is celebrated in the sacred Mardaiya:n ceremony.

You can see from my resource map that alone of all the Lands, only the Wurra:nggilyangba seem to lack the long yam which, next to burrawang, was regarded as a staple food by these Aborigines. The women said that the long yam was in fact found in Wurra:nggilyangba country but that they were very small and not eaten. With regard to the round yam, *murunggurra*, the women said that it wasn't really an important food and they don't eat it any more. Old Lulungu pointed out that it had to be soaked before being used and was now not worth the effort. But the comment is also an indication there were sufficient long yams and other tubers – and in pre contact times sufficient burrawang – that foods of lesser quality were ignored.

In contrast to plant foods and fish, the women would not target areas they considered particularly abundant in a particular species of shell fish. They were "everywhere". The one exception was the rock oysters of Ngamaburra (#110). "Catching" shell fish is quite an operation and you may be interested in how it is done. I took the following excerpt from one of Ruth's 1969 notebooks:

September 2. Today we were out for oysters, two Wurramara women – Janice and Damiya – and seven children. Again they sit with their legs apart, no horror at not wearing pants when I'm around, one little girl playing with the genitals of the boy with real laughter and fun.

They at first discouraged me from going out into the water – but only a little. They find the oysters in the weedy areas with their feet. Comically, I thought, we sort of shuffle around abstractedly 3/4 in H_2O feeling for the flat types of shells which are often in clumps attached to a larger, apparently non-edible, substance.

Within an hour or so two women and I collected two large potato sacks full which we dragged along beneath the water.

On returning we were cold and gladly huddled over the fire. The women covered their bodies in warm sand – an excellent hot-water bottle. Foodwise, immediately we threw shells into the fire and covered them with hot coals for a few moments. They naturally handed me a few, no questions asked, thinking I knew all about it. Unlike the missionaries who try to keep me as far away as possible from what they are doing.

As we ate, they too were eager to hear about my family and stories of Canada. Just back of the shade we built is a waterhole or what have you: you dig down a yard or so in the middle of the sand. Gets gradually wetter until the water appears beautiful tasting slightly chalky in colour, perhaps from the yellow sand.

It's not so much birds that are sought after on Bickerton as their eggs. The only one hunted for food is the brolga and this is because it can be speared (or shot) while it is walking about. Apart from the salt water billabong where Rainbow Serpent(s) made her way into Bickerton, there are no "oases" on the island where birds congregate to be catchable. At one of these, a well-aimed throwing stick in their midst (or today a shotgun blast) would always bag a few. Although there are seagull egg places around the island, one of the best spots for them is the small island deep in South Bay (#82) where that old man is sitting on his rock telling people to go away. No wonder with all those seagull eggs there! It's no coincidence that the island is in "Bad Dreaming" country. The old man is, in fact, acting against the whole foundations of the culture: he has something, and to have something should be to make it available to someone else who has nothing.

The other major seagull egg site is the island of Anggangmadja (#33) off the north-west coast.

Ya:lyiya, or flying foxes, are found in the mangrove swamps and these days are shot. They taste something like a very gamey wild duck.

Rock wallabies, though not highly prized as food, are to be found anywhere in the rocky outcroppings that dominate the central and northern parts of the island. Today they are shot and in pre-contact times speared. The spotted tree goanna/monitor is found in hollow logs anywhere on the island, as is the frilled lizard, though neither are actively sought after.

Sugar-bag, *yilyaugwa*, or wild honey, is, however, and even an old woman like Lulungu will spend many hours with her ax felling a tree with sugar-bag in it once she has spotted the tell-tale bees buzzing about in its upper reaches. Sugar-bag is also sometimes found in the ground or in the rocks conveniently packaged in pellets produced by stingless bees. And that's the way it is eaten: honey, wax and bees and all.

Mengaliga, or pandanus, too is found "all over the place" and is actively sought when ripe. When it turns red it falls to the ground and is opened up and the nut taken out and eaten.

The wildlife on Bickerton has a certain Liliputian quality to it, as if nature had taken a slight detour here and decided to fine tune rather than expand her creations. The only wallabies are rock wallabies. The magpie larks, *dugurrabura*, (*Grallina cyanoleuca*) are of the miniaturized variety and are noticeable as such even to the untrained eye in comparison with their "brothers and sisters" on Groote. The butcher birds *angwurrida* (*Cracticus nigrogularis*) may not be made in miniature but at least seem so here. To wake up to their morning-song each day was sheer delight, so much so that I was moved to tape record their calls back and forth to start the day. (I play it on these cold winter Canadian nights to rekindle the warmth in my soul that each morning at Milya:gburra brought.)

On Bickerton the birds even speak: Duwalya calls, "here is the boat, here is the boat", as if, the Aborigines interpret it, to warn the locals that their peace is about to be disturbed by uninvited guests.

It took about two weeks before I really noticed it, but my whole body began to unwind. I guess it was partly the pace – or lack of it. Getting up at daybreak, lighting your fire, boiling your billy, preparing the damper and tea supplemented by any left-over fish from the previous evening, ambling about waiting for consensus to take us fishing along the beach at Yingelanggwaberangamandja (#92), or in search of root vegetables near Arumandja or mapping sites and resource areas. At some point something would happen;

after a time I didn't really care exactly when myself. Somehow everything always seemed to get done, including my work. I began to feel very peaceful and at ease with myself. I suspect that diet, though, bad much to do with it. Far from the Angurugu store we lived on whatever became available from the bush and sea, supplementing it as the Aborigines did with the aforementioned damper and tea. As well, there were no dogs, no fights and no alcohol – and only a few people: 10 to 20 at the most though the numbers fluctuated as events unfolded or didn't at Angurugu on Groote. After a month I could have stayed forever. The Aborigines must have noticed it, because just before we left to return to Canada, Peter Wurramara, whose Land this was, said we could come back and stay on Bickerton – forever.

Bickerton is an island of about 100 square miles. I had originally hypothesized that you could redraw its internal boundaries around exclusive resources so as to be able to encompass with one what now was encompassed by two. I thought this would demonstrate that there had been an element of choice involved in the delineation of the original boundaries between People/Lands. That hypothesis has since given way to something far more subtle, and indicative that intent is indeed at work here. As you've seen, for one thing I would no longer talk of exclusive resources, but of exclusive abundances. No one Land is without fish, for instance, and most have some kind of fresh water supply however poor its quality. Yet the Wurramara have fresh water in abundance year round, the Wurramarrba an abundance of long yams, the Warnungamadada the best fishing grounds and the Wurra:nggilyangba seem to have the island's major supply of wild apples and would have had its best fishing grounds before the northern strip of their Land was subdivided for the Warnungamadada in the pre-contact period.

It's the Warnungwadarrbalangwa who seem to have least in the way of resources and, interestingly, it's the Warnungwadarrbalangwa who seem to have held jurisdiction over the largest land mass on the island – about 30 square miles (counting Land they have on the south-east and north-east comers). They are followed by the Wurra:nggilyangba at about 25 and the Wurramara at 20, followed in turn by the Wurramarrba at 15 and the Warnungamadada at 10. While I don't want to make much of this we could say that land mass varies inversely with resource base, though I'm not sure how we can measure the Wurramara's fresh water against the Wurramarrba's yams, and the Warnungamadada's Land would have originally belonged to the Wurra:nggilyangba.

Given that, objectively speaking, there is no shortage of food anywhere in this island area considered as an unbounded domain, we must conclude that humans have created "artificial shortages", and compensated those for whom little or no "abundance" could be located with greater areas of Land by drawing boundaries in a particular manner (I could not even begin to compare sea-areas in these terms though each Bickerton Land does also include a large expanse of sea). As I pointed out in the Introduction, Bickerton could have been an internally undifferentiated island belonging to but one People; indeed this would seem "natural" from our point of view. But no.

Even more than this, and certainly in keeping with the basic principle behind it, there is evidence that these Aboriginal people actually squeezed a large population into a small area(s) in order, again, to preclude the possibility of self-sufficiency on the part of any one segment of them and to promote interdependence between them. An estimate of the Groote Eylandt area population, including Bickerton but not the adjacent mainland, is available from Tindale for 1925. He puts it at 300. In 1941 Rose estimated the islands' population at between 300 and 350 or one person for three square miles. This is high when compared to other parts of Australia, particularly the Centre, and is particularly high when compared to that of other hunting and gathering peoples around the world. But it is low compared to what it probably actually was. We must take the reports of a major epidemic sweeping through here seriously and consider that the population may have been reduced by as much as a third – two-thirds if recent estimates by Noel Butlin in his book *Our Original Aggression* of the effects of smallpox on the Aboriginal population in the first few years of contact in southern Australia are any indication.

Interestingly, the only estimate I have of Bickerton Island's pre-contact population puts it at about one person per square mile. It comes from Old Galiyawa. I had asked him if he could remember how many people were living on Bickerton when he was a young man before the Wurrabalanda or white man came. He remembered the time when his grandfather was alive. What he gave me was a list of men's names and their Lands. There were 10 men in all, one from the Wurra:nggilyangba, two from the Murungun, one from the Warnungamadada, two from the Wurramara and four from the Wurramarrba. My Promised Land histories showed that these 10 men had a total of 27 wives and 62 children, making a grand total of 99 people.

I am certain of the accuracy of Galiyawa's estimate of the number of men because he did not simply give me a list of all the men on the generation in question. There are those on my histories he did not mention but whose names he knew; presumably they had died by the time he was thinking about or perhaps had been living elsewhere. Furthermore, among the 10 were two single men who died before marrying which indicates he did not simply leave out any whose line did not continue down to the present generation. What I cannot be sure of is whether the wives and children on my histories were contemporaneous with the time period he had in mind. Allowing for this, we can say with some certainty that the pre-contact population density of Bickerton – long after the epidemic – was more likely to be higher than that estimated by Rose.

Each bit of data, by itself, would not allow us to draw a firm conclusion about the way Amagalyuagba economics works. But together, all the bits add up to a consistency and it is this: people imposed a type of scarcity on abundance so that social consequences of a certain kind would follow. Taking it all to its logical conclusion, stripping away all qualifications and hesitations based on "real-life" situations, we can say that what they did was impose abstractly conceived blocks and lines of "empty" Space on the material landscape so that each People had more of one thing within their space than others bad within theirs while at the same time being denied (wholesale) access to it. This not only rearranged the relations among People but also the material landscape itself by transforming it into a landScape.

Either the Aborigines grasped the law that from "nothing", or renunciation, peaceful relationship flows and consciously implemented it as policy, or they were moved unconsciously by historical forces to implement it despite themselves. But there is a third alternative: they were guided in a certain direction by perception in interaction with nature. This brings us back to the question of "Spirit".

A means to the realization of relationship as I have just outlined it, however imperfectly realized in practice, is the identification of Species with Person(s) through common source in Spirit which carries the implication that therefore the species in question is denied to you as food. It is not so much that species are sung because they are important as food, as they are important enough to be prohibited as food and therefore a catalyst to interdependence in social relationships. This implies that, to Aborigines, life-givers themselves have life, are animated by Spirit, and are therefore sung. I can't test out whether species sung have greater food value than the unsung, having no means of measuring the relative weights attached to foods in the pre-contact period. But I can fall back for support on the Aborigines' own perception of the issue.

In 1969 we were camped overnight on Adrrunggurra (# 119) which is little more than a sand bar in the sea dotted with a few whistling pines. I selected what I thought was a good sleeping spot on the far side of the fire but noticed that my Aboriginal companions were not joining me. Suddenly I felt the reason why: a sharp pain began to penetrate my lower back. Just as suddenly Galiyawa was beside me and with his hand knocked something off me. It was a scorpion (*ma:rribura*). I had lain too close to a nest and disturbed one of them. If you don't disturb them, as my companions would not, there was no problem. You couldn't camp where there were no scorpions because on this island they were everywhere. The point is Galiyawa's comment on my subsequent question. Still in pain but always the professional, I had asked him who sang scorpion. "Nobody," he replied, "Rubbish thing."

Burrawang was a staple and its Spirit is commemorated in the sacred Mardaiya:n ceremony. Bickerton land animals are not sung and are eaten, but not a great deal of importance is attached to them as a food source. But the highly prized "salmon" and turrum are sung as are turtle and dugong. On the other hand, shell fish are not sung, with the exception of baler shell which is also used as a receptacle. But "rubbish things" like *denena*, mosquito, are sung, this one by the Warnungwadarrbalangwa. There is something to my thesis, then, but this is obviously not all there is to it. As to what more there might be, we will have to await our return to Angurugu after this sojourn on Bickerton is over.

Where Spirit fits more solidly into the Aboriginal economic scheme of things is in its ability to allow you to move out from where you have "nothing" to where something is available, as well as to move back to where you have "something" in order that you can make it available to someone else.

Spirit as a substance permeating a stretch of land, sea and air as well as yourself is the linchpin in the whole enterprise. Without it nothing in a literal sense is possible. Let me illustrate by way of an example.

You remember that supposed famine on the west coast of Bickerton which apparently drove the Warnungwadarrbalangwa over to Groote. If my economic thesis is true, how can one possibly suffer from famine? Isn't something somewhere else where there is no famine automatically made available to you? The answer is "yes", but not "simply".

In the first place, a famine is not just going to hit one part of Bickerton and not another. But areas with an abundance in something are going to experience less hardship than those without an abundance. The Warnungwadarrbalangwa on Bickerton were without an abundance. There's no doubt that the Warnungwadarrbalangwa would not be denied what had become less of another Land's abundance. The trick, though, is how to gain access to it via the rules that have developed over the millennia to activate the "s/he who has nothing is due something" principle. The only ties the Warnungwadarrbalangwa have to the other Peoples of Bickerton which would allow them a right of access to their Lands is marriage. And marriage ties link them to but two other Lands – one in any given generation – those of the Wurramara and the Wurramarrba. These they marry in alternate generations. These ties may not be enough when a crisis in resources hits. One of the People you marry, for instance (and for whatever reason), may decide to allow more access to the other People they marry rather than to you. Perhaps they wish more access to their Land than to yours. But there is a safety valve. And the Warnungwadarrbalangwa used it. It is the Songstream.

The Warnungwadarrbalangwa follow Ya:ambirrgwa, Parrot Fish, and Bara, West Wind, not to mention Dambul, Ghost Pulling Ceremonial Posts, to the Warnungwudjaragba on Groote. A part of the Djaragba's Spirit is the Warnungwadarrbalangwa's and vice versa. Both are predisposed to access one another. There is no need even for one party to set up shop permanently in the midst of the other. They can simply remain there as visitors until the crisis at home passes and return. This is the advantage that Spirit affords. You can leave it behind you when you go while carrying it with you wherever you may wander, secure in the knowledge that where you came from is still "yours" to go back to – as the people with whom you are staying are secure in the knowledge that you have no designs on the Land that is "theirs". As host and guest we live in peaceful co-existence together yet always, when judged by this other dimension, in a sense apart.

This is the route the Warnungwadarrbalangwa chose to go – on the invitation (as is appropriate under circumstances leaving them with "nothing") of the Warnungwudjaragba. Indeed, the Warnungwudjaragba went so far as to subdivide their country on Groote Eylandt on Bara, the West Wind, giving the part where he touched down to the Warnungwadarrbalangwa as a permanent Promised Land, keeping the rest to the east for themselves. What the Nambirrirrma story is trying to do, I think, is convince the Warnungwadarrbalangwa that the marriage route is still open. The remaining Bickerton Peoples are now the ones with "nothing" – no marriage system – now that one of the four Peoples there have departed. But not to worry, the Warnungamadada will come over from the mainland to fill the gap by subdividing Wurra:nggilyangba Land on Stingray. And through all this the Warnungwadarrbalangwa still retain their Lands on Bickerton, the Warnungamadada theirs on the adjacent mainland.

No indeed, Amagalyuagba is by no means an island entire unto itself. On the contrary (Map 5): the Lands it contains are a particular manifestation of something quite universal and eternal.

VII

Songstreams

Agwilyunggwa

A few weeks into my stay on Bickerton I was called back to a funeral at Angurugu. My *diyabarrga* (elder sister) had died and Gula was to lead the Singing. He insisted I be there.

Nawgulaba:na used to be a young reprobate; now he is an old reprobate. I love this old man. He has never said hello and he has never said good-bye. Right from the outset he has known we would spend the rest of his life, at least, knowing each other. He knows that I think he knows that his culture hasn't got a chance. He also knows that knowing that is why I came back and why, having come back, he keeps on teaching me. He also knows that he can only teach me so much and he also knows the reason why. If he can't teach me, Europeans just can't be taught. That's why they call him, but not me, "the Professor".

Gula drinks too much. The sparkle in his eyes has given way to a heavy dullness. The voice isn't as clear now, as other Aborigines put it. But the wisdom is still there. Everyone knows that, including Gula. He cultivates the impression with a long white beard and carefully arranged coiffure – and three wives. The wisdom is why no one tries to do anything about the drinking. There's the respect, of course, but there's also fear – fear that no one else will know as much when he dies. No matter what front I put on, no matter how much I encourage him in his genius, he knows that I think he knows that his culture hasn't got a chance. And he knows I'm wrong. It's his *people* who don't have a chance, not his culture. That will still be there whether there are people to practice it or not. What will still be there is Amawurrena, Spirituality, on the "other side" and the source of what is on "this side". Gula described his experience of Amawurrena while singing in Agwilyunggwa, a phase of mortuary ceremonies.

> You can look and see the place in your mind. You can see it, but it's not there in front of you. Same with Stingray following Central Hill's track. Then it's Yinemawurrena – it means a shadow in your brain.

Like *awarrawalya* – shadow. If it was Dove it would be Damawurrena.

Old Badjura [of the Amagula], Baima [of the Warnungwamalangwa], Banjo [Gula's father] could do it. Nanggulilya [his brother]? Not quite. Alan [another brother]? Not quite. Murabuda can do it. Old Quartpot [of the Wurramarrba] could do it more than Galiyawa [Murabuda's father]. Alex [Quartpot's son] can do it.

The shadow in your mind is like the real fish, but it's a shadow.

I used to love to sit and sing with my father. I was nervous in front of Wanadjamaiya, Wanaiya, Baima and the old men. My father told me to take it [the Song]. But I was too shy. But finally I opened up when Admiral's [his brother] daughter died. My father said, "I won't sing any more. You can take it" [Alumera, Silt, and Amalila, Dry-Itchy Place].

And another time he said:

I can't draw it in a book or even in the sand. I can't draw the Stingray, when I see the Stingray in Song. I can't draw the Silt, but it is in my mind. That thing comes out from my brain. I can see with my brain. Not with my eyes but with my brain.

You see Amawurrena in one form when you sing in Agwilyunggwa and other phases of mortuary ceremonies where the Spirit of the dead person is taken through to the "other side", the fifth dimension. But you have to be a Songman to see it. I learned more from Murabuda:

When you Sing you see a shadow in your mind. When I Sing Ship it is bouncing up and down on the waves, going along all happy. I see my *numerarrga* [grandfather] way back. His face and what he looked like even though I've never seen him. He looks different from anyone I know. I feel … [at this point Murabuda let out a big heavy sigh]. Everyone sees something different.

Murabuda now tried to explain to me what the difference was. We had been talking in Anindilyaugwa but slipping into English every time he sensed I was stuck. Such a time was now. Murabuda looked up and glanced out the window of my "office". He asked me what I saw in the eucalyptus tree just beyond the verandah. Sensing he was testing my sensory capabilities I pointed out a bit of light here, a bit of shadow there, the contrast with the blue sky behind, the lightness of the tree up high compared to lower down. He just smiled and said, "The tree is a garden. Do you see that it's cold? I didn't. "Do you see the smokiness around the tree?"

"The what?"

"Angwura ubera". Of course I didn't. Murabuda said he loved the tree. That was the difference between Aborigines and Europeans. The "smokiness around the tree" was a manifestation of Amawurrena. That's what he loved about the tree.

I have seen Arnawurrena three times – once as an "inside experience" of the kind Gula is referring to, and twice as an "outside experience" in the way Murabuda just mentioned. In this book I'll only talk about the outside experiences and on both occasions they occurred on Bickerton. At least I think what I saw was what Gula and Murabuda were talking about. I'll never be absolutely sure.

A phrase in one of the Songs I had recorded in 1969 and transcribed for my 1974 book had always stuck in my mind. It was *megamainggamandja,* "the sea is laughing with whitecaps". It occurred in a Wunamara Song about the Rainbow Snake(s) in his/her/their Channel. Now how do waves "laugh"?, I had asked myself when I worked out this translation. The answer was no more illuminating when I asked my informants. I was, however, told the conditions under which waves laugh. It is in dry season, Mamariga or South-East Wind time, in the afternoon when the wind comes up and the tide is coming in.

My puzzle over the phrase came to mind one afternoon on Bickerton because the wind had come up particularly strongly and I knew from fishing the previous day that the tide was coming in. I rushed over to Gilbert's hut and asked him if I could borrow the Toyota and, jumping in, I drove down the bush track toward my own personal favourite spot on the island, A:nemurr-emadja (#7), on the south-east corner of the island. Before it, stretching back down the Gulf, was a channel of open water between Groote and the adjacent mainland. If I was going to see waves laughing anywhere it was here.

I parked the Toyota back along the track which had now become little more than a sand dune. To continue on down to the beach in the Toyota was to risk getting bogged. I was by myself and wouldn't chance it. As I walked down off the dune and on to the beach I looked up at the sea. The waves were laughing. I don't know how to explain it, but they were. So was I: chuckling away deep inside myself. The whole sea was alive. I don't know if you've seen the Japanese painter Hokusai's "The Great Wave off Kanagawa" (in *Masterworks of Ukiyo-E* by Narazaki); I don't mean the whole scene with the boats at the base in the foreground, but just the wave itself (Plate 12). It was like looking at a million such waves arranged within a grid, each precisely the same, each with the same wisp of whitecap spitting from its peak, each chuckling away to itself. The impression was of something in motion which was at the same time at rest. I became overwhelmed by a sense of Form over and above the individual waves themselves. What I now saw was waveForm(s) through which real water was flowing. I just sat there on the beach – beaming.

The next day the conditions seemed to repeat themselves. And again I raced off in the Toyota, this time armed with my camera and taking Ruth. Well, the conditions were the same all right, but the waves weren't laughing. We just stood there and looked out onto a choppy sea on a windy day. I felt the camera in my hand and realized how stupid I had been. Cameras only record what we have seen before and see now in a material sense. The chemicals emulsions of film are designed to reflect what the average European sees, not what an Aborigine sees. Even if I had seen the waves laughing again how could a camera possibly record the impression? We headed back to Milya:gburra. It was far too windy even to do any fishing.

Plate 12 (above). Hokusai's "The Great Wave Off Kanagawa"
Plate 13 (below). Lawren Harris' "Pic Island, Lake Superior"

An account of the second time something like this happened to me will have to wait until we return to Amagalyuagba in 1987. But let me draw a preliminary conclusion from the two together: at least some of the Aboriginal people actually see another dimension to what we regard as the "real" world – material existence, empirical events. Though this "Amawurrena" can only be truly grasped while singing Agwilyunggwa, enough of it is evident in everyday experience to confirm them in their deeper cosmological beliefs. This is the experience of illuminated Form or Presence I mentioned above. If we Europeans can't see it then there's something lacking in us, in much the same way as, from an Aboriginal point of view, dogs are lacking in fully human capabilities though able to achieve at least the potential for higher things. For this they are rewarded with personal names on "rubbish places". Fortunately for our own self-esteem, our own potential in Aboriginal terms, we Europeans are Wurrabalanda and are worthy of names, if on our own places.

Can women see it? I don't know for sure and neither does Ruth. It's not something a man can discuss with women or women discuss with each other. I do know, however, that women can't lead the singing, nor can they "pull" the *yiraga,* or dronepipe, which accompanies the singing. Very old women may be allowed to accompany or "come in on" the Singing, but only on the sidelines and not as active participants. They do, however, have full access to the Song texts, though they may not have access to the real meaning of a text during a performance. But then, neither does anyone but the lead Songmen themselves.

It is the origin-Songs whose meaning the men keep privately "secret" as they sing in public. These are not really "origin-Songs" in the sense that they locate "the beginnings" of a People/Land or a particular custom or ceremony at the dawn of time. They are "origin" in the sense of locating which people sing what Songs and why. It is locating what Song is being sung at the moment that is the difficult part. Even if you hear the name of a particular Creative Being in a Song and its activities described, you may be fooled. To give you an example, take Derrarragugwa. Derrarragugwa is Peaceful Dove, but it is also Spider, and unless you know virtually everything there is to know about "Dreamtime" Doves and Spiders as well as real doves and spiders, there is no way you can tell which is being Sung by whom at any given point in time.

The real meaning of the Songs was the sole thing men kept from the women in traditional times (ignoring for the moment the Songs of the introduced Mardaiya:n, Gunabibi and Marndiwala ceremonies which are held in seclusion away from the women). By allowing women to hear the Songs and know the stories behind them, the men could check the extent to which they were actually succeeding in keeping the subtleties of the Singing from them. Hence they had a standard against which to hone their skills.

If this sounds like gender bias, it really isn't, because the old men kept the same knowledge from the younger men – even those within the Songman's own People/Land – and only *some* of the younger men ever came to realize the fullness of the Truth. Most only got it to a degree. But, then, so did the women. The older men in one Land kept their own brand of the Truth from the older men in other Lands through the same means. What was the point of this? It was to anticipate the unfolding of a "revelation" to the "uninitiated" later in life. Without going into detail at this point, the point was to lull the young, and the women, into believing that unity was the predominant organizing principle in both the real and the Spiritual world. Men in other Lands were lulled into believing that this is what you in your Land believed. You were lulled into believing, for example, that Doves and Spiders were the same. And if they were the same, then it would follow that the Peoples/Lands singing them were the same.

To take another example, the Wurrawilya People sing Angwura, but then so do the Wurramarrba, the Amagadjeragba, the Durila and the Mamariga. Angwura is Fire or Smoke. Yes but … not really. The Wurrawilya sing a fire that didn't work, as we saw when we translated the meaning of the place Nemabergunga merugura (#6) on Bickerton. The Warnindilyaugwa sing Angwura as Smoke on the South-East Wind. The Wurramarrba sing Angwura as the "Fire of a Shooting Star", that is, its tail. So do the Warnungamagadjeragba. The Durila sing the Shooting Star itself, Dangalarridjanga. They can "come in on" Angwura, but they can't themselves lead in the singing. Only the Wurramarrba sing Angwura as Fire and Smoke as such and they sing it in such a way that it is very hard for someone who is not Wurramarrba to know when they are singing which.

The untutored, then, are lulled into thinking that the Wurramarrba are so stupid that they confound in culture something which is differentiated in reality, such as smoke and fire. The Wurramarrba gain great satisfaction in letting them think this, knowing that all along they alone know the Truth.

Nobody lies, nobody cheats, nobody (well, almost nobody as we'll see) steals. They simply perform the Truth and dare people – challenge them really – to crack the code to it. "Challenge", because when they do crack it they can participate in it.

When I was out on Bickerton I decided to take a chance and finally test this out on a woman to see just how much she really knew. I would ask Old Lulungu, the oldest women remaining in the area, who it was that sang Angwura. She herself was Murungun. As I wrote in my notebook following the incident, "I asked Lulungu whose Song Angwura was. She looked at me and at the fire in front of her and with a perturbed look on her face, started talking about something else."

Murabuda told me that he first learned of the Ship story from his *dunggwarrga* (grandmother). This is an origin story telling what People/Land really has the right to sing smoke and fire and what is the difference between smoke and fire. The woman who told it to him was from Murabuda's mother's mother's Land, not his own. My question to Lulungu, then, was rather a naive one. It may be that everyone knows what's what but no one lets on they know. Who knows?

I have to believe that the women see what the men see of Amawurrena in the world around them. As to whether they see the same fullness of it that some of the men see when they are Singing, I don't know.

Because men and women see something of it under everyday circumstances, and because I have seen it, for however brief a moment, I have to consider it real. (The "non-religious" can relax: whether real or merely an idea, the consequences for material existence are exactly the same.)

The Agwilyunggwa at Angurugu was for Balalya, my *diyabarrga* ("elder sister"). She was Nandjiwarra's wife. Of all the people I had known in 1969, Nandjiwarra was the one who had now visibly changed the most. He had been a powerfully-built man, in the mould of Gudigba. It was Nandjiwarra who had really made it possible for me to come to Groote Eylandt. And it was Nandjiwarra who had created quite a stir in Australia's daily newspapers when he announced at the conference he was attending in Perth, Western Australia, in 1968 that the missionaries had been "playing about" with the Aboriginal women and it had better stop. He was referring to an isolated incident but that's not the way it came out in the newspapers. It was Nandjiwarra who made sure we were able to stay at Angurugu to "write their Bible" in 1969. When the Mission superintendent told us that no suitable accommodation was or would be available it was Nandjiwarra who organized the elders to demand otherwise – by threatening to go to the *Sydney Morning Herald* with more stories. A quick petitionary prayer on the steps of the Council office and we were staying.

Since I had last been here Nandjiwarra had been awarded the MBE (Member of the British Empire), for his contribution to Aboriginal development. If it had been intended that this would shut *him* up it hadn't worked very well, because he was still railing away against both Europeans and his own Peoples who did not see things his way. In matters anticipating the disastrous consequences of further contact with Europeans, he was usually right.

In his outspokenness Nandjiwarra was unusual amongst Aboriginal men. Politically, he was always ahead of his time, in much the same way as Gula was always ahead of our time in a Spiritual sense. Only Nandjiwarra's "time" included Europeans. He had learned European rhetorical devices such as over-assertiveness and was applying them to dealings with his own Peoples. Though this was resented by most of the elders, nobody could do anything about it. There was the wisdom factor here too. But Nandjiwarra had also suffered a massive heart attack and now resembled a victim of the neurological degenerative "wasting disease". Most of his life was spent sitting around with his wife – and playing cards.

Balalya's death represented a tremendous loss to him and he took it hard. The men thought that he would not last six months. Her Agwilyunggwa was to be a major happening. People would be invited over from Numbulwar on the adjacent mainland and from Aurukun in Queensland where two of Nandjiwarra's daughters had (unsuccessfully as it turned out) married. Balalya had visited these places. She, like the Creative Beings when they traveled about in the long, long ago – and contemporarily in another dimension – had left something of herself – her Spirituality – in these places when she visited. This would have to be "cleaned up", with the help of those in the host country.

Agwilyunggwa is one of four stages of the mortuary rites that follow the death (Nidjungwa) itself: first, taking the Spirit away (Ngarrilya:namerra); second, burning the deceased's possessions (Ngarrima:yadaga); third, painting those in the same Land and generation (Agwilyunggwa); and, fifth, burying a lock of the deceased's hair (Mamungba). A fifth stage, Amunduwurrarria, or "remembrance" used to be performed a few years after the person died in the pre-contact era but this has been dropped, or really absorbed by the Mardaiya:n ceremony introduced from the mainland. I won't repeat the details of all this here as I did so in my 1974 book, *Tradition and Transformation*. Even then a "short way" was distinguished from a "long way" of performing mortuary ceremonies. In the "short" version, sequences one and two are collapsed and performed on the same day and may be combined with the sequence two of other persons recently deceased who have not yet completed this part of their journey. I say "journey" because the Songmen pick up the Spirit of the dead person from the place where s/he is buried and transfer it to Braulgwa, what I initially took to be the Land of the Dead.

Braulgwa is said to lay beneath the sea beyond Amburrgba, North-East Island, off the coast of Groote. On the way there the Songmen pick up the deceased's ancestral Spirits – and their own if they are from a different Land – and bring them along on the journey. The major innovation I had noted in 1969 was that for some, the journey was now to "Heaven" in the sky, rather than to Braulgwa in the sea, and the jump-off point on that journey was Central Hill on Groote, not North-East Island. This had been so irrespective of Peoples' Promised Land affiliations. Even in pre-contact times all Peoples used the North-East Island route once they had left their own respective countries with their ancestral Spirits (in this manifestation of Amawurrena, referred to as "Wurramugwa").

Some of the traditional "jumping off points" for the various Peoples/Lands were as follows: for the Wurramara, Malurba on Bickerton; for all the Wurragwagwa (Lalara, Wurra:nggilyangba etc.), Yandarranga or Central Hill on Groote and Galerrunda a Central Hill manifestation on the mainland; for the Warnungwadarrbalangwa Manggudja, a Bara or West Wind place on the mainland; for the Wurramarrba, Yinbiya on Bickerton; for the Warnindilyaugwa, Aiyawalyamandja in Dalimbo country on the South-east corner of Groote; for the Wurrawilya, Marangguwida, on South Point over on the other corner of Groote. Amburrgba or North-East Island was properly the "jumping off point" for the Warnungamagadjeragba and the Warnungwamalangwa.

In addition, each People/Land has other places – also the names of important old people and Creative Beings – referred to as *alara* (lit. "big name") where they paint up to conclude the first two parts of the ceremony. Those who share (or at least use) the same *alara* in their Songs paint up together. They are "one Company" as the Aborigines refer to them in English, having no proper name for the groupings themselves Three such names for the Wurragwagwa are Yinunggwawiya (a Personal name), and Amandjuwa:na and Amumbugwadja (both places in Warnungangwurugwerigba country on Groote Eylandt). Four of those used by the Wurramara and the Warnungamagula are Amagbarranga, A:rrirra:gba and Nambirr-irrma (names on Arumandja on Bickerton), and Angwinjuma (a place in Amagula country in the south part of Groote). Affiliation with *alara* is the basis of the division of the People/Lands into four Companies. As they were given to me by Gula in 1969 they were (reading from the mainland to Groote):

1. Nundirribala – Wurramara – Amagula = on Madalyuma, Sea Channel.
2. Mirniyawan – Wurramarrba – Warnungwamalangwa (Bara Bara) – Warnungamagadjeragba = on Midjiyanga, Ship, and Derrarragurgwa, as Dove.
3. Ngalmi – Warnungamadada (Lalara) – Wurra:nggilyangba –Warnungangwurugwerigba = on Yandarranga, Central Hill.
4. Murungun – Wurrabadelamba (Warnungwadarrbalangwa) Warnungwudjaragba = on Dambul.

In comparison with the list in Table 2, which is my own composite compilation, you can see that three of the Groote-Bickerton Lands mentioned there, the Wurramaminyamandja, the Mamariga and the Wurrawilya, are not mentioned here. The Wurramaminyamandja are one of the only two Peoples/Lands who share *all* their Songs with another, in this case the Warnungamadada. They "come in on" the Stingrays, Sawfish and Parrot as well as the derivatives Silt and Dry-itchy Place – with one qualification: they have their own Tunes for these things. The Amagula likewise share their Songs with the Mamariga and they are an offshoot of that People/Land in fairly recent times, though there was some differentiating of Songs going on between the two by 1969 (with Mamalerrbirra, Mungarrarnbilya and Amalgamura [all Hooked Spears], as well as Amureba [Stringybark], Yinigarrbiyama [Caterpillar], Delada [South Wind], and, of course, Madalyuma [Rainbow Serpent(s)' Sea Channel] and its Shallow Pait [Yilyerra], becoming the primary responsibility/right of the Amagula). This process seems largely to have drawn to a halt for reasons we will come to in Part III.

The Wurrawilya seem not to be affiliated permanently with anyone at all, though in 1969 they were leaning toward the Warnungwadarr-balangwa although they were said to have ties to the Nemamurdudi of the mainland on the Milky Way. This would link them indirectly to the Wurramaminyamandja.

"Coming in on" the wrong *alara* is a Songman's greatest fear. Gula, who himself has access to six, said if he makes a mistake and mentions the wrong one – or someone else's – at the wrong time or in the wrong place, he will have to pay dearly, these days in the form of money or goods. What the other Songmen around you are watching for is the chance that you might sing "too far into" someone else's Place, thereby implicitly extending your jurisdiction. The lesson is, you had better know your own Songs in their most minute detail so you can countermand this practice if necessary.

If you now compare the above list of Companies with the so-called "clan groupings" used today for purposes of representation to the Angurugu Community Government Council (page 42) you will see considerable consistency, the "couples" there containing the People/Lands most closely linked in Spiritual terms here. The Wurra:nggilyangba and the Warnungangwurugwerigba, however, seem to have merged as "Wurragwagwa", though this is only for purposes of representation on Council, the former being very few in number. The lone-wolf Wurrawilya have been combined with the, by now virtually extinct, Wurramaminyamandja. The basis of this association, though, is anomalous: common residential affiliation (the criterion deplored by Nambirrirrma). The Wurrawilya are said by others to be "moving in on" the Wurramaminyamandja, not by Song but by an association of "grandfathers" who camped together in Wurramaminyamandja country. By the same token, the Warnungamadada and the Wurramaminyamandja are drifting apart as the latter fear the former are moving in on them too far – by Song.

If others are watching to make sure you don't "move in on them" with your Song they equally are waiting for you to "make a space" for them to move into if your own knowledge is lacking. How they are going to do this is not something of which they wish to forewarn you. As a result, everyone is on their toes. In a non-literate culture such as this such intensity is what keeps that culture continuing.

A special term *ayerrderra* refers to the language of "catching people out" in the context of Singing. This is the language of leading another Songman on to see if he is bluffing and keeping it to yourself when you find out. This is the language of giving someone enough rope with which to hang himself.

Balalya died, I believe, on the Wednesday in Gove. This, however, didn't stop some of the men – including Gula – from going drinking at the club at Alyangula on the same day, and Nandjiwarra was mad. This meant they'd been drinking when they returned to sing his wife that night. To make his point he persuaded the Mining Company to close the club to Aboriginal drinkers and the Council to close the shop at Angurugu. Now Gula and a lot of other people were mad. If people are mad, the Spirit of the person won't leave. It would all have to be sorted out.

Gula had begun singing as soon as news of his sister's death reached him. He went down to Yenbakwa in Amagula country where she had been living then began gathering up all the ancestral Spirits from his own country – or rather Hell. The innovation I mentioned earlier about some Singing to Heaven carried with it the implication that up to that point they had been mistakenly singing the Spirits of the dead to Hell. The place the old men knew about couldn't have been Heaven because they didn't mention God or Jesus. The fifth dimension, then, had two planes and the implications were clear. The Wurramugwa were "devils".

The innovation was made by Wanaiya of the Warnungwadarrbalangwa and Gula, along with some of the other Mission Aborigines, had followed it. The Aborigines at Umbakumba hadn't. In 1986 I found this situation unchanged, except for the fact that some Aborigines, like Nambadj of the Amagula, were Singing "two ways": to Heaven when the leading Songman insisted on it and to Braulgwa when the leading Songman didn't. No one had as yet resolved the issue as in a sense there was no issue to resolve. Accommodating the difference was more important.

I joined them on Saturday night. Gula and the Lalara were in the middle of a line of Songmen and *yiraga* players with their Nunggubuyu counterparts flanking them on either side. One of these was Giningai of the Ngalmi, an important sacred-ceremony man. They were all facing toward the north-west following the Spirits of the Dead on a journey through their country. By now they had reached the Armadadi coast and were preparing to cross the Gulf to Groote. All the men were joking and apparently happy.

If you are sad the Spirit of the dead person will linger around, realizing that the ties it has in its human form are too close to break. But one old woman, listening to the Singing in the group beside the campfire at the house on our left, was wailing away to herself.

I noted later the apparent incongruity of the men Singing in the light of a campfire through which flickered the shadows of petrol sniffers passing by on the road on the other side, while in the camp in front of us the sound of rock music blared forth from the kids' ghetto-blasters.

Sunday there was no singing, though I knew from Isaac, Nambadj's son and the chief *yiraga* player (the role assigned to those in Lands unconnected to the dead person's Songstream), that one had been planned. Where was Gula? Playing cards? His daughter said he was in his house, mad about the club being closed. In any event, on Monday Gula and the lads were back at it again, singing away. That's the day I had walked into my "office" and found I was sharing it with the empty coffin. They had just finished it at the shop and no one else wanted to live with it.

By Tuesday the Aurukun people had arrived from Queensland, and that night and the next they sang Songs in their part of the camp in harmonies that I associate with the South Pacific islands – very unaboriginal to my ear, but then I am biased toward Groote Eylandt music. I was told they were singing hymns.

The funeral was set for Thursday at 10 a.m. Things though got complicated when someone sang the shop and the club at Alyangula late Monday night. The Spirit he had put there on the doorstep first had to be sent back to where it had come from before the funeral could begin. There had also been some illegal drinking and subsequent fighting. Back in 1969 this would have been enough to postpone events indefinitely. But this was 1986 and too much had gone into the preparations. Those with the appropriate authority turned a blind eye. Fortunately the 'plane carrying the body was delayed until noon which gave the organizers the breathing space they needed. When it finally landed they were ready.

From the airport into the cemetery the road was lined with piles of grass and leaves. I was sitting beside Gula with the other Songmen just in front of the airport when the 'plane touched down. Nandjiwarra and some of the *djunggwaiya:* of Balalya's Land helped him off-load the body into the coffin. So far all was relatively calm, though you could feel the electricity in the air. The coffin was placed in the Council station wagon and the entourage set off for the cemetery. This, the funeral procession, I had never seen before; the innovation apparently had been introduced a few years earlier. The idea of the fires along the way was a traditional adaptation by the Umbakunba people. What happened just before the funeral procession took place was more familiar: the *djunggwaiya:*, in a line, came at the body with their spears cocked on their spear-throwers acting out Duwalya, Curlew, a Lalara Creative Being: one foot forward, the other foot up in the air, then that foot down and the other foot raised. The dance imitates Duwalya's behaviour at night. The spears, cocked and then thrust down into the ground, represent Duwalya pecking for grubs. I had seen the same dance at a mortuary ceremony at Umbakumba in 1969.

The entourage moved along the road with the *djunggwaiya:* lighting the piles of leaves and grass just ahead of them, as I had done for Milurndum on Bickerton to make the path safe for him to follow. As they did so, again something new to my experience happened. Nanggabarra of the Wurrabadelamba began wailing and gashing himself on the head with a knife. A few of the older women joined him. Soon a chorus of grief trailed beside the entourage. Some of the *djungwaiya:*, visibly shaken, moved to console them and lead them away. Disapproval showed on the faces of the Songmen. We were at a dangerous stage in the proceedings and this would only make it more difficult for them to release the Spirit.

When we reached the cemetery the procession stopped and the *dunggwaiya:* repeated the Duwalya dance. Then the station wagon drove the body and Nandjiwarra through the cemetery to the gravesite for a burial service conducted by Aringari. With few exceptions, most of those who attended were women. Most of the men had moved across the river to the settlement where Gula would lead the Singing of Balalya's Spirit to Heaven (to another dimension, in any event). I stayed at the service for a time – until Aringari had succeeded in calming the older women down sufficiently to proceed with the service – and then made my way over to join Gula and the lads in the Singing. I did note, though, that Balalya's grave had been dug in a straight line with others of her Land, anchored at the far end by old Banjo, Gula's father.

By the time I arrived back in the camp, so far as I could make out Balalya's Spirit had already been taken away and the ancestral Spirits were on their way to the spot where we were seated – simultaneously an *alara* in

Balalya's country. Country can move in Song too. This, however – Singing the Spirit away before the ancestors had arrived – was new to me. It was apparently done in case there were any further overt displays of grief by any of the men. The plan now was to burn her personal possessions and smoke the things she recently had been in close contact with – the station wagon, her bedding, a motor boat, the house she stayed in – and then begin the return journey of the Spirits to their various countries/Hell or whatever.

I was sitting to the left and slightly behind Gula when the *djunggwaiya:* brought in the large grinding stones and ochres. What was a thick line of people facing south to Nandjiwarra's house and the approaching Spirits slowly began to rearrange itself into clusters of sub-lines – Lalara with the same father and mother here, Lalara with the same father but a different mother there and so on. An apparently undifferentiated mass was becoming differentiated; "the law" was unfolding as the ancestral Spirits approached. The phenomenon was not unfamiliar to me: during the Marndiwala circumcision ceremony I witnessed in 1969 where the women turned the young boys over to the men as an undifferentiated mass, all painted in the same way in contrast to the men who were painted in their individual/Land designs. As the night progressed the boys were differentiated into their own various lines.

I looked to the far end of the assembly and saw Nenindilyaraugwagwa and realized I was in the wrong sub-line. In 1969 I had been affiliated with "Johnny" and his line, primarily because his camp was adjacent to where we had pitched our tent. Here I was now sitting with Gula. On the other hand, Gula had insisted. I was there, I thought, as the "official anthropologist" of Balalya's Agwilyunggwa. Because it was Nandjiwarra, they wanted the ceremony "covered." Then I turned and looked ahead past Gula to the perimeter. And suddenly it dawned on me just what was going on. There was Nawurawinya of the Wurramara sitting there grinning at me from ear to ear and twisting his wrists back and forth alternatively in the grip of either hand. As a *djunggwaiya:* he was overseeing the performance and one of the performers was going to be me! The parallel to Marndiwala was much closer than I had thought.

I had two choices. Either I could make a point of picking up my camera and leaving the assembly as if to find a better vantage point from which to photograph the proceedings – in other words I could feign ignorance and thereby avoid offending anyone. Or I could stay in the assembly and get painted up not knowing the full implications of doing so. I sat there, feeling.

Then I realized: deep down I wanted this to happen and my greatest fear was that it wouldn't.

The Singing began to build up signaling the approach of the Spirits. The *djunggwaiya:* seated beside the grinding stones began to pour a few drops of water on them and rub in the red ochre. An invisible message passed between Gula and the *djunggwaiya:*. The fires over at the house were lit and the *djunggwaiya:* began painting the Lalara up. Most received just a strip of red ochre around their wrists. Those closer to Balalya, however – those in her line – were painted with a more elaborate design. It consisted of a band of red ochre bounded by white stripes around the wrists as well as the calves and a herringbone design on the front and back of the trunk of the body. The latter is associated with a Mardaiya:n, or sacred ceremony, Song. A facial design can be added which consists of a circle of white around the perimeter of the face bisected with a line under the eyes over the bridge of the nose.

Across the way women similarly close to Balalya were being painted with the calf and wrist design. The *djunggwaiya:* to my right was from Numbulwar. He finished painting a band of ochre around the wrists of those seated with me and then hesitated, seemingly uncertain. Gula, who had his back to us, suddenly interrupted his singing and turned to the *djunggwaiya:* to his left, just behind me. I couldn't see who it was. "Him too" (in wrong sub-line or not), he said, and the *djunggwaiya:* came over and painted me up. Gula then returned to the business of getting those Spirits away from here before they could do any damage. That, of course, was the real purpose of the smoke.

I was really feeling satisfied. It was like being admitted into Sunday Morning Hockey in my home town of Perth in Canada (see Turner 1992).

The next day, however, I was brought back down to earth with a bang. I found out what the implications were! I was heading over to where Milurndurn was staying to find out when we would be going back to Bickerton. Gudigba who had come over from Bickerton to be painted up intercepted me. He had been drinking. A "bush club" had followed the Agwilyunggwa. I had never seen Gudigba under the influence before. He looked pretty serious and for some reason I felt a bit nervous. We went around to the side of the house.

"Why did you come back?" he asked aggressively. Before I could respond he followed on with: "Now that you've been painted up you can't leave."

This is what I had been worried about even as the ceremony proceeded. I knew it would have some implication like this, though I was hoping it would not be this extreme. After some discussion with Gudigba on this point he at least qualified his ultimatum: "If you leave you will have to pay." Difficult to deal with as this was, I was intrigued by the idea. We would think of paying for the privilege of staying! Here you paid to go because you were taking something of yourself away and had to leave something of yourself behind to fill the gap. He said something else that was the reverse of our way of thinking: "From now on you have nothing. Everything we have is yours." We would expect the second sentence to have run, "Everything you have is ours". The way Gudigba put it at least confirmed my economic thesis about the "renunciation" of resources even if the implications for me seemed mildly disturbing. But then what did I expect? Everything to go along on my terms as it had up to now?

On the other hand, what use was I to them inside, if I could ever really be inside? Outside connected in I could at least mediate with officialdom on their behalf. I went to talk to Murabuda about "the problem".

No worries, he said. Being painted up means you are welcome here any time. Yes I could go away – he was the *djunggwaiya:* and he determined what went on, not Gudigba. This latter remark only served to rekindle my anxieties. Would Gudigba and others resent my appeal to a *djunggwaiya:?* This would not be the end of the matter.

One thing the painting up did mean was that if Gula died first I would have to come back for his Agwilyunggwa. But they would pay my fares. If I died first they would come to my home in Canada....

In Balalya's case the burial, singing the Spirit away, burning the possessions, and painting up were all held on the same day (there is no sequence four, Mamungba in the case of a woman). In 1969 things were never speeded up to this extent. And when they were speeded up to some extent it was largely because a number of people had died in a short space of time – six during my stay there – and they were having trouble keeping up. The Agwilyunggwa for Balalya, however, does not reflect a weakening in tradition. In the first place, women were *always* more likely than men to be "done" the short way. In the second place, Nandjiwarra wanted to put on a good show, particularly for the Aurukun people from Queensland. Collapsing sequences like this produced exactly that. The whole event was finished off with, as the Aborigines themselves phrased it, "a barbecue" on Friday night.

In fact, the Agwilyunggwa phase itself had not been completed. It still remained to "clean up" Balalya's Spirit-matter in places she had frequented in her recent past. This meant smoking the houses she had stayed in elsewhere as well as painting up any "brothers and sisters" she had, who had not been able to attend the ceremony. This meant going off to Aurukun.

Now I don't want to be cynical about this, but ... they did charter a DC-3 at considerable expense; they did have it wait for them at Aurukun over the weekend until the job was done; and it did return half empty because some of them decided to stay in Aurukun for a holiday to be chartered back later also at considerable expense. On the other hand, it was mining royalties' money. If you had money you spent it or gave it away, if you didn't ... *"mama"* which in Australianese translates as "she'll be right". If you had *big* money you simply spent it on bigger things. Anyway, how better to spend money than on renewing your ties to other People at the very point when the tie-er had vanished. These, like yourself, were people who had been indelibly imprinted with the Presence of the deceased when alive, now and forever shall be, and to whom you would always be linked.

Yes, I was learning. That's why I was so worried that I might have to stay!

Not that there weren't significant changes in the ceremony at Angurugu in 1986 compared to 1969. Late that night, after Balalya had been laid to rest, the petrol sniffers sneaked into the church and performed their own ceremony for her. What the substance of the ceremony was I don't know, but they did steal a chalice from the altar so obviously whatever they did they intended to repeat. The major change in the ceremony from 1969, then, was that only a segment of the society as a whole now performed it.

The dwindling number of potential performers was matched by a dwindling number of old men of Gula's calibre. In 1969 there were at least half-a-dozen more qualified than he at Angurugu alone: Badjura, Baima, Balrumba, Crosby and the like. Now there was just Gula. What this has meant is that the People of other Lands might have to rely on a few like Gula to help them maintain their own traditions. In the course of Singing over a 30-year period, Gula and a few others have picked up a great deal of knowledge about other People's Songs, though they were not allowed to perform them themselves.

If they are to be the teachers, however, this will lead to some diminishment since they will not be party to the full details of the multiple-meaning singing characteristic of another People/Land. For them to be teachers, the other People/Lands will have to relax the rules about only passing on Songs down the male line in the People/Land in question.

With people from other Lands helping the "hosts" out as they sing in mortuary ceremonies it might appear to the untutored observer that "everyone sings just about everything". Nothing could be further from the Truth.

Life's Logic Present
I was puzzled by something I had recorded in 1969 and published in my *Tradition and Transformation*. On page 73 I had mentioned that Mangiyanga, Shark, was sung by the Warnungamagadjeragba of Groote and connected them to Woodah Island and thence to the Durila People. At the same time I was told that Mangiyanga was also sung by the Murungun of the adjacent mainland. How could this be?, I wondered. They were People/Lands that intermarried. Such a Spiritual connectedness implied that you couldn't intermarry with the Wurramara (and formerly the Warnungmurugulya) who did likewise. In 1986 I came back to this question. I asked Gula about the "sharks".

Both the Warnungamagadjeragba and Murungun sharks were *mangiyanga*, but the Murungun shark was hammerhead shark, *mungwarra*, whereas the Warnungamagadjeragba Shark was *baungudja*, tiger shark. But not really ... *mangiyanga* referred to any shark with a round face, *baungudja* to any with a pointed nose (Figure 3).

In other words, *mangiyanga* was not a superordinate class – and yet it was. *Baungudja* could be included within it and yet it had a pointed nose. And there was more to come: in his list of *baungudja*, Gula names *yimurrbunga* which refers to brown-spotted cat-shark, among others. In fact it refers to this fish specifically as well as to any that is a "savage animal in the sea". These are the fish everyone is frightened of when they go spear fishing in the shallows. But the term can *also* be used to refer to *yimaduwaiya* or diamond stingray which isn't a shark at all. Or is it? That it isn't is just our way of looking at it.

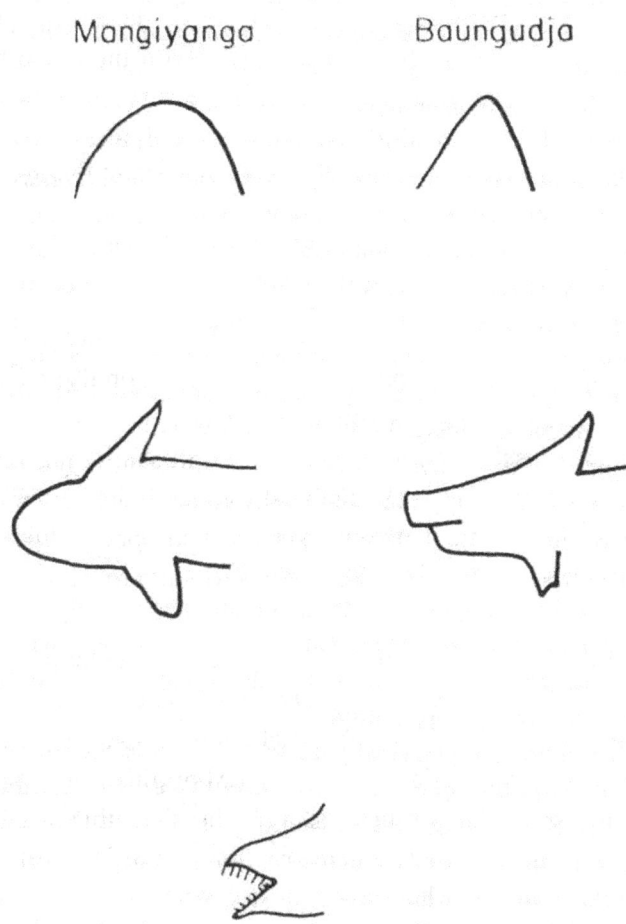

Figure 3. Gula's Drawing of Sharks

Finally I began to clue in, with Gula's help of course: "We call them all *mangiyanga* because they have the same teeth," said Gula. *Mangiyanga*, then, was an attribute of something, not its general form. *Baungudja*, pointed nose and all, could be considered *mangiyanga* for this reason. But *mangiyanga* also referred to any shark with this tooth formation with a round face. There was a general class there, but it was not all-inclusive. The very idea of "all inclusiveness", of unity on a universal level, was an anathema to these Aboriginal people. Every time they reached that plane they qualified it by also referring back to something less inclusive on the plane below. Their means of doing this was to use an attribute or part of something on one plane to define the whole of something on another which already was pre-differentiated from something else. This is why affiliation with *baungudja* did not carry the implication that the Murungun and the Warnungamagadjeragba were Spiritually connected. At the level of *baungudja-sameness*, sameness simply did not exist.

The contradiction which is at first apparent, then, is not real. What is real is paradox – something that continually comes back on itself. Just when you think you've got it, it escapes you. Just when you think you have located a superordinate class in *yimurrbunga* – since all sharks are dangerous, the term might be a term for all sharks – they go and stick stingrays in! To us this reflects an inability to mutually exclude and oppose. To them it is the Logic of Life. It's the logic of relationships which transcends exclusion and opposition.

The "List of 'totems' principally associated with Bickerton local groups" I provided in *Tradition and Transformation* (Table 15) should have been labeled "list of Songs sung first by Bickerton People in their own sector of the Songstream in question". Again, the Aboriginal logic of relationship confounds the issue of who sings this and who sings that. A People or Person doesn't Sing something exclusively; nor do they share the same Creative Being with others, though they do share the same Songstream which, however, is meaningless in and of itself as a grouping principle without a manifestation being specified and this is always something sectorialized and particular. Let's take the example of Yandarranga, Central Hill.

All those singing Central Hill's path are "Wurragwagwa", but not really. Wurragwagwa also refers to those on the last leg of his journey from Bickerton to Groote. The Lalara are only Wurragwagwa when actually singing on Central Hill. When they are not they are themselves; that is to say they are singing other things. The Lalara "come in on" Central Hill when singing Stingrays. The Stingrays, Yimaduwaiya and Yilyanga, joined Central Hill as he entered Bickerton and became part of him as he traveled across, becoming themselves again once he reached Arawura on the other side where he threw them off into the sea. From there, with Yugurredangwa, Saw Fish, they made their way to the Angurugu River where they were joined by Magaberramera, Shovel-nosed Ray, in their quest to cut the Angurugu River. Shovel-nosed Ray is sung by Warnungwadarrbalangwa. Does this mean that the Warnungwadarrbalangwa and the Lalara are one Company? To the contrary, Shovel-nosed Ray is an anti-connector, there to demonstrate the absence of connection. He tries to cut the River and fails, turning back to the sea, leaving the job to Sawfish who swims through followed by the Stingrays (my 1974 account of this tale in *Tradition and Transformation* is garbled because I had failed to grasp this principle).

When Central Hill was in the sea coming over to Bickerton from the mainland he had to decide whether to follow Dugurrurrgwa, Brolga, or Yilyanga. He chose Yilyanga.

But Shovel-nosed Ray didn't do anything, create anything, with the trio on that stretch of Land and Sea. The trio did, but only a trough through the place, which is the only part, properly speaking, that belongs to them. In Angwurugwerigba country to the east they met up with Central Hill again who, in the meantime, had cut his own trough across Groote from the north west coast. The trio "settled with" him there, but this time together, apart. Instead of becoming a permanent part of Central Hill, as they potentially were when crossing Bickerton, the trio climbed to the top of him to have a better look at the Land before becoming Lake Hubert, their tail(s) forming the outlet of his salt water lake to the sea.

This makes sense in culture, but what is the logic of the connection of Central Hill to the Stingrays in nature? 1 was stumped on this too until one day I was telling Murabuda how Ruth caught that stingray on Bickerton. It was as if my theoretical question had already occurred to him. Cooked stingray (culture) and raw stingray (nature) were in two different forms. Cooked stingray was like (raw) Central Hill, Murabuda said, insofar as it was rolled up and moulded into "little hills". A transformed aspect of one, then – flesh of Stingray – was correlated with the untransformed "other" to effect the relationship. Again, the principle at work was this: an aspect of one was seen as analogous to an aspect of another and juxtaposed to establish a connection.

This is what Creation was/is all about – it too put a part of one in the other and vice versa without affecting the integrity of either. For a Creative Being merely to have visited a country was not enough. To have passed by and called out the name of a country was even less connecting. On the other hand, to Create in a foreign place to the extent of completely re-Creating it in one's own image was entirely unacceptable. Hence the differentiation of each branch of the Wurragwagwa from each other and from non Wurragwagwa.

The Lalara, then, are differentiated as singing first on Dangerous Snakes, which refers to the King Brown (Ya:ya:rrindangwa), in particular and to this Snake plus Brown (Yanggamamindangwa), and Death Adder (Dedadda, prob. Aboriginalized English) in general. They also sing first on the Stingrays and Sawfish, though the Wurra:nggilyangba can "come in on" Yilyanga, Shovel-nosed Ray. While the Lalara sing first on Mamalagunda, Fresh Water Spring in Sea, the Wurra:nggilyangba Sing Ederra, a particular Cave near the Spring, causing them to come in with each other. The Wurra:nggilyangba can also come in with the Lalara (or vice versa) on Merrua or Tide on Stingray, on Alumera or Silt and on Amalila or Dry-itchy Place. Wurrawa:ba, Parrot, is really Wurra:nggilyangba first, but Wurruwa:begba or Big Parrot is Lalara first; both, though, come in on each other's Songs. The Wurra:nggilyangba sing Yuwa:ba, Meat Ant, first and also Yinimanenga, Wild Apples, not to mention Magarda, Sea, on Parrot. The Lalara sing first on Mabunda, Softwood and Duwalya, Curlew.

With the Ngalmi the Lalara sing Central Hill on the mainland and take over as he moves out into the sea. With the Ngalmi too they sing Dijirradudi, a Small Bird with a Long Beak, as well as Malbunmggu (Bush Turkey), Dilyangbulyuwa (Small Stinging Fish), Yunggwurna (a Fresh Water Fish), Yingagiya (Goose), Wurrawuminya (Duck), Dubulguma (Merten's Water Goanna) and King Brown Snake, all of these on Central Hill and all Songs of mainland origin.

I haven't worked out the intricate "part of one in the other" connections for all of these, nor included the Warnungangwurugwerigba's Songs on Groote. But it can still be done if you and your collaborators have the patience. Here I merely want to point out the complexity of relationship and the error that would result from designating different People as singing the "same" or "different" Songs. The best illustration of my point, however, is the Wurramaminyamandja of Groote who, as I have pointed out, do sing precisely the same Songs, equal first, with the Lalara, but still insist on differentiating themselves by choosing different Tunes or melodies, *Augway-agayama,* on which to do it.

Ask a woman, though, and you will gain the impression that the Wurragwagwa are one People sharing the same Songs. I did ask Didjidi of the Wurra:nggilyangba and this is what she told me. But I also asked her brother Nawaradidja and saw my own impression of differentiation confirmed. This is not due to "contact" but is built into the culture as we saw when we examined how men's knowledge is different from that of women.

If I may digress for a moment into theory, in nature it is women who represent "relationship" the way the men conceive it, being in and of themselves the Logic of Life. Pregnant, they alone are an indivisible yet ununifiable "two". Here, a part of the one is in the other and vice versa without affecting the integrity of either. And the men know it; why else would they perform sacred ceremonies in secret simulating the women's reproductive processes? I am thinking here of the Gunabibi ceremony held on the mainland and in which the Groote and Bickerton Islanders now participate. The men, then, pursue and covet intellectually and rationally what the women *are* physiologically and intuitively.

I can't go into the details of the Gunabibi ceremony precisely for the reason that the ceremony has sacred-secret aspects (just as I cannot go into the Marndiwala circumcision ceremony, also of recent mainland origins, through which I was put symbolically in 1969). But I can say that another level of relationship between Peoples/Lands does exist which I have not mentioned as yet but which these ceremonies justify/brought into being. Anthropologists refer to it as a moiety division effecting a division into two. On Groote Eylandt the Aborigines have no names for these divisions of Peoples/Lands, just as they have no names for the four Companies. But they do exist.

On "our side", *yirra:nigaberra* (from my Lalara point of view), connections were formed by the Gilyirringgilyirring, a "Mob of Men and Women" who traveled down the coast on the adjacent mainland, Creating and Relating as they went. Their exploits are celebrated in the Gunabibi ceremony. However, the Mob never quite made it to Bickerton or Groote and thus don't really join us all into one Company. Our Company thus remains distinct from that in which the Warnungwadarrbalangwa are situated. Nevertheless we perform Gunabibi with them. There is, however, a rumour amongst the mainland Gunabibi Peoples that the Mob called out the name of South Point as they passed down the coast, thereby establishing some kind of a connection between us and the Wurrawilya in the other Company, but we have not yet accepted this as Truth. Nor had we in 1969. The "other side", *wurra:nigaberra,* are linked into one and perform a different ceremony, Mardaiya:n, which celebrates the fact of their connection in Song.

On the "other side", however, the connections are somewhat more firmly established, though less firmly so than between Peoples/Lands within the same Company. The links in question here were forged by Blaur or Djadjabul as he walked from Dilyargurrba on the south-east corner of Groote along the south coast and thence by sea to Bickerton, passing through Wurramara country and into the sea again at North Bay, from there making his way to the mainland. At least that's the Groote and Bickerton peoples' version; the mainlanders have him going in the opposite direction. But that's another story.

In any event, as he moved he called out the names of all the Peoples/Lands in the two heretofore separate Companies in question which include the Wurramara in one and the Wurramarrba in the other. However, Blaur actually only Created in Lands in one of these Companies, the one containing the Wurramara, the Mamariga and the Amagula. These were already linked on the Madalyuma or Sea Channel of the Rainbow Serpent and the relation consolidated by an exchange of countries at either end. A piece of the Wurramara's just offshore at Milya:gburra "went" to the mouth of the Amagula River and a piece of the Amagula's at the mouth of the Amagula River "went" just offshore near Milya:gburra. In his travels, Blaur merely called out the names of the Peoples/Lands of the other Company which does not include the Wurramara.

As far as I can piece the story together, the origin of the Mardaiya:n ceremony lies with a Mimiyawan man on the mainland who found a carved wooden figure floating in the sea and Dreamed it as something to do with Blaur's journey (among other things). The news eventually got over to Groote. The Warnindilyaugwa did not know that Denalua, Spoon Billed Turtle, had become a man and that this man was Blaur. In fact, the story in the dream says that they actually denied the possibility when Spoon-billed Turtle had suggested it to them. As a result, Turtle had gone back into the sea and returned to the land only when the Warnindilyaugwa were absent. As Blaur, that's when and where he made Munenga or Burrawang. Moving along and singing in Anindilyaugwa Blaur eventually reached the Amagula

River and moved out into the sea and on to Malurba in Wurramara country on Bickerton, calling out the names of the Groote Eylandt Lands in the Wurramarrba's Company as he went. When he reached Malurba he looked back, signifying an important point of differentiation, and began speaking half Anindilyaugwa and half Nunggubuyu. He made a similar break on reaching the mainland and began speaking in Nunggubuyu alone.

The Mimiyawan People, so the story goes, revealed the story and the ceremony to the Warnindilyaugwa People as compensation for having killed some of their numbers in a skirmish. The ceremony was a remembrance for the dead and that's how the Groote and Bickerton Islanders adapted it, whether to something similar already in place in their culture or from nothing, we don't know. However, the final episode of Agwilyunggwa, *mamungba,* where they take a lock of the dead person's hair and sing it to a special burial ground (one for each Land), is a "remembrance". Mardaiya:n could easily have been seen as an extension of this. In fact, there may have been an indigenous ceremony of such a nature called Amuduwarrarria which Mardaiya:n replaced.

This newly-established link between the Mimiyawan and the Wamindilyaugwa, however, created some problems – and still does – because the Amagula branch of the Wamindilyaugwa was in the same Company with the Wurramara on Bickerton who were linked to the Nundirribala of the mainland and not the Mimiyawan. The Mimiyawan were linked to the Wurramarrba. During the Mardaiya:n ceremony the People/Lands divide on a Company basis as well as a moiety one. The Groote and Bickerton Islanders were, and still are, unsure of which shelter to enter, much to the bemusement of the mainlanders.

This confusion over how the Groote and Bickerton Islanders' Songstreams intersect with those of the mainlanders is also what caused the problem for the Durila who had come to Groote from the north-east Arnhem Land coast via Woodah Island in the pre-contact period. On Groote they were associated with the Warnungamagadjeragba People/Land who came to be in the Mardaiya:n moiety established by Blaur. The Durila's mainland compatriots, however, were on the Gunabibi side. Once the Durila had married with Groote Eylandters on the basis of the error, the mistake was irrevocable. This problem hadn't moved any closer to a solution by 1986 than it had in 1969, except that the Durila, some of whom have renamed themselves "Wanambi", are slowly drifting back to north-east Arnhem Land and the settlement at Yirrkala, I presume trying to leave their problem behind them. However, the nature of their ties on Groote being what they are, the Groote Eylandters they have married are going with them, thereby perpetuating the problem, though the burden of guilt will now fall on the Groote Eylandters as the Durila reassume their traditional place in Yirrkala society. The Durila had previously attempted to consolidate their position on Groote – and also the mistake – by "moving in on" Angwura, Fire, and on Dangarridjanga, Shooting Star, Sung first by the Wurramarrba. But the attempt has so far failed, all other Peoples not wishing to see the error eternalized.

Though the ties forged by Blaur across two of the area's four Companies are much weaker than those within the Company, they nevertheless now do exist and provide the basis for a new emphasis in the culture (which explains why in the "clan couples" represented on Council [p. 42] the Nungumadjbarr can be in with the Mirniyawan while being associated with the Wurramara on Groote). What's more, the form Blaur's journey took, establishing Creative links between some, but only "recognition" links between others even in the same Company, in effect established a hierarchy with the Mirniyawan, as the founders of the ceremony, at its apex.

Implicit in the Mardaiya:n alignment, then, is hierarchy and unity, an anathema to all I have been saying about the traditional culture of the Bickerton (and I think also the Groote Eylandt) People. What's more, there is but one Songman in Mardaiya:n and he is Mimiyawan. Everyone else just dances. The Songman sings secret words of which only he knows the meaning.

However, a caveat must be repeated: the ties Blaur formed are of a very weak type – even his Creative Acts were few. So long as the base of People/Land/Songstream relations remains intact, Mardaiya:n remains but a theoretical counterpoint to the traditional culture. But strip that base away and....

(Contrary to Mission's and previous anthropologists' beliefs, the moiety principle does not regulate marriage to the extent of the Lands and the Companies. Else why would a category of People in the moiety opposite to your own be prohibited to you [as *warnigarangbidja*]?)

I won't write any more about Mardaiya:n, not just out of respect for Aboriginal sensitivities regarding the publication of secret/sacred material, but also out of a sense of self-preservation. This ceremony has become the final stage of initiation. It's the one they want me to stay for next. They know I've seen bits and pieces of it – but not the whole thing, though I've talked to the old men about the whole thing. I'm afraid, after what Gudigba told me following my initiation into Agwilyunggwa, that if I do go through this one 1 really won't be able to leave, not without paying out a huge amount of money anyway! Thinking this way as I still do, means that I'm not really ready yet to go through it. On the other hand, given the nature of Mardaiya:n, it might also mean that I might have to pay to stay *and* revisit!

In "The Economics of the Dreaming" I introduced a theory of Song species/resource-surplus classification. Aborigines' abstract intervention in nature in the Form of bounded jurisdictions, created artificial surpluses and these surpluses were prohibited to certain People/Lands as food. While the theory is neater than the facts that support it, I believe there is something to it. But there definitely is more to it than this. Many things Sung are not edible or useful, or even species, at all and I have already listed some of these. Furthermore, things Sung may be purely metaphorical such as Wurrawinya:mba, Fight of the Blue-Tongued Lizard on its way to Braulgwa, the fifth dimension, which is a Warnungwudjaragba Song. It is as if certain Songs had been selected out because they completed a pattern. The squeezed-together "hills" of Yilyanga's flesh which linked it analogically to Central Hill is an example of how such a pattern could be completed by use of an artificial construct.

I hypothesize that surplus-resource Songs form a base or grid into which other things of a purely symbolic nature are put and that both together explain the basis on which Song-species/subjects are selected. I explored this question with Murabuda.

Of Ships and Doves and Spiders and Things

Ya!Wa! a:n' alwudawarra	Midjiyanga langwa narrimanga:gburragama langwa	
"Dreamtime story about	Ship	about where they made it

ningimaginamerra.	Wurraginl	nalalegarna	warnungwaragbagiyawiya
telling	Those people	they went on and on	those people of a long, long time ago

wurralawudawarra	narrimana:gburragama	Midjiyanga.
those "Dreamtime" people	where they made it again	Ship

Wurragin' warnamamalya	naya:ya:ngbidjadjungwunama		warnamabalda:ya
Those people	they call themselves		Balda:ya people.

Balda:ya langwa.	Nawurragelegarnima	wurragina	namerndagelegarna
from Balda:ya land to the west: Macassar	They all kept on going	those people went	they all went and

ngaw' bi....ya.
after a while

"Angaba langwa?"	Dugwa	nalegarnemerra
From over there	Perhaps	they came (from there)

"Ngarningbala."
We don't know

Biya	wurragina	yaugudjina	nuwanggirriga magina.
And then	those (Aborigines)	in that place	they heard the noise (of the boat)

Nemagburrum-num-num-num	midjiyanga	adenubawiya.
The ship is making a big noise	ship	in the beginning

Biya naya:ma		"ga ga ga ga"
And they (the Aboriginal people) said		keep quiet

"Miyemba:na magina.	Nemagburruminamerra	nawurrageya: ma
What's that	that's making a big noise	What are they doing

warnemabalda:ya	warnamamalya."
those Balda:ya people	those people

Nawalelegarna　　　　nawagwugwadangwo... ....yaugudjina　　nara
They went and went　they came closer　　　　to that place　"No" -- here
　　　　　　　　　　　　　　　　(indicating a stop and change in emphasis)

"ma:ma' aragba nemagwudangwadena -danemagburruminamama", naya:ma.
it　　now　　it (ship) is getting　　it is making a lot　　　they said
　　　　　　nearer and nearer　　　　of noise　　　　　　　　(wondering
　　　　　　　　　　　　　　　　　　　　　　　　　　　　　　what kind of noise)

"Agina　angalya Waldar　amegira".
That　　place name

Yadigina wurragina　　　　　　nawurragwarmadjuwa　　Waldar langwa
From then those people on　　they all got up　　　　　from Waldar
　　　　　　　　　　　　　　　　up and went (Aborigines
　　　　　　　　　　　　　　　　and Balda:ya people)

nalegarnema　a: na: nuwa　　ayanggudarrba.　　Namerndamernda gelegarna
they went　　to this　　　　　island (Bickerton)　All those people went

wurragina　　ngawa biya　　narrarragulyam'　　　　　agina wurra:nigaberra
those ones　and then　　　　they went along　　　　　that place (past)　their
　　　　　　　　　　　　　　past the ghosts of　　　　　　　　　　　　　　side
　　　　　　　　　　　　　　the Murungun
　　　　　　　　　　　　　　People at Windanga (#155)

yirra:nigaberra　　angalya.
our side　　　　　　places (on Bickerton)

Nalegarna　　wurragina　　bi....ya　　　Yinbiya.　　　　Biya nara-maga
They went　　them　　　　all the way　　Wurramarrba　　They didn't want
　　　　　　　　　　　　　　　　　　　　place, #129

garriminga:gbarraga　Yinbiya　magarda　mandja.　　Narrimanga:gberragama
to make the boat　　　　　　　　near the sea　　　　They made it on the beach

195

a:ra:gba mandja Narrimardirranga magina   narrimanga:gminga:gberagama
They nailed the   that one   they were still making it
wood together

biya....   nemandabuda.   Wurragina-ga   warnamamalya
then   they made the Boat   Those ones   those Aboriginal people

wurramindjirradada-ga   adenigbawiya   wurramindjirradada
white people (then)   in the beginning   white people

narringma:gburragama langwa   narrimadeguma.
where they made it   they (the Balda:ya people) smoked the
                               Boat (to make it dry and lighter)

Narrimalunggwa:numerra   agina.   Yaugudjina   wurragin'
They painted the Boat   that one   At that place   those

narragungwadadjuwa   angwarra   wurramerndagagina   warnamamalya.
they are all black   smoke   all of them
from the burning

Biya   aduwaba   ngarna   ngarnamalyeduma ngarna.
Then   today   we   we are all black we

Ngarrimindjirremurridjunguma   warnamaugwulya.
Where we black people became black
Narrimanga:gburragadya:ya.
Where they made the Boat

"Ma:m' aragba   augudangwa   magardamandja   ma:ma-da", naya:ma.
This   now   close to he sea   this one   they said

Narrimarrgarrgarna   wurragina   narrimaduwarga   angaluba   wideramurra.
They (Aborigines)   those   they tied rope   from over   with a
pulled the Boat   people   to the Boat   here   special rope
to the sea

David H. Turner

Narrimarregegarna	wurraugwala	arndadiga-ni -arndadiga:na
They pulled again	those others (black people)	side by side, on each side of the Boat (some pulling the rope, some using their hands)

narrimarregegarna	wurraugwalama:rra-murra.	Biya nawurrageya:ma
they pulled again	those others with a rope	Then they all said

"Li li li li li li....li li li li li lill,"   nawurrageya:ma wurragina.
we are all set to go   they all said those ones

Biya....	nimilyigerangama ma:rra	magina.	Biya....	namenurringgadja
Then	the rope broke	rope	that one	Then	they looked at each other wondering what to do

wurragina menba	yaugudjina	magarda	mandjanemilyigerangumandja.
those people eyes	there looking at each other	in the sea	at the place where the rope broke

Nemilyigerangma	ma:ma	ma: rra-da.
The rope broke	this	rope

"Augwa ngaladjanemarumadina	ma:ma	magarda?	magarda mandja
And it is the sea, high	this	sea	in the sea

mangaba?	Ah!	Nemugularra:na ma:ma	midjiyanga-da,"	na:ya:ma.
over there		it is leaking this	Boat	they said

"Agiyamargina ngarremelalega?",	naya: ma
What shall we leave the Boat	they said

Aba' narremelalega	magina mandja midjiyalya-da	aginamandja angalya
Then they	left the Boat on the beach	at that place place

Yinbiya amegira.	Narremelalega	aga:n'	nawurragelawurradina
name	They left the Boat	and	they (the Balda:ya people) returned

Balda:yuwa	aberralangwa	angalya	abinuwa	narriberadadumulangwa
to Balda:ya	their	place	to it	where they started from

Balda:ya agin'amegira.	Magin'	narremanga:gburrigamamandja	agina
that name	That one	at the place where they made the Boat	it

awalya	agina	nawanggwudaduma	ngawa	narra:gburrigama
black, sooty smoke	it	where the fire is smoking	still	they made the Boat

narrimanga:gburrigama	yaugudjina	narrimangwudangama	magina.
they made the Boat	at that place	the fire and the smoke are still burning over there in Ship place	that Ship place

Agin' amalawudawarra	nuwardjiya	yaugudjina Angwura.	Angwura
That (Fire) Dreaming	stands up	there Fire	Fire

agina	amamalya.	Nara dagin'	dagilyingarridjanga --	Angwura
that one real		Not that one	Shooting Star	Fire

gaina	Wurramarrba	amegira	Angwura	ama:ba agina.
that one		name	Fire/Smoke	song that one

Agin' ngawa-da! That's all

This is a "Dreamtime" story about Ship. It's about where people made it, those people of long, long ago. A people called the Balda:ya came from the west, the Aborigines don't know exactly from where. The Aborigines at Waldar on the mainland in Mirniyawan country heard a noise, a big noise, but they didn't know what it was. Finally, a ship came carrying the Balda:ya people. From Waldar the Aborigines and the Balda:ya people went across to Bickerton past the place where the ghosts of the Murungun People are. They went past the Lands of one moiety and of the other all the way through to Wurramarrba country. They wanted to make a boat so they moved off the beach and went inland. There they nailed wood together and made it.

Those Aboriginal people were white at the time. The Balda:ya people smoked the Boat to dry it out and make it lighter. Then they painted it. But the smoke turned all the Aborigines black, all of them. That's why Aborigines are black today.

The Aborigines pulled the Boat to the sea and tied rope to it, special rope. They pulled the Boat side by side, some on the rope and some using their hands. But just as they were all set to go off in it the rope broke. Then the Boat started lo leak. They didn't know what to do, so they left the Boat on the beach at Yinbiya. Then the Balda:ya people went back to where they had come from.

The place where they made the Boat is where the fire is smoking still. The fire and smoke are still burning over there in Ship place – real fire, not the Shooting Star Fire. Fire and Smoke belong to Wurrarnarrba. That's their Song.

That's also the end of the story.

Yes, but not quite all of it. For one thing, Murabuda didn't mention how the rope broke. It was Yabongwa, Rainbow Serpent, who bit it. This act of anti-connectedness confirms that the Wurramarrba and the Wurramara Amagula are not on the same Songstream. Why does that need emphasizing here? Because the Story of the Ship is a capital-D differentiating story. It explains why Aborigines are different from Macassans and it explains why some Aborigines are different from others – the Wurramarrba from the Wurramara-Amagula: "our side", the Blaur side, from "their side", the Murungun's, who are mentioned in the tale. By the same token, it explains why the Waldar People, the Mimiyawan, are connected to the Wurramarrba on the same Songstream. The Macassans picked some of them up, brought them to Bickerton, and then took them back again (a detail omitted from this version). But the story also confirms differentiation between Peoples/Lands within the same Songstrearn: Fire/Smoke is sung first by the Wurramarrba, not by those who sing it on Shooting Star like the Durila (because its tail is like Fire).

It is tempting to see the broken Ship, the one the Aborigines Sing, as an admission of inferiority and the basis of a class division between Black and White – the teclmologically superior Macassans and the technologically inferior Aborigines. But there is no hint of this in the way the Aborigines tell the tale, including the way Galiyawa, Murabuda's father, told it to me in

1969. In fact, in both versions it is the Macassans and the Aborigines who together make the new Boat, though it is the Aborigines who pull it to the sea.

In this tale can be discerned a certain logic, though it's not as clearly defined as in another version of the tale recorded by Peter Worsley in 1953 and which I analyzed in *Life Before Genesis*. There the sense of unity at the outset is much more pronounced, with all the Aboriginal Peoples of the region linked by the Macassans' journey. But mention of the Murungun People in the above tale, who are linked neither to the Wurramarrba nor the Wunamara but to those on "the other side", as well as mention of both "sides" themselves, during Ship's journey hints of an overall unity too. This includes the Balda:ya people. All at the outset are white. The possibility of unity, then, is the potential problem dealt with by the story.

The tale begins with a statement of mediation. The Balda:ya people bring some of the Mirniyawan People over to Wurramarrba country and appear to "go between" both "sides" while doing so. While the "vertical", if you will, lines separating Aboriginal Peoples into Lands begin to become blurred in the tale, a new line, this one "horizontal", begins to emerge. In the episode concerning the building of the Boat, it seems that it is the Balda:ya people who do the skilled work, the Aborigines the hewing and drawing. The division is symbolized by the transformation of white Aborigines into black and, later, by the breaking of the rope, Aborigines at one end, Balda:ya people at the other. But I reiterate: the storytellers seem not to judge this. It simply is a Fact of Life. The fact that the rope breaks is a reaffirmation of differentiation within the Aboriginal population. The Wurramarrba and the Wurramara-Amagula are not on the same Songstream. In the final analysis, Mirniyawan and Wurramarrba, Macassans and Aborigines, separate and withdraw from each other, that is, they differentiate on another plane.

A potential "class" situation is, then, avoided. Unity at all levels is rejected, but then so implicitly is subordination. As the historical record indicates, the Macassans did not colonize and settle and the Aborigines did not drive them away. They lived together, apart, side by side, neither in major competition nor cooperation.

The same logic of *mediation* ==> *separation* informs the structure of most Songstream tales in this Aboriginal culture including that of Central Hill. Central Hill travels through the countries of four Peoples and, to the

European mind at least, is a common denominator linking them all into one. This, apparently, was also the implication to Aboriginal People; the difference was, they abhorred it! Central Hill eventually becomes primarily affiliated with but one People/Land, the Warnungangwurugwerigba of Groote by transforming himself into a high hill in their country, and each time he threatens to settle down in some other country he manages to "pull himself out of the mud" and move on. In the course of this journey Central Hill also brings to mind all that Aboriginal society potentially is not.

On entering Bickerton the Stingrays become an undifferentiated part of Central Hill, the implication being that all joined in the same Songstream are one. In Wurra:nggilyangba country Central Hill enters into a co-residential, co-production relationship with the Blind Woman, Dimimba, helping her in her gathering activities. But before the relationship is consummated in what would have been an incestuous relationship within the same Songstream, Central Hill escapes to Groote, Dimimba's spears falling harmlessly in the sea behind him. By the same token, he "resurrects" the Stingrays and throws them off into the sea. Unity on an intra-Land level, and by implication in the Songstream as a whole then, is an alternative to be avoided at all costs. Instead, the Lands remain separate but interconnected without losing their respective integrities. This aspect of the tale is reinforced by the way Central Hill and other "connectors" are sung – a different tune for each leg of their respective journeys. And it is reinforced by the ending. Not only does he become primarily affiliated with but one People/Land, but the Stingrays settle down beside him.

It would be a mistake to think that we have recorded all there is to sing about Ship in the above version. Narrative accounts are without the influence of A.mawurrena, if I can put it that way, in the sense that they lack the engagement and insight of an actual performance and hence its inspiration and detail. There are no "Paddles" mentioned in this version of the tale, nor any "Sails", yet these are both sung by the Wurramarrba as part of the Ship cycle. In fact, "under" Ship in the Aboriginal scheme of things, are Miya:dja (Paddle), Dumbala (Sail), Na:ningumagadja (Macassan Sailor), Djangadjanga (Rooster), Mamugilyigarrguwuruma or Aeroplana (Aeroplane), Brabella (Propeller), Angwura (Fire), Angwura (Smoke), Amarnina (Ashes), Ma:rra (Rope), Dumungarniyenda (Dragonfly), Galugwa (Coconut), Moarra (Driftwood), Yingabarranga (Cut-leaved Palm).

Until you read this list you might have been tempted to think that all items introduced by foreign contact, including coconuts which also are not indigenous, come under the "Ship" heading and for obvious reasons. The Macassans were the Aborigines' first experience of non-Aboriginal outsiders for tens of thousands of years. But Dragonfly? Palm? This is where "pattern" comes in as well as a principle of classification fundamental to Aboriginal culture, indeed the whole way of life.

Dragonfly comes under Ship because Dragonfly has a "motor" – it's the way its wings move when in flight. Propeller comes in, not so much because it is a contact item, but because it has Dragonfly Wings/a "motor" and assumes the shape of a Paddle. Dragonfly Wings are Paddles too. Now these are not Yimendungwa or Cypress Pine Paddles which are Sung first by the Warnungwamalangwa but are Ship Paddles which are made out of different woods. Paddle to Paddle, though, is one way the Wurramarrba relate to the Warnungwamalangwa in the same Songstream.

So even some items which appear to be lumped together because they are economically significant or useful are associated because they complete a logical pattern, a symbolic whole. And the principle which organizes this pattern is, "an aspect of one is fit to an aspect of another and vice versa". These may be real aspects, such as the propeller of a boat and the propeller of a 'plane, or they may be formal or symbolic aspects such as the shape of a paddle and the shape of a dragonfly wing. Just this one example will confirm my point about how incredibly difficult it is to tell at any given moment in a Song just who is singing what. It becomes impossible for the untutored to understand when it turns out that there is more than one Ship and Ship(s) starts crossing over into Dove and Spider!

First, Dove and Spider are both "Derrarragugwa". The "new name" for Spider is Dagwarargwa which literally means "Thread" and refers to the weave in a piece of cloth, *dumbala*. Dumbala brings us back to Sail and Ship. Thread is like Ma:rra, String, and String is what Dove pulled around on her journey. But it wasn't really String; it was a piece of Wurrumilya:a or Burney Vine. Wurrumilyalya comes under Spider because Spider Webs are like clusters of vines. Yimurralya or Green Ants come in under Spider because vines are where you find them. Spider Webs are like the weave in a piece of cloth, are made of threads, are like the piece of vine pulled by Dove which is what Ship was pulled with. Dove String broke just like Ship "Rope Broke" (Nemenenggarma:ra, which is sung) and at the same Place.

Yet there's a differentiation into lines here too: under Dove come Ma:rra (String) strictly-speaking, and Dumarnda (Reef Heron, whose connection to the rest escapes me except to say that Heron made part of the same country that Dove did), while under Spider comes Burney Vine, Green Tree Ant and Dragonfly. Between them both are the Long and the Round Yam.

I've already dealt with the complexities of Angwura, Fire/Smoke, but it is worth pointing out here that Angwura connects up to its complementaries by the same process as the others. A part of the Shooting Star, the tail, is equated with the blaze of the Fire. The Smoke from the Fire is carried on the South-South-East Wind, Amarrba, which blankets all Wurramarrba country though being primarily associated with one, Rrarrarrarra (Map 3, #139). As to how the Wurramarrba of Bickerton come in on the same Songstream with the Warnungamagadjeragba of Groote: the latter sing Miyarruma which is a plant food that floats in the sea and is eaten by turtles. In June and July it floats out on the sea on the East Wind all lined up just like Macassan Ships returning home to Macassar (Plate 14). The East Wind connection here has recently been used by the Warnungamagadjeragba People (actually Person) to justify a switch in Songstream affiliation to the Mamariga. This may have been a mistake because the Mamariga have seized the opportunity to use the connection to move in on the Warnungamagadjeragba whose Land is adjacent to a part of theirs in the north-east corner of Groote.

It would be a mistake, however, to see Ship as a superordinate Song streaming its bits and pieces down to Create other Songs below. It is more that Ship and Spider/Dove are co-existent equals whose bits and pieces shift back and forth and occasionally down each line in search of correspondences and linkages.

We could say the same things about Central Hill and Stingrays amongst the Lalara and their Companions, and about Fresh Water and Rainbow Serpent(s) amongst the Wurramara and theirs. Here, the reflection of Rainbow Serpent(s) in the clouds links them to the rain which falls into the Fresh Water Pools of Malurba, the same rain that brings Nambirrirrma to earth at Arumandja. Fresh Water Pools, Amara, are the Head of the Rainbow, and contain the Frogs, Leaches and Mermaids which are Sung when the Pools are in Flood after heavy rains, washing them all down toward the sea. Frog's eyes, when they blink, flash like Lightning, as do people's eyes when they cough. Hence the reason why Wurramara and the extinct Warnungmurugulya are on the same Songstream. Wurramara Lightning, striking as it does on the east coast of South Bay, is "good" as distinct from Nemarnurdudi Lightening on the mainland which is "bad" and the source of sorcery there. This explains from the Aboriginal point of view how these two Peoples could be in opposite moieties and intermarry despite apparently sharing the same Song *(ama:ba),* and solves the problem I had with the list of "totems" I obtained at Ngukurr in 1974 (see Chapter 2).

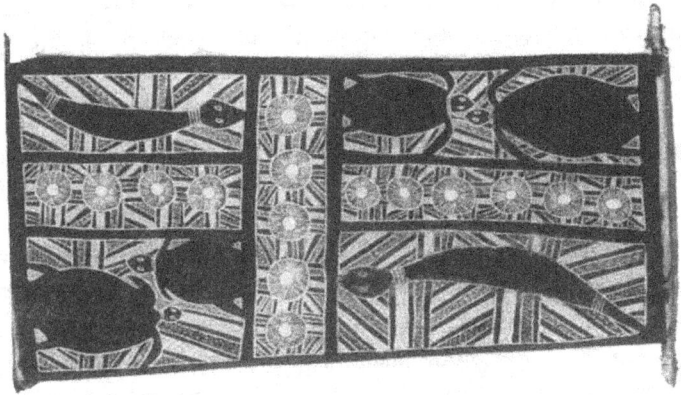

Plate 14. Gegender Durili's bark painting of Miyarruma, Turtle Food

Plate 15. Iain Baxter's "Reflected Landscape"

I worked out much of this while checking the "totems" I had listed or located in Songs in my 1974 book, spurred on by some listings by Julie Waddy in her thesis (Table 6.7 "Groote Eylandt clan totems") which didn't make any sense to me at all, collapsing as they did "shared" items that to me could be further differentiated. In the course of these checks I found that the list on page 88 of my book contained one major mistake: the Warnungwadarrbalangwa didn't sing Mamungwulya, Sea Weed, or at least Sea Weed strictly speaking. They did, however, sing Marraugwa, Sea Fan. Mamungwulya was sung by the Mamariga, the Wurramarrba and the Durila. The "Anema" or "Black Mangrove" on my list turned out to be one of those contextual items which could be sung not only by the Warnungwadarrbalangwa but also the Wurramara while carrying no common Songstream implications. Ya:embirrgwa turned out to be sung first by the Murungun of the adjacent mainland, second by the Warnungwadarrbalangwa and third by the Warnungwudjaragba of Groote. Yimendungwa, Cypress Pine, is sung by Wurramarrba first, WarnungwamaJangwa second. Yingag-barrnga, which I have as Coconut, is "really" Cut-leaved Palm, but the two are confounded in Song.

So far I have examined a material and a logical basis for the classification of Song-species/subjects. But there is another basis, and this is sociological. "Species" may be selected and set in a certain relation to each other because of certain prior structural arrangements at another level. For instance, if you are going to designate Peoples who intermarry by two Winds it would make sense to select contrasting ones and leave complementaries to designate those within each Company and moiety who do not intermarry. Once you select one with this purpose in mind, the other should "naturally" suggest itself: North-West Wind, Bara, People do in fact marry South-East Wind Mamariga People.

(Despite this consistency, though, is there not a contradiction here, one that becomes all the more apparent were we to substitute, say, animals for winds. Sea Eagle People [Wurrawilya] can marry Hawk People [Wurramara], but in nature Sea Eagles reproduce with other Sea Eagles, Hawks with other Hawks. However the apparent contradiction here really only highlights a consistency: the principle of Spiritual transmission of Peopleness or Landness, Amawurrena, is through the male line [it would work the same way through the female line]. Sea Eagles do reproduce other Sea Eagles – using Hawks as a "receptacle" in which to do so.)

To return to the Winds, they all seem to fall into place around the sociologic of marriage. Those to the right of a north-east to south-west axis (the dry winds) do not intermarry; those to the left (the wet winds) of the same axis also do not intermarry. Those on either side marry each other. This is diagrammed below (figure 4).

The symbolic situation reflects the sociological situation, with one exception. There is no Wind for the Lalara People and their Songstream mates. Bara, Mugrrerraga and Lungwurrma are sung by two Peoples on the Lalara's "side" but in a different Company. The interesting thing, though, is that a space has actually been left for them on the "compass": west-south west, the direction from which Central Hill traveled to Bickerton. Is this because the Lalara are latter-day arrivals? Perhaps, but this wouldn't explain the absence of Wurra:nggilyangba and Warnungangwurugwerigba Wind affiliations.

The pattern then – gap included – fits the sociological reality. The Warnindilyaugwa on South-East Wind marry the Warnungwadarrbalangwa or the Warnungwudjaragba then switch over to the "blank" sector on the Warnungwadarrbalangwa's side to marry the Lalara or one of their Companions, coming back to the other sector in the next. From the other side, the Warnungwadarrbalangwa marry Warnindilyaugwa or Amagula in one generation then switch to one of the Peoples on a "weaker" Wind on the Warnindilyaugwa side of the axis, returning to one on the "stronger" Wind in the next. The only inconsistency here is Delada which is Sung by Amagula as well as Warnungamagadjeragba. They are in different Companies, though this is changing as I have indicated. A note of qualification as to my translation of the two "weaker" Winds on the south east side, however, must be introduced. Dunggwarra seems to be a "something added" to the South-East Wind which makes it blow very strong, though its separate nature is indicated by the fact that the two Winds together are Yiniyaruma, Very Strong South-East Wind. By the same token, Amarrba seems to be "something subtracted" from the South-East Wind to make it weaker. I'm not so sure these two Winds can be given specific locations.

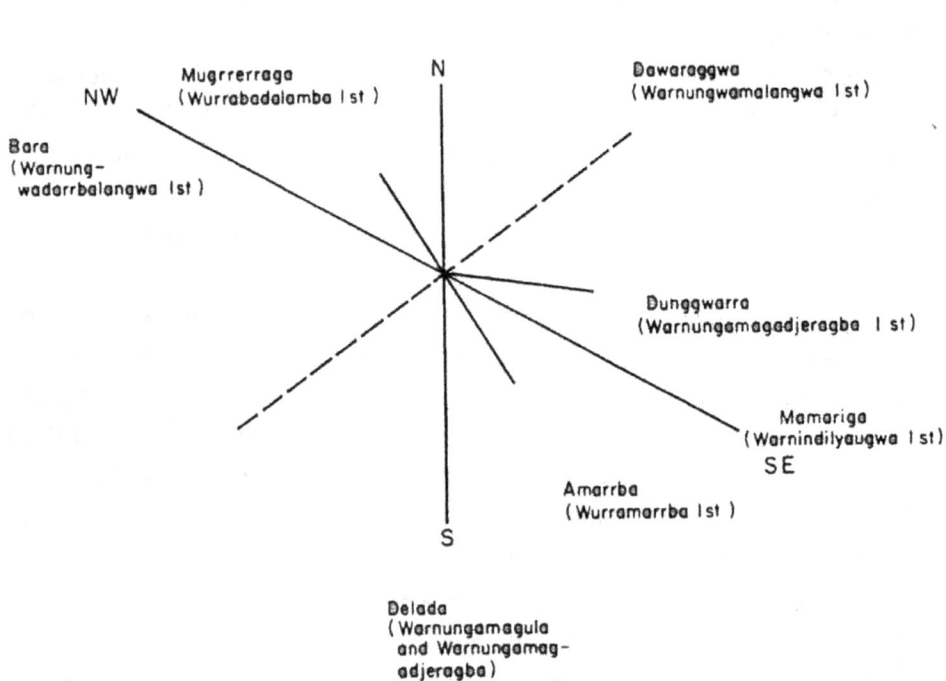

Figure 4. Wind Songs and their People/Lands

Some Song "species", then, appear to have been selected on a sociological basis. Or was it the other way around? Were the Winds arranged to fit the People/Lands or were the People/Lands arranged to fit the Winds? Certainly they are now, now that the arrangement is in place. People consciously "follow" the Winds, "follow" the Song-species in arranging marriages. The broader question this addresses is, does culture determine nature or does nature determine culture? Have the Aborigines imposed a cultural vision on nature, or has their cultural vision been derived from close observation and analysis of nature? We are not helped any in investigating this through the Aborigines' classification of the natural environment as such because it seems to proceed basically according to the same principles as we have already located in the Song-species and social organizational domains. There is the same lack of completed hierarchy or superordination, the same simultaneous general and specific referents, the same "aspect of one correlated with aspect of other" that we find elsewhere. This we illustrated in the way Aborigines classify things like "shark/s".

Augwalya is the general term for "animals" of any kind; but it also refers to the narrower category "sea animals" and within this to the category "fish" and, within this, "bony fish". *Adidira* refers to shellfish in general; but also to the hermit crab in particular. Only *yimenda* among life forms of the sea stands only for something in general, and that is turtles. Wurradjidja refers to animals of the air in general, including flying mammals; but it also refers to insects, ticks, spiders, scorpions and centipedes.

Yinungungwangba refers to land animals in general including mammals, reptiles and frogs; but it also refers specifically to four-footed land manunals.

Yingarna refers to snakes, legless lizards and eels, but it also refers to brown snakes and death adders in particular.

The same kind of non/discrimination goes on in relation to the plant world.

Amarda is a plant of any kind; but is also any non-woody plant, flowering plant, fern, green algae, brown algae and red algae.

A:ga is any woody plant; but it is also any flowering plant. By the same token an element of hierarchy is also a part of the way Aborigines arrange things. Taken in its general meaning of "flesh foods" the term *augwalya* does subsume the three kinds: "flesh from animals of the sea" *(a:ningumagardumandja),* "flesh from birds and flying mammals" *(wurradjidja)*, and "flesh from land animals" *(yinungungwangba)*. The first category in turn subsumes "fish" *(augwalya* again), "shellfish flesh" *(adidira)*, "squid flesh" *(dilyimba)*, and "turtle flesh" *(yimenda)* in the first case and "python flesh" *(dingarna)* and "flesh of four-footed land mammals and reptiles" *(yinungungwangba* again).

As Waddy points out in her study of Groote Eylandt plant and animal classification (1984: 288), this reflects a hierarchical logic which divides fleshy foods from non-fleshy foods, classifies fleshy foods "as a subset of the biological classification of the animal kingdom", and classifies non-fleshy foods as "contrasting with the biological classification of plants and based on the part of the plant which is eaten." On this aspect of the Groote Eylandt classification system I refer the reader to Waddy's soon-to-be published account.

My point here is that we are not dealing with two systems of classification, the one superior or inferior to the other, as "scientific" to "symbolic", but rather with one that sees the poles of hierarchy versus equivalence as untenable (unreal?) in any domain. Rather, a "part of one in the other" principle is applied equally to the Aborigines' classification of the natural worlds as it is to the cultural – whether looking across or up and down to relations between classes. As there is an element of equivalence in their natural classification system, there is an element of hierarchy in their symbolic classification system. (It's beyond my ken to locate what aspect of each fits in to what aspect of the other to account for the apparent confounding of levels and categories in the Aboriginal system of natural classification here but it could be done.)

In both spheres of application, the natural or the cultural, the basic principle to be abstracted is that no category is autonomous with respect to the reality it represents, no category has meaning except with reference to the reality it represents, no category has meaning except with reference to some property of that to which it refers. Nor are these properties unique to the referents of those categories. For example, "Warnindilyaugwa" is sometimes used to refer to all the Aborigines of the area who speak the Anindilyaugwa language; but it is also the name for the largest of the Peoples/Lands on Groote. On a symbolic level, Yabongwa is the name for Rainbow Serpent and simultaneously its multiple manifestations in the Madalyuma and on Amagalyuagba.

The real issue, then, is whether the principles of Warnungamagalyuagba classification and social organization are an artificial imposition on nature, or whether nature has suggested them to these Aboriginal Peoples and they then applied them to classifying nature and organizing society. Here we enter a highly speculative area, fraught with many dangers. For if we answer "yes" to the first question we insult Aboriginal Peoples as misguided, and if we answer "yes" to the second we insult ourselves as not up to their achievement. Perhaps an appeal to "God", or some Cosmic Principle, is the only way out of this dilemma.

VIII

Cosmo-logic

Arumandja Revisited

On my way back to Bickerton and Groote in 1987, having worked out something of the Aboriginal Logic of Life, I happened to come across Fritjof Capra's book *The Tao of Physics* in a Canberra bookshop. Reading it on my way to Darwin I was intrigued to find that Aboriginal concepts, Aboriginal ways of interrelating, were even more in line with the new truths of physics than were the Taoist or Buddhist ways he was discussing. In the first place, they were at least as difficult to communicate in conventional language. As Capra observes of physics (p. 53), "Quantum theory and relativity theory, the two bases of modem physics, have made it clear that this reality transcends classical logic and that we cannot talk about it in ordinary language."

In Aboriginal studies it is the logic of binary discrimination and duality as-opposition that ultimately fails to grasp the reality encountered. This is the logic of the dialectic characteristic of Western philosophy. But, by the same token, the logic of "undifferentiated, undivided, indeterminate suchness" (p. 36) characteristic of Buddhist thought, also fails to grasp the Aboriginal reality. Comprehension of the Aboriginal reality requires a concept of "relation", yes; but not "relation" in the form of undifferentiated unity, though there are ambiguities in Buddhist thought about the internal nature of that unity. But first to the world of physics, our point of departure in this discussion.

A few definitions from the world of physics are necessary to aid in this summary. Physics examines the behaviour of "particles" which can be differentiated as to mass. "Photons" and "neutrinos" are massless; "electrons" are the lightest massive particles; "muons, pions and kaons" are a few hundred times heavier than these; the rest (including neutrons, sigmas, omegas) are one to three thousand times heavier than these in turn. All particles with mass are referred to collectively as "hadrons". "Mesons" are the lighter variety. Atoms are constituted out of these particles. Mass, though, is not a substance but a form of energy. We cannot therefore direct our attention to relations between atoms because atoms themselves are relational. To quote Capra (pp. 76–77):

Rutherford's experiments had shown that atoms, instead of being hard and indestructible. consisted of vast regions of space in which extremely small particles moved, and now quantum theory made it clear that even these particles were nothing like the solid objects of classical physics. The subatomic units of matter are very abstract entities which have a dual aspect. Depending on how we look at them, they appear sometimes as particles, sometimes as waves; and this dual nature is also exhibited by light which can take the form of electromagnetic waves or of particles.

Quanta, the basic "units" of matter (you can see how familiar language begins to fail us), are energy packets of heat radiation. Matter can be simultaneously particle and wave because it only shows tendencies to exist at definite places. Waves, in the language of physics, are probabilities of interconnection. Particles do not move in wave patterns. In a water wave, particles move in a circle as the wave passes by. What is transported along the wave is a disturbance.

Nature, then, is not composed of "building blocks" but of "a complicated web of relations between the various parts of the whole" (p. 78), though again, use of a term like "part" distorts the reality. The solid appearance of matter derives from the fact that particles move around when confined to a small area of space. The smaller the space, the faster the movement. High velocities make the atom appear as a rigid sphere.

The chief characteristic of matter is its transformability: particles emerge from energy and vanish into energy, change into other particles and interpenetrate. Each time they probe deeper into the nature of matter, physicists discover that what they thought might be base-units dissolve into webs of relations.

How, then, are relations established in the sub-atomic world? Basically by interaction in force fields. In an illustration of Capra's (pp. 239–40, reproduced by permission below), two electrons approach each other, one of them emitting the photon (y) at the point A, the other absorbing it at the point B.

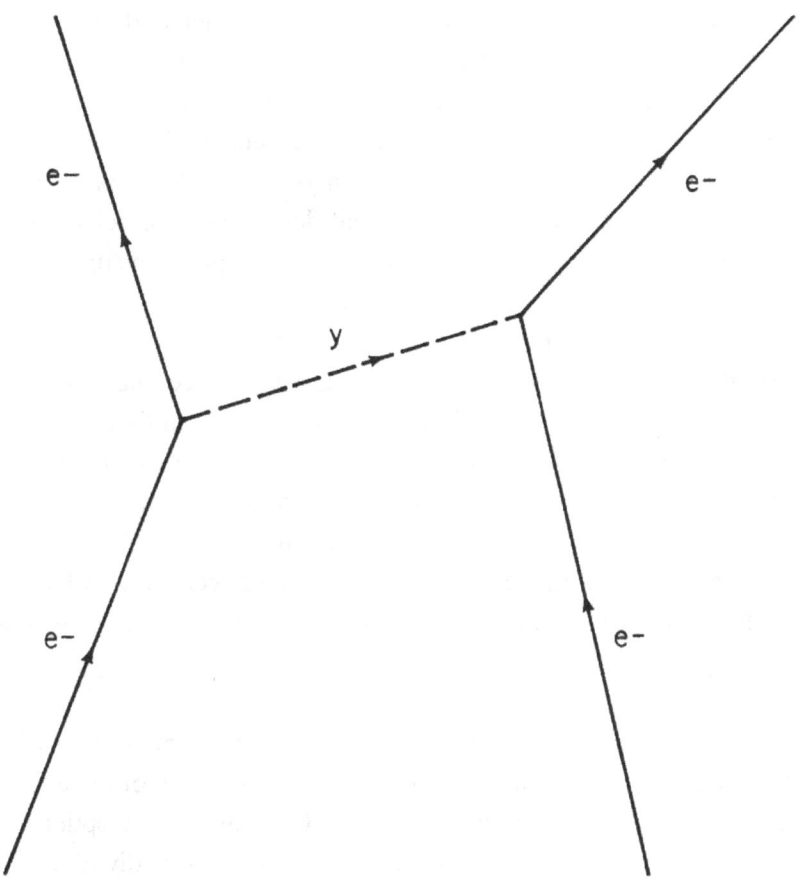

Figure 5. Particle Interpenetration

To quote Capra, "When the first electron emits the photon it reverses its direction and changes its velocity ... and so does the second electron when it absorbs the photon. In the end, the two electrons fly apart, having repelled each other through the exchange of the photon."

In reality, then, there is not so much a "force field" as interaction between particles mediated through fields constituted of other particles. The binding force holding "things" together appears as the exchange of particles. Both "things" and particles are hadrons. Hadrons "involve" one another in a dynamic and probabilistic sense. They "interpenetrate". The nature of this interpenetration is such that it is simultaneously local and part of a larger whole. It is the activity of the whole that determines the behaviour of the "parts" (if indeed we can still speak of "parts"). Capra sums up:

> According to Bohr, the two-particle system is an indivisible whole, even if the particles are separated by a great distance; the system cannot be analyzed in terms of independent parts. Even though the two electrons are far apart in space, they are nevertheless linked by instantaneous, nonlocal connections ... they transcend our conventional notions of information transfer. (pp. 345–46)
>
> In Bohr's view, the real world is structured according to the same general principles, with the whole being enfolded in each of its parts. (p. 352)

Capra's point is not so much the physics as that Eastern mysticism's vision of ultimate reality approaches modem physics' conception of material reality. The crux of the matter according to Capra is Buddhism's conception of "relationship". "Ignorance" in Buddhist philosophy consists of dividing "the perceived world into individual and separate things" (p. 107) in an effort to confine the fluid forms of reality in fixed categories." But beyond the real world of distinctions and opposites, is *acintya*, "the unthinkable, where reality appears as undivided and undifferentiated "suchness" (p. 106). This "undivided and undifferentiated suchness", however, is no simple "unity", but rather a domain where opposites are united in their polarity. In other words ultimate reality is differentiated but the differentiation is confounded. The relations extant here are expressed as Yin and Yang (the classic representation of Chinese Taoist origin is presented below).

Yang is the strong, male, creative side; Yin is the dark, receptive, female side. The two sides are opposed as black to white and yet are complementary in the sense that one presupposes the other, brings it into being. This can be illustrated if you rotate the circle as a one-dimensional whole: the point where the white sector fills the space left by the black is the point where the black sector fills the space left by the white. The relation of interdependence between opposites that is asserted here is expressed on three planes: the one just noted, the spot of white in the black and the spot of black in the white, and the circle containing the whole. They are also its limitations. Circle "contains" a force which, if unleashed, is wholly destructive. This can be illustrated by rotating the circle over its "base", that is, by imagining the two dots as windows open to something resting permanently below. Yin has now become uniformly and exclusively "one" (white) as Yang has become uniformly and exclusively "other" (black). The interdependence and harmony of the universe has been fractured and the forces of opposition released. But, according to Buddhist thought, while this might happen in the "real" world, it does not occur in the world of enlightenment. As Capra puts it (p. 158),

> In the East, a virtuous person is therefore not one who undertakes the impossible task of striving for the good and eliminating the bad, but rather one who is able to maintain a dynamic balance between good and bad.

The believer's task, then, is to transcend "ignorance" for a deeper Truth. Capra's belief is that this is the same Truth that modem physics finds hidden below the apparent world of material "solids".

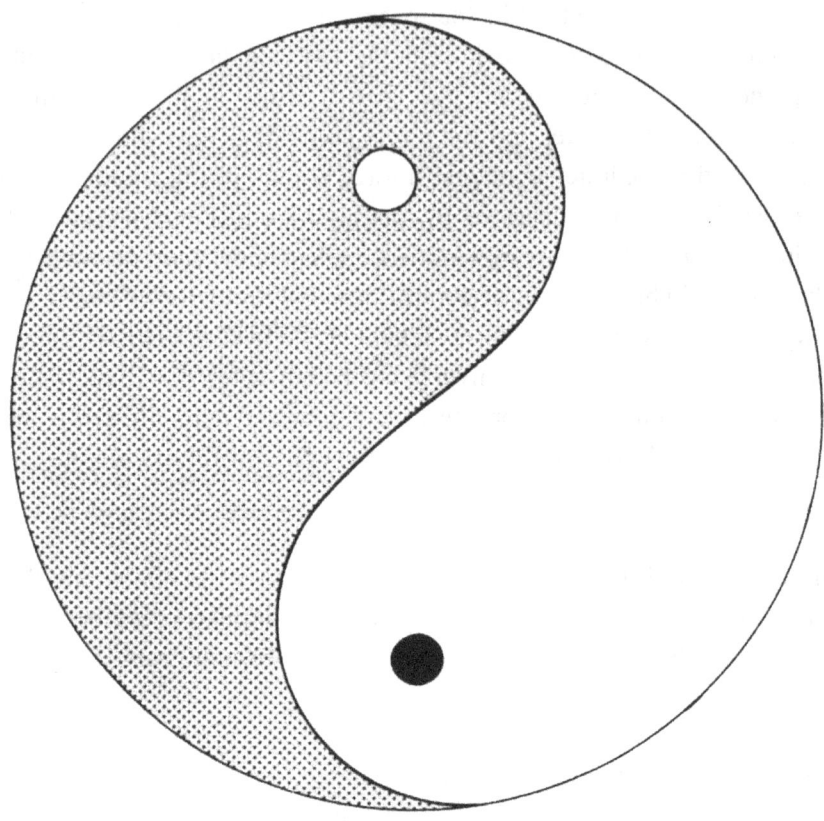

Figure 6. Yin and Yang

Granted that some Eastern mystics experience the world as an indivisible whole of mutually interdependent parts, as do physicists. But the question still remains: are the nature of the interdependencies comparable in both cases? It is difficult to know because Eastern mysticism declares the details of connectedness to be ultimately unfathomable. Or rather, it declares them to be overlapping and confounding. Aboriginal ideas of relationship are somewhat more precise: they are through "a part of one in the other and vice versa without loss of integrity of either", mutually renunciative, process.

In Groote Eylandt and Bickerton Island Aboriginal symbolic representation, no circle is employed to represent the enfolding of parts into a whole because there is no whole, only an unbounded stretching of interrelations to infinity, represented by line. And without circle, "rotation" to reverse the interpenetration of the part of one that is in the other in the Yin Yang case is impossible. That is, the part of the one that is in the other in Aboriginal society has permanently "interpenetrated" any dualities or oppositions to defuse them and render them merely paradoxical—no longer worthy of the name "opposites" at all.

But perhaps the most significant fact about Aboriginal conceptions and those of many other ways, including those of many Eastern mystical ways, is that those of the Aborigines' are not just conceptions: they constitute the real everyday world in which people participate. The Aboriginal realization does not require the separation of a class of mystics, priests or monks to engage in full-time pursuit. The realization is general and matter-of-fact.

To jump from here, though, to an assertion that Aborigines have looked deep into the nature of matter to discover its true essence, as physicists have done, is the worst form of reductionism in disrespect of what the Aborigines themselves claim to have encountered. What are we to suppose? That Aborigines are born with microscopic vision? That they simply see more deeply into material reality? But this is not what Aborigines' claim. They claim to have grasped a transcendent Truth about reality—its foundation in Forms and its ultimately Spiritual, not material, nature.

Essentially this is the problem with Capra's approach to the insights of Eastern mystics which also claim transcendent status. The problem for his argument is that physics is an inquiry into the nature of the material world by means of artificial, sensory mechanisms which probe deeper into, but not beyond, the world of sensory experience. Eastern mysticism and Aboriginal religion, by contrast, offer us statements about the non-material as such. (Since I have raised this matter only to show the line of inquiry untenable, I must apologize to both Buddhists and physicists for treating their fields in such a summary and cursory fashion.)

We end up in much the same reductionist blind alley when we attempt to posit sociological causes of Aboriginal Spirituality, such as I may have seemed to be doing when I pointed out that the Creative Beings leave "stuff" in their wake much as people leave a part of themselves in the memories of those they encounter wherever they go. The impression would have been heightened had I also added the sociological truism that we leave much more of ourselves in the places where and amongst those with whom we interact most frequently. This is precisely where and among whom the Aboriginal Creative Beings deposited most of their "stuff".

This said, however, there is a sociological context from which we can proceed without risking the charge of reductionism. In the midst of fundamental conflict where opposition is both real and destructive, an impasse may be reached. The forces—people—in question may be in equal and opposite reaction. Some may now reach out to a "neutral" plane of existence as a point of reference for negotiation and reconciliation. Hence the possibility of transcendent awareness. This could also occur when two or more parties, themselves opposed, are threatened by a third.

The reason why this line of inquiry does not become reductionist is because, even if the sociological aspect is valid, we still have to account for the "neutral plane" that is encountered in the process, and this makes no reference at all to the sociological domain. To explore this question in more detail I would like to take you with me through my second experience of Amawurrena, again on Bickerton Island, but this time in June of 1987.

When I returned to Groote Eylandt in 1987 I invited John McLaren, a friend from Darwin, over to stay for a few days. I thought it would be interesting to show him the site of Nambirrirrma's incarnation, seeing as I had talked to him so much about its significance.

We arrived at Milya:gburra outstation and the next day set off down the beach for the site, but it wasn't long before I realized I had lost my bearings. I wasn't sure exactly where the grave was located. After unsuccessfully searching about on the higher ground back of the beach for a bit I was going to call it quits and went back toward the water to meet John. I was embarrassed to say the least. As we walked along the beach I chanced to turn and look out at the bay. A funny feeling suddenly swept over me. There was a certain unreality to what I was seeing; like there was another dimension to the bay I had never seen before. And then I realized that I was at a point of perfect symmetry. I think John realized it too.

"This is where it is," I said.

I turned and walked directly inland up off the beach and there was the site—the depression and the baler shells. I looked up to the escarpment, now horizontal in front of me, and then turned and looked back at the bay. The same feeling swept over me again. I can't really put it into words. But this was a special place.

When we returned to Milya:gburra I took out my copy of *Tradition and Transformation* and showed John the Nambirrirrma story. Then I turned to the two drawings of Bickerton Island executed for me by Galiyawa Wurramarrba and "Crosby" Wurramara respectively (Figure 2).

Immediately John said, pointing at Galiyawa's representation of Bickerton as a "horseshoe": "That one was drawn from that spot we were just at on the beach." I had realized that Galiyawa had drawn Bickerton Island as the water line of the bay and added the inland "countries" as islands around it. But I hadn't realized that it had been drawn from the perspective of someone looking out from the place where Nambirrirrma had sat down. Nor had I realized that the line of water around the Bay could also have represented the Form of the Bay, this quality I had just experienced.

"It is the only way someone would see the curvature of the bay without the advantage of an aerial perspective," John had said.

I looked at "Crosby's" drawing beside it (Figure 2). It consisted of two straight lines in the form of a cross with a curved line extending from the focal point to the north-east, and a straight one extending from the bottom of the vertical line directly west. Dots on the line marked "totemic" sites, I had been told. But it had always puzzled me that different sites on the same line sometimes belonged to different People/Lands. Now I realized: the focal point was the place where Nambirrirrma had sat down. The lines traced the various episodes in the tale. Nambirrirrma constructed physical space for these old men. Lamentably they had now passed away and I couldn't check it out and deepen my understanding; but then there was no need to. I now just "knew".

It was then that it occurred to me to take the Nambirrirrma tale at face value, forgetting about the theory of the Macassan visitor, about the possible historical context of the story, about searching for any materialist explanation. What had happened? A man had come down from the sky on the rain to two men who recognized him as a different kind of person, though one speaking the same language as they did and knowledgeable about their culture. This man set down or reiterated the law, then he married, had a son, died and was buried. As I had found out since, the son also married but had no children and died. As in Nambirrirrma's case, his body was placed on a platform and the bones buried at the site.

Taken at face value the story follows this course: *nothingness* --- > *being* => *relationship*. Expressed even more abstractly: *anti-thesis* --- > *thesis* = = = > *plurality* or complementarity. This, as some of my readers will immediately realize, is also the course of the "Christ event" (see pp. 235–240).

I hadn't bothered to translate the word at the time, but at the point in the tale where the two Aborigines were puzzling over where this stranger had come from, Galiyawa had inserted, *"nalarra wurragina* God *dugwa"*. That is, "perhaps he fell from God". I took the mention of "God" as Galiyawa's own embellishment, something he had picked up from the missionaries, though he spoke very little English. To that point in the story, debate had centered on whether Nambirrirrma had come from the adjacent mainland or from northeast Arnhem Land, indicating that if he was a different kind of person, he was at least a different kind of *Aboriginal* person (there is no mention in the story that he might have been Macassan). Apart from this, it never occurred to me to have the English in his story translated, or what that translation might reveal. When I returned in 1987, though, I asked his son Murabuda what his father would have meant by "God" in the context of the story.

"He meant Nambirrirrma is Amawurrena", he said.

As we have seen, there is really no English translation for this. The missionaries at Angurugu, however, have translated Amawurrena as "Holy Spirit". Jesus Christ is "Jesus Christ" and God is "God" as well as "Nungwa (Father), Na:nugwa (Son), and *amawurrena* (Holy Spirit)". From my point of view the missionaries have selected the right terms but have them back to front. They should run, Amawurrena --> Nungwa-Na:nugwa, that is, Holy Spirit --> Father-Son. Father-Son becomes the means by which "Holy Spirit" is transmitted and made manifest in humans over time (though the means could equally be, and in some parts of Australia actually is, Mother Daughter). To "Arnawurrena" I would add the term *alawudawarra* which in Aboriginal thought is the dynamic aspect of Amawurrena, its transforming power.

I now realized that I really had written the "Bible" that the Aborigines had wanted from us in 1969. In my book *Tradition and Transformation* I had proceeded from the Nambirrirrma tale to an ideal model of Aboriginal inter-relationships and moved on from there to show how Bickerton Island culture was embedded, *a priori,* in a wider matrix of ties to the east and west, showing something of the basis of these ties in the Songs of mortuary rites. What I had come to think of as the weakest aspect of my book, a theoretical perspective which insisted that "experience" was mediated by "cultural categories" to effect a behavioural response, now proved to have been its strongest. Weren't "cultural categories" merely ideological constructs predicated on a materialist-sociological base? I had reflected. Wasn't my "theoretical" perspective thus mere tautology?

What 1 now realized was that one "cultural category" was determinative rather than derivative and that was Amawurrena. Amawurrena was a cosmological rather than an ideological construct. But it was it really cosmo-*logical*? Did it have anything to do with logic at all? Was it even a "construct" at all? If not, then what was it? To answer these questions we will have to re-examine my "experience" of the Horseshoing South Bay. Instead of reiterating the experience in words, it may be more appropriate to present you with an image. This is Canadian Group of Seven painter Lawren Harris' "Pie Island, Lake Superior 1924" (Plate 13; in Bess Harris' and R.G.P. Colgrove's book, *Lawren Harris*). The "island" is an abstract form which seems to "float" above the waters of the lake while still somehow remaining attached to it. Now imagine if you will this representation simultaneous with the real scene, the one superimposed over the other and yet visible through it, and you will gain some idea of what I saw.

It's interesting that it was Northrop Frye who wrote the Introduction to the Harris and Colgrove book because another representation close to what I experienced – though not as close as the Harris painting – hangs in the foyer of the Victoria College Library at the University of Toronto. It is of a Northrop Frye figure "floating" in abstract space. Professor Frye is Canada's premiere literary critic and University Professor known for his own abiding interest in the Spiritual, if in an abstract-academic sense.

What I saw, then, was pure Form – "perfect symmetry". I saw it because I "moved into" it from asymmetry and already had some predisposition, or training, to see it from my experience with "laughing waves". I think this is what the Aborigines see all the time. The thing about it is that it's really there. This is no figment of the imagination. It is not ideology. It is not a construct, ideological or cosmological. Amawurrena is a concept, but it's referent is not another concept or category; it is an experience of "Nothing", the Emptiness that is the illuminated, outlined, Form.

This would explain a lot of things. For one, it would account for the Aboriginal emphasis on establishing natural points of differentiation as the boundaries between different countries. These would establish the parameters of the form of the land, transforming it into Land. It would also explain why Aboriginal life proceeds from a base of two and why the two are in complementary rather than opposed relation. One form takes its definition only in comparison with another: the form established between two points takes its definition as much from the forms extant on either side of these points as from something intrinsic to itself. In other words, Form is also the space between Forms.

The perfect symmetry I saw in the Bay was simultaneously Sea and Land, one circumscribing the other; the two were a simultaneous differentiation with the same symmetrical, transcendent, quality.

Pure symmetrical form bisects along its axis and "folds over" to mirror itself, a part of one in the other. As form circumscribed by a differentiated form it simultaneously separates into two as it is "folded". The resulting "unfolded" impression is something akin to the photographic essay "Reflected Landscape" (Plate 15) by Iain Baxter in the collection of the Ontario Art Gallery where the landscape does literally reflect itself. Since the camera doesn't "see" the way Iain sees so he has to intervene and rearrange the landscape to make it do so. What's real here? The image the camera records? the unarranged landscape? or the landscape as rearranged by Iain? Aboriginal "cameras" – Galiyawa's and "Crosby's" drawings – say the latter. The landscape is rearranged abstractly to bring it into harmony with itself.

This explains why on Bickerton the Wurramarrba People have "one country" which is divided between two points of land on opposite sides of the mouth of the bay; why the Wurramara have "one country" which extends around the bay but is differentiated into Bad Dreamings on the one side and

Good Dreamings on the other (and even into Wurramara and Warnungaung-geragaba). The two mirror as one—or rather the four (each side is bisected horizontally) mirror as two.

A film-maker friend of mine, Keith Bushnell, formerly of Darwin but who now works out of Sydney, discovered what appears to be a manifestation of this on the level of language. He was editing some Arnhem Land Aboriginal audio tapes when he noticed a word that sounded exactly the same played backwards as it did when played forwards. He was astounded. He experimented and found a few more. How could this be? How does one sound a word backwards as well as forwards, one which is phonetically equivalent either way, particularly without the aid of a tape recorder? Maybe it had some deep significance and maybe it didn't. I thought it did. Perhaps it signified particularly important places – places such as Rrarrarrarra in Wurramarrba country on Bickerton where Wind, Smoke and Fire all interpenetrate. Such words effectively mirror themselves or run back and forth through themselves, a one-word-as-two. (Keith also thought that this "mirroring" might have something to do with the Aboriginal talent for "imitating" animals and humans. I wonder if it doesn't also have something to do with their choice of the dronepipe as a musical instrument which requires one simultaneously to breath in and breath out in order to play it.)

This is all going to be difficult to grasp for those of you who live in such a mobile society as ours. But imagine the situation of people who have lived in contact and continuity with the same place for hundreds if not thousands of years. Given that the parameters in question are fixed by nature, though signified by culture, it is perhaps easier to understand how people could come to see the f/Form of the land – the Land as well as the land – as a mere geographical entity.

For example, for a few years I lived in a cottage on a lake near my home town of Perth, Ontario, in Canada. There was an island a couple of hundred yards off shore right out in front. I began to notice that the summer and winter solstices were marked by the passage of the sun along the length of my island. At the height of summer the sun reached the island's easternmost point in the channel between it and another island. It then began its return journey to the west, reaching the other extreme end of the island before reversing its path. This observation transformed my perception of the sun. For me now the sun travels laterally as well as vertically (though, of course, it does nothing of the sort). This in turn relativized my sense of time. I began to equate one rising and setting of the sun with one complete movement along the solsticial plane. Time and space became a continuum rather than discrete entities. So too in Aboriginal thought: the noun substitute for "place" (*angalya*) is *alarrge* which is a partial reversal of the noun-substitute for "time" (*anggawura*) or *agelarr*. A "noun substitute" can be used in another word to constitute a related meaning, as in *alarrgemidjiyalya,* a place on the beach (*midjiyalya*).

What my "observations" also did that was very Aboriginal was cause me to see two "boundary points" in the natural environment – the west end of the island and the channel – between which a Form began to take shape.

This theory of Forms also explains how Australian Aboriginal culture is a universal culture with particular manifestations as well as how each part is determined by a whole and how People and Lands could have linked up by direct or indirect means all across the continent (and in theory beyond) without proceeding from a fixed starting point, or point of invention, outward from "self" to "others" by imposition or otherwise. The Forms as an *a priori* "two" were seen simultaneously by all, everywhere. All that was needed was for people to interpret or identify them to each other. The result was an abstract arrangement of Forms that contained people in a relatively stable accommodation across the continent.

The "transcendent" nature of this order constituted a fundamental break with nature – with material determination – which permitted matter as people, species, resources and artifacts to move between these Forms at this and the Land level, thereafter becoming subject to the Forms into which they moved and being attracted back to the Forms from which they originated in turn. Nature moved between culture alternatively as host to guest.

This would help to explain why Warnungamagalyuagba culture has remained basically unchanged from 1940 to the present day despite prolonged contact and a fundamental alteration in the society's economic base. We see here a culture predicated on a theory of Forms with an experiential, empirical base which is at the same time non-material.

If this all sounds somewhat Platonic or Aristotelian it should because it is simultaneously both at once. For Plato (as in Buddhist thought) the material world is transitory, shadowy, constantly in flux. Over and above it is the world of Ideas or Forms, the ultimately real. Here is to be found unity, stability, constancy. It is a world to be reached, not by mystical transcendence, as in Buddhism, but by contemplation and rational thought. For Aristotle, on the other hand, Ideas or Forms did not exist in a transcendent realm, divorced from things, but were rather contained within those things. In Aboriginal thought/life, things are a manifestation or incarnation of Forms while simultaneously expressing them (though the Forms are not conceived of as Ideas). In this sense so-called Aboriginal religion is both imminent and transcendent. This brings us back to the question of the Nambirrirrma event as a "Christ event".

As I said, the "Christ event" too follows the *anti-thesis* ---> *thesis* => *plurality*, or, *nothingness* --- > *being* ===> *relationship* scenario. However, Jesus is moved this way twice, the initial sequence ending with his death at the hands of his enemies whom he loved. The second begins with his crucifixion, proceeds (at the level of the text) to his resurrection and reaffirmation of his relationship with his disciples, and ends with his ascension. To me the death and resurrection part of the sequence are significant for their form, not their content. There may be many more ways to be "nothing" and then "being" than to die as an adult and then be reborn as an adult three days later. To me what is important is that a statement is being made about the necessity of transcending our material circumstances or limitations. There may be many ways to do so other than by actual death and rebirth.

In the context of "sequence", then, death and resurrection, nothingness and being, are equivalent sets of terms. Nambirrirrma, insofar as he represents an incarnation of Amawurrena, is structurally equivalent to Christ (he is also physically equivalent insofar as, like the resurrected Christ, he appears as a "different kind of person" to those around him, to those who should know him). In the context of sequence two, "crucifixion" and "ascension" in the Christ event/story are equivalent terms. To me, their occurrence in the Christ event/story, like the Badjuini part of the Nambirrirrma tale, are significant as a statement of pessimism, a recognition of the odds against permanently establishing "the Kingdom of Heaven" here on earth, a recognition of the vulnerability of, in Jesus' case, Love. What were the grounds for this pessimism in Jesus' case?

Those closest to Jesus in kinship/ethnic/religious and even class terms, those we would have expected to love him the most, to be the most receptive to his message, the people amongst whom he was born and raised, loved him least, rejected his message and engineered his death (even the Disciples denied him in the end). Those farthest away in these terms, those we would have expected to love him least, to be the least receptive to his message, namely non-Jewish Gentile pagans and even Romans, came to love him the most and were most receptive to his message. (Here we locate another parallel with Nambirrirrma: like his Aboriginal counterpart, Jesus belonged to one "ethnic group" yet spoke to all.)

Nambirrirrma was not put to death by his fellow man, own or other, but he did die, though nothing is made of this in the tale. It is his son's life that ends on a pessimistic note. What is the basis for this relative optimism compared to Jesus? Nambirrimna's was an institutional solution to the problems of his People; Jesus' was personal. Why Jesus did not go the institutional route we may never know. Perhaps he was so appalled by the traditional idea of a Chosen People in a Promised Land that he failed to see how the idea could be pluralized on a world-wide basis. Perhaps he realized that on theoretical grounds even the idea of Chosen Peoples in Promised Lands was bound, in the end, to fail. All we do know for certain is that there is no mention of Peoples and Lands – Promised Lands – in the singular or plural in the New Testament; there is virtually no mention even of the appropriate religious institution within which Jesus' ideas could be contained and continued, that is, of a Church. "All" there is, is "Love one another as I have loved you" (John 13: 34). How – or whether – you generalize and apply this beyond the personal is, apparently, up to you.

Jesus' first appearance, his birth and life on earth thereafter, is, we might say, low on "incarnation", high on "relationship". His second appearance, after his crucifixion, is high on "incarnation", low on "relationship". By this I mean that in the first instance, Jesus is a manifestation of "God" but born of a human agent, Mary, if not Joseph. In his words and his deeds thereafter, however, Jesus exemplifies Love in the sense of concern for "other", to the absolute point of giving up his life for those, not who love him, as we might expect, but for those who hate him. His second appearance is directly out of death itself without the intervention or mediation of a human agent. His words and deeds on this occasion are, however, minimal. Save for a brief sojourn with the disciples, more to establish his Presence than to re-relate and reiterate, Jesus departs, somewhat hastily to my mind, for "Heaven".

By contrast, Nambirrirrma appears but once and this appearance is both high on "incarnation" and high on "relationship". He doesn't require a human mediator to be brought into human form. If anything, Nambirrirrma is born through "country": the bay in the depths of which he originated is called *mulgwa* or womb by the Aborigines and even assumes the appropriate physical shape.

Given the structural or sequential similarity of the "Christ event" to the Nambirrirrma event, were their respective revelations also structurally similar (disregarding the question of the level to which they were to be applied)? What was this thing Jesus called Love? How were "I" and "You" (to be) related?

Jesus modeled his Love for others, theirs for each other, on his own with his Father's. Turning to John (quotations are from the Revised Standard Version "Common Bible") we find him saying:

14:10 Do you not believe that I am in the Father and the Father in me? The words that I say to you I do not speak on my own authority; but the Father who dwells in me does his works. Believe me that I am in the Father and the Father in me.

And again in 14:20:

In that day you will know that I am in my Father, and you in me, and I in you.

There are many more references of like kind, almost all expressing relationships in the form of overlap and concurrence – that is, not quite "unity" (if unity were your intent, why separate "you" and "me" at all?), and yet not quite separation either. The one (I think) exception to this rule is revealing. Again, John:

15:7 If you abide in me, and my words abide in you, ask whatever you will and it shall be done for you.

The passage is followed almost immediately by another of like kind:

15:11 These things I have spoken to you, that *my joy may be in you,* and that your joy may be full.

The italics are mine. Unlike the rest, these passages locate a type of relationship in which a part of the one is placed in the other, as in the teachings of Nambirrirrma and in Aboriginal culture in general. But there is no *vice versa* in these passages. No part of you comes back to "me", Jesus; no part of "you" comes to "me" independently of Jesus. It is rather implied that "you" and "I" merge together through common affiliation with Jesus; not only is unity still implicit, then, but so is hierarchy. Relationships, even of Love, involve hierarchy?, one over the other?:

14:6 I am the Way and the Truth and the Life. No one comes to the Father except through me.

But again, as in the language of relationship, there is ambivalence here too: does "through me" mean "me" as a person or what "I" represent? It could be said that Jesus represents "God" and "God" is Trinity: Father, Son and Holy Spirit. Trinity is plural. Could this mean the path to "redemption" is through somethlng like Amawurrena, Spirit, in differentiated form? Again, there is a problem. The Christian Trinity runs backwards as if still building Towers of Babel, still trying to reach transcendent Truth from the ground, from material existence, up.

My point is that in the Christian New Testament there is but a hint of a type of relationship that appears full blown in Nambirrirrma. The same hint occurs at the beginning of Genesis too, likewise an unreciprocated part of one in the other: Eve is made from a part of Adam but in her attempt to reciprocate she gives Adam, not a part of her self, but one thing for them both to share – the forbidden fruit. For this they are both expelled and doomed to a life of unity as man and wife, a Chosen People and so on.

No matter what your religious beliefs, or lack of them, you must admit that there appears to be something in Nambirrirrma, in Aboriginal culture, that clarifies, indeed completes, what is the crucial point of the Christian message. Though I cannot do this question full justice here, I can at least outline the kind of marriage that is possible between them.

Assuming True Love is of the "part of one in the other and vice versa without loss of integrity of either" kind, that is, without hierarchy; assuming that this clarification/completion is acceptable to Christians, we could say that all that is lacking in Christianity is a vision of Love in institutional form. This would be some means of predisposing people to act as if they loved one another whether or not they actually did so. Aboriginal culture for its part, though possessing these institutional means, seems to lack a positive, personal, concept of Love (although persons do love each other). Love seems directed more at Amawurrena than at people. The difference between a European and an Aboriginal, I was told by Murabuda, is that the European sees a beautiful tree and finds it pleasing to the eye; the Aboriginal loves the tree. S/he sees in it shades of differentiation, of forms, of another dimension reflective of eternity and humans' proper place in the scheme of things. This is, appropriately, the object of veneration and Love.

The final parallel I have to offer between Nambirrirrma and Jesus, however, puts the possibility of such a marriage in its proper cosmo/logical perspective. Nambirrirrma is no longer the figure he used to be amongst Aboriginal people on Bickerton Island, Groote Eylandt and the adjacent mainland. In importance he has been superseded by the more "Dreamtime"-like figure, Blaur, who traveled between Groote and the mainland, linking half the People and Lands of the region – including the Wurramarrba and Wurramara of Bickerton – into one exogamous, or out-marrying, Company or moiety. In contrast to Nambirrirrma, Blaur did not speak to those in Lands of the other "half". His travels are associated with the spectacular Mardaiya:n secret-sacred ceremonies which originated on the mainland and now involve the Bickerton and Groote people. As Jesus is downplayed by his own People, the Jews, so Nambirrirrma is now downplayed by his own People, the Wurramara, and by Aborigines of the area generally.

The first term in our incarnational sequence, *anti-thesis,* may be "death", as in the Christ-event case. This we take to be "nothingness". But it may also be Nothingness, a positive affirmation of "non-existence". As Capra observes (p. 234) in reference to Buddhism,

> In the Eastern view, the reality underlying all phenomena is beyond all forms and defies all description and specification. It is therefore often said to be formless, empty or void. But this emptiness is not to be taken for mere nothingness. It is, on the contrary, the essence of all forms and the source of all life...
>
> In spite of using terms like empty and void, the Eastern sages make it clear that they do not mean ordinary emptiness when they talk about Brahman, Sunyata or Tao, but, on the contrary, a Void which has an infinite creative potential.

Amawurrena, Contentless Form(s), as a force for "differentiating" and "federating", a part of one in the other, is this "infinite creative potential" in Aboriginal life/thought. It is neither in nature nor in humankind but in humankind in interaction with nature in interaction with humankind. Whether you want to call this "God" or not and posit the existence of an afterlife as Aborigines and Christians (if not Buddhists) do is up to you. But if you do I hope you will at least take your cue from these Aboriginal Peoples. Aboriginal thought recognizes no Form of Forms. In fact, it emphatically denies it at every turn. There is no "Laughing Wave" from which all lesser Laughing Waves derive. Rainbow Serpent is ultimately plural, one simultaneously two, tail-to-tail in the Madalyuma, one the inside-out of the other, as in a reflection.

If contentless Form is to be "God", then "God" would have to be *a priori* plural, properly differentiated and "federated", a part of one in the other. "God" would have to be pure paradox.

To return to the question of culture and nature, determination and derivativeness, we must distinguish ideology from cosmology and experience. Then we can conclude that the former is usefully referred to as that ideational plane which is derived from the perception of other levels of human activity such as the economic, the political and the sociological, albeit the resulting constructs are sometimes reinserted into those levels to partially reconstruct them in turn. Cosmology is ideas about experiences whose ultimate nature admits no categorical expression. The experience is simply there to be realized by those who can grasp it, "good" when it is grasped, neutral in its moral implications when they do not, "evil" when grasped imperfectly (or not at all). On this latter point I am thinking of the man sitting alone on his Island in "Bad Dreaming" country on Bickerton who has got it all wrong, telling people to keep away and hoarding all the island's resources for himself. This is why he is in "Bad Dreaming" and not "Good Dreaming" country.

Anti-thesis, not only as contentless, differentiated and federating Form(s), but also as a principle in and of itself, was not only perceived but also employed by Aboriginal people as a tool for forming (re-forming) society. We saw it most clearly in the economic domain where boundaries seem to have been drawn about "surpluses" of resources so as to preclude self-sufficiency on the part of any one segment of the population, the resources in question – and later others – then being forbidden as food to those in whose domain they predominantly occurred. This is to realize the cosmological principle that relationship to others is founded in renunciation, in self-denial.

It is not so much putting others first that is at issue as removing your "self" as a potential object of other's desires. This is to renounce what you "have" – all or most of something you have that others do not – thereby putting you in a situation where you not only have nothing more to give but also nothing to be taken from you. Under the circumstances others also renounce; or at least that's the theory of it.

This also makes sense of that other most fundamental of human activities, procreation, which, when set in an Aboriginal context, seems bizarre indeed – women bearing children who are not "their own" but belong to their husband and his People/Land. Is it not that a woman bears children who are her own whom she then "renounces" to thereby prompt complementary renunciation on the part of another? – again, concrete content passing between Forms.

Anti-thesis, not only as contentless, differentiated and federated Form, but also as a principle in and of itself, is also at the basis of the Aborigines' highest intellectual/aesthetic accomplishment: musical composition. Now I don't know much about music, not having been trained in it, but I know what I hear. I hear Gula telling me that he Creates his Tunes (though not the words to his Songs) from "nothing": *"nar' a:bina"*. I hear him telling me that he "slices" something off his father's or grandfather's tunes and "twists" it in to the one he has created: *"gemalyangarrengama"*. And I hear Gula's tunes.

The Language of the Gods

To Aboriginal People, the Songs are "out there" to be picked up, accompanied, followed, in the context of performing mortuary rites. Songs aren't really Amawurrena but the Forms of Amawurrena. As such they have "content" and the content "moves", though here as Forms within Forms. This is how the Songmen can "carry" a place like A:rrira:gba on Bickerton (Map 3, #85) around with them as they sing – can be where they are and in another place at the same time. It's also how Songstream sectors are linked, a part of one in the other. In the context of a performance there's kind of an inversion of reality where concrete content, the physical persons of the Songmen, stay put while Form, as Forms within Forms, moves.

The Songmen begin a performance by going out and getting their respective Songs. Then they follow them along, the Songs carrying the Songmen along rather than the other way around. As Gula put it:

> You make sure there's three words in front of you. When you finish the three words you have to think, "Now another two or three words, probably four". Then when you finish the three you can pick up another word. That's the way you can see with your brain, see it out in front of you.
>
> One day when I was young I opened my mind and spread out all the words over my Tune. My father knew I could take the Song now. He was really happy: "That's yours now. That's yours. You can take it over."

The word for Tune is Augwayagayama. Mamera is also Tune but implies voice as well. The Tune Gula is referring to above is Alumera, Silt. This is one Gula had created from "nothing", twisting in something from his father's/grandfather's Tunes. An analysis of the word for "slicing and twisting in", *gemalyangarrengama,* will help us to understand something of the process to which the word refers: *ge* means "I will"; *ma* is the noun class for "Tune"; *lyang* is a noun incorporation meaning "head", *aringga,* and connoting "turn back on itself"; while *arrengama* means "break, tear, cut". Hence, "slicing and twisting with the head or mind", as Gula himself translates the concept. It's the relation between the unincorporated and incorporated noun for "head" that most interests us.

One segment *[a]* has been deleted from the unincorporated *aringga* while the other moves to a position before the *ng.* The *ng* and *g* segments assimilate, which is simply a matter of nasalizing the *g.* The *r* becomes *l* by lowering the sides of the tongue (in distinctive features this is known as [-lateral]). The *i* loses its syllabic quality, becoming *y.* The resulting form is *-lyang-.*

To take another example, *mamarugwa,* road, and its noun incorporated form, *-melagwa-:* the *m* and *u* segments are deleted; the second *a* shifts to a position after *r;* as before, *r* becomes *l* and through some undetermined process, *a* becomes *e* (this is a matter of moving the articulation of the vowel forward in the mouth, raising it perhaps a bit without rounding the lips).

In these examples, then, a part of one word has been "sliced" from another and "twisted" to form a new unit which is then inserted into another word to enrich its meaning. Noun "incorporation" is perhaps the wrong concept to describe the process. Noun "federation" would have been better.

Speaking generally, the Australian linguist Dixon (1980: 436–37) points out that incorporated nouns can be identical to the unincorporated nouns or be completely different as well as being a transformed part. He does see those completely unrelated as possibly affected by taboo restrictions which apply to the unincorporated but not the incorporated form.

Basically, it is this kind of "twisting" that goes on in musical composition, and it is a fully conscious process -- indeed the application of a "law". The really difficult thing, though, was to figure out what Gula meant when he said he created his Tunes out of "nothing". I would have been stumped but for the fact that one of the Tunes Gula had created in this manner was Alumera and to my ear Alumera was melodic in a way that other Aboriginal music I heard was not. Stephen Kossen confirmed my impression. Something in Gula's Tune for Alumera had been borrowed from the Western musical tradition. But before we discuss what that was, a note on the transcriptions.

Because of the nature of Aboriginal melodic patterns, Western means of musical notation are unsuited to their transcription. For the most part, Aboriginal melodies consist of short, repeated patterns, utilizing microtones. Although microtones (quarter tones) can be represented on the Western musical staff, the actual melody (in terms of higher or lower melodic intervals) is hidden. (This emphasis on microtones may very well reflect the Aborigines' superior discriminating/analytic abilities.) A system of accidentals ("diacritics" marking pitch variation) allows a melody that uses three tones (below #1) to be written using only one line or space on the staff, obscuring the intervals, especially to those unfamiliar with the notation system. This may seem unimportant, but when the focus of the investigation is the comparison of melodies and the discovery of repeated elements "federated" into successive melodies, "visibility" of the intervals allows patterns to be seen more explicitly.

Modern Western musical notation uses a staff of five lines. Each line and intervening space represents a different letter-name given to certain tones (using the first seven letters of the alphabet and repeating at each octave). Semitones that fall between these tones are shown by the use of accidentals (sharps and flats) and the best that can be represented by the system are semitones (not including conventions for quarter tones, like the example above), which have not been "standardized". In each octave there are twelve semitones, represented by only eight lines and spaces in total. The staff that has been created for the purposes of this investigation has twelve lines. Each line and space is equal to a step of one quarter tone. The staff represents the twenty-four quarter tones of an octave, with no need for accidentals.

There is no clef indicator, as this staff is meant only to show relative pitch. The time values of the notes are also relative. This was done because of a lack of repeated samples. Showing relative pitch and time will allow for any variation in absolute pitch that may exist from performance to performance, as well as any mechanical effects of the recording. The transcriptions, though, were done together, and each staff represents the same pitch values.

David H. Turner

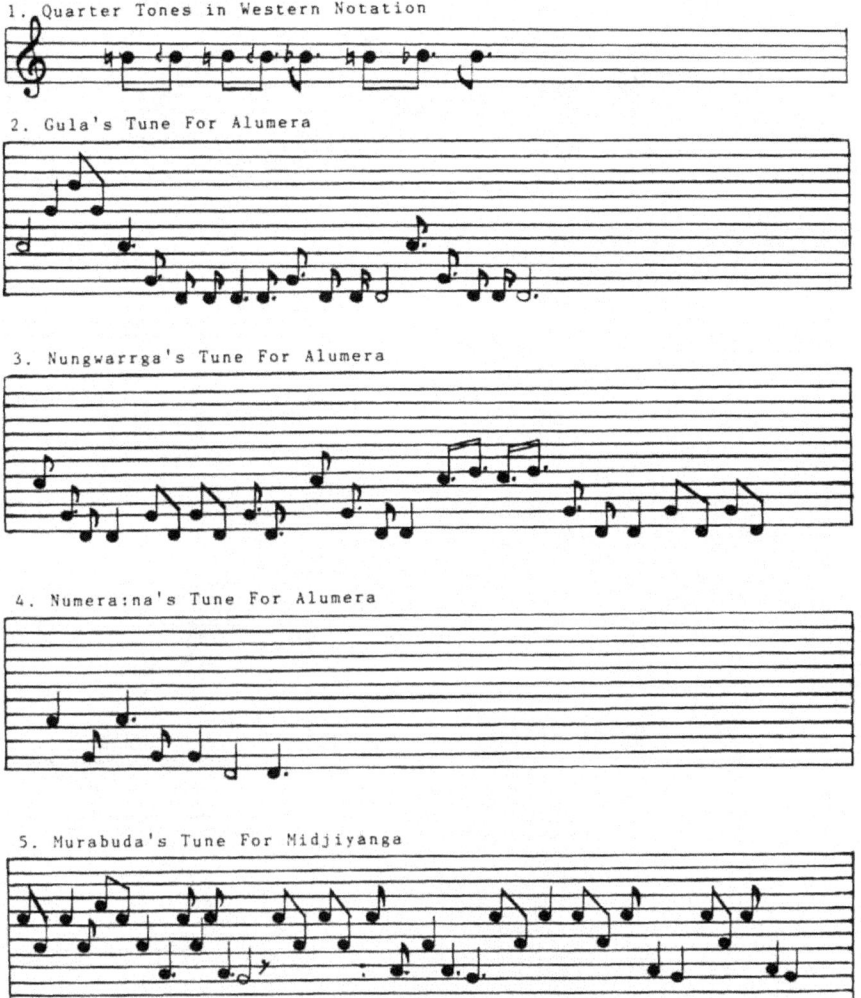

6. Nungwa:nigba's Tune For Midjivanga

7. Numera:nigba's Tune For Midjiyanga

8. Gula Singing Sectors of Yandarranga: a. Ngalmi Sector

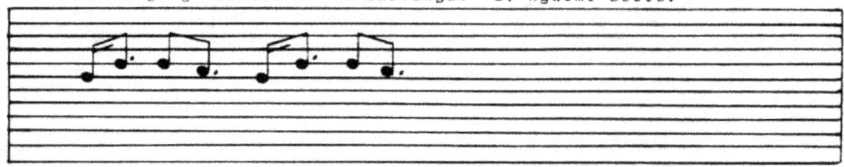

8. b. Warnungamadada Sector

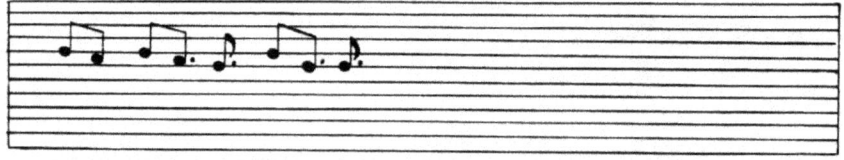

8. c. Wurra:nggilyangba Sector

David H. Turner

9. Mirniyawan Tune For Midjiyanga

10. Nundirribala Tune For Midjiyanga

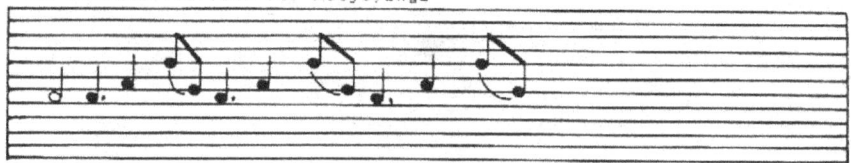

11. Wurramarrba Tune For Midjiyanga

12. Warnunggwamalangwa Tune For Midjiyanga

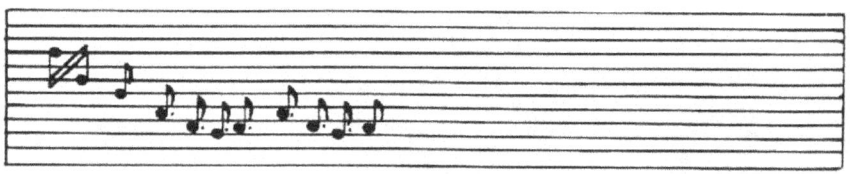

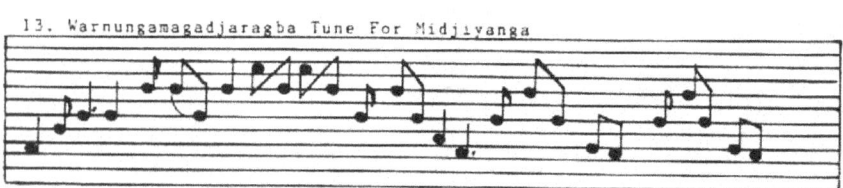

13. Warnungamagadjaragba Tune For Midjiyanga

Gula's Tune for Alumera (#2) is more melodic in the Western sense than any I encountered in my fieldwork. It covers a range of 4.25 whole tones with jumps of as much as 2 tones. By contrast, his father's Tune for Alumera (#3) covers a range of 2.25 tones, his grandfather's (#4) a range of only 2 tones with intervals of just 1.25 tones. What Gula seems to have done is taken the first four "ascending" notes from what we can only term the "parameters" of the Western musical tradition (he says he was inspired by having heard country and western music), looked back to his father's and grandfather's Tunes picking out three tones (those occurring on the space below the first line, on the second line and on the fourth space of the staff), and allowed theirs to flow into his, transforming them in the process. (I apologize for the long sentence but I wish to communicate something of the simultaneity of the creation.)

It is the way Gula's Tune begins with an ascent of more than one tone that is uncharacteristic of Aboriginal music and melodies. Though some of the Tunes recorded here proceed from an ascent, it is of a narrow range. Traditional Aboriginal music characteristically proceeds in a descending pattern, flowing from the "Heavens" down rather than the ground up, like the Aboriginal way of life or perhaps in advance of it, in the sense that it is "incarnational" music proceeding from Spirit to "matter".

The "parameters" of the Western musical tradition, then, is the "nothingness" out of which Gula has created "something" and into which he has "sliced and twisted" something "concrete" out of his and his forbears' tradition.

It is as if Gula has determined the pattern (the shape if you will) of his Tune but had not chosen the actual tones to fill the shape, therein giving it substance. This "substance" he cuts from his father's (and/or grandfather's) and "twists" it in to fill out his own. In a sense he has created a new theme from a variation. Include what his father has done before him and his father before him and you can see that what we have here is three themes from a variation.

Musical creation, generation by generation, would follow basically the same process, the "nothing" from which each one "incarnates" being the parameters or Form of the Aboriginal musical tradition – its possibilities. For instance, if we examine Murabuda's Tune for Midjiyanga (Ship) (#5) and compare it with those of his father's (#6) and grandfather's (#7) we can see that all descend to the same tone but differ in the manner by which they get there. Like Gula's Tune for Alumera, in comparison with those of his forbears Murabuda's expands in two directions: melodic range and length of repeated pattern. Murabuda's grandfather's Tune covers a range of just three quarters of a tone and his father's only one tone. Such small ranges give the appearance of chants. An example of a chant is the mainland Mirniyawan Tune for Midjiyanga (#9).

If we now turn to a comparison of Tunes co-existent in space as distinct from (dis)continuing over time we can see a very different principle at work. We find that Tunes differ from one sector of a Songstream to another, which is precisely how Aborigines say Creative Beings travel between People/Lands: they change their Tune. What similarities there are stem from their situation within a common musical tradition, not by "slicing and twisting", the Groote-Bickerton Tunes being more similar to each other in this respect than both are to the mainlanders. For instance, the mainland Ngalmi's and the-of-mainland-origin Wamungamadada's (Lalara) Tunes for Yandarranga (Central Hill) (#8a and 8b), cover a range of just .75 of a tone and are close to each other in pitch whereas the Wurra:gilyangba's Tune (#8c) has a range of two full tones. (Unfortunately it is not possible to compare the latter's Tune with that of the Warnungangwurugwerigba of Groote because of Gula's reluctance to Sing their segment because they have primary jurisdiction over Yandarranga.)

In comparing the various Tunes for Midjiyanga (#9–13) on a People/Land-to-People/Land basis (really Tunes specific to particular lines within People/Lands), we find a progression along geographical lines from the more chant-like ones of the mainland (Mirniyawan, Nundirribala) to the more melodic of Groote Eylandt (Warnungwamalangwa, Warnungamagadjeragba), with Bickerton being a midpoint between them. But the chant-like mainland Tunes are more similar to each other than to those on the Bickerton-Groote sector of the Songstream.

The Groote Tunes contain similar patterns of ascending and descending melodic segments but differ in the range of ascent and descent. Both start at a lowish point, build to a high point, then have two descending tones, the first of a smaller range and then down to a lower point ending with two descending lines. The patterns are of approximately equal length, but the range distinguishes each as a separate, distinct Tune. The lowest note of a segment marks the end of the descending line, and there is for each an intermediary note(s) that leads up to another descending melodic segment. These cannot really be considered as ascending lines and are more like steps to the descending segment.

The Wurramarrba Tune from Bickerton can be seen as following a similar pattern. It begins with an ascent and is followed by a descent, as if the four descending melodic segments of the Groote Eylandt patterns were compressed into one consisting of only two notes. The brevity of the Bickerton Tune can be seen as a result of being intermediary between Groote and the mainland. It is as if differences of starting point and range of melodic segment are inserted. This "ascend-descend" pattern then, is something which is constant – "out there" – into which differences of statting point and range of melodic segment are inserted.

In contrast to creation over time from "nothing" into "something", in creation in space lines of People/Lands take real differences of content and project them into "nothing", the very way Songmen themselves proceed each time they begin to sing.

To sum up,

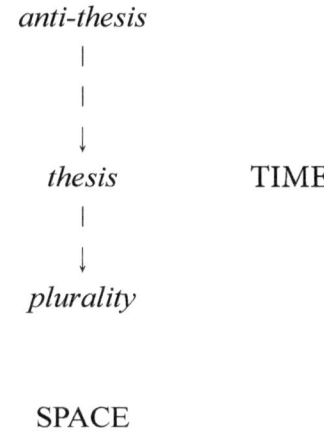

THE FALL

IX

Malara Muwurrariya
(Manganese Nightmare)

Nineteen-eighty-six was certainJy the most rewarding year of my working life. I had not only reached a deeper level of understanding of Aboriginal culture but had been able to contribute something practical to the betterment of Aboriginal and Euro-Australian relations in the Northern Territory. And I had renewed ties with the Warnungamagalyuagba which now included my children. But still there were loose ends and I returned briefly to Groote Eylandt in May of 1987 to tie them up, or so I thought. One task was to complete the survey of marriages contracted since 1969 that I had begun the year before. The other was to assist Professor John Cawte and Dr. Charles Kilburn of Prince Henry Hospital and the University of New South Wales in their investigations into the "mystery illness" that had gripped the Aboriginal community of Angurugu. This was the neurological degenerative disease I mentioned earlier. The implications of the disease for Aboriginal culture were just beginning to make themselves felt, and they were not pleasant for the people or the Peoples concerned. My son Iain had been diagnosed with cancer when we arrived back in Canada the year before and I had a gut feeling that it might have had something to do with being on Groote Eylandt. In many ways this trip was like returning to Umbakumba in 1974 after my earlier experiences on the island in 1969. I wasn't sure if I really wanted to be there.

I arrived in Sydney just as Professor Cawte was sending his preliminary diagnosis of the illness off to be published in *The Lancet* (May 30,1987), an international medical newsletter based in London, England. In it he described the high blood manganese levels of two Aboriginal brothers from Angurugu on Groote Eylandt with the neurological degenerative "bird" disease: 630 and 640 n mol/1 respectively, compared to an adult reference range of I 00-350 n mol/1. A subsequent testing of 20 more Aboriginal people showed highly elevated levels above 600 and 700 n mol/1 in four with the disease and low levels in the order of 150–200 n mol/1 in those without. Such low levels also characterized Caucasians generally on the island. The article also pointed out that the elder brothers had worked in close contact with manganese at the mine on Groote while a younger brother who was unaffected had not. At least 16 people had the illness, though not all had been tested for the manganese factor. Other unusual clinical conditions observable within the local Aboriginal population besides the "bird disease" were "connective tissue disorders, congenital malformations and infant deaths [a still birth–rate of 42 per 1,000 compared to 29.5 for Aborigines in the Northern Territory as a whole], and also psychiatric syndromes, usually expressing acute excitements." The implication was that all these were somehow related.

Comparisons were made with the motor-neurone disease syndromes of the Western Pacific which "are associated with parkinsonian-dementia, described in Japan, Guam Island and West Irian ... located on approximately the same longitude of 137 degrees... However, no parkinsonian-dementia is obvious in the Groote Eylandt cohort." There was, however, a common mineralogical context for these ailments – trace metals such as manganese and aluminium.

Cawte went on to point out that he and his co-authors Charles Kilburn, the on-site investigator, and Graham Hams had progressively eliminated genetic determinants associated with in-breeding, deficiencies of calcium, iron, folic acid and protein and the toxic effects of foodstuffs such as cycad palm nut and cassava. He did, however, point out that manganese, though mined only recently, was a substance long-used in the area by Aboriginal craftsmen and was relatively close to the surface. In fact, Angurugu was located on top of one of the richest deposits of manganese on the island. They virtually lived in the stuff.

John Cawte told me that he had told Murabuda, the Angurugu Council President, of these findings and I knew he would be worried. So I phoned him from Sydney. Yes, he knew the results and so did the Council. So, by the way, did top officials at the mine. But the Council hadn't yet told the community because the people would be afraid, particularly the old men. He asked me if I would speak to Clyde Holding, the federal Aboriginal Affairs Minister, about it and ask him to ensure that the news remained confidential. The Aborigines were still smarting over the Biles Report pointing out the high crime rate on the island and they did not want any more bad publicity. This was a restriction I would have to apply to myself, though Murabuda never said as much.

I made my way to Canberra and saw Clyde on the evening of the 9th. He did not know of the most recent findings or that they were being published. But as a former labour relations lawyer he certainly realized the implications. So would the Mining Company. Neither GEMCO as such nor their parent firm the giant B.H.P. were going to take Cawte's findings at face value. Murabuda willingly got his promise to keep the matter confidential and John Cawte was summoned to Canberra for a conference. Meanwhile I was off to Darwin and Groote.

Murabuda and the Angurugu Community Government Council were indeed worried about the manganese. John Cawte and Charles Kilburn had told them that it might be responsible for the sickness, but the Aborigines needed time to think it all through. One reason was that they couldn't understand how the manganese could be causing an illness in some when all were more or less equally exposed to it. This was also the doctors' dilemma. There were basically two schools of Aboriginal thought on the matter.

One was that the manganese was in fact causing the disease, getting into the blood because of over-exposure and somehow affecting people because it was in the blood. This made sense because there is no recollection of the illness prior to the onset of mining. I couldn't recall having observed the symptoms myself in 1969, though of course I wasn't looking for them. John Cawte had gone through the previous work on the island by Worsley, Rose and Tindale and neither could he find any concrete evidence of it in the earlier period. The issue is complicated by the fact that the Aborigines classify the neurological degenerative disease in with any physiologically disabling illness such as leprosy. They call all *alarndarragawarriya*. Superficial inquiries will appear to elicit evidence of the neurological disease in the pre-mining era when the Aborigines are in fact referring to another particular illness. The issue is further complicated by the fact that symptoms of the disease are also characteristic of someone who has been sorcerized. This brings us to the second school of thought.

The Groote and Bickerton Aborigines insist that sorcery was imported from the mainland in the recent past and confirm that I witnessed the very first act performed on Groote in 1969. This is recounted in my book *Tradition and Transformation* (pp. 106–108). But then it all depends on what we mean by "sorcery". The kind of interference in the world of the Spirit they call *mamadjinga* and translate as "sorcery" and regard as "evil" they also regard as abhorrent because it represents a human intervention into the domain of the Spiritual. Recall the "Bad Dreamings" of Bickerton. Such sites are dangerous – evil in their effects – only insofar as you approach them so closely as to become contaminated by them. Humans cannot use them for evil effect (nor for that matter can they use them for good effect, I now found). Humans can, however, intervene through singing to temporarily resituate (one of) a person's Spirit(s) someplace else, whether this is the Spirit of someone alive or someone dead. They cannot, though, cause a permanent breach between body and Spirit. The Spirit can be caused to "stretch through" to the fifth dimension. But it is (must be) then be sung back.

What these Aborigines translate as "sorcery" and insist is "foreign" takes all this one step further to bring about a permanent breach. This results in death. Cosmologically there can be no question as to the effectiveness of this means of killing.

What sorcery does is remove your own Spiritual part and resituate it elsewhere, thereby leaving you only with parts of others' – your mother's, father's mother's, mother's mother's. To be wholly "other" is to be non-self – *anti-thesis,* no-thing. As no-thing you are dead. What follows from this are the actual techniques of what we may term "Spiritual violence": pointing bones and the like within which to capture and hide a person's Spirit. Sorcery, then, brings about the same transformation of body and Spirit as natural death but before one's time bas come and in the reverse direction. On physical death the body is "extracted" from, or dissolves around, Spirit. Aboriginal people on Groote now believe that any "premature" death, that is, one whose cause is not immediately evident, must have been brought about by sorcery. This no longer includes such European-introduced diseases as measles as it did in 1969. The list of explainables is growing as the knowledge of the Aboriginal health worker, Fred Durila, and his assistants grows.

No one believes that the neurological degenerative disease is caused by sorcery. Some, however, think it may be due to "Spiritual contamination." They observe that the illness runs more in some "clans", as they now call them in English, than in others -- primarily the Lalara and the Bara (Warnungwadarrbalangwa) though there are people with the disease in five different "clans". Since there is no concept of biological inheritance or transmission, except in some vague sense perhaps through the mother, the Aborigines explain the phenomenon of "running in clans" by a form of "contamination" called *auguburda.*

In pre-mission times bodies were raised on platforms until the flesh decayed off the bones at which time the bones were wrapped in bark containers and buried in caves in the deceased's, or a closely related, country. The body-juices, though, were scooped up with baler shells as they fell to the ground and later evaporated over a pile of hot stones. All this was then covered with earth and abandoned. The danger was that someone would come into contact with the body-juices as they fell or were being collected, become "contaminated", and suffer Spiritual injury. This, they insist, is what happened to Mandaga Lalara two generations ago. Now his "fractured Spirit" is showing up in his grandchildren, producing the same effect as if they had been the victims of sorcery. (This thesis has the interesting effect of reinforcing a belief in the reincarnation of the Spirit that I thought had been replaced by a lineal-cyclical notion by 1969.) Having identified the "cause" of the neurological disease in the "clan" in which it is concentrated, however, proponents of this explanation began to "remember" similar causes in the case of everyone afflicted -- afflicted not just with the neurological degenerative disease but with any illness classed *alarndarragawarriya::* "Bugwanda (must have) touched the stuff (a grandchild has the disease), and also Dabbo (who has something like the disease), and Wanaiya's father"... and so on.

Interestingly, Malara Muwurrariya, Bad Manganese Dreaming (Table 3, #102), is used, not by proponents of the Spiritual cause explanation but by those favouring material causes, as an indication that the old men knew there was something wrong with manganese as a substance and that one should avoid contact with it. In terms of their present predicament, at least if it is the manganese there is hope for those who do not yet have the illness. There is no hope for the 16 already with it no matter what the cause of the illness. Once you contract it, eventually you die.

A meeting on the manganese problem was organized for Thursday, June 11th at the Health Department in Darwin. I completed my survey of the marriage system on the previous Sunday, the 7th, as it turned out, just in time. I found that none of the afflicted patients had been born of a *warnigarangbidja* or closer marriage relationship, that is, father of man and mother of woman from the same Land and generation. *Warnigarangbidja* marriages had occurred since 1969 but they represented only a small percentage of the total. Neither, then, had the marriage system broken down as those who would blame the Aborigines for their own misfortune would have us believe. This is not to say that the manganese is causing the disease; it is simply to say that it is not due to "inbreeding" or the like.

The conference papers have been reproduced in the booklet, *Manganese and Metabolism,* prepared by John Cawte and Charles Kilburn, and here I will summarize my own impression of the findings. Neither Professor Cawte nor Dr. Kilburn are responsible for the views hereafter expressed. By the time of the conference another article had already gone off to *The Lancet* in England for publication (June 27, 1987). It concerned the data on high concentrations of manganese in the soils and native food-stuffs around Angurugu. While the world average concentration of manganese in soil was 500 parts per million (ppm), in the old vegetable garden run by the Mission at Angurugu it was 103,000 ppm. In the banana plantation it was 41,900, and in two sections of the old orchard 33,400 and 14,300 ppm respectively. The concentration was also very high, however, in the local, non-cultivated, staple food the long yam, *murndigrriya:rra:* 720 ppm. The world average for a vegetable food-stuff was 0.2-7.7 ppm. Fulther tests at Angurugu showed Paspalum with a concentration of 240 ppm and bananas 31 ppm. The paper concluded that the immediate source of manganese toxicity could be the topsoil rather than the mining, though it pointed out that gardening had all but ceased during the period in which the illness manifested itself and that bush foods were not as sought after in this period as they had been in the past. But the long yam was the one bush food that was still consistently gathered in the vicinity of Angurugu.

At the conference further data were presented showing that manganese in the air at Angurugu was 100 times the world average, and in water 10 times, though the researchers concluded that the intake this represented would be relatively insignificant. In combination with the other factors, though, they could become very significant.

In all likelihood the "cause" of the illness is a cohort of factors of which manganese accumulation/concentration is a necessary but not sufficient cause. Florence, Stauber and Fardy in their paper for the conference list low iron or anemia, chronic infections, high alcohol intake, low dietary calcium and zinc depletion as increasing one's susceptibility to manganese toxicity. All these factors characterize the Aboriginal population. In answer to the question of why all are exposed to manganese yet only some contract the disease, the authors suggest "individual susceptibility" or individual variations in uptake rate and clearance rate of the toxicant in turn affected by the excretion ability of the liver and kidneys.

The source of the manganese concentrations? Admittedly the Angurugu Mission was established on a site particularly rich in manganese and the Aborigines have been living in close contact with it there ever since. But the other fact remains that there is no clear-cut evidence of the disease prior to commencement of the mining in the mid-1960s. Of those with the disease born prior to 1960, onset of the disease (with one exception) was in adulthood. Of those born after 1960, onset was in childhood. Something was triggered by the coming of the mine whether excessive exposure to manganese, a worsening dietary situation, or exposure to debilitating European diseases.

At the conference Professor Cawte stated that he had advised top government officials in Canberra as early as 1984 (see Preface to this edition) that

> it is now my view that Angurugu should be regarded as an unsafe environment until proven otherwise. I believe that every man, woman and child, and especially unborn children, may be at considerable risk.

Had I known this in advance, I would never have placed my own family at risk by taking them back with me to Groote. One of the toxic effects of manganese noted by Dr. Cawte, for instance, which was "not previously recognized nor suspected", was interference with the immune system, "notably the defense against viral infections". Particularly potent viruses can trigger off neuro-blastoma, the kind of cancer with which Iain was afflicted.

After the conference a press release was issued stressing the ongoing nature of the research, the continuing need for the support of all parties including the Mining Company and a call for "further research" to clarify the issues raised by the participants and called on participants to "jointly formulate a properly researched and agreed protocol for future research".

Fortunately, Mike Duffy of the Northern Land Council, who had sat unidentified throughout a conference to which his organization had not been invited, picked up the same point and published it in his account of the proceedings in the following issue of *Land Rights News* (Vol. 2, No. 3). Mike's impression was that despite the evidence of the conference, officialdom still "appear to accept the possibility of a genetic trigger" and "balked at linking this with the natural environment, or with any disturbance to that environment." This article, more than anything else, served to keep the issue from being placed on the backburner. It was picked up by the *Sydney Morning Herald* (June 19) and then by the Trades Unions, worried about the implication for their members working for the Mining Company on Groote. There was nothing in the Company's General Safety Handbook (1986) at all to warn of possible health hazards from exposure to manganese even though some of these are by now well known (see the World Health Organization's 1981 paper, "Environmental Health Criteria for Manganese", Geneva).

John Cawte reproduced Mike's article in his *Proceedings* of our Conference and had the foresight to insist that the press release state that the final decision as to who would henceforth do what and to whom in the way of research would rest with the Angurugu Council.

The Aboriginal response? The Conference passed through Murabuda, Kevin and Djabeni like water through a sieve. They puzzled at me for not having brought up the *auguburda* issue. Here I was, the one person who understood their culture well enough to know the illness could be because of *auguburda* and I didn't say anything. Instead I told the meeting the illness wasn't because of close marriages which, to them, was a non-issue. But what the hell was I supposed to do? Blame the victims? What was anyone to do except trust the experts to come up with a solution. This is what the Aborigines did. As the Conference proceedings reported:

> Mr. Murabuda said that his people were anxious that the research go forward to a successful conclusion. The disease must be controlled to make the people strong and happy. He emphasized that the people did not want any public attention, fuss or trouble. They just wanted their disease understood and relieved. He thanked today's experts for coming to this meeting.

No matter what we throw at these aboriginal people, they remain infinitely accommodating.

Nevertheless, you can feel what John Cawte terms "dread" looming at Angurugu. Murabuda has declined a second term as President and withdrawn to what he hoped would be a gardening enterprise at the mouth of the Angurugu River. But who at the mining Township or at Angurugu is going to buy fruit and vegetables grown in manganese-infected soils? Nandjiwarra and Gula divide over the issue of the cause of the illness, taking their People and Songstream-mates with them: Nandjiwarra charges *auguburda* or, worse, sorcery, Gula claims manganese poisoning which would mean relocation or an end to the mining and its royalties. (I mention sorcery because certain implications are now being drawn from the Wurramara's association with

Lightning and Lightning's association with the Nemarnurdudi, or Sorcery People, on the mainland.)

The frustration builds, a part of one begins to be extracted from the other and vice versa.

John Cawte noted another syndrome amongst the Groote and Bickerton Islanders. It is characterized by excitability and a tendency toward violence. The implication is that it is also environmentally, or even genetically, related. But I don't think so. The syndrome wasn't evident in 1969 and I could locate but one case of death by violent means between 1946 and my first visit and that for infringing "the law". Missionaries and policemen, however, are quick to form an impression that the Aborigines were always a violent people. Admittedly much Aboriginal behaviour implied violent intent. But what missionaries and policemen failed to mention or observe was that rarely was the "intent" ever fulfilled.

Just as Malgari of the Arnagula, for instance, would rush forward in an excited state, his spear hooked to his spear-thrower, his throwing arm cocked, "obviously" bent on killing Djawaranga or whomever, someone would suddenly appear out of nowhere in the nick of time to prevent the spear being thrown or causing it to be thrown off target. Even actual violence was always under control, and it almost always put an end to further violence rather than initiated new instances of it.

I recall the case of a young man from Numbulwar who had come over to work at the mine. He had gone to the bush with a woman promised to Grumadali. Grumadali speared him for it. I know because I was only 20 feet away when he did it. They had appeared out of nowhere running toward my tent, the young man in front, Grumadali in hot pursuit with his spear hooked on his spear-thrower. It was all so close I was able to notice two things. In the first place, the young fellow was pacing himself, dictating the size of the gap between himself and the older man behind. In the second, Grumadali's spear was *mamanugwa,* the unbarbed fighting spear, which meant he only intended to wound. He threw it and it lodged in the fleshy part of the young man's side. Other men now intervened and carried him off to the Mission clinic. Grumadali's honour was saved. The incident was over. But this didn't stop a patrol officer from coming down from the mining Township of Alyangula the next day and arresting Grumadali. He was sentenced to four to six months in jail in Darwin.

Today, though, except for the police intervention, things are different.

There is fighting almost every night and people are getting killed -- more than a dozen since my last visit in 1974. All of the killings, and most of the violence, are under the influence of alcohol. Alcohol doesn't so much cause as excuse aggression. The cause, it seems to me, is the obverse of sorcery.

Sorcery causes a premature death by extracting the victim's Spirit, leaving them wholly "other", *anti-thesis,* no-thing. In the real world of post-contact Aboriginal society, however, "other", I would put it, is slowly being extracted from "self" whether on a People-to-People or Individual-to-Individual basis leaving selves in unmediated confrontation. On a reciprocal basis, unless the extraction is simultaneous, it leaves the one from whom the extraction has been made alone, dependent and vulnerable. S/he strikes out in anguish at what can only be termed a fall into un-humanity. When this happens between a man and a woman, we can say that love is coming apart; in the Aboriginal case, however, it is what Men and Women love that is coming apart.

X

Broken Promises

Ironically, from my point of view at least, it was the Church Missionary Society who brought the mining to Groote Eylandt. Ironic, considering it should have known better in the light of what the New Testament has to say about the evils of pursuing wealth and material prosperity. These lines are from 1 Timothy, Chapter 6:

6   But godliness with contentment is great gain.

7   For we brought nothing into this world and it is certain we can carry nothing out.

8   And have food and raiment let us be therewith content.

9   But they that will be rich fall into temptation and a snare and into many foolish and hurtful lusts, which drown men in destruction and perdition.

10   For the love of money is the root of all evil: which while some coveted after, they have erred from the faith, and pierced themselves through with many sorrows.

To which one might add, "and pierced themselves *and others* through with many sorrows."

Compare these comments with those of Jim Taylor, the ex-Superintendent of Angurugu who, with the C.M.S. organization, negotiated for GEMCO to come to Groote Eylandt and mine manganese (quoted in Keith Cole's book, *Groote Eylandt Stories*, p. 82):

> ... missionaries on Groote Eylandt in the past were always trying to find viable economic projects which could be undertaken in order to find gainful work for Aborigines. Thus when B.H.P. first made overtures to the C.M.S. in the early 1960s to allow them to prospect the

manganese ore body, the immediate reaction of the staff was that here was golden opportunity for proper economic employment of local Aborigines, not only directly in the mining of the ore, but also indirectly in the supply of ancillary services...

As for how to harness the Aborigines to the cause: "until an acceptable incentive is either taught or found [neither money, the desire to raise the general standard of living, nor even working alongside their workmates being in themselves sufficient], we will find that the majority of Aborigines will work irregularly by European standards" (p. 84).

Between C.M.S., GEMCO, and various levels of Government, the Aboriginal people of Groote and Bickerton Island were pushed on to a course that now promises not only to extract the parts of themselves that are in others, but also to institutionalize and even idealize the resulting separations on an individual/group, People/Land, basis (if there are to be People and Lands left here at all) thereafter relying, as we do, on the coercive powers of the state to hold the resulting tensions in check.

You may have wondered why there is no updated detailed map of the Promised Landscape of Groote Eylandt in this book. I had planned on drawing one up on the basis of my 1969 researches, with some supplementary work in the early 1970s. This never having materialized (Chapter 1) it is by now out of the question. The very act of investigating the issue would hasten the separations that are now taking place. Recall my experiences in 1974 when Wanaiya tried to make use of the generalized map of Bickerton in my book to claim Land which he knew to be in dispute. That was before the inauguration of land rights. Paradoxically, the granting of Aboriginal land rights, while easing the tension from the Aboriginal-White point of view, has exacerbated tensions within Aboriginal society – on Groote Eylandt as well as elsewhere. The problem is that no matter how "progressive" we are in our intentions, our institutions are so primitive in comparison with those of the Aborigines that we diminish their culture in any accommodation. Land rights is one example; Community Government, the subject of my consultancy with the Minister of Community Development in the Northern Territory in 1986, is another.

Land(?) Rights

The Aboriginal Land Rights (Northern Territory) Act 1976 establishes Aboriginal Land Trusts to hold title to Aboriginal land for the benefit of those entitled by Aboriginal tradition to the use or occupation of the land in question. These Trusts are to operate under the direction of Land Councils representing those "entitled" by Aboriginal tradition which Section 4 of the Act defines as "traditional owners". These are local descent groups of Aboriginals who have common spiritual affiliation to a site on the land and primary responsibility for that site and are entitled by Aboriginal tradition to forage over the land. Though the Act specifies that a Land Council shall take into account the interests of any other Aborigines with an interest in the land, it is the rights of the "traditional owners" that are primary. Groote and Bickerton Island fall within the jurisdiction of the Northern Land Council. Though they were granted land rights automatically with enactment of the Act and thus did not have to go through a claim process, the terms of the Act have not been without their effects on the islanders.

Soon after land rights were enacted Judith Stokes, the Mission linguist, attempted to draw up a map of Groote and Bickerton Island with the Aboriginal elders setting down proprietary jurisdictions in accord with the terms of the Act, that is, in accord with the concept of "traditional owner". The attempt ended in confusion and bickering and was abandoned. The elders decided instead to treat all of Groote Eylandt and Bickerton Island as a single jurisdiction for purposes of dealings with Europeans and work its internal relations as they always had. But in the course of this exercise they were introduced to the concept of "traditional owner" and some were quick to grasp the implications for "their own" interests (or for realizing a concept of "their own" interests). By 1976 the term had crept into popular use without an Anindilyaugwa equivalent. This is because none is possible.

Property rights in Australian and Western law in general afford an "owner" the right to use and enjoy property, exclude others from such enjoyment, and alienate the piece of property in question. One of the essential tenets of Aboriginal law is that one holds jurisdiction over, on and below land, sea and air in order to make what is over, on and below it in a material sense available to others. We allow for the sharing of property, even multiple rights in property, but not the holding of it for non-owners who in turn hold theirs for you, except perhaps in a Trust relation. But even in a Trust relationship the property in question is eventually turned over to the "rightful owners" once certain conditions such as age of majority are fulfilled. The gulf between ours and the Aboriginal concepts is so great as to be virtually unbridgeable. Virtually, but not entirely. Both share one important element in common and this is the "legal" aspect of the relation: one continues to hold one's property in our society even though it may not be in one's possession. Your house is still yours to come back to even though you have been away from it, say, on holidays. The law and the State will affirm your title over and above that of squatters. In this aspect "property" is somewhat like citizenship in the State. Citizenship gives you a share of jurisdiction in the State and the State is a bounded jurisdiction.

To me, citizenship in the State is more like affiliation with an Aboriginal-style Promised Land than is "property". As embodied in a passport, it allows you to move in and out of your country without affecting your right of re-entry. It allows you a measure of control over what is in your country in combination with your fellow citizens without specifying the form that control might take (such as to make what is in it available to citizens of another Land, as distinct from enjoying it for yourself). It is like being affiliated with the boundary drawn around the country – which is fixed – without being similarly affiliated with what is contained within that boundary. It enables you to treat those who move in with similar affiliations elsewhere as guests and for them to treat you as guests when you move into their abstract space in turn. The essence of the arrangement in both the Aboriginal and our own case, is that neither party thereby poses a threat to the other; peaceful co-existence is thus guaranteed. The main difference between the Aboriginal concept of Promised Land and ours of citizenship is that the boundary that defines the Land in their case has a transcendent, religious quality that implies "expulsion of matter" whereas the one that defines the state in our case, does not.

But neither citizenship nor the concept of a Promised Land were the basis of the Land Rights Act, and it was now 10 years after the Act had been implemented. Its implications had more than just sunk in – they were beginning to be realized in practice. Wanaiya of the Warnungwadarrbalangwa to whom I had "given" land on Bickerton with my mis mapping was, unfortunately, a man ahead of his time. A case in point is the Land within which Angurugu is situated. The whole area between the Angurugu and Yedigba rivers was originally Wurramaminyamandja country. However, when the Warnungamadada (Lalara) moved over from Bickerton in pre-historic times (but after the Warnungwadarrbalangwa migration from Bickerton) they were given what appears to be a share in the jurisdiction of this area by the Wurramaminyamandja. Recall that the two Peoples sang the same Songs but by different Tunes. Everyone agrees on the two men party to the agreement, Numulyarrgariya Lalara (Gula's grandfather) and Nenungwabara

Maminyarnandja, but the details of the agreement differ. Some Lalara insist the whole area was turned over to them, the Maminyamandja agreeing to restrict themselves to a much smaller area south of Yedigba on the east coast. Some Maminyamandja say their country was subdivided, the part along the Angurugu River going to the Lalara, the rest remaining Maminyamandja. The same applied to the area south of Yedigba, half of it remaining Maminyamandja, the other half becoming Lalara. The Maminyamandja at Umbakumba, on the other hand, insist no such agreement was ever entered into and the whole Land in question remains Maminyamandja. The Lalara are there as guests. (Something everyone agrees on, though, is that Angurugu itself was later carved out as a "neutral zone" to accommodate the Mission – a variation on the "guest home" principle we have already encountered in our travels through the Promised Landscape of Amagalyuagba.)

The point is that all of this erupted when the elders tried to draw up the "land rights" map with the concept of "traditional owner" now in the back of their minds. Things became so heated that the Lalara threatened to pack up and return to the mainland unless some support was forthcoming for their position. The debate continues.

It's not just the European definition of "traditional owners" and "land rights" that is at issue, but also the relative worth of land now that Europeans have intervened in the Aboriginal environment. Europeans not only look at land as something owned for the owner's benefit but enforce that outlook on behalf of some Aborigines who have come to look at it that way themselves. "My/our" land, property, or whatever is now a legal possibility in Aboriginal society and there are those who are quick to realize it.

Central Hill entered Groote Eylandt at Amalyigba on the north-west coast and made his way across to the east side of the island. In 1969 the implication was that the part of him that was Wurra:nggilyangba from Bickerton had pushed in to the part of him that was Warnungangwurugwerigba on Groote, thereby establishing the close connection that exists between them. In 1986 the question is, by pushing in did not Central Hill establish primary jurisdiction there for the Wurra:nggilyangba? At least this is the question the Wurra:nggilyangba are asking if not the Warnungangwurugwerigba. If the blood of Dimimba washed up on the north-west coast of Groote, did that not mean the shore belonged to the Wurra:nggilyangba in whose Land on Bickerton it originated? Did not the Wurramara's Lightning linkage to the extinct Warnung-murugulya give them a claim on their now "vacant" Lands?

There is another dimension that Europeans encourage: land used and occupied is land owned. It's a criterion written in to the Land Rights Act as an addendum to Spiritual affiliation. It may also be the basis of the Wurrawilya's recent claim to a share in the Wurramaminyarnandja's jurisdiction over its Lands on Groote. They have rights there, they say, because they "camped together" with the Mamaminyamandja in pre-Mission times. The Lalara, at least, are skeptical.

I talked to Murabuda of the Wurramarrba at length about these shifting emphases. He had been pressing the Wurra:nggilyangba case not only for Central Hill's pathway on Groote but also for the north-west shore of the island as well as for Connexion Island in between Groote and Bickerton. His mother is Wurra:nggilyangba. He had the upper hand until I remembered something his father, Galiyawa, used to do when explaining relation to Land to me. He would clasp his hands together with the fingers of one through the spaces between the others as he talked about Land-to Land relations. So this is what I did while explaining that in his father's time Lands were "like this", while now they were "like this" as I unlocked my fingers and made two clenched fists, banging them together. End of debate.

Things haven't changed significantly in this respect as yet, but as my computer survey confirms, they are slowly changing. The changes in respect of Land/s are perhaps best symbolized by comparing Murabuda's drawing of Amagalyuagba (Figure 2) with those of his father and Crosby Wurramara (Figure 7). The symmetry is still there and Nambirrirrma's landing place is still the focal point in Murabuda's drawing, but Galiyawa's Seascape rendition of the island has given way to one of the Land as such; and Crosby's lines, expressive of "part of the one in the other" or federative logic, have yielded to blocks of separations. More significantly, the landScape of Amagalyuagba is now bifurcated, the basis of the symmetry now the track of the moiety-Being, Blaur.

There is a reason for this. Blaur is associated with the secret-sacred Mardaiya:n ceremony. In the context of Northern Land Council meetings in Darwin, Aborigines from all over the "top end", as the semi-tropical north country is called, have discovered a common point of reference in this and other ceremonies of like kind such as the Gunabibi. Indeed these ceremonies and what they represent have laid the basis for a pan-Aboriginal dual identity focused on the two moieties which has become particularly significant to

Aboriginal people whose cultures have been altered much more by European contact than those of the Groote and Bickerton Islanders. Through Land Council affiliation and a moiety level of "commonality", many Aborigines are reassessing what it means to be "Aboriginal". The more significant these inter-Aboriginal contacts become and the more interaction there is on a wider basis, the more important these dualistic institutions become. Unfortunately, at the local level this threatens to diminish the richness of the traditional culture.

For instance, Culture Heroes such as Blaur normally visit or call out the names of only one or two places within any given Land. There is but one Songman per segment of the Songstream and but one Songstream. The Songman and his Land also assume hierarchical significance and the former is likened by Aborigines to a "high priest" or "bishop" in the fashion of the Catholic or Anglican Church. Now this is not new. I heard such talk in 1969. What is new is that the "Bishop" may become the sole repository of, and the ceremony the sole expression of, Aboriginal culture in many areas. That prospect to me is frightening.

Return to Eden

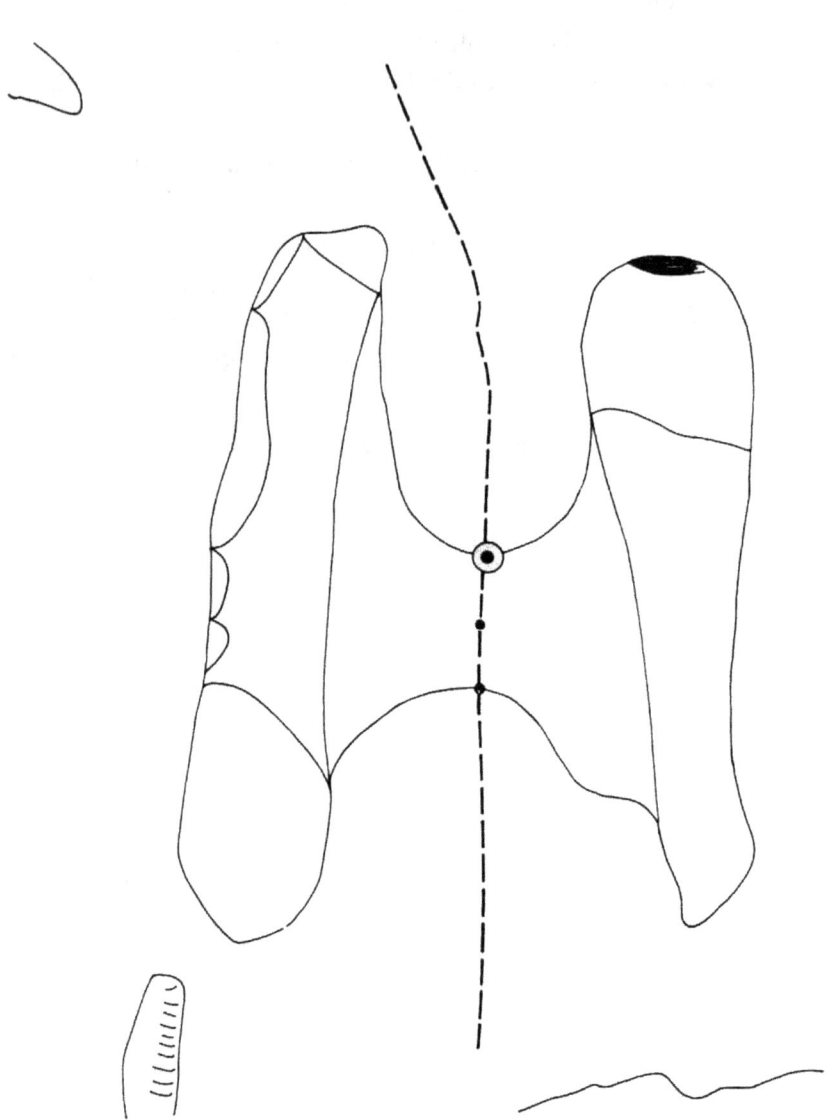

Figure 7. Murabuda's Drawing of Amagalyuagba

It is no coincidence that these ceremonies harbour the more violent expressions of Aboriginal ceremonial life such as killings for ritual transgression. As Tony Swain (1993) observes, such aspects may very well have originated in the dualistic distinction the early Christian Missions introduced into Aboriginal Spirituality between God (as Good) and the Devil (as Evil), not to mention the practice of introducing Aboriginal people to Christianity through the Old Testament, believing these "tribal" people predisposed at least to that chapter of their story. Herein are precedents that "God punishes Evil through human agents like Moses and Joshua" which may well have influenced Aboriginal Spiritual thinking. Certainly today many Aborigines treat both Old and New Testament as equivalent, referring to Moses and the Prophets as "Christians". And when it comes to punishment for ritual transgression the methods employed not only sound Old Testament but are explicitly founded on Old Testament precedent. I won't go into them here.

I am fortunate indeed to be working with Peoples on the fringe of the secret-sacred ceremonial orbit and to have recorded their Spirituality as it existed in its absence. In its absence the sacred is not secret in the sense of removed from view and Spirituality has no Evil side which can be harnessed to human ill through such means as sorcery, though it does have a side potentially harmful to humans if they approach it too closely.

Another reason why I do not want to go through the Mardaiya:n ceremony, by the way, is that I do not wish to be seen reinforcing it.

Working against the indigenous culture on Groote and Bickerton in this respect is increased communication with Aborigines who have come to rely on ceremonies like this in order to preserve any vestige of their traditional culture. Such communication takes place in the context of meetings of the Northern Land Council and in the Mardaiya:n and Gunabibi rituals themselves which take these Aborigines as far inland as Beswick near Katherine on the Stuart Highway running south from Darwin. Nor is their situation helped by the paucity of old men who remain to disseminate their own traditional culture, nor by the apparent paucity of young people willing to receive it. Indeed, the petrol-sniffing 10–20 year-olds who should be engaged in this quest seem bent on creating a secret-sacred sub-culture all their own.

Though I have shied away from studying petrol-sniffing culture, it tends to make its own presence felt. And what I have noticed in it is a weird inversion of the traditional Aboriginal culture married to an even weirder Christianity. First, the sniffing itself produces visions not dissimilar to those experienced by the old men during the Singing though the latter require no stimulant to achieve this. The young men have found they can "get there" without all the work that normally goes into learning how to get there. Rock videos and the like with their dream-like images and confounding of space and time are evidence to them that Europeans "get there" too. Knowing how different European and Aboriginal cultures are in other respects the sniffers attempt to "get there" by inventing their own culture which, they think, will make them more like Europeans.

Instead of singing and dancing in lines, they form into sniffing circles, usually two. If alcohol is an excuse for indiscriminate fighting among men and between men and women in the world of their fathers and mothers, sniffing is an excuse for indiscriminate love-making on the part of their sniffing children. If normal society comes out during the day and sleeps at night, the sniffers sleep during the day and come out at night. As in Mardaiya:n the sniffers have high priests, but they are selected from amongst prominent Aboriginal Christian families. They too hold their services in the C.M.S. church when it is not in use by the Christians.

These are the kids who think that if you act like a European when you are alive, you will come back as a European when you die. That might be a fate worse than sniffing but for the brain damage sniffing causes. If it continues there will soon be few young people left with the intelligence to learn the complexities of the traditional culture even if they decide to come back to it. There's even some doubt whether they will be able to reproduce themselves. Apparently, fifty per cent of the 14 to 24 age group at Angurugu have syphilis.

Mining royalties don't help. It's not as if the Aborigines have been assimilated into the syndrome identified in the passage from Timothy quoted above at the outset of this chapter. Their attitude to money is still very much "if it comes along utilize it, if not, well, *mama,* she'll be right." The trouble is, too much of it is coming along too regularly to be handled.

"Clan money day", July 2nd, is a day to behold. There's over $400,000 in cash in the Council office waiting to be doled out to each and every Aborigine entitled to a share. Those entitled are the "clans" and lines within "clans" of Groote and Bickerton and anyone else these "clans" and lines think should be entitled. This includes mainland people in long-standing association with Groote and Bickerton people such as certain Murungun, Mirniyawan, Nungumadjbarr and Durila people as well as the Herberts, part-Aboriginal people from Umbakumba, and the Blitners, part-Aboriginal people from Angurugu.

The money is doled out on an equal basis to each "clan" or line in a "clan" where numbers warrant. The largest "clan", the Lalara, are subdivided into five lines; the Mamariga, the Wurramara and the Wurrabadelamba into three each; the Amagula and the Wurramarrba into two each, while the remainder stay as "clan" units.

Royalty payments from the manganese mining are administered by the Groote Eylandt Trust containing Aboriginal representatives and European advisors. Though I haven't taken much of an interest in this business I do get the impression that the Aboriginal representatives run things more or less their own way on advice from the wider society. A typical budget apportions the money between the "clan" grants which are handed out directly, support for outstations or homelands, the cost of running funerals and traveling to ceremonies, some medical services, and community activities such as sports and recreation. Basically the Trust retains the principal, now upwards of $9 million, and spends only the interest. This is over $1 million a year. A typical "clan" grant is about $25,000 per "clan" or line. You may have wondered how the Aborigines could afford to bring me over from Canada for the funeral if Gula died. Now you know.

There's nothing particularly "Aboriginal" about the way the Trust is set up. After all, it was instituted by C.M.S. But having been set up the way it is, there's now constant jockeying to "line up" for an "equal share" of the pie. By this I mean, get your line established as a line rather than as a "clan". That way the "clan" gets more than one share. It's within the framework of the Trust that changes which could fundamentally undermine the Aboriginal way of life are being introduced. Already there have been fightings and killings over the allocation of Trust money. It must seem ironic considering that the Trust was founded on a principle of sharing and equality, but that's the way it is.

To get back to "clan money day", early in the morning the vultures begin to descend from Alyangula onto Angurugu with their new and used trucks, cars and boats. Bridge Auto in Darwin has already sent a shipment out to the shop and the vehicles sit there all gleaming and seductive. The Aboriginal men and women begin to congregate in the space out behind the shop, then the office doors open and they file in, one by one, returning a few minutes later with a fistful of dollars. That's when the vultures move in for the kill. Some of the goods are the genuine article but most of it is Alyangula hand-me-downs painted up and priced for the occasion. The older men are more cautious now and compare before buying. But the younger ones are still gullible, grasping for what looks new and flashy. Some completely forget themselves and spend all they have without regard to the others of their line and "clan". That's when the fighting breaks out. Christmas has come to Angurugu.

The missionaries are appalled by this, but it's they who originally brought the mining operations to Groote seeing in economic development the key to the Aborigines—and their own—future. Perhaps it would have come anyway, but because it came before land rights the Aborigines have no real say in the terms of the operation. The Mining Company is looking forward to the 21st century, its leases secured. The Aborigines are looking backward to the past wondering, what with the "bird disease" and all their social problems, if they—the missionaries on their behalf—didn't make a mistake. That's the source of the high crime rate amongst the young people, most of which is directed toward the property of the Mining Company and its employees. All they have to look forward to is the royalty payments and all they have to look back on is forbears who made a mistake.

As the future unfolds it is not only John Cawte's "dread" that is beginning to set in amongst the senior generation, amongst the Murabudas, the Nandjiwarras, Gula, as that peculiar resignation I noticed in the old men in 1969 which appeared not to care that things might be changing for the worse and that their young people might not learn the culture. It is not only the knowledge that the basis of the culture is still there whether there are people to see it or not, but also the attitude that having failed to prevent the trouble in which you now find yourself, you must learn to live with it now that it's here. There's no concept of crisis-management—of an ongoing effort to control events that are always on the verge of getting out of hand—the very foundation on which our own attempt at civilization is built. All there is, is an eternal order which does or does not manifest itself in human affairs. The time is simply not now.

But there is resentment. The attitude of the Murabudas, the Nandjiwarras, Gula, is very much that we Europeans brought all this to them knowing full well the consequences—the mining to poison the environment, the money to encourage greed, the petrol to be sniffed and the brain destroyed. Murabuda speaks to me of "genocide". But they give us too much credit. We assume that they think as analytically and as deductively as we do *with the aim of* preventing social disruption similarly on our mind. They assume we are as capable as they are of grasping the Truth they see in nature and the human condition and of putting it into practice ourselves. In me they see someone who, after nearly 20 years, is still only half-way there.

There is one way to intervene in such a situation: change our side and leave theirs alone. In this I am in sympathy with the Marxists who see the problems of the Third and Fourth World as rooted in the First and Second, the source of expansionary capitalism. However, I am not in complete agreement with their diagnosis—class conflict—and certainly not with their prescription for a solution—class revolution—nor with the world that follows from it. I have come to know that every situation of conflict—class based or otherwise—contains within itself a basis for accommodation; I have come to know that in the very act of revolutionary overthrow the victors become kindred spirit to those they have overthrown whom they now elevate to their own former oppressed status. I have also come to know that without the intervention of Marxist ideology such revolutionary overthrows are far from inevitable. I would hope that the scenarios which generate both Marxist ideology and revolution can be avoided and what Marxists call capitalism, which I would equally avoid, can be deflected—contained—within a permanently accommodating force. It was this hope that persuaded me to undertake my consultancy for the Minister of Community Development of Australia on affairs Aboriginal in 1986, in particular on the issue of Community Government. And it was the concept of citizenship, if a limited form thereof, that I saw as the means through which to forge this accommodation.

The seeds of the kind of blueprint I had in mind for this purpose had been sown by the Territory Government in 1979 when Part XX was introduced as an amendment to the Local Government Ordinance. Its purpose in the words of the Minister at the time, the Hon. Jim Robertson, was to provide "a simplified alternative for local or community government than that which now operates in the major population centres under the municipal or corporation system." Part XX, later amended as Part VIII of the Local Government Act, states that a Community Government Scheme may make provision for, among other things, the boundaries of the Community Government area to which the Scheme applies, the composition of the Community Government Council, the eligibility of persons to be members and to vote, the manner and frequency of elections, the functions to be performed by the Community Government Council and the manner of performance of those functions. No restrictions are placed on any but the last of these provisions. Potential powers of Community Government Councils, however, are listed as "commercial development, communications, community amenities, education or training, electricity supply, garbage collection and disposal, health, housing, relief work for unemployed persons, roads and public works, revenue raising and such other matters as are approved by the Minister." In conjunction with carrying out these functions Councils are empowered to make laws which then become laws of the Territory providing they do not contravene existing Territory laws.

Community Government, then, is a more flexible form of local government than Municipal Government, leaving open as it does the question of the location boundaries and of the criteria of membership within. Suspended, if not transcended, was an entrenched bias about the nature of political organization in our society, namely that rights in a jurisdiction should be determined by simple situation in space. In the Northern Territory, as elsewhere in Australia and the Western world, membership and voting rights are generally exercised on the basis of simple residence, or a few months' residence within the jurisdiction in question. Suspension of this principle in the Territory opened the way for Aboriginal principles of jurisdiction. The scope of Part VIII of the Act, applying as it did equally to European as well as Aboriginal communities, opened the way for non-Aboriginal Australians to enter into the Aboriginal ambiance. But first a few changes would have to be made. And Alan Scott, the Secretary of the Department of Community Development at the time, and Hugh Richardson and John McLaren who worked with him, as well as Minister Don Dale, were prepared to make them. As for Barry Coulter who had brought me over in the first place, I wasn't sure. He was simply willing to let whatever was happening happen without overly reflecting on what was going on so long as it "worked".

One change that had to be put into effect immediately was to abandon the Government's preferred option of the simple residence model as the basis for drawing up a Scheme of Community Government. The Groote Eylandters had already circumvented the intent of that option by making their "clan groupings" the units of representation on Council. It had "slipped through" before anyone realized what was happening. I turned it into a precedent. My aim was to blanket the Northern Territory with a grid of Community Government jurisdictions organized internally along Aboriginal lines and interconnected along Parliamentary lines such that no one of them could act unilaterally independently from the rest. "Along Aboriginal lines" would mean that Aborigines in effect would be granted "citizenship" at a local level and interact on this basis with citizens of other jurisdictions of like kind. Human life would then flow through these jurisdictions with a predictable effect, namely peace and order and economic stability through good government. Actually it wasn't my vision that was at issue but Aboriginal tradition and its effective translation into our terms.

A Community Government Council Association (C.G.C.A.) would be formed on a regional basis focused on Darwin, Katherine, Alice Springs and East Arnhem respectively, the regional boundaries coming to coincide with Territory electoral boundaries. A Community Government Division of the Local Government Grants Commission would be established to distribute equalization and other grants amongst the Community Government Councils and would consist of representatives of the Community Government Association.

Try as I might I could see no way of avoiding an element of hierarchy in the arrangement, nor any way of immediately encompassing the Municipalities—Darwin, Katherine, Tenant Creek, Alice Springs—in the overall scheme of things. This is what I meant when I included my own efforts at accommodation here as also inevitably diminishing Aboriginal culture. The units I had in mind would have to be mediated by second tier (C.G.C.A.) and first tier (the N.T. Government) units which may very well, judging from our own previous history, come to dominate those from which their authority should flow. This is what worried the Land Councils about my proposals. What I thought was that local "citizenship", the grouping of Community Government Councils into a power-block and the coincidence of regional C.G.C.A. and political boundaries, would effectively countermand this tendency. But it was a tendency already built into the arrangement by the proviso that the Minister ultimately held veto power over a Community Government Scheme and that Community Government Council bylaws not contravene those already in existence in the Territory.

There was also the fear that the Minister, the Government of the day, would use its authority in these respects to manipulate Aboriginal Councils on Aboriginal Lands in their own interests, or the interests of those behind them, counter to the wishes of the "traditional owners" and the Land Councils. This fear was founded on the present Liberal-Country Party's ties to the mining industry. My own fear on this account, as expressed to the then Minister Barry Coulter, led to a certain coolness developing in our relationship if not to a complete falling out.

Perhaps I'm too much of an Aboriginal by now, assuming that in the final analysis Europeans will "do the right thing" rather than pursue narrow self-interest focused on greed. Perhaps also like the Aborigines I am destined to be disappointed. As yet it's too early to tell.

It would not diminish the Aboriginal accomplishment to see their sense of jurisdiction expressed at a level above that of their Promised Lands, that is, on a wider, regional basis, so long as the relations between the wider jurisdictions were of a "part of the one in the other and vice versa" nature. I consider a Parliamentary forum to be of this nature. As I wrote in *Australian Aboriginal Studies* (1987, Vol. 1: 81):

> The Northern Territory Local Government Act is not the only path to a greater degree of equality in interdependence—dignity and self-respect—for Aboriginal people in the Territory or in Australia as a whole. The Land Rights Act has positive effects in this respect. So would an arrangement that dissolved the Territory and represented Aborigines and other Territorians through enlarged Shire Councils directly to the federal level. One such jurisdiction could be drawn around Aboriginal lands which would mean it would have to be non-contiguous, but this presents little more than a technical problem. And the powers of such a Shire Council would have to be strengthened, including the power to grant "citizenship" which would then afford membership in the larger Australian State. Two more Shires in the Territory would suffice, some 300 in Australia as a whole. In short, no small-s states at all. Far from being apartheid, the kind of equality in interdependence this would achieve—respecting differences that just won't be assimilated—could become the model for a State in the 21st century. Bureaucratic duplication eliminated, democracy close to the people, security of livelihood ensured, who could ask for more than that? The idea is not outside the realm of possibility. Something similar was suggested by Prime Minister Hawke in his 1979 Boyer lecture. (pp. 18–19)

What the Prime Minister argued for was elimination of the Australian states while considerably strengthening the powers of local government.

With political parties representing class and ethnic interests as such, such a framework of "contentless forms" as I had suggested—"citizenries" neutral with respect to class and ethnicity—could very well accomplish its Aboriginal purpose: the accommodation of fundamental differences which would otherwise explode into violence. For one thing, at the inter- or intra- national levels the rights of citizens would counterbalance those of expatriate owners by transforming them from "co-occupiers" into "guests within-the-host's jurisdiction", thereby eliminating any threat they might pose in this respect. The same conjunction would arrest the class tendency by combining those with different interests together as "citizens" while at the same time permitting ties as "classmates" to cut across jurisdictional bounds.

Of course to work as Aboriginal culture works, all this would have to be complemented by the principle of "jurisdiction in order to make what is within available to others". At our own present stage of development it is highly unlikely we could realize this. We are still at the stage of believing that competition leads to specialization and interdependence of function and that co-operation and sharing are the alternative to this. The Aborigines left these ideas and practices back in the Stone Age (if ever there). As a result, no further Ages opened to them, that dialectic ceasing to inform their lives. This was the essence of their accomplishment.

This accomplishment is graphically represented in the traditional culture by X-ray art where the form of, say, an animal frames the "contents" it contains—its internal organs—and by the hand stencil. Here the form of the hand remains imprinted on the face of the rock after paint has been sprayed over it and the hand removed. At once a uni-form, yet differentiated individually, concrete yet transcendent, and by nature of the hand created by at first containing and then expelling matter, hand stencils perhaps represent "citizenship" in a place. This would explain the frequency of the form.

Finally, in Aboriginal sacred ceremonies such as Mardaiya:n it is the Form of one's forbears, as re-created in wood or stone, that is venerated rather than the forbear as such. This is what Murabuda recognizes as the *numerarrga* (grandfather) he has never seen, as he sings. This is what makes this *numerarrga* different from, but the same as, anyone he has known or knows.

XI

Life's Logic Lost?

In the Prologue I mentioned that they were just hints in my notebooks. I hadn't even seen them there until I had gained a theoretical insight into Aboriginal culture which predicted that the information I did not yet have must be there *(Life Before Genesis,* "Theoretical Interlude"). If my insight was correct there had to be a sense in which Lands were resource specific and so-called "totems" prohibited to their adherents as food. There must be a dimension of reality *(anti-thesis* or Nothingness) devoid of material content and yet experienced at some basic level. I took these questions back to Groote Eylandt and Bickerton Island as hypotheses. They were validated in ways I had not imagined. Amagalyuagba was not a one-people island, the outcome either of groups coming together peacefully to share its diverse resources or of one group coming to out-compete its rivals and situate itself alone in control. It was rather an island where people had bounded relatively large numbers of people in small, resource-specific areas, prohibiting the specific resource for one's own use in order to force interdependencies between People/Lands. These People/Lands were founded on a perception of nature in interaction with culture that I have translated as Forms.

This argues against Economists' claims that maximization of material self-interest is normal and natural and that our institutions should flow with, rather than against, this fact. It also argues against Marxist claims that co-operation and sharing are normal and natural too, as well as both Left and Right claims that the drive to autonomy and self-sufficiency/self determination is basic to the human condition. Neither primitive communists nor anarchistic individualists, these Aboriginal People do seem to have achieved what we only (occasionally) aspire to let alone practice and what should be the essence of "civilization." And they did it not by economic but by "Spiritual" development. Here again, Left and Right fall by the wayside as irrelevant to a description let alone an explanation. The Aborigines' is an eternal order from which material existence flows, not an ideology derived from material existence.

I use quotes around "Spiritual" because the very word conjures up "religion", "belief", and the like and diminishes the Aboriginal reality. This is because these are our concepts not theirs: in respect of the Aboriginal reality we are impoverished in our perception and understanding. I do not for a moment deny that Aborigines predicate ideas on a material base—the way in which they classify nature attests to that. But one domain of expression is different from the rest. We refer to it as "theology" and to that of others as "cosmology", though again our term diminishes the Aboriginal reality by situating it in the realm of "religion" which we contrast with "science". That is, we speak of the "transcendent", the "numinous", as at best an invisible reality beyond our comprehension, at worst a psychological state; whereas the Aborigines actually *see* it. The grid of Forms they see, they utilize to chart material reality. Certainly natural markers define the points of differentiation on this grid, but humanly imposed points of cultural differentiation on the grid also locate natural markers. Recall that the Land subdivided at Laugulalya on Bickerton between the Wurramara and the Wurramanba contained no naturally differentiating feature until it was agreed to subdivide it.

Perhaps Aborigines actually see not only the Forms but also the relation between the Forms and what the Forms imply in a material sense. That is, Forms as a fixed constant within which and between which variable matter moves—an impression afforded by, for example, w/Waves. If Gula is any indication, his Aboriginal forbears seem not only to have observed the phenomenon but also to have grasped within it a theoretical principle and fashioned from it a creative force—a set of procedures by which to direct life. Hence *gemalyangarrengama*, "to slice from something and twist into what 1 have created from nothing": *nar'a:bina*, Form devoid of content. To landForms, speciesForms, were attached continuities of People which were then emptied of their content (as was womanForm) thereby to make them available to someone else. This is the essence, the foundation, of the Aboriginal Way of Life.

The principle, *anti-thesis* ---> *thesis* => *plurality* or relationship, is there to be grasped in interaction with Nature; all it takes is people to come along and grasp it. There can be no material prerequisite for grasping and realizing it—in fact just the opposite, for it can only be grasped if "material" is renounced. I have no idea as yet as to why renunciation compels relationship. I can only observe that it seems to act as a trigger which sets "part of one in the other and vice versa" connectedness in motion.

Marcel Mauss points out in *The Gift* that the essence of giving is that it entails a debt on the part of the receiver, moving him or her to repay with an equivalent amount or with more than they received in order to entail a counter-debt. "Renunciation", however, runs much deeper than this. It is a denial that "the other" is indebted. Perhaps I can explain by way of Mauss' critique of "charity". Charity, he says, is demeaning because it entails a debt on the receiver's part that cannot be repaid. But could it not be demeaning because the one who has given does not now have nothing as you had before receiving?

It is also hard to speak of renunciation in an Aboriginal context as "exchange" because, whether one is speaking of a woman belonging to one Land becoming the wife of another, a bounded resource or a Song-species Spiritually attached to one People and thereby available as food to another, the movement of the part in question is preordained, established prior to one's own existence and repeating itself in the same form after it. "Exchange", on the other hand, implies an on-going, pragmatically determined process.

"Exchange" reflects a theoretical formulation which reaches to the very heart of Western history and ideas. It runs *thesis* ---> *anti-thesis* => *synthesis* and is predicated on a materialist "me/mine first" base followed by "you/yours second" and, in this case, "we resolved", or at least accommodated through an exchange between the two. The formulation will be familiar to some readers as the Hegelian/Marxist dialectic. My point here, though, is that there is no way you can arrive at renunciation via this scenario. To arrive at renunciation you must proceed from *anti-thesis*, from a denial of self, an emptying of content leaving only Form, and in so doing you relinquish a materialist starting-point. Only having done so are you able to pose "other" first. If, as Mauss says, there is something human about "exchange", in renunciation, there is something Divine.

The concept of "equality" suffers from the same limitation as "exchange" when examined in an Aboriginal context. What is the basis for this concern? To have everything balance, come out 50-50. Is it a willingness to share, or is it a consequence of greed, emerging out of a determination that if you cannot have more than someone else then you will do your best to ensure that they cannot have more than you. "Equality", whether of economic condition or of political power, may very well reflect the ideals of a crisis-management society which functions to maintain greedy people in stable equilibrium. Indeed, if it were not this way then why else would inequality lead to struggle? If indeed egalitarian societies do exist in which greed and self-seeking are balanced in this manner then they are not all that different from inegalitarian societies like our own where the ability to satiate greed is imbalanced and in need of institutional control. One subtle means of control is to relativize inequality by ensuring that the most disadvantaged within your society are still better off than the most advantaged without. (Thus the American Way.)

It seems to me that a law can be abstracted from the Fall of the Warnungamagalyuagba into our society: peace and order would seem to vary inversely with economic progress in the sense that the more you pursue the one the less chance you have of achieving the other. What is beginning to happen to the Aborigines for negative reasons—fracture and individualization—we promote as positive prescriptions for economic growth. And we are right. This is precisely what the freeing of competitive market forces does achieve, if some higher authority has occasionally to intervene by force of arms or by law to maintain a modicum of order amongst the competing individuals, or cooperating classes of individuals, at issue.

I had originally thought that Aboriginal culture might have emerged in recoil against such conflict and competition to permanently arrest the forces at issue and remain thereafter at a hunter-gatherer level of subsistence in splendid isolation on the Australian continent. Certainly the earliest observers were impressed not only by the Aborigines' undeveloped economic state but also by their lack of interest in advancement in these terms. Captain James Cook noted their indifference to his material possessions (quoted in Gray 1981: 100-101) and Donald Thomson (1962) later recorded that the Cape York Aborigines were familiar with the bow and arrow and gardening culture of the neighboring Torres Straits Islanders but did not borrow them.

But there is another explanation for Aboriginal culture. At some stage the whole world was arranged along Aboriginal lines and that first fatal step out of hunting and gathering as a mode of subsistence fractured those lines forever and set us on our various self-determining courses to repeat the same mistake again and again and again. The problem with this explanation is that there seems to have been another hunter-gatherer way of life (which anthropologists call "band society") with features very different from the Australians', geared as it is to maintainjng self-sufficiency and economic progress within a territory held, rather than "owned" in the Australian sense. Such a society is forever at odds with its neighbours in times of resource population crisis (see "Theoretical Postlude"). Whether the Aboriginal Way emerged negatively out of crises in the midst of such a society or whether it was "created" positively out of a certain perception of reality independently of such circumstance, is not known.

Whatever the situation, we – humans at large – have been trying unsuccessfully to (re)establish a universal framework for peaceful co-existence ever since. I ended my book *Life Before Genesis* with the speculation that we in our present circumstances in the West have left the Secret of the Tree of Life behind us and that it remained still half hidden within the world of the first Australians. Our metaphorical ancestors Adam and Eve may not so much have been expelled as left the equally metaphorical "Fallen" Garden-of-Eden-in-the-singular looking for it. That is because the Secret of the Tree of Life is that the tree isn't there – or rather is there to be made available to someone else!

Edens?: Just before I went back to Groote Eylandt in May of 1986, I happened across an article in *The Weekend Australian* (May 3–4, p. 17) which startled even me. It was entitled "Was Adam an Aussie?" It was based on "The disclosure last week that shellfish remains found on a small cliff face near Warrnambool in Victoria may contain evidence suggesting human occupation in Australia dating back 85,000 years." Some were even suggesting dates of 130,000 years and hypothesizing that *homo sapiens, sapiens,* modern man, may have originated in Australia (though having originally come there from some other place as something else) spreading out northward from there to the rest of the world—the eastern world at least. Perhaps they were some kind of historical source.

* * * * *

Trying to work all this out really got me down about my own so-called "civilization", about myself as one of its representatives and my failure to live up to my own discoveries. We are so far gone that not only do we see competition and conflict as endemic to the human condition but also that competition and survival of the fittest are the means to human betterment. In the end, armed with nuclear weapons, no one survives the struggle. In other words, even if "survival of the fittest" is true as a law of nature we still have to transcend it. Why do we continue to see "boundaries" as "barriers" and fail to grasp the significance of citizenship within the State? Why can't we grasp the idea of boundaries as distinct from their material contents, and the implication of a world of constantly interacting hosts and guests? Why do we see the path to world peace as through amalgamation and unity instead of differentiation and re-relationship? Hasn't history, never mind the Aborigines, taught us time and again that the attempt to amalgamate differences that are real is as much at the basis of our troubles as is resignation to their separation?

What kind of people come to places like Australia and elsewhere to be welcomed as guests only to seize the invitation as an opportunity to appropriate everything from hosts who would have been only too willing to surrender them the material things of life had they but made their needs known? Does it merely reflect man's inhumanity to man, or does it reflect some men's non-humanity? Have some of us not quite got there yet? Are the Aborigines something more than just an aberrant isolate? Could they have been diminished culturally and physiologically as they migrated north many millennia ago?

I was quickly brought back down to earth (or up to the Heavens) by Murabuda. "Haven't we all got the same eyes, the same nose, the same mouth?" he admonished. Whatever the difference between Aborigines and the rest of us, it wasn't because we lacked the same Form (recall his perception of the first foreign visitors to Groote Eylandt as humans because they had faces). Everyone has enough of "God" in him or her at least to be able to look down from outside him or herself to discover that they are not alone.

It's all out there to be seen and realized if only we would stop to see it. But can we? Fritjof Capra pins his hopes for the West on the ecologically and socially conscious "Greens" who, taking their cue from the North American Indians, proclaim that "the earth is our church". But theirs is a "band society". An Australian Aborigine would more likely say "the Church is our earth". But how is that "Church" to emerge in the presence of our materially-advancing society, whether on the Right or the Left, in the absence of the Aboriginal example, and increasingly in the absence of the Aboriginal people themselves, whom it fails to recognize and is in the process of destroying? I really don't know.

THEORETICAL POSTLUDE

Theoretical Postlude

The theoretical side of this journey really began in 1977 with a comparative study of the Warnungarnagalyuagba and the Shamattawa Cree of northern Canada in collaboration with Paul Wertman, then an M.A. student at the University of Manitoba. There and in many subsequent publications, including *Shamattawa,* "Ideology and Elementary Structures", *Dialectics in Tradition* and "Hunting and Gathering: Cree and Australian", I have analyzed hunting and gathering and other societies into two distinct modes of production revolving around the problems of autonomy and self determination (self-first), vs. relation to others, and continuity vs. mobility. The two modes I called "production group diversity/kinline confederation" and "production group unity/locality incorporation". The Australian "federative" arrangement results in on-the-ground production groups whose members (minimally, those conjoined by marriage) have divided loyalties, originating as they do in different, so-called "clans". The Cree "incorporative" arrangement results in on-the-ground production groups whose members (again, minimally those conjoined through marriage) are unified, particularly in an ideological sense but in a form that oscillates with fragmentation.

I suggested that the Australians rejected autonomy and self determination to the degree that they reached a stable accommodation between groups and individuals. The cost, however, was a lack of dynamism in technological and economic affairs which conventional "band" or locality-incorporative societies enjoyed as a result of allowing socioeconomic relations to flow from proximity in space, encouraging (collective) self-interest and permitting a greater degree of pragmatism in economic activities though directed by authority when this individualism threatened the integrity of the group. In the Australian case, stable accommodation was achieved by federative mechanisms (placing part of one in the other and vice versa) at the institutional (the so-called "clan" and "section") levels, in the form of intermarriage, trade, totemic prohibitions and a spacing process which placed relatively large numbers of people in relatively *small* blocks of territory. In the first instance, the parit of one that was placed in the other was men and women moving between "clans", in the second it was items such as natural resources and ceremonial objects, in the third the edible "matter" of the "totem" itself.

Then, in 1985, in my book *Life Before Genesis,* I added the possibility that "clan", or what I came to term Promised Land, boundaries were drawn around exclusive resources. These boundaries, as distinct from the land they contained, were Promised in the sense of being "abstract, eternal jurisdictions" ordained in place by events of the "Dreamtime" over, above and under the land in the form of lines or blocks. Hence, Land, that is, the transcendent quality of land as well as the land itself. In this book I took the comparison one step further by proposing a theoretical articulation of my two types which involved the introduction of this apparently cosmological/transcendent level of determination in the Australian case. In the sense that the theory renounces material determination when it comes to explaining the Australians, it sits outside the (Marxist/liberal) materialist problematic.

The theoretical formulation that "explains" the Australians runs *anti-thesis* ---> *thesis*===> *plurality* and can be seen as an offshoot, at the point of "contradiction", of the monist materialist dialectic, *thesis* ---> *anti-thesis* ===> *synthesis* and its attendant expressions relating to forces and relations of production, class conflict, and so on.

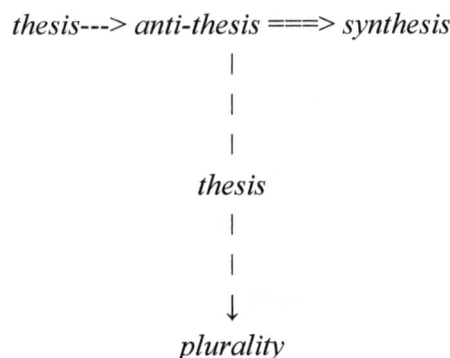

Thesis ---> *anti-thesis* === >*synthesis* is the materialist scenario, asserting "matter", "I", first, and "anti-that-matter", "You", second, ending finally in "me over you, you over me" or "us together", third. Economic and cognitive expressions of this dialectic manifest themselves in history and are discussed below. I term the history in question "monist", meaning proceeding from and reducible to "one". This scenario represents the forces of economic progress and violent confrontation.

The theory predicts that at the point of contradiction in monist materialist history – where conflict between real people is at its height – some, perhaps the weaker amongst them – withdraw and combine in a new relation setting them off on another course. The basis for that new relation is attachment to a "neutral plane" devoid of the content of which formerly divided them.

I suggested that the Australian Aboriginal perception/Idea (in the Platonic/Aristotelian sense) of Form as translated into abstract, eternal, jurisdiction as sanctified by the Dreaming and writ *a priori* in the plural, a sector for you and a sector for me, was a force capable of transcending and transforming the monist materialist dialectic and setting those in it on a new historical course. Evidence of this course was arrested technological and economic development, the absence of organized warfare, a mode of thought which signaled "separate and withdraw" in the face of impending conflict, styles of symbolic expression utilizing line and square over circle, all features of Australian Aboriginal societies (with some qualifications I will not go into here except to say that they are concentrated in Western Desert societies which exhibit some "band" features).

To explain briefly the nature of some of these transformations, in monist history (e.g., mainstream Western history), as in locality-incorporative society, we find an ego-centred, singular universe in which autonomy and self-sufficiency are driving forces. And, indeed, this is perhaps why technology appears as a first priority in the economic order of things – the means to these ends on an individual (Right Wing) or collective (Left Wing) basis. But technology is always capable of benefitting more people than the existing relations of production will allow. Classes vie with one another within society for control of these benefits. The advantaged class overcomes the disadvantaged, the disadvantaged overcomes the advantaged or the two merge together into a new whole *(thesis ---> anti-thesis===> synthesis)*. In monist history, amongst people under threat, or in pluralist history with mutually respected jurisdictions in place, however, consideration of people's respective positions in the production process takes precedence over technological change as such. People are separated into interdependence, each to his or her own (people, resources, functions). Human accommodation now becomes the driving force in history with technology assuming a secondary role in the process.

In monist history, as in locality-incorporative society, thought (in a logic located by Levi-Strauss), in an attempt to resolve oppositions that are real, seeks to avoid the revolutionary implications by substituting weaker terms for each pole in the opposition through a process of analogical reasoning which allows for the appearance of a mediator to effect the illusion of a resolution to the original opposition. By contrast, in pluralist history or federative society, with mutually respected jurisdictions in place a different thought process emerges. In response to opposition that may only *potentially* emerge to undermine complementarity, thought inserts mediators to stand on guard while the elements of the arrangement are dissected and analyzed in an effort to reach the root of the potential problem. But in so doing, the weakeners that maintain the arrangement intact must be removed and, once they are, opposition that was heretofore merely potential all of a sudden appears real. Thought separates and withdraws from its terms.

What distinguishes pluralist history, or federative society, is not only that the "other" is defined separately in institutional relations to "self", but also the way "other" is defined so as to act as a brake on "self", that is, acts to qualify his/her/their ability to act autonomously in a self-determining way.

To return to the Australian-Cree analysis, it may be well to reiterate a comparative point I have made many times before, namely that the Australians relate to people structurally before they form alliances and produce while the Cree and others like them form alliances and produce before they relate to people structurally. But before we can assume this entails a degree of constraint on economic activity in the Australian case, a degree of dynamism in the Cree, we have to define the nature of the "structure" at issue. In my view concern for "other" in the Australian case is in fact built into the nature of a "structure", but, as we have seen, this structure is not kinship-based. Indeed, it is questionable whether kinship plays a role in it at all beyond providing a pathway for the exclusive transmission of something immaterial over time (as in from father to son and daughter or mother to son and daughter). Even here, to Aborigines so-called kinship implies no material linkage between parents and children. The linkage is Spiritual, or Formal, between man as husband, woman as wife, and children. What is at issue, then, is a "structure" based on affiliation with Forms – abstract eternal jurisdictions – neutral or "empty" as to their material contents, but full of Spiritual substance, Amawurrena.

In my view, no historical explanation of the Australian situation is possible so long as one remains intellectually within the monist stream and oblivious to the pluralist side-track. No functional explanation is possible so long as one remains within the materialist problematic unless, of course, one wishes to admit to a cosmology founded on "Nothing" and expressed ideologically as abstract, eternal jurisdictions being in the final analysis determinative. But given the un-real nature of these jurisdictions in Australia, there is no need to admit this. Nor does it trap us in the domain of "theology".

It should not have surprised me, but it did, to discover in 1986 that Aboriginal people themselves are aware of the theoretical formulation that I had intuited as "explaining" their society in both an historical and a functional sense, articulate it summarily in their language, and use it as a creative force. Amongst the Warnungamagalyuagba the formulation, as we have seen, is termed *gemalyangarrenama* -- *ge* (I will) *ma* (noun class for tune) *lyang* (noun incorporation meaning "head") *aringga* (turn back on itself) *arrengama* (break, tear, cut). The term is used primarily with reference to musical creation and can be translated as "to slice something off something and twist it into something else to make a new creation". The "something else" in question is literally "nothing", *nar'a:bina,* that is, no thing in particular but rather the parameters of one's own, here musical, tradition. In other words, its Form.

This Aboriginal term, like my own theoretical formulation, *"anti-thesis ---> thesis ===> plurality,"* could be translated in less abstract terms as *"nothingness ---> incarnation of something ===> this something being federated into something else, a part of one in the other."* Put another way, it also could be translated as *"nothingness ---> being===> relationship."*

"Nothingness" is contentless Form – in an Aboriginal context the stuff of the "Dreaming" (Amawurrena). In more "earthly" terms it is "abstract, eternal, jurisdiction". What is actually in your Form – for instance, a surplus of a particular material resource(s) often marked "totemically" and prohibited as food – is then "expelled" to someone else and *vice versa.* This matter is preordained to move by the very way "Dreamtime stuff" has been situated over the landScape and bounds the resource(s) and People/Lands in question. In this sense, the process cannot be characterized as "exchange" between people, if by exchange we mean "a pragmatically determined process to effect a relationship".

To return to my/Aboriginal theoretical formulation and its ethnographic basis, we can say that renunciation proceeds from *anti- thesis,* from what we call the "Dreaming" but what are really Forms emptied of everything but symbolic contents. To thus proceed is to proceed from a denial of self, or at least a transcendence of self, and in so doing relinquish a materialist starting point. In fact, only having proceeded thusly – from *anti-thesis* – am I able to pose "other" before "self". In so doing "I" find a neutral plane through which to relate to "other". Having done so, "we" end up as an indivisible, ununifiable, two: you and me, a slice of the "plane" through which we now relate for each of us.

Material circumstances, however (such as are experienced in the midst of class conflict), may trigger the "emptying" process. For instance, threat from a third party or an outside force may move those threatened toward one another in a positive way to search out and find a new plane of association devoid of the content that divides them and thereby reach a stable accommodation. The renunciative material implications simply follow from the "emptiness" established.

In pluralist history, that is, with "contentless Forms" in the plural already in place, this order of things would be reproduced by direct perception of the Forms in question and by their successful determination of material relationships.

To return to the Australian example, within their particular pluralist framework, it could be said that a woman renounces her own children to her husband and his Land or it could be said that matter emerges within woman-Form which is then "sliced off" and "twisted in" to something else. That is, *gemalyangarrenama.* The same could be said of resources within landForm as well as a resource successfully hunted by manForm.

Even with this brief synopsis it can be seen that Australian Aboriginal society/culture or whatever we want to call it, cannot be appropriated to a materialist paradigm, Marxist or otherwise. Our materialist paradigms more appropriately apply to locality-incorporative peoples and those in the monist tradition where economic activity informs Idea-logical expression rather than the other way around (the capital I implying the Formal/Emptiness dimension to this concept/experience).

In the Australian case, as we know it from the ethnographic record, apart from the question of origins, we are dealing with an interactive mode, of perception in interaction with nature, of contentless Forms that are really there to be grasped and the implications realized. The fact that they are imbued with religious significance is immaterial and theoretically irrelevant. Terms like "communal", "sharing", "co-operation", as I suggested in *Life Before Genesis,* and here, are appropriate to histories and societies informed by the monist/materialist mode. So is the drive to appropriate. But what also informs the monist mode is the possibility of transformation and transcendence in an Australian direction. What informs this pluralist mode is the possibility of a Fall into monism, as in the Aborigines present circumstances and as I hypothesized for Eden out of Edens in the Book of Genesis:

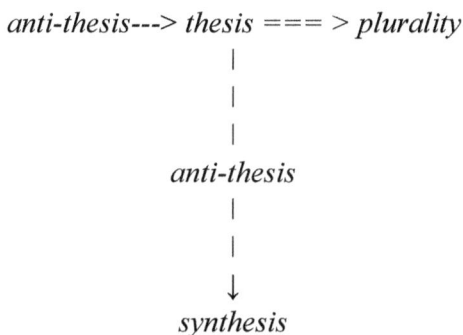

Again, I will let the Aborigines have the last word on the subject by repeating my summary of an Aranda myth as cited in *Life Before Genesis:*

> ... humanity emerged in a shapeless mass of half developed beings all grown together and undifferentiated. Mangarkunjerkunja, the Gecko, however, came down from the north to separate this mass into individual men and women and taught them the eight section system (four "clans" with the sections in each combining alternate generations into one category). But after he left the people fell into incestuous unions. Another culture hero, Katukankara, the Sandhill Wallaby, then came from the north to reinstitute the Law. (p. 161)

Does this mean an original "monism" from which Aboriginal "pluralism" emerged, or does "half developed" imply an original "pluralism" with "monist" tendencies? It seems the Aborigines are as ambiguous on the issue as I.

In a recent review of *Life Before Genesis* in *Australian Archaeology* (1988/24: 73) Deborah Bird Rose concluded that the paradox, the challenge, of the dialectic *(thesis --->)* and the *anti-dialectic (anti-thesis --->),* proposed here is that in their articulation, "each threat is a new potential. The paradox, and the challenge, is the same paradox regenerated again and again in the book of Genesis: how to revolutionize our way of thinking and doing without reproducing the same revolutionary dialectic that led us to require revolution". She goes so far as to suggest that the scenarios outlined in *Life Before Genesis,* the paradox in question, record the history of *homo sapiens* as a species. I would agree, so long as one keeps the Aboriginal perspective on the issue always in mind.

Either way—whether "in the beginning" or "derivative"—the basic question we have addressed here remains: is "institutional pluralism" recoverable/realizable and, if not, have we much longer to live on this planet?

References

"Australia: Northern and Southern Aboriginal Music", 1980. In Stanley Sadie ed., *The New Grove Dictionary of Music and Musicians,* London: Macmillan, pp. 713–728.

Bamborough, Renford. 1963. *The Philosophy of Aristotle.* New York: Mentor Books.

Barnard, Alan and Anthony Good. 1984. *Research Practices in the Study of Kinship.* (A.S.A. Research Methods 2). London: Academic Press.

Bayton, John. 1965. *Cross Over Carpentaria.* Brisbane: W.R. Smith and Peterson.

Butlin, Noel. 1983. *Our Original Aggression.* Sydney: George Allen and Unwin.

Capra, Fritjof. 1976. *The Tao of Physics.* London: Fontana.

———. 1984. *Green Politics: The Global Promise.* New York: Dutton.

Cawte, John and Charles Kilburn eds. 1987. *Manganese and Metabolism.* St. Lucia: University of Queensland Printery

Charlesworth, Max and Kenneth Maddock eds. 1984. *Religion in Aboriginal Australia.* St. Lucia: University of Queensland Press.

Cornford. F.M. ed. 1964. *The Republic of Plato.* New York: Oxford University Press.

Dixon, R.M.W. 1980. *The Languages of Australia.* Cambridge: Cambridge, University Press.

Elkin, A. P. 1938–40. "Kinship in South Australia", *Oceania,* 8: 419–52; 9:41–78; 10: 196–234, 295–349, 369–388.

Gray, W.R. 1981. *Voyages to Paradise: Exploring in the Wake of Captain Cook.* Washington, National Geographic Society.

Harris, Bess and R. G. P. Colgrove eds. 1976. *Lawren Harris.* Toronto: Macmillan.

Hawke, R .J. L. *The Resolution of Conflict.* (1979 Boyer Lectures). Sydney: The Australian Broadcasting Commission.

Kiloh, L. G., A. K. Lethlean, G. Morgan, J. E. Cawte and M. Harris. 1980. "An Endemic Neurological Disorder in Tribal Australian Aborigines", *Journal of Neurology,* Neurosurgery, and Psychiatry, 43: 661–668.

Levitt, Dulcie, 1981. *Plants and People: Aboriginal Uses of Plants on Groote Eylandt.* Canberra: Australian Institute of Aboriginal Studies.

MacKenzie, C.S. 1987. *The Trinity and Culture.* New York: Peter Lang.

Maddock, Kenneth. 1972. *The Australian Aborigines.* London: Allen Lane/Penguin Press.

Mauss, Marcel. 1969. *The Gift: Forms and Functions of Exchange in Archaic Societies.* London: Cohen and West.

Narazaki, Muneshige. 1968. *Hokusai, Masterworks of Ukiyo-E.* Tokyo: Kodansha.

Peterson, Nicolas ed. 1976. *Tribes and Boundaries in Australia.* Canberra: Australian Institute of Aboriginal Studies.

Rose, F. G. G. 1960. *Classification of Kin, Age Structure and Marriage amongst the Groote Eylandt Aborigines.* Berlin: Akademie-Verlag.

Shkilnyk, A. 1985. *Poison Stronger than Love.* New Haven: Yale University Press.

Smith, Gavin and David H. Turner, eds. 1979. *Challenging Anthropology.* Toronto: McGraw-Hill Ryerson.

Stanner, W. E. H. 1979. *White Man Got No Dreaming: Essays, 1938–1973.* Canberra: Australian National University Press.

Strehlow, T. G. H. 1947. *Aranda Traditions.* Melbourne: Melbourne University Press.

———. 1965. "Culture, Social Structure, and Environment in Aboriginal Central Australia". In R. M. and C. H. Berndt eds. *Aboriginal Man in Australia, Essays in Honour of Emeritus Professor A. P. Elkin.*

———. 1981. *Songs of Central Australia.* Sydney: Angus and Robertson.

Stokes, J. 1981. "Anindilyakwa Phonology from Phoneme to Syllable". In B. Walters ed., *Australian Phonologies: Collected Papers* (series A, Vol. 5). Darwin: Summer Institute of Linguistics.

———. 1982. "A Description of the Mathematical Concepts of Groote Eylandt Aborigines". In *Language and Culture* (series B, Vol. 8). Darwin: Summer Institute of Linguistics.

Swain, Tony. 1985. *Interpreting Aboriginal Religion: An Historical Account.* Adelaide: Australian Association for the Study of Religion.

———. 1993. *A Place for Strangers.* Cambridge: Cambridge University Press.

Swain, Tony and Deborah Rose eds. 1988. *Aboriginal Australians and Christian Missions.* Adelaide: Australian Association for the Study of Religion.

Taylor, James. 1982. "Industrialization and Aboriginal Welfare". In Keith Cole ed., *Groote Eylandt Stories*. Parkdale Vic.: Church Missionary Society.

Thomson, Donald F. 1963. In Helen Sheils ed., *Australian Aboriginal Studies*. Melbourne: Oxford University Press.

Tindale, N. B. 1925–26. "Natives of Groote Eylandt and of the West Coast of the Gulf of Carpentaria". *South Australian Museum Records*. Vol. 2, No. 1: 61–102; Vol. 3, No. 2: 103–34.

Turner, D.H. 1973 "The Rock Art of Groote Eylandt and Bickerton Island in Comparative Perspective". *Oceania*, Vol. 43, No. 4: 286–325.

———. 1974. *Tradition and Transformation*. Canberra: Australian Institute of Aboriginal Studies.

———. 1978a. *Dialectics in Tradition: Myth and Social structure in Two Hunter-gatherer Societies*. Occasional Paper 36 of the Royal Anthropological Institute, London.

———. 1978b. "Ideology and Elementary Structures". *Anthropologica,* Vol. 20, Nos 1–2: 223–47 (special issue, "The Social Appropriation of Logic: Essays Presented to Claude Levi-Strauss on his 70th Birthday").

———. 1979. "Hunting and Gathering: Cree and Australian". In *Challenging Anthropology* (Gavin Smith and David Turner eds.). Toronto: McGraw-Hlll Ryerson.

———. 1981. *Australian Aboriginal Social Organization*. New York/Canberra: Australian Institute of Aboriginal Studies.

———. 1984. *Report to the Strehlow Research Foundation*. Adelaide: Strehlow Research Foundation.

———. 1986a. *Transformation and Tradition: A Report on Aboriginal development in/on the Northern Territory of Australia*. Darwin Government Printer.

———. 1986b. "The Warnindilyaugwa Relationship System: A Computer Simulation". In Gisele de Meur ed., *New Trends in Mathematical Anthropology.* London: Routledge and Kegan Paul.

———. 1992. "The (S)Pacific Effects of Sunday Morning Hockey: A Participant's Observation". *Culture*, Vol. 12, No. 3: 77–85.

———. 1985/87. *Life Before Genesis: A Conclusion.* New York: Peter Lang.

———. 1988. "The Incarnation of Nambirrimna". In *Aborigines and Christian Missions* (Tony Swain and Deborah B. Rose eds). Adelaide: the Australian Association for the Study of Religion.

―――― and Paul Wertman. 1977. *Shamattawa: The Structure of Social Relations in a Northern Algonkian Band.* Ottawa: National Museums of Man.

Waddy, Julie, 1984. "Classification of Plants and Animals from a Groote Eylandt Aboriginal Point of View". (PhD thesis, Macquarie University, to be published by the Northern Australian Research Unit, Darwin).

Warner, W. L. 1937/64. *A Black Civilization.* New York: Harper Torchbook.

Worsley, P. M. 1953. "The Changing Social Structure of the Warnindilyaugwa". (PhD thesis, Australian National University).

Thematic Index

Amawurrena-alawudawarra-, concept of in Aboriginal religion 48, 165–67, 222–27, 231–33; experience of as "laughing waves", 167–70; as "horseshoeing bay", 220–22; and Songs, 233–34.

Anindilyaugwa language, general, xxi; noun incorporation, i.e., federation 234–35.

Berndt, R. M., 7–8, 16–17.

Book of Genesis, xxvii, 279, 289–90.

Capra, Fritjof, 213–20, 280.

Christianity and Aboriginal religion, general, 222, 227–32; the Christ-event and the Nambirrirrma-event, 222, 227–32; negative effects of missionization, xxix, 22, 49, 257–58, 263–66.

citizenship, Western notion of, 260; in comparison with Aboriginal idea of jurisdiction, 259–60, 268–60, 269–72.

"clan", critique of concept of in Aboriginal context, xxviii, 42, 66.

C.M.S. (Church Missionary Society), general, 3; history of at Roper River, 19–21; at Angurugu, 55–57, 268; and permits to enter Aboriginal Reserves, 8–18.

Community Government, general, 269–72; Act of inauguration of, 269–70; Angurugu Community Government Council, xxv, 40–43, 49–50.

"Companies", as "clan"-People/Land groupings, 42; Gula's list of, 175–76; and Songstream, 70–71; relevance to marriage, 82; relevance to migration patterns, 162–64.

contraception, 58–59.

Cook, Captain James, observations of, 278.

Coulter, Barry, 35–37.

dialectic of monism (incorporation), general, xxix–xxx, 2–3, 284–88, concept of locality—incorporation and, 285.

dialectic of pluralism (federation), general, xxix-xxx, 222, 227–31, 231–34, 243, 276, 287–90; concept of kinline confederation and, 283, 286.

"Dreamings"/Songspecies, general, 26–27, 24–25, 186–89; naming on, 59–62; prohibition on consuming species associated with, 140–47, 169–72; principle of classification of, 187–89, 201–206; principle of classification of species associated with, 206–11.

dreams, 59–60.

Eastern mysticism and Aboriginal religion, 216–219.

Form, concept of, xxx, 228–29, 233–34, 276–77; experience of, as "horseshoeing bay", 220–22, as "laughing waves", 167–70; material determination by, general, xxx, 287–88; of Land, 135–38, 161, 277, 223–226, 232–33; and Songs, 233; and Aboriginal art, 273.

Form/content relation, xxviii, 161–64, 275–87.

GEMCO (Groote Eylandt Mining Company), BHP, see under "mining".

genealogical method, inapplicability of, 66–67, 72–78, 83.

gender relations, 84–91, 170–72.

Gula Lalara, xxiii, 143, 165–66, 176–78, 180–81, 241–42.

Land rights, as defined under the Act, 268–69; in conflict with Aboriginal forms of, xxv, 31–33, 133, 260–61.

Macassans and Aborigines, 149.

Mardaiya:n and Gunabibi, 189–93, 262–65.

Marriage, system of, 39, 80–91; changes in, 31–39, 85–87, 90–91.

Milya:gburra outstation, 43–44, 47–48, 93–94.

mining, by GEMCO, xxv, 3; negative effects of, xxv, 17, 27, 38–40, 247–48, 251–56, 266–68; Aboriginal employment in, 50.

Murabuda Wurramarrba, xxiii–xxvii, 19–20, 91, 140, 144, 166–67, 222, 241–42, 262, 273, 288.

Nandjiwarra Amagula 27, 43, 49,172, 268.

Neurological degenerative disease, among Aboriginal people, xxii-xxvii, 38–40, 51, 247–56, 268–61.

Nunggubuyu people, "clans"/People Lands of, 21–25; "Dreamings"/Songspecies of, 24.

People Lands, defined, xxviii, 109–17; boundaries of, 135–38; mapping of, 110–116; Lands within: Lands/countries within countries, 130–32; traditional disputes of boundaries between, 114; distribution of resources within, 140–46, 149–54, 156–64.

petrol sniffing, general, 46–47, 265–66; and juvenile crime, 49.

procreation, beliefs about, 58–59, 62–3; and naming, 59–63.

Promised Lands (see also People/Lands), xxviii, 294.

relationship system, terms, 68–70; system of, 45–46, 71–80; changes in, 74–79; basis in myth, 97–110.

renunciation, general, 277–78; as defined by Aborigines, 181–82; as basis of way of life, xxx, 232–43; of resources, 141–49; hypothesis relating to, 47–48, 139–40, 159, 161–63, 275.

Roper River (Ngukurr), 19–20.

Rose, Deborah, xxix.

Rose, F. G. G., xxviii, 84–86, 154, 161.

section system, 22–23, 84–86.

semi-moieties, 21–22.

singing, and naming, 60; spirits of the unborn, 62–4; spirits of the dead, 64; secret meaning of, 170–71, 184, 188–89, 201–04; and mortuary ceremonies, 62, 172–84; songForms, 233–43.

sorcery, general, 249–50, 255–66; Christian origins of, xxix.

Songstreams 71, 190–93.

Spirituality (see also Amawurrena, Form), general, 62–64, 76; as souls 62–64; transmission of across generations, 63–64, 66; reincarnation, 62; soul loss/spiritual contamination, 94–95, 250–51.

Stokes, Judith, xxi, 259.

Strehlow collection, 35–36.

Swain, Tony, xxix, 265.

technology, precontact, 143, 149.

"totems" (see "Dreamings"/ Songspecies)

Umbakumba settlement, 43–45, 84.

Waddy, Julie, xxi, 206, 210.

Welfare Branch, Northern Territory Administration, and permits to enter Aboriginal reserves, 7–8, 30.

Worsley, P. M., xxviii, 74, 154, 200.

www.ingramcontent.com/pod-product-compliance
Lightning Source LLC
Chambersburg PA
CBHW051525020426
42333CB00016B/1782